Ideographia

Ideographia

The Chinese Cipher in Early Modern Europe

DAVID PORTER

Stanford University Press
Stanford, California

Stanford University Press
Stanford, California
© 2001 by the Board of Trustees of the
Leland Stanford Junior University

Printed in the United States of America
on acid-free, archival-quality paper

Library of Congress Cataloging-in-Publication Data

Porter, David.
     Ideographia : the Chinese cipher in early modern
  Europe / David Porter.
        p.   cm.
     Includes bibliographical references and index.
     ISBN 0-8047-3203-5
     1. Europe—Civilization—Chinese influences
  I. Title.
CB205.P67   2001
303.48'24051'09031—dc21   00-54776

Original Printing 2001
Last figure below indicates year of this printing:
10   09   08   07   06   05   04   03   02   01
Designed by Eleanor Mennick
Typeset by BookMatters in 10/13 Sabon

For Lani

Acknowledgments

Although research and writing may often seem, by necessity, a lonely process, the isolation is only intermittent and partial. A project such as this one owes in large measure its completion to the many friends, mentors, and colleagues whose contributions belie the appearance of a solitary production. I would like to begin by thanking my teachers Sherm Cochran, who first introduced me to the intrinsic perplexities of East-West encounter, and Herbert Lindenberger, Terry Castle, and John Bender, who provided invaluable guidance and encouragement in my early efforts to sort through the encounter's permutations in the early modern period. My colleagues at the University of Michigan have been exceptionally supportive of this project; for their generosity of spirit and incisive readings, I would especially like to thank Julie Ellison, Lincoln Faller, Andrea Henderson, John Kucich, Marjorie Levinson, Adela Pinch, Yopie Prins, Michael Schoenfeldt, Valerie Traub, and James Winn. The many others to whom I am indebted for their thoughtful critiques of all or substantial portions of the manuscript at various stages include Elizabeth Bohls, Laura Brown, Gerald Cooke, Hans Ulrich Gumbrecht, Elizabeth Kowaleski-Wallace, Pericles Lewis, Robert Markley, Alexander Ogden, David Palumbo-Liu, Bruce Redford, Timothy Reiss, Haun Saussy, Patricia Meyer Spacks, Nicolas Standaert, and John Tinker. For their generous assistance in other crucial respects, I thank Bliss Carnochan, Joe and Laurie Dennis, Robert Gordon, Marcel Lieberman, Tobin Siebers, Martha Vicinus, and John Whittier-Ferguson.

The project could not have been completed without the financial support of the Mellon Foundation, the Stanford Humanities Center, the U.S. Department of Education, the Mabelle McLeod Lewis Memorial Fund, the National Endowment for the Humanities, and the Institute for Advanced Study in Princeton, New Jersey. I am grateful also to professional librarians at the following institutions for their expert research support and assistance: Beijing, Stanford, and Princeton Universities, the

University of Michigan, the Bancroft, Sutro, and San Francisco Public Libraries, the Institute for Advanced Study, and the British Library. Parts of earlier versions of Chapters 3 and 4 first appeared in *Studies in Eighteenth-Century Culture* and *Eighteenth-Century Studies*, respectively; I thank these journals for permission to use this material.

My parents, however inadvertently, laid much of the groundwork for this enterprise, and their continuing advice and encouragement have helped to sustain me through it. A final word of special thanks goes to my sons Nathaniel and Nicholas for their wonderfully ebullient spirit, and to my wife, Lani, for her patience, warmth, and good humor. I would like to thank her especially, though, for having shown me the way to China and, ever since, mediated and enriched my own cross-cultural encounter with the Far East.

D.L.P.

Contents

Illustrations

Since [the Chinese] never name themselves with moderation, they would have no right to complaint, if they knew that European authors have ever spoken of them in the extremes of applause or of censure: by some they have been extolled as the oldest and the wisest, as the most learned and the most ingenious, of nations; whilst others have derided their pretensions to antiquity, condemned their government as abominable, and arraigned their manners as inhuman, without allowing them an element of science, or a single art, for which they have not been indebted to some more ancient and more civilized race of men.

Sir William Jones, *Dissertation on the Chinese*, 1792

Introduction

The late twentieth century will be identified by future historians with the rapid globalization of American culture. Even where the incursions of the Internet, MTV, and the English language have been relatively limited, the economic system, political ideology, and popular culture of the United States have achieved an unprecedented, if ambivalently regarded, prominence as highly visible points of reference in the collective imagination of societies across the globe. If any one distant place could be said to have exercised a comparable grip on the collective self-consciousness of Western Europeans in the seventeenth and eighteenth centuries, that place, without a doubt, would be China. From the time of the first successful Jesuit mission in 1583 until the disastrous failure of the final British trade embassy in 1816, the cultural practices of a great civilization halfway around the world transfixed the attention of philosophers and theologians, architects and designers, venture capitalists and social critics. Its direct influences upon European culture were many and profound, ranging from Chinese teahouses in palace gardens to adaptations of Chinese plays for the popular stage, from calls to restructure the civil service on the model of Chinese meritocracy to the use of Confucian precepts in the moral education of children.

More significant, however, than even such readily visible gestures of imitation and appropriation are the interpretive strategies that accompanied them, the complex and deeply motivated processes by which those responding to the unfamiliar and often enigmatic artifacts of Chinese culture coaxed them into familiar forms of meaning, thereby engaging them in the emergent discourses of European modernity. What patterns can be traced among attempts to decipher perplexing and provocative signs of foreignness in the various spheres of encounter that comprised this history? How might one compare, for example, the experiences of radical illegibility in Europeans' initial confrontations with the Chinese writing system and the architectural design of Buddhist temples? How was early modern culture in Europe transformed through its contact with the world beyond its borders, not only through the direct channel of assimilated influences but also in the less obvious sense that an active engagement with the cipher of the foreign itself constitutes an act of cultural formation?

In both its historical and geographical situation, the particular encounter that is the subject of this book occupies a distinctive place among more familiar stories of cross-cultural contact, a place that is uniquely well suited to addressing the kinds of questions posed above. On a historical time line, the period covered by this study is largely removed from a medieval tradition of romance travel writing that gave Marco Polo's fabulous account of his journey to China in the thirteenth century the fondly jocular nickname *Il Milione* and has led to enduring doubts as to its credibility even today.[1] At the same time, it definitively predates the most recent, explicitly colonialist phase of China's relationship with the West that began with the humiliation of the first Opium War (1839–1842) and ended only with the return of Hong Kong and Macao to Chinese sovereignty in the final years of the twentieth century. Although both missionaries and traders strove mightily during this precolonialist phase to achieve some measure of influence over Chinese religious and economic policies, their efforts typically ended in frustration and failure. What limited successes they claimed were often local and short-lived. Meanwhile, the profound fascination with every aspect of Chinese civilization that their accounts generated in Europe took on a life largely independent of the original purpose of their journeys, creating an imaginary landscape of far more richness and complexity than would normally have been warranted by a naked quest for untapped markets and unredeemed souls. To make sense, then, of the vast body of writings on Chinese subjects these two centuries produced requires at least a provisional bracketing of familiar colonialist paradigms and the articulation of an alternative, less teleologically predetermined model for exploring the dynamics of cross-cultural encounter in the early modern period.

Just as the historical particularity of this phase of the East-West relationship resists easy categorization, so too China occupies a distinctive place in the geographical imagination of seventeenth- and eighteenth-century Europe. In marked contrast to the "primitive" cultures of sub-Saharan Africa and the Americas or to the legendary fallen empires of Egypt, Mexico, and Peru, China was acknowledged the seat of a great and ancient civilization whose cultural achievements not only reached back four thousand years but also continued to rival those of Europe into the current age. Only the Mughal and Ottoman Empires could compare with China in scale, splendor, and stature, but as bulwarks of the Muslim world, their place in the Western imagination was inevitably circumscribed by the collective memory of centuries of bloody conflict with the infidel. Early merchant travelers to India, moreover, proved far less effective than the Jesuits in China in cultivating European understanding of their host country, with the result that India, although geographically more accessible, remained far more obscure than China until the latter half of the eighteenth century and the consolidation of the British colonial presence. The Levant, considerably more familiar to European readers and travelers, typically attracted interest by way of its rich associations with antiquity, while its living inhabitants—the Turks in particular—more frequently appeared through the lenses of shimmering exoticism or haughty contempt. China stood alone, then, on the oriental horizon as a civilization sufficiently well known and admired to sustain a richly varied array of interpretations and responses throughout the early modern period.[2]

In making this case for the uniqueness of China's place in the imaginary geography of the West, there is some risk that the history of this encounter will appear as a quaint but largely irrelevant exception to the predominant narratives of conquest and exploitation, romantic idealization and imperialist epistemology that largely shaped these early centuries of European contact with non-European peoples. While recognizing such a risk, I would propose that developing alternative narratives corresponding to distinctive historical and geographical contexts will not only enrich our appreciation of the variety and specificity of the discourses generated through individual encounters, but also may yield more generally applicable paradigms that will illuminate the workings of transcultural contact zones in other times and places. My purpose in this book, then, is to read broadly across early modern responses to Chinese cultural artifacts for interpretive patterns at once specific to their context and suggestive of larger trends beyond it. My interest, finally, lies less in cataloguing Western images of the East or Eastern influences on European culture than in tracing the origins of hermeneutic strategies, their historical evolution, and their own culturally transformative potential.

Edward Gibbon, the great eighteenth-century chronicler of the demise of the Roman Empire, begins his autobiography with a few instructive reflections on family history. The popular success of his earlier masterwork had amply testified to his generation's fascination with its cultural forebears. As he turns his probing gaze inward, he ponders the appeal of genealogy on a more personal scale. "A lively desire of knowing and recording our ancestors so generally prevails," he proposes in the opening paragraph, "that it must depend on the influence of some common principle in the minds of men." Religion and philosophy may help to allay fears of one's own mortality, but "we fill up the silent vacancy that precedes our birth by associating ourselves to the authors of our existence." Just as he had originally been inspired to devote his life to writing *The Decline and Fall* by the sight of Franciscan friars singing vespers on the ancient site of the Roman capitol, so we all "seem to have lived in the persons of our forefathers . . . nor does the man exist who would not peruse with warmer curiosity the life of a hero from whom his name and blood were lineally derived."[3] To identify with the historical authors of our existence, whether among the ruins of empire or the branches of a family tree, is to recover some part of our own meaning there. An awareness of origins enlivens and provides a purposeful form to the silent vacancy of the past and, in doing so, Gibbon suggests, may shape one's experience of the here and now.

The search for these origins, as a result, proceeds not without the apprehensions of a certain vested self-interest. To begin with, the warmest curiosity and, presumably, the most generous indulgence are reserved only for ancestors of heroic proportions. As Gibbon observes, "The longest series of peasants and mechanics would not afford much gratification to the pride of their descendent. We wish to discover our ancestors, but we wish to discover them possessed of ample fortunes, adorned with honourable titles, and holding an eminent rank in the class of hereditary nobles." The mythological burden one casts upon forebears, fraught as it is with existential doubts and longings, is a weighty one, and only those of the highest stature and purest pedigree are fit to carry the load.

But the discovery of an illustrious line of noblemen among the distant tendrils of a family tree is only the first step. The second precondition for achieving genealogical redemption is to establish that such a line is genuinely one's own. Only a lineal derivation of name and blood can justify an heir's claim to ancestral glory: vanity is falsely served by the admiration of someone else's forebear. For Gibbon, this precondition can finally be satisfied only through a substantial leap of faith. Virtue, after all, cannot be reliably transmitted through the generations alongside estates and titles, so that "even the claim of our legal descent must rest on a basis not perhaps sufficiently firm, the unspotted chastity of *all* our female progenitors."[4]

The search for personal meaning among the ancestral authors of one's existence, then, can be a potentially perilous undertaking on which one stakes the very legitimacy of one's being. In the likely absence of heroic origins, the dreary meanderings of a family line can afford little sustenance to the spirit of its most recent progeny. And even if a baron or a prince turns up among the distant founders of the line, a knowledge of the vagaries of human passions unsettles the certainty of one's own descent. But lest the outlook appear too bleak for the genealogically inclined, Gibbon offers an instance from the international annals of family history calculated to restore the reader's faith in the redemptive power of the past.

The family of Confucius is in my opinion the most illustrious in the world. After a painful ascent of eight or ten centuries, our barons and princes of Europe are lost in the darkness of the middle age: but in the vast equality of the Empire of China, the posterity of Confucius has maintained above two thousand two hundred years its peaceful honours and perpetual succession; and the chief of the family is still revered by the sovereign and the people as the living image of the wisest of mankind.[5]

With a pedigree such as the noblest of European lords could only dream of, the family of Confucius marks the apogee of Gibbon's fantasy of genealogical legitimacy. A lineage could claim a no more exalted origin than a renowned sage of antiquity, after all, and could hope for a no more compelling affirmation of its true and honorable descent than continued public recognition and acclaim.

When Gibbon refers a second time to the Confucian family in the next paragraph, he buttresses his renewed assertion that it is "the noblest upon earth" with recapitulations of its claims to legitimacy of both origin and descent. Lest a skeptical reader suspect that legend may have played some role in the reconstruction of the line, he affirms that "seventy *authentic* generations have elapsed from that philosopher to the present chief of his posterity" (emphasis in original). And lest a philistine impugn the stature of a philosopher as unworthy of all the fuss, Gibbon points out that this same heir also "reckons one hundred and thirty-five degrees from the Emperor Hoang-ti, the father, as it is believed, of an illustrious line which has now flourished in China four thousand four hundred and twenty-five years."[6] Gibbon justifies his admiration for this illustrious line, in other words, on the grounds, first, of its authenticated descent over thousands of years and, second, of its origin with two founding fathers of truly epic proportions: the progenitors in China not only of philosophy but of empire.

Gibbon's passing allusion to Chinese history is hardly surprising in itself. His *Memoirs*, written in the early 1790s, came at the end of two centuries of sustained European fascination with the great civilization of the Far East. Beginning in the early 1600s, missionaries, traders, and travelers picked up where Marco Polo had left off in 1295, flooding Europe with descriptions, anecdotes, and artifacts that stimulated a lively interest in every aspect of Chinese culture from language and religion to the arts and commerce.[7] As I will demonstrate in chapters devoted to each of these four spheres of encounter, references to Chinese examples abounded in contemporary writings, regularly achieving a rhetorical currency that a man of Gibbon's erudition could scarcely have overlooked.[8] Language projectors and reformers took the Chinese script as a paragon of linguistic rationality. French philosophes found in China's secular society an enviable model of religious freedom and tolerance. Artists and architects among the followers of rococo and gothic styles, meanwhile, discovered in Chinese gardens and porcelain fantasies an aesthetic that broke exuberantly free from neoclassical conventions. Even Chinese hostility toward foreign trade achieved a widespread notoriety through the accounts of those commercial adventurers who had attempted to overcome it.

Still more revealing, however, than the reference to China in Gibbon's rhapsodic rendering of the Confucian family tree is its use of a trope of legitimacy to mediate the encounter with the foreign. Gibbon characterizes China as a uniquely privileged site not only of genealogical but also of what one might term representational legitimacy, a place, that is, where the myriad signs and symbols that constitute culture were reliably grounded in a fixed, originary source of meaning and therefore not subject to the corrupting vicissitudes of common language and history. I would suggest that, in doing so, Gibbon adopts an interpretive paradigm established by Western observers of Chinese culture during the previous two hundred years. In each of the four spheres of encounter I have mentioned, Europeans consistently projected onto China—and onto the enigmatic ciphers they discovered there—a framework of representational legitimacy that served both as a precondition of cross-cultural legibility and the basis of their own emergent self-definitions in relation to Chinese difference. The pattern that emerges with remarkable consistency through two centuries of European assessments of Chinese culture is an insistent preoccupation with the tendency of its artifacts either to conform to or to flout flagrantly the ordering principles of origin and descent. As the predominant focus of European interest shifted in the early eighteenth century from the language and religion of the Chinese to its aesthetic models and trade policies, the prevailing attitude toward China gradually evolved from one of reverential awe to one of increasingly dismissive contempt. Throughout this entire period, however, an implicit model of legitimacy in representation remained a constant point of reference, a common conceptual and rhetorical thread woven through the varied cultural discourses comprising the European experience of the encounter.

A closer analysis of a passage from Gibbon's text will help to clarify how, in general, a genealogical principle of legitimacy might serve as a useful category of analysis in the representational domain. While Gibbon's immediate concern in the opening pages of his memoir is to rationalize his own personal interest in family history, his presentation of the Confucian lineage simultaneously suggests a second, more figural reading of the reproduction of meanings in Chinese culture. Gibbon's language seems to imply an analogy between the reproductive potentiality of sexual and textual processes. Not only does he imagine one's ancestors as the historical "authors" of one's existence, he also describes his own authorship of *Decline and Fall* in decidedly procreative terms as a process initiated in a "moment of conception" and completed in an "hour of final deliverance."[9] Comparing this analogy to the case of the Confucian family tree reveals a representational corollary to the genealogical legitimacy he so admires there. When Gibbon describes how the current chief of the Confucian family is revered as "the living image of the wisest of mankind," the phrase "living image" evokes a suggestive ambiguity between genealogical and symbolic connotations. The documented authenticity of the heir's succession, on the one hand, assures that his personal traits—his biological inheritance, as it were—literally reproduce to a certain degree the renowned qualities of the sage, making for a "living image" in the sense of a genetic simulacrum. The considerable diluting effect of seventy intervening generations on this process of replication, on the other hand, would suggest that the reverence accorded the head of the family arises in large measure from his role as a symbolic, rather than simply biological, incarnation of the Confucian spirit, a "living image," that is, in the sense of an unusually potent icon or metaphor.

The "vast equality of the Empire" over the millennia, in other words, makes possible both the endless perpetuation of the blood line of its founders and their full and immediate "representation" in the bodies of their heirs. If genealogical legitimacy relies on a combination of exalted ancestral origins and verifiable descent to provide for a comforting vindication of a descendant's existence, then the notion of representational legitimacy implies the presence of an originary wellspring of meaning that gives rise to a succession of grounded signifiers in which the living image of that origin is fully and immediately present. The absolute authority of the founding moment would be fully vested in each of these semiotic progeny; they would be legitimate in the sense of being entirely free from distortion, slippage, or ambiguity. While the prospect of a discourse comprised of fixed and fully embodied signifiers might come across as insufferably tedious to postmodern sensibilities, one can readily imagine that the fantasy of such a semiotic spectacle, with its attendant promises of epistemological order, coherence, and certitude, might particularly appeal to the perplexed observer of a bafflingly foreign cultural landscape in a less gleefully skeptical age.

Gibbon's principal concern in the *Memoirs* is autobiography, not cross-cultural interpretation. And yet his passing encounter with the foreign, however brief, reveals the mediation of a powerful hermeneutic tool. China comes across in these opening passages as a place where, in the vast equality of time, scarcely a ripple disturbs the memories of the ages. It is a place where the passage of thousands of years is marked only by the honorable succession of a founder's glory, and where present lives are legitimated by the immediacy of their connection to lives in the distant past. The dominant relation is one of perfect identity; representation seems to function only with reference to a single, omniscient source of meaning. All of this, one might observe, makes for a dubiously coherent conception of more than four thousand years of history. But China was not Rome, and few Europeans would have been moved to chronicle its history by the vespers of its native monks. A vastly reductive conception was in some sense a necessary one, and as an interpretive apparatus, the paradigm of representational legitimacy Gibbon shared with his contemporaries was one of the few that could have rendered such a vast expanse of unmitigated foreignness minimally legible to observers at their cultural distance from the scene.

Faced with an impenetrable wilderness of alien signs, intrepid European philologists and missionaries, in particular, sought to assimilate the written language and religious practices of China within familiar Western frameworks. Invariably, these frameworks were genealogical in structure and placed a pronounced emphasis on the paired topoi of origin and descent. By arranging the chaotic universe of Chinese representation according to the symmetrical hierarchies of a family tree, these European observers, anticipating Gibbon's belated gesture, projected a legitimizing order onto Chinese cultural institutions that rendered them both legible and responsive to the exigencies of the observer's own historical moment.

The title of this book is intended to foreground the importance of such specific strategies of interpretation in assessing the origins and effects of a society's responses to foreignness. If an "ideograph" is a symbol expressing the idea of a thing without conveying its name, as in a traffic sign or a hieroglyph, and "ideography" is the direct representation of ideas by means of such graphic images, then by "ideographia" I mean to suggest both a plurality of ideographic systems and a symptomatic proclivity to discover such systems in otherwise meaningless configurations of signs. Most Chinese characters are not, properly speaking, ideographs; their form rarely conveys sufficient semantic information to establish the meaning of a word, while they often do provide significant phonetic clues as to their pronunciation. The early history of Western responses to the Chinese script, however, reveals a long-standing, almost compulsive desire to read it as an impossibly pure form of signification and to systematize its notations in a relentless quest for an originary and transcendent order. I take this fantasy of specifically linguistic legitimacy as paradigmatic of the type of interpretive projection that determines Western responses to Chinese culture more generally during this period. Responses in other spheres resemble the ideographic fantasy insofar as they presume a similarly transcendent representational system as the basis of their assessment of Chinese religion, aesthetics, or economic and social policy.

This book is divided into four sections, each devoted to one of these four spheres of encounter. Although even the earliest responses to the Chinese language are themselves premised on Jesuit accounts and thus are in a strictly chronological sense secondary to the story of the first Jesuit missions, I open with a chapter on language issues in order to foreground from the outset the central problem of cross-cultural legibility in the context where it is most directly and explicitly engaged. As I noted in the case of Gibbon's *Memoirs*, the idea of legitimacy not only facilitated a certain kind of reading of Chinese culture but also satisfied, in its uniquely

Chinese instantiation, a longing for a model of continuity, stability, and authenticity that could not be found at home. In this first chapter, I argue that just such a longing took shape among philosophical circles of the seventeenth and early eighteenth centuries. The decline of Latin as a lingua franca, the corresponding rise of undisciplined vernaculars, and the call for modes of speech and writing suited to the rigorous exigencies of science prompted efforts lasting from Bacon's until Johnson's day to create, discover, or restore thoroughly grounded, originary, and potentially universal forms of language. It was a quest that led with remarkable consistency to the Chinese script, a form of writing whose antiquity, changelessness, and apparent grounding in originary philosophical meanings seemed fully to satisfy the period's pressing demand for viable models of representational legitimacy.

The missionaries whose writings I take up in the second chapter approached China with their own version of this demand. Rather than a panacea for a perceived crisis in language, however, they sought a stable cultural foundation for the edifice of Catholic theology they hoped to erect on Chinese ground. Through their readings of the ancient Confucian canon they discovered religious representations that seemed firmly rooted in a pure and authentic revelation of the divine. If the policy of accommodationism they subsequently developed was premised on the theological legitimacy of certain Chinese religious practices, this legitimacy in turn derived, like that of the Chinese script, from an originary and authoritative source of truth. In both cases, the apparent validity and legibility of a cultural artifact were products of a genealogical framework that, while answering to a historically specific and discursively delimited Western need, nonetheless contributed to that generalized conception of Chinese cultural legitimacy to be found in Gibbon's work and countless other laudatory depictions of the Far East.

If China's conformity with a model of representational legitimacy constituted the prevailing paradigm for the interpretation of its culture in the first half of the period I am considering, then the predominant outlook in the second half discovered within the same culture an outrageous and thoroughgoing defiance of the legitimating principles of origin and descent. The resulting cast of cultural illegitimacy first emerged in the writings of the same Jesuit priests who had so vaunted the ancient religion of the Chinese. However appealing it had seemed to their own sensibilities, Confucian doctrine, they discovered, could claim no monopoly on Chinese souls. The plethora of competing sects and cults that made up the rest of the religious landscape in China appeared to these early Jesuits as an irredeemably cluttered and confusing morass. The tangled web of heresies they saw in Buddhist doctrine, in particular, disrupted their designs for a unified Chinese theology under the auspices of the Catholic Church. In its resistance to legibility, Buddhism called upon itself a charge of illegitimacy figured in terms of sexual debauchery and semiotic proliferation that precisely negated those used to exalt its favored counterpart. By dismissing Buddhism as a bastard religion whose ignoble origins were reflected in the beliefs and practices of its adherents, the Jesuits demonstrated the utility of a genealogical model of legitimacy in containing even those cultural codes it proved unable to crack.

The lesson was not lost on the Jesuits' opponents within the Catholic Church. In their condemnations of the Chinese sects, the Jesuits had perfected a potent rhetorical tool that their enemies could use, in turn, to discredit the accommodationist premises of the Jesuit mission. The Rites Controversy at the end of the seventeenth century raised the question of whether the now commonplace denunciation of these sects on the grounds of their seeming illegitimacy ought to be extended into a proscription, on the same grounds, of Chinese religious culture as a whole. The Jesuits' ultimate defeat on this question testified, however ironically, to the power of the interpretive paradigm they had brought to bear in the course of their engagement with East Asia.

In the third chapter, I argue that the rhetorical terms of this paradigm carry over in Europe from the theological to the aesthetic sphere. By the beginning of the eighteenth century, a rising tide of imports had stirred an interest in Chinese culture among a class of artists and collectors less concerned with the interpretive legibility of the foreign than with the sheer thrill of its exoticism. The fanciful style in interior decoration and garden design in Europe that came to be known as chinoiserie presented Chinese aesthetic practice, in its seeming rejection of classicist norms, as a deliberate subversion of the representational ideals that an earlier generation had found embodied in the writing system and ancient religion of the Chinese. The delicately painted porcelains and ornate furnishings of the Chinese style were both admired and reviled as an extravagant celebration of the same kind of unsettling proliferation of ungrounded signs that the Jesuits had so roundly condemned in the renegade religions of the Chinese. As the longing for authentically grounded meanings gave way, with the popularization of the Chinese taste, to the delights of engaging foreignness for its own sake, the bucolic vision of China as a land of noble

lineages in the semiotic domain increasingly succumbed to a bacchanalian fantasy of a pleasure garden of the senses where the very conditions
of representational integrity were sacrificed on the altar of aesthetically
mediated desire.

Classicist denunciations of the chinoiserie style, I suggest in the final
chapter, found a strangely distorted echo in the discourse of that East
India trade whose imports had fueled the craze. In the light of an eighteenth-century commercialist doctrine that posited the free circulation of
economic and cultural capital as the basis of progress and prosperity,
China's restrictive trade policies and social norms appeared artificially
confining. Countless impediments to the free flow of goods and ideas
seemed, in the eyes of English merchants and ambassadors who visited
China, to disrupt processes of exchange that were ultimately grounded,
according to Adam Smith and his predecessors, in the natural order of
things. Within this new commercialist framework, the genealogical
notion of historical origin was replaced by economic determinism and
that of mimetic descent by the ceaseless circulation of signs. Nonetheless,
the representational ideal evoked by the living image of the Confucian
heir remained intact. When this version of the ideal was projected onto
China, however, the systematic obstruction of natural circulatory
impulses in Chinese society seemed to undermine the legitimacy not only
of trade contracts and diplomatic negotiations but also of family ties, the
public sphere, and ultimately the Chinese state itself. The charge of illegitimacy stemmed this time not from the boundless proliferation of signs
but rather from their complete and deathly stagnation. If a genealogical
failing threatened China's continued vitality at the close of the eighteenth
century, then its mark appeared not in the fallen virtue of a female ancestor but in the impotence of a palace eunuch.

While the historical scope of this study is considerable, there remain
important dimensions of its subject that I do not cover here. To begin
with, this is a book about early modern Europe, rather than Ming or
Qing dynasty China. I make only limited claims to sinological expertise,
and as my concern has primarily been Western strategies of interpretation
and their origins in and consequences for seventeenth- and eighteenth-
century European culture, my treatment of the encounter is largely mono-
logical and does not draw upon primary Chinese sources. A number of
invaluable recent studies do systematically address the responses of con-

temporary Chinese to their Western visitors. I refer the reader in particular to Jacques Gernet's *China and the Christian Impact*, James Hevia's *Cherishing Men from Afar*, and Lionel Jensen's *Manufacturing Confucianism*. Secondly, this book does not pretend to be an exhaustive survey of Western responses to Chinese culture during this period. I limit my discussion to Britain, France, and Germany and do not address such potentially noteworthy topics as Quesnay and the French physiocrats, Montesquieu's political theory, early Portuguese and Russian embassies to China, or the widespread adaptation of Chinese materials for the eighteenth-century stage. Other scholars, including William Appleton, René Etiemble, Basil Guy, Donald Lach, and Virgile Pinot, have amply documented the extraordinary range of such responses, and I am indebted to their often more comprehensive overviews of these two centuries of East-West contact. I have chosen, instead, to focus on four specific discursive domains, and within each a limited number of representative figures, in order to reconstruct in some detail their epistemological premises while simultaneously reading across the seemingly incongruous array of written and visual evidence they present for recurrent motifs, fixations, and interpretive gambits suggestive of unexpected resonances among them and the contours as well, perhaps, of a deep structure underlying the discourse of the encounter as a whole. Where my selection of examples is weighted toward British materials, this is owing both to the occasional need for a sustained contextual focus and the historical fact that Britain produced the greatest range of imaginative and material responses to Chinese ideas and artifacts across both the entire period spanned by my study and the cultural spheres with which I am primarily concerned. While the British experience of the encounter cannot be taken as wholly representative, the interpretive methods and paradigms that emerge in its various phases help to illuminate more broadly applicable patterns of response.

Finally, while my project is indebted in obvious ways to the early work of Edward Said, it is situated toward the margins of the field of postcolonial studies that has emerged in the twenty years since the publication of *Orientalism*.[10] As I have indicated above, there clearly are aspects of early missionary and merchant interventions in China that might profitably be read from within a colonialist framework. And to the extent that the Cartesian subject of Enlightenment humanism emerges, in part, during this period, through the pursuit of self-serving, sovereign knowledge of the alien and unfamiliar, even the more benign speculations of the first protosinologists may well conceal an implicit violence in their negation of autonomous difference. One might, in other words, construct a plausible narrative from the materials I have gathered here that would highlight the coercive potentiality of the forms of knowledge they represent and demonstrate their contributions to a latent imperialist project that would culminate in the mid-nineteenth-century Opium Wars. Such an approach, however, would forsake the relatively unique opportunity afforded by an early modern contact zone that is *not* overtly or predominantly colonialist to examine other, equally interesting kinds of cultural work the discourses of encounter may perform.

While this book, then, does not share the explicitly political orientation of much recent postcolonialist scholarship, my own search for paradigms better suited to the historical particularity of my subject has remained in dialogue with a number of the methodological premises underlying this scholarship. As will by now be clear, I am similarly concerned to explore the cultural conditions of a society's responses to foreignness, the relations of interdependence these conditions promote, and the forms of hybridity they may entail. My own approach, in its emphasis on interpretive practices over images and influences, likewise shares with postcolonialist criticism a tendency to privilege the discourses of encounter over their material conditions. Finally, the fundamental problem this study addresses is one that I take to be at the very center of postcolonial theory: the problem of how cultural self-definition is renegotiated in the wake of a transformative encounter with difference. The twentieth-century history of modernization and revolution in China bespeaks an ongoing engagement with the challenge of Western hegemony. In an earlier era, however, the challenges crossed both ways, and Europe found itself compelled by the force of its own cultural anxieties to realign its inward gaze within the contours of ideographic fantasy.

CHAPTER ONE

Linguistic Legitimacy and the Interpretation of Chinese Writing

And what if the primordial language in Paradise was
Chinese—as some have thought and as is permissible to
conjecture—is it then not possible to imagine that the
Blessed Ones converse with each other in that language?
How will you rejoice, dear Sir, if you shall find that the
language which you are studying so assiduously now is
the principal language in Heaven?

—Ignatius Koegler and André Pereira, letter to T. S. Bayer,
    ca. 1736

China, as a construct of the Western imagination, has always been col-
ored by the historical situation of its observers. From the fantastic tales of
the Venetian Marco Polo to American media accounts of the tragedy at
Tiananmen Square, depictions of the earth's most populous nation have
inevitably reflected the collective longings and fantasies of the societies
that produced and consumed them. When reports from the first Jesuit
missions in China began making their way back to Europe in the seventeenth century, the context within which they were interpreted and
debated was one of profound crisis and upheaval. The Thirty Years War,
fueled by the mutual suspicions of Catholic and Protestant leaders,
engulfed most of Europe from the Baltic to the Rhine Valley in a bloody
conflagration that dominated continental politics for the first half of the
century. In England, religious conflict erupted in civil wars culminating
in the execution of the monarch in 1649 and precipitating a constitutional
imbroglio not fully resolved until the Glorious Revolution forty years
later.

The response to prolonged periods of turmoil, then as now, was a widespread yearning for new sources of order and stability. One of the striking patterns in seventeenth-century cultural history is the persistence of a pronounced ordering impulse across so many fields of endeavor, from the rationalist metaphysics of Descartes to the founding of the French Academy, from the elaboration of mercantilist economic theory to Le Nôtre's triumph in the formal gardens of Versailles. When Europeans looked eastward to China during this period, this same impulse informed their gaze, so that the idealized, quasi-utopian society they read into Jesuit missionary reports emerged as a model of the continuity and order they so craved. In China they discovered (or so they believed) a form of government that had endured, essentially unchanged, for thousands of years and that had, furthermore, documented its achievements in countless tomes of meticulous historical records. Here was a state bureaucracy based on principles of wisdom, integrity, and respect for the past and known for its rational organization and efficiency. Here was an officially sanctioned moral doctrine that had for millennia promulgated values of virtue and obedience across an expansive empire while remaining untainted by violent sectarian dispute. And here, finally, was a peculiar form of writing that seemed to transcend the fatal transience and ambiguity of Western vernaculars to convey the timeless essence of ideas and things in themselves.

Ever since the confusion at the Tower of Babel, something of the hubris of its original architects has persisted in ambitious proposals to recover, restore, or if necessary recreate the unity and perfection of the language of Eden. In *The Search for the Perfect Language*, Umberto Eco traces the history of this project and the impulses behind it from Plato's *Cratylus* and the spirited defense of spoken Gaelic over Latin on the part of seventh-century Irish grammarians to the emergence of the modern international languages Volapük and Esperanto. The history of Europe begins, Eco argues, with its linguistic fragmentation after the fall of the Roman Empire, and the distinctive culture of the continent "arose as a reflection on the destiny of a multilingual civilization." Such a history implies an undercurrent of deep linguistic nostalgia; indeed, for Eco, "the dream of a perfect language has always been invoked as a solution to [the] religious or political strife" that, perhaps, this postimperial history made inevitable.[1]

Never was this tendency more pronounced than in the seventeenth century, which was inclined, to a remarkable degree, to regard such strife as having both its origins and proper remedies in language. The curse of Babel—in the form not only of the sheer multiplicity of tongues but also of linguistic ambiguity and uncertainty of every kind—was seen as lying behind the tumult of the times; peace and stability could only be attained if language could be once again made whole. The amateur Egyptologist Athanasius Kircher wrote wistfully of his desire that the peoples of the world who had been dispersed by the confusion "be called back together . . . for a new linguistic and ideological reunification." The Czech educational reformer and theologian John Amos Comenius, after traveling through war-torn Europe, proposed a world council that would establish the perfect state by means, in part, of its promulgation of a new universal language whose fixed definitions and antirhetorical strictures would forever eliminate the ambiguous use of words. And the German polymath Gottfried Leibniz, driven by his conviction that religious unity would provide the only lasting basis for universal peace, postulated a philosophical algebra that would resolve theological disputes with mathematical certainty, by providing a "language [that] will make argument and calculation the same thing."[2]

The scope of language reform efforts in seventeenth-century England was no less ambitious. A tradition extending from Bacon to Locke posited an essential equivalence between linguistic and philosophical standards of clarity, precision, and transparency of thought as the basis of a new empiricist epistemology. Moreover, as Robert Stillman has persuasively argued, the rationalist regimes imposed on language within this tradition reflect not only the new ordering of experimental knowledge promoted by the Royal Society but also a fundamental commitment on the part of its adherents to reinforcing and legitimating the authority of the state. The disorderly condition of language was no mere metaphor for political instability, but rather a significant underlying cause. The universal language schemes of Bacon, Wilkins, and others "emerged as rival authority structures designed, in great measure, to contain and control the disorders of words because such disorders threatened chaos in the historical world of things."[3]

Given the urgency of this preoccupation with language issues throughout the period, it comes as no surprise that when Jesuit reports from China began to circulate in Europe, as they did in ever-increasing numbers during the seventeenth century, accounts of the curious, nonalphabetic writing system in use there were singled out for scrutiny and speculation. These early accounts of the Chinese script captivated the imagination of their readers in several ways. The characters of the script, they suggested, rather than depicting a merely arbitrary sequence of sounds as in alphabetic writing, bore an intrinsic and logical, if still somewhat mysterious, relation-

ship to the ideas they represented. As a result of their semantic independence of the spoken language, these characters had achieved a regional universality among China's neighbors, providing a written lingua franca for
groups whose speech was mutually unintelligible. Finally, their geographical range was matched by a historical continuity that made it possible for
present-day readers in China to access an original corpus of works composed hundreds or even thousands of years in the past.[4] Such claims—to
some degree of nonarbitrariness, universality, and resistance to change—
could not fail to capture the attention of language planners whose own
quests so often embodied a similar set of ideals. Indeed, the best-known
figures of the seventeenth-century language reform movement—Bacon,
Comenius, Wilkins, and Leibniz—all refer prominently to the Chinese
example; of the dozen or so lesser-known universal language projectors
there is scarcely one who fails to cite the Chinese script as a precedent or a
point of reference.[5] Taken separately, these references to a foreign example
can appear as merely incidental and have been generally treated as such in
recent scholarship. When taken together, however, they reveal a consistent
set of assumptions concerning the properties of the Chinese script and the
principles that the script seemed to embody, as well as a broadly shared
tendency to regard the Chinese character as a nearly sacred emblem of
what I am calling "representational legitimacy."

Since the time of Sir John Mandeville, China had been regarded as the
privileged domain of a higher form of law, and one whose power seemed
to inhere in its material written form. In his *Travels* (ca. 1356), Mandeville
speaks with wonder of the four clerks who sit at the Chinese emperor's
feet while he is eating, recording his every word in order to endow it with
the force of law, "for everything that he says really must be done."[6] For
the Jesuit compiler Juan González de Mendoza who wrote toward the end
of the sixteenth century, Christian teachings have displaced imperial edicts
as the highest law in China. But in describing the enduring viability of the
gospel centuries after its first appearance in China, Mendoza retains in a
central metaphor the imagery of scribal authority: the doctrine of St.
Thomas, he writes, "dooth remaine printed in their hearts," and "beareth
a similitude of the truth."[7] Although by the eighteenth century sacred doctrine had been largely displaced, in its turn, by natural law, a similar figure
appears in this typical encomium to Chinese civilization by a Frenchman
posing as a Chinese philosopher in 1762:

When I compare the history of China with that of all other foreign peoples, how
pleased I am to have been born in this country. Opening our history, I observe a

vast and ancient empire, established by laws that seem to have been dictated by nature and reason. The duty of children towards their parents, a duty which nature engraves in their hearts, is the sustenance of this government that has sub-sisted since time immemorial. One can say, in consequence, that the entire state resembles a family of which the Emperor is the protector, the father, and the friend.[8]

Once again, one encounters a figural inscription vested with the tran-scendent authority of an acknowledged lawgiver. As in each of the two previous cases, the image of the written word takes on, in an imaginary Chinese context, the aura of unquestioned validity or authenticity as a result of its immediate grounding in an originary wellspring of law or truth. One might describe the special status of such privileged forms of writing as their "legitimacy" in the etymological sense of the Latin *legit-imus*, "lawful," or *legitimare*, "to declare to be lawful," in that their spe-cial force and authority arise precisely from their immediate association with a primal source of law, whether a charismatic leader, divine revela-tion, or the Book of Nature.[9]

A second, closely related sense of "legitimacy" is evoked by the well-worn analogy in the final passage between the patriarchal family and the state.[10] In the domestic context, of course, the term denotes the status of a child who is lawfully begotten, or created in accordance with legally sanctioned forms of reproduction. The legitimate child is an emblem not only of the orderly transmission of genetic information but also of the transmission or descent of a particular legal status and, hence, in effect, of the law itself. To describe a form of writing or, for that matter, any form of representation as legitimate, then, would suggest not only the purity of its originary source of meaning but also its regulated derivation from that source and faithful reproduction of its authority. The efficacy of the emperor's commands, in the first passage, depends upon his every word, precisely as it is spoken, being recorded by four clerks whose very redun-dancy underlines the importance of perfect accuracy in preserving the legitimacy of the law in this sense of the term. In the third passage, like-wise, imperial authority arises from the reliable historical transmission of a doctrine of filial piety within the family unit and its political reproduc-tion in the properly reverential attitude of the citizenry toward the emperor. The legitimacy of language, finally, is a function of its derivation considered both as origin and process, a duality that will be fully manifest in the richly metaphorical characterizations both of this ideal in the abstract and of its specific imaginative incarnation in the Chinese script.

In his book *Origin and Authority in Seventeenth-Century England*,
Alvin Snider suggests that "a desire to establish the legitimacy of the present through the recovery and representation of origins" deeply informs
much of the literature and philosophy of the seventeenth century.[11] I will
argue in this chapter that such a desire also shaped the early modern
European encounter with the Chinese written language, leading reformers, universal language projectors, and philologists alike to seek within
this inscrutable foreign script material evidence of the possibility of legitimacy in representation. Whether it was credited with being the original
language of mankind or an enigmatic cipher of divine revelation, with
embodying a perfectly rational philosophical system or the fundamental
principles of all the sciences, Chinese writing served an embattled age as
an emblem of the prospect of redeeming the authority of language, of the
feasibility of forms of knowledge and communication that were reliably
grounded, universally valid, and absolutely true.

The origins of this collective fantasy lie, as I have suggested, in a
heightened contemporary awareness of the various inadequacies of common forms of language and, more broadly, in the pervasive longing for
order in a period of widespread social conflict and political uncertainty.
The cultural contexts of both these phenomena have been treated extensively by Snider, Stillman, and other scholars, and I will not attempt to
duplicate their work here.[12] Although I will suggest connections between
readings of the Chinese script and seventeenth-century language theory, I
will focus primarily in what follows on the internal structure and development of the Chinese language myth—its foundational axioms and historical variants and permutations—with the aim of developing a more
broadly generalizable model for interpreting the reception and assimilation of foreign and specifically Eastern cultural artifacts. I will approach
the response to the Chinese language, in other words, as a foundational
case of ideography, understood as the domestication of the foreign sign,
the process by which the unintelligible is rendered legible and interpreted
within a more familiar matrix of meanings, and contributes, in turn, to
shaping it. To describe a Chinese character as an ideograph, a written figure symbolizing the idea of a thing, is already to participate in such a
process. My purpose in proposing the term "ideography" to describe this
process, and in beginning a book on early modern responses to Chinese
culture with a chapter on interpretations of its script, is to suggest that the
response to the Chinese character is paradigmatic of other aspects of this
encounter and provides a useful conceptual framework for examining the

Western response to equally obscure symbolic lexicons in other cultural domains.

The Formation of an Ideal

If, as I am suggesting, a prevailing sense of linguistic crisis informed early European responses to the Chinese language, then examining the terms in which language reformers decried the corruptions afflicting their own language will help to account for both the strikingly impassioned nature of this response and the often fantastical interpretations that it entailed. This section will briefly survey the diagnoses of a fallen language offered by five representative figures—Bacon, Sprat, Wilkins, Swift, and Johnson—with a view toward identifying their rhetorical common ground and to reading their recurrent metaphors for insights into how the imperfections of language were imaginatively conceived by those most urgently concerned with overcoming them. The language of legitimacy figures prominently in their writings, a reminder that they span a period of British history in which those crises of political and religious legitimation underlying so much linguistic debate were perennial, the Gunpowder plot, rebellions in Ireland, dissolutions of Parliament, civil war, popish plots, Scottish invasions, the South Sea Bubble, and countless foreign conflicts marking only a few of the more spectacular disruptions of domestic tranquility. Stillman, Markley, and others convincingly demonstrate the specific historical connections between political and religious crisis and language reform initiatives on the part of some of these writers, as well as the omnipresence, more generally, of political interest behind contemporary appeals to notions of progress and natural truth.[13] To these scholars' richly historicized readings of these initiatives I would add a layer of rhetorical speculation in proposing that questions of legitimacy provide not only the political impetus behind the arguments of Bacon and his successors but also, crucially, their metaphorical structure. The common association to be found in these writings between improperly grounded meanings and an often femininized notion of linguistic illegitimacy allied with principles of deceit, decadence, and proliferation will provide a discursive template for discussions of the Chinese language and will evolve later into one of the shaping metaphors of the Western encounter with Chinese culture as a whole.

As James Knowlson suggests, much of seventeenth-century language theory can be traced back to Francis Bacon's denunciation in the *Novum*

organum (1620) and *De augmentis scientiarum* (1623) of the "idols of
the marketplace," or errors in understanding that arise in the course of
human interaction from "the ill and unfit choice of words" that "throw[s]
all into confusion and lead[s] men away into numberless empty controversies and idle fancies."[14] In particular, Bacon warned of usages in which
res and *verba*, subject matter and word, failed to correspond, resulting in
"names of things which do not exist" or "names of things which exist,
but yet confused and ill-defined, and hastily and irregularly derived from
realities."[15] The proper derivation of names and knowledge from material
realities was, of course, essential to Bacon's larger project in these texts:
the creation of a new system of natural philosophy within which scientific
understanding would be founded upon direct access to the facts of nature
and things in themselves by means of rigorous experiment and correct
observation. Bacon recognized that the translation of sensory observation
into a useful form of understanding was a process intrinsically fraught
with hazards. Errors in the collection and processing of data might arise
from the failings of human perception, psychological factors, or precon-
ceived philosophical notions. But it was in the communication of results
that the risk of straying from natural truths was greatest. However fastidious the investigator's experimental technique, if he chose his words
carelessly or indulged in groundless abstractions or flowery rhetoric in
presenting his observations, his work, far from contributing to new
knowledge, would distort or distract from the matter at hand, leading
only to a multiplication of error. The purpose of natural history, Bacon
urged, was not "the pleasure of the reader," but "the formation of true
axioms." Its practitioners would be best served by observing a strict economy of style, setting down essential points "briefly and concisely," and
purging their work of needless citations, sensationalist descriptions,
superstitious stories, and, above all, rhetorical language, which he ban-
ishes in terms that would appear again in classicist satires of the Chinese
taste in the following century: "For all that concerns ornaments of speech,
similitudes, treasury of eloquence, and such emptiness, let it be utterly dismissed."[16]

   The reliability of scientific language, then, is for Bacon rooted in an
immediate correspondence between words and the natural phenomena
they describe. The Bible having been decentered, as Markley argues, "as a
logocentric guarantee of interpretive and ideological authority," nature
stood alone as the ultimate linguistic referent, the "parent" of all meaning,
the sole guarantor of the truth and legitimacy of speech. Bacon justifies his

claim to be "nature's spokesman," for Snider, through his advocacy of "a
style that proclaimed its proximity to an absolute beginning" such as only
material nature could now offer.[17] In *The Advancement of Learning*
(1605) Bacon had proposed the rigorous definition of terms as an important step toward achieving semantic stability, resolving disputes, and
defending thought against the "false appearances that are imposed upon
us by words." But by the time of the *Novum organum* he viewed definitions as grossly inadequate as a basis for common understanding or as a
corrective for the lack of correspondence between words and things,
"since the definitions themselves consist of words, and those words beget
others [*verba gignunt verba*]" in their turn.[18] Just as Bacon rejects the syl-
logism as a precarious edifice of vague and hastily abstracted words and
notions in favor of the grounded linearity of inductive reasoning, so too he
rejects the logical circularity of attempts to anchor linguistic meanings in
the shifting sands of words in favor of an appeal to the originary authority
of the nature of things. His choice of metaphor, evoking the specter of a
boundless proliferation of badly begotten, bastard words, suggests that
Bacon's prescription for the reform of language stems from a fundamental
anxiety regarding the irregular derivation and lawless descent of meanings
as well as a corresponding attempt to control the Babelian confusion that
results by insisting on the accountability of language to an original prelin-
guistic progenitor. If Bacon draws upon reproductive imagery to describe
the lexical illegitimacy he so deplores, he imagines the rationalist regime he
offers as a necessary antidote in equally sexualized terms. He characterizes his natural philosophy as the product of a "legitimate, chaste, and
severe course of inquiry," one that promises to unite the mind "with *things*
themselves in a chaste, holy, and legal wedlock."[19] Representational legitimacy is allied here with the suppression of pleasure and desire in a for-
mula that will resonate through the language theory of the next century
and its enthusiastic heralding of the Chinese script.

When the Royal Society was first established in 1660, it incorporated
Bacon's precepts on language into its grand designs for "the Benefit of
humane life by the Advancement of *Real Knowledge*." Thomas Sprat's
History of the Royal Society (1667), an official defense of the group's
work against its early detractors, transformed them into a new gospel
creed, accompanied by a more dazzling display of rhetorical virtuosity
than one might have imagined possible in ostensible defense of plain
speaking. Like Bacon, Sprat situates nature as the ultimate lawgiver and
stresses the orderly reproduction of her teachings: members of the society

are exhorted "to make faithful Records of all the Works of Nature or Art, which can come within their reach." And like Bacon, he expresses concern at the untoward begetting of false meanings entailed by the prolixity of ornamental language. The only remedy, he writes, for "this vicious abundance of *Phrase*, this trick of *Metaphors*, this volubility of *Tongue*, which makes so great a noise in the World," is a return "to the primitive purity and shortness when men deliver'd so many things almost in an equal number of words."[20]

In the third book of *Gulliver's Travels* (1726), Jonathan Swift would parody this stoical impulse toward linguistic mastery in his famous account of the school of languages at the Lagado Academy of Projectors. Purposes of brevity and health would both be served, Swift's academicians suggest, were words simply abolished altogether and replaced in conversation by the things they represent, bundles of which could then be assembled in advance as required for each day's business. In contrast to most of the projects of the academy, which, like the scheme to extract sunbeams out of cucumbers, turn out to be exercises in futility, this new universal language is actually employed by many of the "learned and wise" of the kingdom. The only obstacle to its more widespread use has been the staunch resistance of the women, who, together with the "vulgar and illiterate," had "threatened to raise a rebellion, unless they might be allowed the liberty to speak with their tongues."[21] Swift's association of flawed forms of speech with the unruly masses is not surprising given the political contexts of recent attempts to impose order and discipline on language. The prominence of women among the Lagado rebels is more remarkable in that it hints at a distinctly gendered dimension to the empiricist critique of rhetorical language and to the ideal of linguistic legitimacy that lay behind it.

Evelyn Fox Keller, Susan Bordo, and Londa Schiebinger have treated at length the historical associations of the Baconian project with a specifically "masculine philosophy."[22] The point I wish to stress here is that both Bacon, in his warnings against unlawfully begotten words, and Sprat, in his longing for a primitive purity of expression, convey a profound mistrust of any process of linguistic production or reproduction that is not subject to rigorous regulation and control, a mistrust perhaps best captured by the marked irony of the all-knowing Prospero's qualified assurance to Miranda, "Thy mother was a piece of virtue, and / She said thou wast my daughter."[23] In language planning, as in patriarchy, privileging the value of legitimacy and certain knowledge translates into hostility toward that locus of uncertainty and desire that is represented as the feminine. The implicit ideal here, as elsewhere in the language reform movement, is a self-sufficient, masculine realm of representation that remains religiously faithful to the original truth of things through a chaste renunciation of suspect practices of linguistic reproduction.[24] For Sprat, the most dangerous incursions of the feminine into this realm of autonomous "male *virtus*" are those temptations posed by the pleasures of the aesthetic, and he is even more adamant that Bacon in urging their rejection. He refers to rhetorical eloquence as a form of "beautiful deceit" and insists that members of the Royal Society have been fastidious in their endeavors "to separate the knowledge of Nature from the colours of Rhetorick, the devices of Fancy, or the delightful deceit of Fables." The seductive delights of language play, like the Sirens' call, threaten the ruin of their heroic enterprise; were it not for the members' diligence in avoiding them, "the whole spirit and vigour of their Design had been soon eaten out by the luxury and redundance of speech."[25] To dread the emasculation of philosophy at the hands of rhetoric is simultaneously to venerate a curiously autogenetic ideal of language, one whose legitimacy is finally premised on the rationalist repudiation of "female" generativity in the production of meaning.[26]

Twenty-two years later, John Locke would take up a similar ideal, repeating Sprat's denunciation of "the beautiful deceit" of figurative language in terms that would explicitly foreground the gender coding of the natural philosophers' quest. In Book III of *An Essay Concerning Human Understanding* (1690), a chapter entitled "Of the Abuse of Words" ends with a series of reflections on the difficulty of weaning the mind in search of "dry truth and real knowledge" from the habitual pleasures of the aesthetic. While acknowledging that "Pleasure and Delight" may constitute justifiable ends for a limited range of discourses (such as poetry), Locke insists that the project of true understanding requires their complete renunciation. But in a tone of striking resignation, he laments the futility of such a prescription, given mankind's manifest preference for "the Arts of Fallacy" over the "improvement of Truth and Knowledge." The temptation of pleasurable deceit is an irresistible one and, like the rebels of Lagado, poses a decidedly feminine challenge to the orderly reproduction of truth in language. "Eloquence, like the fair Sex, has too prevailing Beauties in it, to suffer it self ever to be spoken against. And 'tis in vain to find fault with those Arts of Deceiving, wherein Men find pleasure to be deceived."[27]

The ideal of scientific purity of expression and the corresponding mistrust of rhetorical excess articulated by Bacon and Sprat and elaborated later by Locke and Swift underpin much of the speculation on universal languages that emerged as the predominant interest of language planners in the mid- to late seventeenth century. These later proposals, however, raise the issue of linguistic legitimacy to an entirely new plane. For Bacon and Sprat, language reform largely came down to a matter of prose style: if deception entered into language through thoughtlessness or vanity of expression, then it could be purged through a writer's conscientious adherence to the proper methodological and rhetorical principles.[28] For the prophets of universal language, however, a fundamental corruption was intrinsic to the nature of existing languages, whether or not they were being diligently employed in the service of natural philosophy. A mere reformation in the practice of writing would be insufficient to guarantee the legitimacy of expression; what was needed was an entirely new, artificial language constructed to assure from the outset the requisite correspondence between words and things.

The apogee of the universal language movement was John Wilkins's *An Essay Towards a Real Character and a Philosophical Language*, published by the Royal Society in 1668. Based on a comprehensive classification of things and concepts "according to their respective natures," his scheme derives both the pronunciation and symbolic representation of each of the words comprising his artificial language according to its position in his taxonomic tables, which in turn is determined by the attributes of the object or idea itself. Thus, for example, "the word *diamond* doth by its place in the Tables appear to be a Substance, a Stone, a precious Stone, transparent, colourless, most hard and bright," and each of these qualities is conveyed by the word's spoken and written forms in Wilkins's system. By embedding the description of objects within the words and "real characters" used to represent them, Wilkins aspired to incorporate the Baconian ideal of linguistic precision within the structure of the language, thereby assuring "the distinct expression of all things and notions that fall under discourse."[29]

Most of the several flaws that Wilkins identifies in existing languages stem from their tolerance for the disorderly reproduction of meaning. As for Bacon and Sprat before him, rhetorical excess and the habitual decoupling of words from precisely grounded meanings appear to Wilkins as the first and most obvious culprits. He associates metaphors and ornamental phrases not only with "ambiguity" and "false appearances" but also with a dangerously feminine fickleness and fecundity, attributing the destruction of "solid Knowledge in all professions" to the fact that, "like other things of fashion, they are very changeable, every generation producing new ones."[30] In the theological realm, the volatility of midcentury conflicts between the established church and Catholics, Quakers, atheists, and dissenters of all descriptions lent, for Wilkins, an undeniable urgency to a project that would

contribute much to the clearing of some of our Modern differences in Religion, by unmasking many wild errors, that shelter themselves under the disguise of affected phrases. . . . And several of those pretended, mysterious, profound notions, expressed in great swelling words, whereby some men set up for reputation, being this way examined, will appear to be, either nonsense, or very flat and jejune.[31]

A second source of corruption in modern language might be seen as a continuing historical legacy of its biblical fall from grace. Whereas learned languages that "remain only in Books, by which the purity of them is regulated, may . . . continue the same without change," the vulgar languages are subject to constant alteration from their "original purity" as a result of commerce, royal marriages, and military conquests, as well as "the common fate to which all . . . human things are subject." Semantic mutation, in other words, results not just from individual acts of rhetorical irresponsibility, but from the situation of these acts within the tumultuous cauldron of history. The only hope for restoring language to its native wholeness is to reconstruct it according to "the Rules of Art," a set of philosophical premises sufficiently universal as to transcend the particularity of any given cultural context.[32]

This brings me to the final source of linguistic confusion that Wilkins identifies, and the only one that marks a significant departure from a model of representational legitimacy based on the regulated reproduction of meaning. Whereas rhetorical superfluity and historical change evoke a temporal break in the lineage between bastardized sign and the purity of an original referent, the entirely arbitrary and disorderly construction of existing languages suggests an a priori structural flaw. Wilkins faults the ordering of letters in alphabets as "inartificial and confused, without any such methodical distribution as were requisite for their particular natures and differences; the Vowels and Consonants being promiscuously huddled together, without any distinction." Far preferable would be a regular alphabet in which they were "reduced into Classes, according to their several kinds, with such an order of precedence and subsequence as their

natures will bear." Ambiguity, while often arising from the use of metaphor and other "affected ornaments," can likewise be traced to a structural "deficiency" resulting from inadequate distinctions between elements of the language, as in the case of homonyms or equivocals, "which
are of several significations, and therefore must needs render speech
doubtful and obscure."[33]

The remedy for all this linguistic promiscuity is the taxonomic arrangement of words and things that serves as the "great foundation" of his
design. If the purity of the learned languages was assured by their ossifi-
cation in the classical canon, then the corruption of the vulgar tongues
might be corrected through the systematic enumeration, classification,
and naming of things and notions according to a schematic analysis of
their characteristics. The legitimacy of Wilkins's language would thus be
guaranteed by a regimen of clearly defined distinctions that would serve
as the philosophical basis of the system, "it being the proper end and
design of . . . Philosophy to reduce all things and notions unto such a
frame, as may express their natural order, dependence, and relations."[34]
Within a theoretical discourse saturated with imagery of conception and
generation, "dependence" and "relations" stand out as particularly suggestive terms here. As Mary Slaughter points out, the philosophical
"frame" that Wilkins proposes is that of Aristotelian taxonomy, a model
within which the transmission of essential identity is conceived as
genealogical in a very fundamental way:

> It is not insignificant that taxonomic concepts and constructs take as their point
> of departure the most primitive and basic form of order that we have, the order of
> the family. The word *genus* comes from a word originally related to family, "what
> something derives from." . . . The genealogical family is our first (and perhaps our
> last) intimation of connection, relation, and order.[35]

To premise the remediation of language on its taxonomic ordering, then,
is to conceive of representational legitimacy in terms not only of the regulated descent of individual signs from an originary source of meaning
but also of the regulated relationship among those signs. Robert Markley
argues that Wilkins's discussion of the category of "Economical Posses-
sions" in the *Essay* reveals an underlying conception of "natural order"
that "privileges the patrilineal family as a literate, landholding, and
legally constituted entity" and that structures all subsequent social relations according to this model.[36] I would suggest that Wilkins's understanding of linguistic order as premised on a hierarchical and rigidly dif-

ferentiated system of categories likewise derives from a familial and indeed patrilineal paradigm. Whereas Bacon and Sprat emphasized a relationship of vertical descent—the immediate derivation of scientific prose from the observable nature of things—as the guarantor of authenticity in language, Wilkins proposes a multidimensional ordering system of both derivational dependence and metonymic relations among the terms of his branching taxonomical frame. In doing so, he reconfigures the idea of legitimacy he inherits from Bacon by placing the internal, structural consistency of a representational system on a par with the purity of its epistemological pedigree. Both of these standards will figure prominently in the idealized conceptions of the Chinese language that emerged alongside these language reform proposals.

By comparison with the projects of Bacon and the Royal Society, the ambitions of early-eighteenth-century language reformers appear markedly more modest in scope. After having reached a peak in 1668 with the publication of Wilkins's *Essay*, interest in linguistics among members of the Royal Society declined in the latter part of the century. John Locke's *Essay Concerning Human Understanding* (1690) signaled the death of the century's universal language movement with its argument that words ultimately referred not to things in themselves at all, but rather only to largely arbitrary ideas in the minds of individual speakers.[37] Under the shadow of Locke's subjectivist epistemology, the ideal of linguistic purity began to fade, and the fantasy of a rational, philosophical language was replaced by the rather more quotidian aspiration for "the improvement of knowledge and politeness."[38] Later writers like Jonathan Swift and Samuel Johnson remained concerned about the imperfections and corruptions that plagued the English tongue, but the emphasis in their work shifted from curing the disease to arresting its course and halting or slowing the seemingly inevitable process of decline. By resigning themselves to intrinsic deficiencies in the nature of language and focusing instead on the problem of historical change in their efforts at reform, they implicitly developed a third conception of linguistic legitimacy, this one emphasizing values of permanence and stability rather than linear derivation or taxonomic ordering.

Ever since the establishment of the Académie Française by the Cardinal de Richelieu in 1634, prominent writers in England, including Dryden, Evelyn, Sprat, Addison, and Defoe, had called for an equivalent institution to preserve their own language against the forces of decay. The leading proponent of such a plan in the early eighteenth century was Jonathan

Swift, who in his *Proposal for Correcting, Improving, and Ascertaining the English Tongue* (1712) laid before the Lord-Treasurer Oxford a series of urgent observations on the imperfection and continual decline of the language.[39] He contends that in spite of the literary efforts of his peers, "its daily improvements are by no means in proportion to its daily corruptions; that the pretenders to polish and refine it, have chiefly multiplied abuses and absurdities; and that in many instances it offends against every part of grammar." He is concerned, as well, with the lack of refinement of English when compared to the Romance languages and worries that its precipitous decline may presage the fate that befell the original Roman tongue.[40] The imagery he uses to portray the agents and processes of this deterioration preserves the overtones of illegitimate reproduction introduced by his predecessors. The current decline of the French language, for example, Swift attributes to "the natural *inconstancy* of that people, and the affectation of some late authors to introduce and *multiply* cant words, which is the most ruinous corruption in any language" (emphasis added). London, he claims, is never short of dunces of sufficient credit "to *give rise* to some new word, and *propagate* it in most conversations, though it had neither humour nor significancy . . . while the men of wit and learning . . . were too often *seduced* to imitate and comply with them" (emphasis added).[41]

Like the planners of the previous century, Swift views the corruption of language as arising from the irresponsible use of words, a habit of linguistic debauchery that perennially plagues the public sphere. But whereas Wilkins considered unregulated change and proliferation inevitable features of all natural languages that could be remedied only by replacing them altogether, Swift rejects the assumption of essential mutability and submits that the same static perfection sought by Wilkins in his artificial language might somehow be attained by English. "I see no absolute necessity why any language should be perpetually changing," he writes and then suggests that if English "were once refined to a certain standard, perhaps there might be ways found out to fix it for ever, or at least till we are invaded and made a conquest by some other state." The standard he proposes is the English spoken during Queen Elizabeth's reign; although the period was no stranger to "very ill taste both of style and wit," such shortcomings could be overlooked in the name of stability: "It is better a language should not be wholly perfect, than that it should be perpetually changing."[42]

In his willing accommodation of imperfection, Swift offers a pragmatic revision of the previous century's dream of legitimating language through an appeal to an originary or transcendent authority. The legitimating impulse remains intact, but the mythic point of origin is firmly historicized, and the transcendent authority of nature and philosophy is replaced by the merely cultural and political stature of a monarch. The emphasis in his scheme, as a result, shifts from radical reformation to the preservation of a modestly altered linguistic status quo. Legitimacy becomes a function of constancy, and precedent the sole basis for judgment. If only the users of the language could forego linguistic novelty to remain faithful to an accepted standard, the English tongue—and good taste too—might endure intact through countless ages. The price of fickleness, by contrast, could only be precipitous decline under the ominous shadow of Rome.

Although Samuel Johnson refers dismissively to Swift's *Proposal* as a "petty treatise on the English language," he nonetheless shares a number of its premises. In his own struggle in the monumental *Dictionary* project (1755) to tame a language "copious without order, and energetic without rules," Johnson, like Swift, envisions a firmly historicized context for his linguistic nostalgia, searching out the "pure sources" of "English undefiled" as an antidote to the spread of "fugitive cant."[43] He is even more insistent than Swift, however, in imagining the emergence of modern forms of language in terms of natural processes of generation. In offering his thoughts on the "descent of our language," Johnson notes that the original "progenitors of our speech" are likely to be found in every corner of the world.[44] The fact that these progenitors were of human rather than divine origin accounts for the corruption that plagues language while the things it represents remain immutable, for "words are the daughters of earth, and . . . things are the sons of heaven."[45] Johnson justifies his emphasis on etymology in the *Dictionary* precisely as a response to this fallen, bastardized condition of language:

By tracing in this manner every word to its original, and not admitting, but with great caution, any of which no original can be found, we shall secure our language from being over-run with cant, from being crowded with low terms, the spawn of folly or affectation, which arise from no just principles of speech, and of which therefore no legitimate derivation can be shewn.[46]

If English cannot be entirely purified and embalmed, in other words, at least it can be purged, through an appeal to historical origins, of its most flagrantly misbegotten progeny.

Johnson's association of corrupted speech with colorful figures of excess—"over-run," "crowded," "spawn"—recalls the pronounced concern with the rhetorical "extravagance" and "superfluity" observed in the lamentations of Bacon, Sprat, and Wilkins. Critics have noted the degree to which Johnson was influenced in his vision of language reform by seventeenth-century language projectors, and it seems clear that he inherited from their writings this imagery of chaotic profusion, illegitimate representation, an illicit and uncontrolled reproduction of meanings that jeopardizes an established order of signification.[47] If the defilement of such an order is attributed to the profligacy of signs, Johnson's etymological remedy suggests that its preservation depends on the certification of pedigree. In a linguistic order continually being undermined by the "colloquial licentiousness" of its users, a "settled test of purity" is required to detect "adulterations" and restore the "propriety" of the language.[48] The test that he prescribes is essentially a genealogical one: just as kings derive their legitimate authority from an established royal lineage, so the words in his dictionary owe their claims to validity to their verifiable derivation from an acceptable source.

Johnson's genealogical mappings extend in two dimensions. On the one hand, he attempts to provide each word with an etymology in the diachronic, historical sense by tracing it back to a Roman or Teutonic original.[49] On the other hand, he also proposes a kind of synchronic taxonomy for each word based on a precise division and ordering of its multiple senses under distinct categories according to their degrees of figurality.

In explaining the general and popular language, it seems necessary to sort the several senses of each word, and to exhibit first its natural and primitive signification; as,

To *arrive*, to reach the shore in a voyage: he *arrived* at a safe harbour.

Then to give its consequential meaning, *to arrive*, to reach any place, whether by land or sea; as, he *arrived* at his country seat.

Then its metaphorical sense, to obtain any thing desired; as, he *arrived* at a peerage.[50]

This short example of a progression from literal to metaphorical sense, while illustrative, hardly does justice to Johnson's practice. He admits to having been "convinced of the necessity of disentangling combinations, and separating similitudes," but at times he carries his near obsession with the distinction of subtle nuances so far that, for Robert Demaria, "the most salient feature of his book, besides the amount of quotation, is the number of senses into which he divides each definition." However many the "metaphorical acceptations" of a given word, though, they are all rigorously subordinated to "the original sense" even if that original sense is no longer in use. Thus, he explains, although "ardour" and "flagrant" no longer mean "heat" or "burning," because these remain the "primitive ideas of these words," they are set first in the list of definitions.[51]

In establishing etymology as the basis of his notion of linguistic legitimacy, Johnson draws upon all three of the earlier conceptions of this idea that I have discussed to this point. First, his appeal to the original or primitive meanings of words as a source of absolute authority, his acknowledgment of the merely human provenance of such authority notwithstanding, recalls in form Bacon's insistence on the accountability of language to the origins of meaning in observable nature. Second, his synchronic mapping of degrees of figurality as a means of indicating distinctions and affinities among words is the lexicographic equivalent of Wilkins's emphasis on philosophical taxonomy.[52] And finally, although he ultimately comes to recognize the impossibility of linguistic stasis, his frequent invocations of tradition in his attacks on the vagaries of modern usage and indeed the teleology of the dictionary project reflect a profound sympathy with Swift's desire to "fix" the language, to anchor usage to a fixed point in an idealized linguistic past.

Over the course of this century marked by efforts at language reform, the ideal of legitimacy appears in various guises, but the underlying concerns regarding false uses of language and the metaphorical framework through which they are articulated remain remarkably constant. The creative capacities of language—its tendencies toward proliferation and fanciful innovation—are described as promiscuous, seductive, out of control. When faithless words are no longer wedded to their original senses, the generation of meaning becomes an illegitimate process that undermines truth, good taste, and the integrity of the language itself. Each of the reform efforts that I have explored here is premised on a conception of linguistic legitimacy that seeks somehow to restore this lost integrity and to ground the production and reproduction of meanings in stable, sanctioned relationships between signifiers and their scientific, historical, or philosophical contexts. The contemporary responses to the Chinese language treated in the remaining three parts of this chapter will reveal a remarkably similar longing and the emergence of a conceptual paradigm that will substantially determine the ways China is successively imagined and reimagined in the West from the founding of the first Jesuit missions to the opening salvos of the Opium Wars.

The Legitimacy of Chinese Writing

The third part of *Gulliver's Travels*, as noted above, offers a trenchant satire of those projectors and reformers who had become intoxicated by the quest for a perfectly grounded language. Although Swift's barb may have been intended for the followers of the Royal Society, the attention given to the language schemes of the Lagado academicians and the other linguistic curiosities in Gulliver's tale—the slanted writing of the Lilliputians, for example, the Laputans' musical language, or the notable absence of words for lying or falsehood among the Houyhnhnms—reminds one of another dimension of the search for superior forms of expression during this period: the fascination with accounts of exotic languages discovered in the course of travels to real or imagined foreign lands. Authentic reports informed many of the more fantastic tales of linguistic practices, and as Paul Cornelius suggests, "the languages of these imaginary states were—each in its own way—related to a number of trends in the history of language in the seventeenth century," owing to their creators' frequent involvement in real-world language reform projects as well.[53]

By far the most important foreign model for European speculation on alternative languages during this period was Chinese. Cornelius and others have emphasized "the extent of the 'Oriental' influence on the language ideals of seventeenth-century Europe," especially the notions of universal and philosophical languages.[54] It is certainly clear that early descriptions of Chinese introduced a number of novel ideas—concerning, in particular, the supposed special properties of the written characters—into contemporary linguistic discourse. What is perhaps less readily apparent is the degree to which Western interpretations of the Chinese language were themselves informed by elements of this same discourse. If the Chinese model influenced seventeenth-century linguistic thought, it did so through its apparent convergence with the contemporary intellectual quest for legitimate forms of representation. The Chinese script, in other words, did not so much provide new answers in its own right as serve as an endlessly evocative case study for the interpretive hypotheses that demanded them. The centrality of the problem of legitimacy in contemporary language theory shaped the European encounter with the characters, giving rise to a composite vision of a uniquely "Chinese" mode of representation as fantastic as the fictional language of any imaginary kingdom. Ultimately, as I will show in subsequent chapters, the form of this ideographic fantasy extends into the European interpretation of other representational elements of Chinese culture and provides the framework for the dizzying reversal of China's fortunes in the eighteenth-century imagination.

Two influential missionary works published within a thirty-year span during Bacon's lifetime provided the groundwork for a century's speculations on the nature of the Chinese language. In 1585, the Augustinian monk Juan González de Mendoza published his *Historia de las cosas mas notables, ritos y costumbres del gran reyno de la China*, a compilation of the accounts of Portuguese and Spanish priests into a single volume that for the first time attempted to bring together, at the request of Pope Gregory XIII, a "history of the things that are known about the kingdom of China."[55] An English translation—the first detailed work on China in the language—appeared three years later under the title *The Historie of the great and mightie kingdome of China, and the situation thereof*. By 1600 the book had been reprinted forty-six times in seven European languages, making it one of the best-sellers of its day and the first book on China since Marco Polo's *Travels* to reach a wide European audience. According to editor C. R. Boxer, "it is probably no exaggeration to say that Mendoza's book had been read by the majority of well-educated Europeans at the beginning of the seventeenth century."[56] European readers encountered actual Chinese characters for the first time in this compendium and surely would have found their curiosity piqued further by the author's intriguing account of them:

You shall find very few in this kingdom but can both write and read, yet have they not the alphabet of letters as we have, but all that they do write is by figures, and they are long in learning of it, and with great difficulty, for that almost every word hath his character. . . . They do use more than six thousand characters different the one from the other. . . . It is a kind of language that is better understood in writing than in speaking (as the Hebrew tongue), by reason of the certain distinction of points that is in every character differing one from the other, which in speaking cannot be distinguished so easily. . . . It is an admirable thing to consider how that in that kingdom they do speak many languages, the one differing from the other: yet generally in writing they do understand one the other, and in speaking not. The occasion is, for that one figure or character unto them all doth signify one thing, although in the pronouncing there is difference in the vowels. The character that doth signify a city is this 城, and in their language some do call it Leobi, and others Fu, yet both the one and the other do understand it to be city; the like is in all other names. And in this order do communicate with them the Japonese, Lechios, . . . and other borderers unto them: whereas in their speech or language, there is no more understanding than is between Greeks and Tuscans.[57]

The three distinguishing features of the written language that Mendoza introduces here—its difficulty, its precedence over the spoken tongue, and its role as a shared medium of communication among a number of linguistic communities within and around China—were largely responsible for the considerable interest generated in Europe by its discovery and would remain the cornerstones of both speculative and investigative responses to the script for the ensuing two hundred years.

It is worth noting that, in contrast to the more fanciful notions of some of his successors, Mendoza's general claims about the language are remarkably accurate. Although more than 49,000 distinct characters are listed in the Kang Xi dictionary of 1716, fewer than 10,000 have been in common usage at any one time. And although modern scholars have argued against the "indispensability myth," which suggests that large numbers of characters are necessary to provide distinctions among words not available in the spoken language, it remains true that native speakers of the language can sometimes be seen, as they could in the sixteenth century, tracing a written character on their palm in order to clear up an ambiguity in speech.[58] Finally, the uniformity of the characters does provide for some degree of communication across otherwise daunting linguistic divides. Speakers of mutually unintelligible Mandarin and Cantonese share a common literary script, while the history of Japanese, Korean, Thai, and even Vietnamese adoption of Chinese characters has long facilitated other forms of cultural transmission between China and her neighbors.

The second key source of information about China at the turn of the seventeenth century was the journal of Matteo Ricci, the founder of the first successful Jesuit mission to that country. Ricci lived in China from 1583 until his death in 1610 and was one of the first Europeans to become thoroughly versed not only in the language but also in the intellectual tradition of the Chinese. A profound understanding of the host culture was for Ricci the cornerstone of a successful missionary enterprise, and the intimate knowledge of the foreign that animates his diaries no doubt contributed to their widespread popularity among European readers. First published in Rome in 1615 by Father Nicola Trigault, who had brought the manuscript back from China and translated it with some revisions into Latin, Ricci's account of the history of the mission appeared in multiple editions in Latin, French, German, Spanish, and Italian from 1616 to 1648 and was excerpted in *Purchas his Pilgrims* in 1625.

In a chapter devoted to the state of learning in China, Ricci confirms and elaborates Mendoza's claims concerning the language of the Chinese.

Because of the complex tonal structure of the spoken language, "it is the most equivocal language that exists." The sheer size of the lexicon, which Ricci estimates at between 70,000 and 80,000 characters, means that no one has ever mastered it in its entirety. The primacy of the written language is owing in part, as Mendoza suggested, to the role of characters in resolving the homophonic ambiguities of speech, but also in part to the historical emphasis on its development: "In ancient times this nation gave much more attention to good writing than to good speaking, and even now all their rhetorical eloquence is to be found in their writing rather than in their speech." Finally, Ricci reiterates the status of the script as a lingua franca among East Asian nations, asserting that although the Chinese, Japanese, and Koreans pronounce the characters according to their particular dialects, they interpret their meanings in the same way.[59]

Before turning to the question of how these early accounts of the Chinese script were received by individual scholars in subsequent decades, it may be helpful to consider in more general terms some of their points of intersection with the central concerns of the contemporary language reform movement. Most obviously, the notion of the cross-cultural legibility of the Chinese script anticipates the seventeenth-century European dream of overcoming the crippling consequences of Babel; indeed, Cornelius and others have identified an awareness of this aspect of the Chinese language as "one of the most important influences behind the movement for a universal language which developed during that time."[60] To the extent that language reformers referred explicitly to the Chinese model, one might expect that assertions of its regional universality would encourage them to seek within this model—or, indeed, to project onto it—other corroborating signs of that representational legitimacy that was the ultimate object of their quest.

To take but one example, one might consider the intriguing possibility that the purported difficulty of learning Chinese would have held a certain perverse appeal to those troubled by the thoughtless ease with which the trustees of European vernaculars seemed to be mumbling their way into oblivion. Where could one find a better antidote to Sprat's alarming visions of decadent rhetorical abandon and careless abuse of words than in the spectacle of legions of stoic scholars, heads bowed reverentially over ancient scrolls, devoting lifetimes to the painstaking mastery of a lexicon of tens of thousands of characters? In a context where linguistic competence is more closely aligned with habits of righteous self-sacrifice than of decadent self-indulgent pleasure, there might well be less to fear from dilettantes taking liberties with words. Ricci's own comments on the moral advantages of literacy in China are explicit in this regard:

[Scholars] begin to study the characters as children and continue until their old age. While the necessity for such study cannot be discounted as an impediment to the flourishing of the sciences in this kingdom, the degree to which it occupies their souls also prevents them from giving themselves over to the desire for pleasure to which the nature of men is inclined.[61]

The moral fastidiousness demanded by a sustained and rigorous study of Chinese will increasingly, in subsequent decades, come to inflect perceptions of the language itself, thereby contributing to the identification of Chinese with a linguistic ideal that was often itself imagined in starkly moral terms.

A European audience obsessively concerned by the spreading lawlessness of speech was bound to be transfixed as well by the notion of a predominantly scribal culture in which the written forms of language take clear precedence over the verbal. The very dichotomy between spoken and written Chinese in Jesuit accounts corresponds to the fundamental opposition underlying narratives of linguistic decline and redemption in the West. When Mendoza speaks of "the certain distinction of points that is in every character differing one from the other, which in speaking cannot be distinguished so easily," he implicitly addresses what would become a central issue of the language reformers' campaign: how, in a discursive sphere fraught with ambiguity, rhetorical mischiefs, and the accidents of linguistic and historical change, to establish a fixed and unequivocal correspondence between words and the meanings they are taken to represent. For Ricci, the Chinese writing system offers not only a remedy for ambiguity but also the basis of a clear and concise literary style, another cause that would be famously championed by the Royal Society. Their method of writing has enabled the Chinese "to create a beautiful and eloquent manner of composition in which with very few syllables they can express far more than can ever be conveyed in one of our long speeches."[62] Ricci finds in Chinese writing, in other words, precisely that economy and exactness of expression that Sprat would call for in exhorting English writers to renounce their habits of prolixity in favor of "deliver[ing] so many things almost in an equal number of words."[63]

Finally, the affinity of Chinese writing with the contemporary ideal of legitimacy in language is reinforced by the historical association of the script with the bearers of the mantle of legitimacy in the social and political spheres. Whereas English reformers could only lament the subjection of their common language to the shameful depredations of the lower orders, the distinguished class of literati in Ricci's China succeed in preserving the purity and stature of the classical literary language that is the mark of their privilege and authority by refraining from writing in the colloquial idiom altogether.[64] In Mendoza's account, this same written language serves as the guarantee of judicial probity and fairness, in that "in all matters of law . . . the judges do nothing but by writing," a practice that by extension comes to certify the legitimacy of the political order itself. "In matters of great importance . . . the judge will not trust the scrivener or notary to write any information; but they with their own hands will write the declaration of any witness. . . . This great diligence is the occasion that few times there is any that doth complain of any ill justice done."[65] It is not only the nature of the script, then, but the social institution of writing in China that marks Chinese literary culture as distinct, in these missionary accounts, from its Western counterparts. The very act of writing is an emblem of status and authority that serves to reinforce political structures and class distinctions, thereby achieving that legitimation of the social order through a rarefied form of language that underpinned the dreams of the language reform movement in Europe.

Up to this point, I have outlined the context of domestic political and linguistic concerns that would shape the reception of the Chinese language in Europe and identified in early Jesuit accounts attributes of this language that might be expected to spark substantial interest within such a context. I turn now to those philosophers and philologists who interpreted missionary depictions of the script for the European public, and whose often extravagant fantasies about the Chinese "ideograph" would shape Western paradigms for reading "China" more generally until well into the nineteenth century. I will attempt to show not only how the contemporary European concern with linguistic legitimacy informed various interpretations of this deeply perplexing script, but also how the prominence of this ideal in debates on a single essential component of Chinese culture might begin to color, in Western eyes, the appearance of the whole.

Bacon's remarks on the Chinese writing system, although brief, are important in that they are among the first to incorporate the Chinese example into a more general argument on the theory of language. In the second book of *The Advancement of Learning* (1606) he notes that words are only one of a variety of media available for the expression of thought and the transmission of knowledge. Language, he argues in a passage that presages a central axiom of Saussurian linguistics, is premised on a system of sustainable distinctions: "For whatsoever is capable of sufficient differences, and those perceptible by the sense, is in nature competent to express cogitations." He cites the gestures employed by the deaf and mute or improvised by two speakers of mutually unintelligible tongues as one example of an alternative communicative system; another is the writing of the Chinese:

> And we understand further, that it is the use of China, and the kingdoms of the High Levant, to write in characters real, which express neither letters nor words in gross, but things or notions; insomuch as countries and provinces, which understand not one another's language, can nevertheless read one another's writings, because the characters are accepted more generally than the languages do extend; and therefore they have a vast multitude of characters, as many, I suppose, as radical words.

The term "characters real" in this passage is a new coinage on Bacon's part, and one that reflects his central preoccupation with their mode of signification. Like bodily gestures, these graphic figures bypass the intermediary stages of letters and spoken words to express meanings directly: the immediate access they provide to things in themselves makes them "real." Unlike gestures, however, or hieroglyphics, which both rely on "some similitude or congruity with the notion" to convey their sense, Chinese characters, in Bacon's view, share with spoken words the quality of being "*ad placitum*, having force only by contract or acceptation."[66] Although they do designate meanings directly, in other words, they do so without recourse to figural representation; the correspondence is a purely conventional rather than a sensible one.

Bacon never makes the connection explicit, but it is clear how his interpretation of the Chinese script might be read within the framework of his critique in the *Novum organum* of rhetorical language and the human "idols" that plague perception and communication. The idea of a "real character" would seem the perfect antidote to the false correspondence between *res* and *verba* that he diagnosed in the casual use of language. The word "real" in the sense of "having an actual existence" itself derives from the Latin *res*, or thing, and indeed one would expect that a writing system anchored in the realm of things and notions would free the understanding of the deceptions imposed by "names of things which do not exist," "fantastic suppositions," and the other bugbears of quotidian prose. Moreover, Bacon's explicit rejection of any pictographic basis to these characters suggests a parallel with the rigorously nonfigural language of his scientific ideal. When "all depends on keeping the eye steadily fixed upon the facts of nature and so receiving their images simply as they are," any indulgence in figural description is a surrender to a false eidolon, or mental fiction. "Similitudes," like metaphors and other ornaments of speech, are condemned as mere "emptiness" to be "utterly dismissed."[67] In this light, Bacon's emphasis on the nonfigural nature of Chinese writing appears as a further guarantee of its potential legitimacy as a representational system.

Bacon's professed hostility to ambiguity and word play notwithstanding, his own writing is at times sufficiently rich in metaphorical nuance that one cannot refrain from scrutinizing a phrase as suggestive as "characters real" more closely in this light. The word "real," as it was employed in the seventeenth century, claimed two distinct etymologies. Apart from the familiar sense rooted in *res* noted above, a "real" was also a silver coin of the Spanish Empire whose name derived ultimately from the Latin *rex*, or king. John Donne puns on these two distinct senses of the term in his poem "The Canonization" (1633): "Observe his honour, or his grace, / On the Kings reall, or his stamped face." That Chinese characters might have suggested to Bacon a similar confluence of meanings is suggested by the self-justifying aside with which he concludes his discussion of the topic. Although the inferiority of gestures and Egyptian hieroglyphics as forms of communication may make their study largely useless, "yet because this part [of knowledge, that is, language] concerneth, as it were, the mint of knowledge (for words are the tokens current and accepted for conceits, as moneys are for values, and that it is fit men be not ignorant that moneys may be of another kind than gold and silver) I thought good to propound it to better inquiry."[68] What gives a coin "current and accepted" status is its backing by the state whose emblem it bears. Coins, in other words, derive their legitimacy from political authority (*rex*), just as words, for Bacon, derive their legitimacy from the material authority of things in themselves (*res*). For Bacon to describe Chinese characters as "real" is, in this context, to infuse the latter process with the metaphorical overtones of the former. The appeal of the Chinese writing system in a time of dangerous social unrest was precisely the unmediated relationship with a source of absolute and transcendent truth that it seemed to represent.

It would fall to John Wilkins to pursue Bacon's characterization of the Chinese script to its logical conclusion. In his *Essay Towards a Real*

An

HISTORICAL ESSAY

Endeavoring a Probability

That the

LANGUAGE

Of the Empire of

CHINA

is the

Primitive

LANGUAGE.

By *John Webb* of *Butleigh* in the
County of *Somerset* Esquire.

LONDON,
Printed for *Nath. Brook*, at the *Angel*
in *Gresham Colledge.* 1669.

1. Title page of John Webb's *Historical Essay Endeavoring a Probability that the Language of the Empire of China is the Primitive Language*, 1669. Courtesy of the Department of Special Collections, Stanford University Libraries.

Character and a Philosophical Language, Wilkins not only borrows
Baconian terminology and aspires to the Baconian ideal of "the distinct
expression of all things," but also founds his entire system on the same
three principles that Bacon had stressed in the Chinese case: a direct correspondence between things and words, nonfigurality, and universality.[69]
At the crucial moment in his essay where he attempts to defend the very
possibility of a "real universal character, that should not signify words,
but things and notions," the Chinese example clinches his argument: the
Chinese "have for many Ages used such a general Character, by which
the inhabitants of that large kingdom, many of them of different tongues,
do communicate with one another, every one understanding this common
Character, and reading it in his own Language."[70] Wilkins maintains that
on account of their number and complexity the Chinese characters themselves "come far short of the advantages" of the system he has designed.
But the fact that they serve as a standard of comparison at all, combined
with the evident satisfaction Wilkins takes in noting how the "philosophical" basis of certain Chinese characters resembles his own scheme,
affirms the prominence of the Chinese script among his own thoughts
as he designed his philosophical language, and illustrates the degree to
which "the China character and language so much talked of in the
world" were in fact being talked of precisely in the context of attempts to
address the most critical linguistic problems of the day.[71]

If the "real" quality of Chinese writing and its widespread currency
contributed to its aura of legitimacy from a political and philosophical
standpoint, historical investigations into the purported antiquity of the
language only confirmed its stature in the eyes of those, like Swift and
Johnson, who found the cardinal linguistic virtue in continuity with tradition. Just as the immediate correspondence between a Chinese character
and the object it designated guaranteed its recognition across vast
expanses of territory, so its antiquity suggested an originary validity that
had preserved its form and meaning unchanged across equally vast
expanses of time. By 1669 any number of writers had commented admiringly on the remarkable historical continuity of the Chinese language and
speculated that it predated those of the Egyptians and Phoenicians.[72] The
year was remarkable in that it saw the London publication of a work that
distilled from such claims the ultimate fantasy of linguistic origins that
lay behind them: this was John Webb's *Historical Essay Endeavoring a
Probability that the Language of the Empire of China is the Primitive
Language*. The first extensive treatise on the Chinese language published

in Europe, Webb's essay drew widely from biblical scholarship, missionary accounts, and the historical writings of Raleigh, Vossius, and others to construct a case for the Chinese language as the original birthright of humanity. While fanciful in parts, the two-hundred-page treatise was fastidiously researched and firmly based, as the author insists, "upon sacred truth and credible history."[73]

Webb's argument, as he encapsulates it in his dedication to Charles II, is straightforward enough. Before the episode at Babel, all the peoples on Earth shared an identical language. China was already populated by this time, and its inhabitants spoke this same original *lingua humana*. The biblical confusion of tongues affected only those peoples who were on the scene at the time, which the Chinese, according to Webb's historical sources, were not. As a result, their language retains to this day a continuity with the Adamic language spoken by all of humankind before their pride got the better of them.[74] Although Webb never contradicts scriptural accounts outright, his story does depend, as one might imagine, on a number of rather extravagant speculative leaps. Noah, for example, not only built his ark in China but also resided there before and after the flood, peopled the land with his posterity, and brought with him the basic religious teachings that underlie Chinese "knowledge in divine matters, [and] of the true god especially."[75]

More relevant to my purposes here, however, are Webb's remarks on the nature of the Chinese language and on the cultural and historical factors that have led to its miraculous preservation over several millennia. Contemporary writers on the problem of the primitive language had agreed upon "six principal guides to be directed by, for the discovery thereof": antiquity, simplicity, generality, modesty of expression, vitality, and brevity.[76] In Webb's assessment, Chinese proves exemplary in each. No language could be more ancient, after all, than one spoken by the first of men, nor more modest than one that harbors no obscenities. Although the evidence Webb cites for the superiority of the Chinese language by each of these measures is addressed to the specific polemical aims of his title, his argument is clearly rooted in contemporary discussions of more general linguistic ideals and resonates in particular with the several conceptions of legitimacy in language so prominent in this discourse.

To begin with, Webb's presentation of the antiquity of Chinese recalls the Baconian impulse to establish the legitimate descent of representation by grounding it definitively in an originary source of a priori truth. But while for Bacon, who was skeptical of fallen humanity's ability ever to recover the prelapsarian wholeness of the Adamic tongue, the sensible and secular world of nature served as the best such source available, Webb's interpretation of biblical events enables him to posit for Chinese a more immediate access to the divine: "It was Nature that from God taught them their language."[77] In the Baconian scheme, the doctrine of linguistic groundedness offered the hope of purging fallen language of its habitual deceptions. But because for Webb the Chinese language had retained the purity of its origins, it remained graced as well with a structural simplicity that spared it the need for such reform. In a formulation that anticipates Sir William Temple's famous characterization of Chinese gardening as creating beauty without rules (which I discuss below in Chapter 3), Webb writes that Chinese "is destitute of all those troublesome aids that are brought in to the assistance of Art; for they have no Rules either for Grammar, Logic, or Rhetoric, but what are dictated to them by the light of nature." To have no need for rules is, presumably, to exist in a state prior to transgression, whether linguistic or moral. The force of Webb's argument depends precisely on conflating these two domains, and he draws liberally on Edenic metaphors in cementing the association between the antiquity and the artlessness of the Chinese language.

> Therefore being it is so nakedly free from those superfluous [grammatical] guides which we are constrained to search after in learning whatever other Language; we may well conceive that it was at first infused or inspired, as the PRIMITIVE Language was into our first Parents, and so from them received, rather than otherwise invented and taught the Chinois. . . . For, without all peradventure it is a perfectly natural speech, and was a Language before the World knew . . . what that, which we now call Art, meant.[78]

Webb shares with Bacon the ideal of a language grounded in nature and purged of art, and he shares as well Bacon's intuition of an authenticity about Chinese writing that approaches this ideal. But whereas for Bacon this special quality inhered in the "reality" of the characters, the immediacy of their legitimizing relationship with things, for Webb it emerges from an historical rather than epistemological congruity with an originary wellspring of authentic meaning.

The prelapsarian context Webb evokes in defending the historical legitimacy of Chinese serves him well when he turns to the moral litmus test for a primitive language claim: that of modesty of expression. Not surprisingly, he finds that the transcendent origins of the Chinese language are reflected not just in its grammatical and rhetorical structure but in the delicacy of its lexicon as well. This is one area where other contenders come up short. Whereas ancient Hebrew contains "many somewhat obscene words," disqualifying it on the grounds that "the PRIMITIVE Language, was an harmless and in nothing immodest speech," Chinese, in all its naked simplicity, fits the bill perfectly (202–3). In the poems of its native speakers, love is treated

in such chaste language, as not an undecent and offensive word to the most chaste ear is to be found in them. And which is more, they have no letters whereby to express the Privy parts, nor are they to be found written in any part of all their books, which cannot be said of any language under the concave of heaven, besides. (98–99)

The scolding judgment implicit in the final clause recalls the typically indignant response to the precipitous decline of contemporary European languages so common among Webb's contemporaries. In particular, his emphasis on the specifically sexual innocence of Chinese places his account squarely within a discursive tradition that frequently rendered linguistic phenomena through metaphors of reproduction and sexual morality. The tendency toward promiscuity and corruption that characterized the English and French tongues in the minds of contemporary reformers is averted in the Chinese case not through the moral restraint of its speakers, but through the preservation of a primordial legitimacy within the lexicon itself.

The very durability of the Chinese language over several millennia further strengthens Webb's claim. Not only had the language of Adam and Noah survived the confusion at Babel, it had also resisted, with a tenacity that would be the envy of a Samuel Johnson, even the less dramatic changes that typically attend the vagaries of human history.

Nothing is more exposed to mutation than languages. . . . It is my intention in this scrutiny to appeal for the uncorruptedness of the language of China to their characters, which have remained in writing on record, throughout all times since their beginning to be a people. . . . We may safely conclude that the MOTHER or NATURAL Language of the Empire of China, perdures in its Ancient purity without any change or alteration. (145, 189–90)

The Chinese script had proven so resistant to mutation owing largely to the reverence with which it had always been regarded by the Chinese people. The Chinese, after all, had elevated calligraphy to an art form of such stature that they could not abide the sight of a handwritten scrap of paper lying on the ground, and would "give willingly great sums of money for a copy of their ancient characters well formed" (176–77). The value ascribed to the traditional forms of writing was reinforced in turn by the national examination system through which aspiring scholars earned their degrees and passed into the ranks of the civil service. According to Webb's account, candidates were tested not only on their knowledge of the classical canon but also on the integrity of their script,

> so that, if in making their compositions upon such themes as the examinator gives them, they write not the character most exactly true (being not so fanatical as the Europeans, to be weary of their old words, but using all possible means to preserve them in their ancient purity) they are dismissed without taking their degrees, how excellent so ever otherwise their composures be. (133–34)

This scriptural essentialism serves for Webb as the mode of descent that has enabled Chinese to transcend the accidents of history and to preserve its divine birthright through the countless generations that have followed. The convergence in the civil service examinations of political and linguistic legitimizing functions, like the combined authorizing force of *rex* and *res* in Bacon's "characters real," situates Webb's reading of Chinese writing within a discourse where the pursuit of such equivalences was a matter of urgent concern, and the interpretation of the foreign a crucial source of exemplars in the service of pressing domestic needs.

The second circumstance accounting for the miraculous continuity of the Chinese script in Webb's account is China's historical isolation from foreign influence. According to the Jesuit interpretations Webb drew upon, strict laws had for centuries discouraged travel and commerce with outsiders and natural barriers had kept military invasions to a minimum. Even when foreign rulers such as the Tartars succeeded in subduing the kingdom, the inertia of the native culture tended to overwhelm that of the conquerors, leaving the Chinese language and its supporting institutions essentially intact.[79] For a seventeenth-century reader obsessed with the compromising entanglement of language in history and of English society in an ever-expanding network of foreign trade partners, such a circumstance must have appeared nothing short of utopian. Webb responds by indulging over several paragraphs in an idyllic reverie on China's splendid isolation that anticipates Rousseau in restaging the scene of prelapsarian purity for an age of commerce and discovery.

> Both Policy and Nature have contributed the means, whereby not in learned Greece or pleasant Italy, but in the remote and hitherto unknown China, are now at last found out, the true Indigenes, that ever since the flood of Noah, being born and bred within their own country, never permitted or admitted conversation

with foreign people. But living contentedly at home, in all abundant prosperity, under their own vines, and under their own fig trees . . . have consumed at least four thousand years without conmixture or commerce with other Nations. . . . Thus hath been fully manifested, that commerce and conquest, the two principal Agents in all sublunary mutations, have had no influence to extirpate, alter, or change either the Laws, Customs, or Language of China.[80]

If the naturalness of Chinese in Webb's account satisfies a Baconian notion of linguistic legitimacy and its changelessness over millennia answers to a Swiftian or Johnsonian standard, then the pure etymological structure of the language fulfills Wilkins's requirement that an ideal language demonstrate a coherent order among its parts. Within Wilkins's scheme, the sense and legitimacy of individual signifiers derived from their determinate position within a rational taxonomy of meanings. By replacing lexical genealogies with philosophical tables, Wilkins's program, as I have argued, aspired to transcend the historical dimension of language altogether. In contrast to Johnson, for whom the nuanced derivation of words from historical antecedents was the unique determinant of their authenticity, Wilkins proposed an anti-etymological framework that would privilege synchronic relationships over diachronic descent. Webb's analysis of the elements of signification in Chinese writing takes this ideal of transcendence one step further by replacing Wilkins's contrived taxonomy of complex hierarchical principles with a more elegant basis for meaning in the identity of words and roots. Although Webb shares Bacon's intuition that the characters are not based on any system of formal congruencies in that they are "composed by no art or rule," he does not view them as entirely the product of arbitrary convention, as they appear to him "fitted . . . to the Infancy and Simplicity of Time." Their primeval origins, in other words, endow them with a quasi-mystical organic wholeness that far surpasses anything in the projector's or the lexicographer's art.

The Chinois are never put to that irksome vexation of searching out a Radix for the derivation of any of their words, as generally all other Nations are; but the Radix is the word, and the word the Radix, and the syllable the same also . . . which persuades a facility in their speech not to be paralleled by any other language, and that the true, genuine, and original sense of things seems to remain with them. (192)

In this passage, as in Webb's account more generally, one finds an unusual synthesis of historical and structural conceptions of linguistic legitimacy and of the complementary axes on which they are played out. On the one hand, the characters are rooted in antiquity; yet on the other, their transmission has proceeded ahistorically, without mutation or evolution, thereby guaranteeing the continued integrity of their significative basis. This, I would argue, is the apotheosis of the linguistic fantasy that has been the subject of this chapter: a vision of perfect connectedness between words and a point of origin in the distant past that remains untroubled by those flawed modes of production and reproduction—words begetting other increasingly hollow and meaningless words—by which the present fallen state of language in the West had come about.

A Scholarly Obsession

From Bacon, Wilkins, and Webb I turn now to a second generation of Western students of Chinese whose writings will reach into the first half of the eighteenth century. Drawing on a far greater wealth of linguistic expertise than was available in earlier decades, their interpretations of the language moved beyond grandiose generalizations to detailed, if still somewhat fanciful, analyses of individual characters. The implicit paradigm, however, remained a familiar one: like their predecessors, these scholars shared a conviction that qualities of original groundedness and authenticity gave Chinese characters a privileged place among human writing systems. But by this time, the paradigm had largely taken on a force of its own. Although the concern with legitimacy in language continued to resonate with political debates well into the eighteenth century, the more striking convergences were with other emerging discourses about China itself, especially those concerning its religious traditions, artistic influences, and trade policies that are the subjects of the subsequent chapters.[81] Having been overdetermined by the confluence of linguistic and theological imperatives in the seventeenth century, the broadly imagined association between China and pure, legitimate forms of cultural authority served, in an inverted form, to define the terms of the dominant discourses of encounter in the eighteenth.

The most eminent intellectual to reflect seriously on the nature of Chinese writing at the turn of the eighteenth century was Gottfried Leibniz. Throughout his adult life he was deeply interested in Chinese civilization, and from the 1680s to his death in 1716 he intensively pursued his studies on the topic. On the basis of Leibniz's wide-ranging intellectual contacts and the more than fifty volumes on China and Asia in his personal library, one authority claims that the savant was probably aware of every significant work on China produced in Europe in the seventeenth century.[82] He took a particular interest in the ecumenical efforts of the Jesuit mission in China, which he termed in a letter of 1697 "the greatest undertaking of our time," and wholeheartedly supported the order's accommodationist position during the heated controversy over the interpretation of ancient Confucian rituals and beliefs. His hopes for cultural exchange and collaboration between Europe and China were based on the firm conviction that each side had something significant to learn from the other. "It is a commerce of light," he continued, "that promises to bring to us all at once their work of several thousand years, and to bring ours to them, thereby doubling the true wealth of both sides." Nor was the emphasis on reciprocality a mere rhetorical nicety. As his choice of metaphors suggests, Leibniz was the product of a self-consciously enlightened age, one generally disposed to acknowledge the shortcomings of European societies and to seek alternative models of social and moral codes wherever else they might be found. In the Preface to his *Novissima Sinica* (1697), one of the few published works to emerge from his years of sinological studies, he writes, "The condition of our affairs, slipping as we are into ever greater corruption, seems to me such that we need missionaries from the Chinese who might teach us the use and practice of natural religion, just as we have sent them teachers of revealed theology."[83] While few Chinese missionaries answered the call, the following decades saw no shortage of European writers who, like Oliver Goldsmith in *Letters from a Chinese Philosopher* (1760), adopted the pose of the Confucian sage to dish out secondhand morsels of Eastern moral wisdom to an enchanted and perhaps overly credulous audience.

Leibniz himself, however, gave far more attention to what the West might learn from a close study of the Chinese language. From the 1670s onward he became interested in various aspects of the Chinese writing system and at different times entertained a number of theories concerning its origins, structure, and ultimate meaning. He remained skeptical of Webb's claim that a primitive language could have survived to modern times and, like Wilkins, eventually dismissed Chinese as a practical model for a universal philosophical language. Nonetheless, he sustained until his death a hypothesis that the characters concealed mysteries beyond their modern accepted meanings, and that they were ultimately grounded in a foundational logic that had since been lost by the Chinese themselves. Given that his twenty-year correspondence with Jesuit missionaries conversant in the language failed to turn up the corroborating evidence he so hoped for, his very persistence in entertaining such a view provides some indication of the imaginative force exercised by the legitimacy paradigm in shaping conceptions of Chinese writing among even the most respected intellectual circles in Europe at this time.[84]

In January of 1679 Leibniz learned of the invention of a *clavis sinica*, or key to the Chinese language, by a Berlin theologian, Andreas Müller. Müller had spent ten years in England working on universal dictionary and comparative language projects, possibly in association with John Wilkins. His key, pieced together in 1667 from clues discovered in obscure Arabic texts, would, he promised, enable European traders and missionaries to learn to read and speak the Chinese language with ease.[85] Perpetually frustrated, however, by his inability to secure what he considered just compensation for his efforts, Müller refused to reveal his secret and finally burned his papers before he died without their ever having been examined or published. In his *Monument of China* (1695) he hints at the disappointed expectation that no doubt hastened his end: "Indeed, I really wish I could be as certain of a stipend from the official or ecclesiastical lists, as I am certain that even women by studying Chinese characters for a year, or a shorter space of time, will be able to read Chinese and Japanese books." Although his reticence understandably led to skepticism from some quarters, Müller was respected as "one of the outstanding authorities on Chinese subjects." Leibniz thought him "capricious" and capable of hyperbole in his efforts at self-promotion, but he never ceased to regard Müller as a thoroughly learned and capable scholar of foreign languages, or his *clavis* as a fully achievable if not yet entirely realized goal. Ten years after Müller's death, Leibniz was still lamenting the loss of the famous key and reaffirming his conviction that Müller's claim was no fraud, but rather the result of significant discoveries in his researches.[86]

Müller's conception of the Chinese language as a logical cipher requiring a heretofore hidden "key" for its solution would have seemed not only eminently plausible but also quite appealing to Leibniz. His own research had led him to agree with the Dutch orientalist Jacob Gohl that Chinese was an artificial language, "invented all at once in order to establish verbal intercourse between the large number of different nations," and presumably characterized, as a result, by the sort of intrinsic rationality that Müller had clearly assumed.[87] Whether or not Müller had actually discovered the correct key, Leibniz was convinced that he was on the right track, and that the characters were certainly formed according to regular rules of composition and derivation. He rejected, however, Kircher's hypothesis that an analysis of the characters along these lines would point to a common origin with Egyptian hieroglyphics, precisely on the grounds that the rational basis of the Chinese script set it apart from the merely figural writing system of ancient Egypt:

As it seems to me that the Egyptian characters are more popular and too closely based on a resemblance with sensible objects like animals and other things, and hence are too allegorical, whereas Chinese characters are perhaps more philosophical and appear to be based on more intellectual considerations, such as those having to do with number, order, and relation, conveying only abstract characteristics.[88]

The intellectual basis that Leibniz attributed to the Chinese characters led him to consider their analysis as a task of the utmost importance, in that it would unlock all the ancient knowledge of the Chinese and illuminate fundamental philosophical truths as well. As a writing system, then, the characters bore a clear affinity to his own quest for a "universal characteristic," a philosophical notation that would provide a means of "painting not only words but thoughts in the manner that algebra does in mathematics." Leibniz went so far as to propose that his characteristic might somehow be combined with the hexagrams that he believed to have provided the original basis of the Chinese script.[89] The actual existence of a logical key to the Chinese script would have been of tremendous significance to his own enterprise, both in demonstrating the possibility of representing complex ideas through a system of combinatory symbols and in affirming his own intuitions regarding the philosophical determinacy of Chinese writing.

Given the paucity of details concerning his scheme from Müller's own hand (his 1674 pamphlet entitled *Propositio Clavis Sinicae* gets no further than the reasons for his own recalcitrance), the list of fourteen questions that Leibniz directed to Müller in June 1679 provides perhaps the best illustration of the possibilities and expectations that the idea of the *clavis* may have represented to both these men. Leibniz asked:

1. Whether such a key is unfailing and certain as in reading our A, B, C's or numbers, or whether from time to time one is in need of help, as often happens in reading hieroglyphics.

2. Since Chinese writing, as is well known, is worked out not on the basis of words, but rather on objects, so I should like to know if

the characters are always made according to the constitution of the object.

3. Whether the whole language is based on certain common elements, or a basic alphabet from which the other characters are evolved.

4. Whether inanimate objects are expressed in terms of the animate.

5. Whether the Chinese language was artificially constructed, or whether it has grown and changed by usage like other languages.

6. Whether the Chinese language was also artificially constructed on a certain key.

7. Whether H. Müller therefore believed the Chinese to be unconscious of the key to their own language.

8. Whether he thinks that this language can be introduced easily and beneficially into Europe.

9. Whether those who constructed this language understood the nature of things and were highly rational.

10. Whether the characters take notice of such natural objects as animals, plants, and stones, and whether thereby the characteristics of objects differentiate one object from the other.

11. Whether and to what extent is the bare nature of objects added to.

12. Whether the person having this key and using it can understand everything written in the Chinese language no matter what material it comprises.

13. Whether the person having the key can also write something in Chinese and whether such writing could be understood by a learned Chinese.

14. If one should ask several Chinese and several holding this key to translate something word for word (like "Our Father") from our language into Chinese, whether their translations would be so similar that a person holding one up against the other could detect that for the most part they were one.[90]

On reconstructing from Leibniz's fourteen questions the hypothetical conception of the Chinese language that would seem most likely to have produced them, one finds a novel interpretation of the Chinese writing system informed by familiar components of seventeenth-century language theory. To begin with, Leibniz seems to imagine the characters as being grounded in the flawless logic of a thoroughly rational system that proceeds by the orderly classification of objects according to an "unfailing and certain" scheme. The schematic organization underlying the language endows it, in other words, with the form of structural, synchronic legitimacy encountered in Wilkins's universal language plan. Implicit also in the list of questions are suggestions of that second form of legitimacy rooted in an originary source of truth, although Leibniz speculatively replaces Webb's alliance of God and Nature in this role with the authority of "highly rational" human agents who "understood the nature of things."

Notably absent, however, from this sketch of a hypothetical and highly idealized language is any reference to historical continuity. For Webb, of course, and later for Swift and Johnson as well, the endurance of a language over time assures a measure of fidelity to the purity of its ancestral forms and meanings, permitting, in Webb's reading of the Chinese characters, "the true, genuine, and original sense of things seems to remain with them." Leibniz seems to assume (in question 9) that Chinese was artificially constructed at some point in the distant past, and to imply (in question 5) that such an origin would most likely render it immune to growth and change. But for Leibniz, this supposed immutability, far from legitimating the language and guaranteeing its users continued access to the original sense of things as it did for Webb, only heightens the shameful tragedy of their own current ignorance of its encoded philosophical treasures, as the Chinese are, he surmises, "unconscious of the key to their own language." The admiring notion of a culturally sustaining historical legitimacy found in Webb is thus transformed in this new conception into a considerably less flattering vision of culturally debilitating historical amnesia. China, as reflected in her language, is no longer a contented and autonomous bulwark of isolationism, but rather a nation severed from a legacy it no longer understands and bound to surrender to those who do.

This negation of historical memory is even more pronounced in a second major phase of sinological research Leibniz undertook twenty years later, in the course of his extensive correspondence with the Jesuit figurist Joachim Bouvet between 1697 and 1707. Through these letters, which David Mungello calls "one of the most important sources for the study of cultural relations between Europe and China" in the period, Leibniz collaborates in the development of a theory concerning the ancestral form of Chinese writing that elevates the conception of the language as an originary source of true and universal knowledge to unprecedented speculative heights.[91] But as ever more profound and abstract meanings are attributed to these characters, the connection with the living language of modern China is steadily eroded, and the tenet of its speakers' ignorance of its internal logic is made to bear ever more of the theory's weight until these native speakers are replaced altogether by Western scholars as the true inheritors of the primal legitimacy attending the creation of their astoundingly evocative script.

The correspondence focuses largely on the ancient Chinese text known as the *Yi Jing* (also romanized as "I Ching"), or *Book of Changes*, which Bouvet in a letter of 1700 credits with being the oldest written work in China and the true source of all of her sciences and customs.[92] Originating in ancient practices of divination, the book consists of an elaborate system of abstract symbols and their explanations, which together were taken to account for various events and processes in the natural, familial, and social spheres. The symbols themselves are combinations of solid and broken horizontal lines, representing the male principle *yang* and the female principle *yin* respectively; the book includes the eight possible arrangements of three lines, called trigrams, as well as the sixty-four possible arrangements of six lines, called hexagrams. Each symbol is traditionally associated with a number of related concepts, both concrete and abstract, which taken together comprise what Needham calls a "cosmic filing system" within which any conceivable object or phenomenon might be classified and understood. The second hexagram ䷁, for example, known as *khun*, consists of six broken lines, and connotes earth, maternal, people, supporting, containing, docile, and receptor; the tenth hexagram ䷉, called *li*, is made up of two solid lines, one broken, and another three solids, and represents shoe, to tread, slow advance, or "hazardous success attained by circumspect behaviour."[93]

Bouvet first brought the *Yi Jing* to Leibniz's attention in a letter of 1698. He had discovered the true key, he wrote, to these original characters of the Chinese nation, an analysis showing them to "represent in a very simple and natural manner the principles of all the sciences," a complete metaphysical system originally conceived and encoded in the hexagrams by the ancient Emperor Fuxi (also romanized Fohi), but long since forgotten by the Chinese themselves.[94] A significant breakthrough in the two men's understanding of the *Yi Jing* came three years later, when Leibniz described in a letter to Bouvet the system of binary arithmetic he had discovered in 1679. Bouvet soon noticed a "marvelous connection"

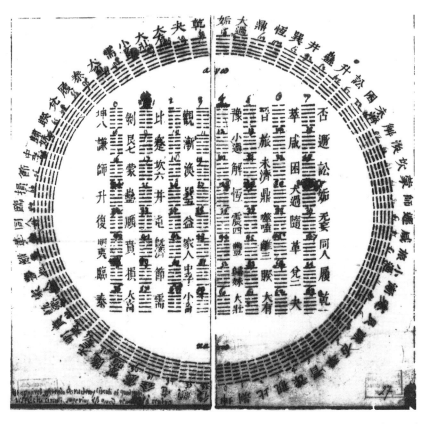

2. The Natural Hexagram Order, enclosed with a letter from Bouvet to Leibniz of November 4, 1701. Courtesy of the Niedersächsische Landesbibliothek, Hannover.

between the two systems: namely, that both were dyadic, or base-two counting systems made up of varying combinations of two basic units. If one substituted "1" for solid lines in the hexagrams and "0" for broken lines and read the hexagrams from top to bottom, they corresponded in one of their circular arrangements to the numerical ordering of the numbers 0 to 63. Moreover, Leibniz had attached a religious significance to his discovery that Bouvet could read as a corroboration of his figurist views. For Leibniz, the binary system provided an "admirable representation of creation," in that its two digits, 0 and 1, corresponded to the formless void and divine spirit from which the entire universe, according to Genesis, had first arisen. For Bouvet, this analogy between "the generation of numbers" and the "production of things" was precisely that which underlay the numerological science he ascribed to the ancient Chinese and its derivation of all knowledge from a mathematical system.[95]

Although Leibniz remained skeptical of certain aspects of Bouvet's interpretation, he seems to have been deeply impressed by the notion that the original precursors of Chinese characters were ancient mathematical symbols of which his own binary arithmetic was the unknowing heir. Summarizing their findings in his *Discourse on the Natural Theology of the Chinese* (1716) he writes:

> Reverend Father Bouvet and I have discovered the meaning, apparently truest to the text, of the characters of Fuxi, founder of Empire, which consist simply of combinations of unbroken and broken lines, and which pass for the most ancient writing of China in its simplest form . . . the 64 figures represent a Binary Arithmetic which apparently this great legislator possessed, and which I have rediscovered some thousands of years later.

After a brief description of the similarity between the two systems, he continues with an account of the fate that has befallen the founder's legacy in the interim.

> So it seems that Fuxi had insight into the science of combinations, but the Arithmetic having been completely lost, later Chinese have not taken care to think of them in this [arithmetical] way and they have made of these characters of Fuxi some kind of symbols and Hieroglyphs, as one customarily does when one has strayed from the true meaning. . . . Now this shows also that the ancient Chinese have surpassed the modern ones in the extreme, not only in piety . . . but in science as well.[96]

Leibniz's reading of the *Yi Jing* as an original template of the Chinese writing system, like his understanding of its modern derivatives, retains most of the hallmarks of foundational legitimacy observed in his predecessors. He modifies one aspect of previous interpretations by positing as the authorizing framework of meaning a mathematical rather than religious or philosophical system. More importantly, he elaborates here the charge of cultural amnesia implied in his interrogation of Andreas Müller. Rather than serving as a site of linguistic conservation and refinement, history has now become an agent of careless self-deception and betrayal. The symbolic patrimony of the ancient Chinese as manifest in the hexagrams equals in stature the imaginary origins of earlier accounts. Their modern descendants, however, in straying from the "true meaning" of the hexagrams and the originary source of their legitimacy, have permitted a degeneration in the symbolic order akin to that which seemed to Bacon

and others to have befallen European tongues. The rift between ancient
and modern that Leibniz introduces into what had been a timeless continuity in the history of Chinese writing corresponds closely to the sharp
distinctions Jesuits had long drawn among Chinese belief systems in the
service of their missionary enterprise. Ultimately, as I will argue, the
image of wayward, illegitimate forms of representation that emerges in
linguistic and theological discussions as a foil to the authoritatively
grounded ideal within the Chinese context will come to inform the
increasingly contemptuous Western outlook on China that will emerge in
subsequent decades.

The more immediate consequence of Leibniz's view of Chinese history,
however, was that it placed him in a position to redeem it: what the
Chinese had once lost could now, with his discovery, happily be recov-
ered. Leibniz had originally sent details of his binary system to Bouvet in
the hope that their religious and mystical associations might be of use in
persuading members of the Chinese literati to accept Christianity.[97] Once
he had been made aware of his Chinese precursor in Fuxi, however, the
significance of his discovery to the missionary enterprise became all the
more apparent. If the Chinese could be convinced not only that the secret
of creation was contained within this "science of combinations," but that
this same science provided a means of deciphering the forgotten mysteries
of the hexagrams, then they might prove more receptive to the religious
teachings of its Western creators. Leibniz's own characteristic, if it were
presented as rational calculus following upon Fuxi's philosophical system,
would make an ideal vehicle for this scientific evangelism:

> This secret and hidden characteristic would also give us the means of insinuating
> among the Chinese the most important truths of theology and natural philoso-
> phy in order to facilitate their road to Revelation, which, as new and different as
> it might be from their own, will be favorably received owing to the association
> with Fuxi, and will ultimately come to resemble the privileged language of the
> highest class of enlightened literati among the followers of Fuxi, to the point
> where it will merit its own associations and schools.[98]

The Chinese cultural elite, having forfeited through centuries of neglect
the mantle of legitimacy originally attached to their language, would now
find it restored to them as a freshly refurbished cloak concealing the precepts of an alien religious creed. Such an approach served, in essence, as
the basis of the Jesuits' controversial policy of accommodation in China,
relying as it did on the appropriation and recasting of native sources of

ancient truth as a means of insinuating Christian teachings into a hostile, or at best indifferent, cultural context. The workings of this process and the impassioned responses to Chinese religious traditions that it entailed will be the subject of the following chapter.

Leibniz's views on Chinese symbology, like those of Bacon, Wilkins, and Webb, were largely derivative: although he clearly had read much of what was then available in Europe about the written language in particular, he never undertook a serious study of it himself. The two final scholars I will discuss in this chapter developed theories that built upon the approaches Leibniz pursued with Müller and Bouvet, but that were informed by a more serious and sustained knowledge of the language. Their writings not only testify to the compelling power of the period's assumptions regarding Chinese writing but also help to explain the profound psychological and philosophical investments that reinforced them. Finally, as misguided as their conclusions must inevitably appear in retrospect, they stand as monuments of original scholarship in the field of Chinese linguistics unmatched until the development of modern sinological studies in the nineteenth century.

As the credulity of Leibniz's response to his claims makes evident, Andreas Müller was no lone eccentric in his belief in the possibility of a *clavis sinica* that would unlock the mysteries of the Chinese language. The seventeenth-century quest for a universal language, along with the increasing availability of East Asian materials in collections like that of the Elector Friedrich Wilhelm in Berlin, inspired any number of attempts to develop such a key. The second major effort at "solving" the Chinese language problem in this manner came from Müller's successor in Berlin, Christian Mentzel (1622–1701), whose *Clavis Sinica, ad Chinensium Scripturam et Pronunciationem Mandarinicam* (Key to Chinese, to Chinese writing and Mandarin pronunciation) drew upon the Chinese lexicographic convention of classifying characters according to their radical elements and these latter according to the number of strokes they contained. Mentzel believed that this system of lexical categories contained not only clues regarding the evolution of the characters, their pronunciation and meaning, but also the secret to the logical structure he presumed to underlie the language as a whole.[99]

The work of Müller and Mentzel provided the starting point for the most eminent sinologist of the eighteenth century, Theophilus (Gottlieb) Siegfried Bayer (1694–1738). A Prussian classical scholar at the academy of St. Petersburg and the author of the first textbook of Chinese to be

printed in Europe (*Museum Sinicum*, 1730), Bayer spent the last twelve
years of his life studying the Chinese written language, experimenting
with methods for analyzing and arranging its characters and trying to discern the rational system he was certain lay at its core.[100] He had no doubt
been influenced in his choice of a life project by his godfather Gottfried
Bartsch, an engraver who had worked with Müller in Berlin. But Bayer's
delightfully candid account of the discovery of his calling reveals a distinctly personal passion for the subject that extends well beyond a merely
derivative curiosity.

In the year 1713, while I was staying in the country, something happened to me—
all of a sudden I was overwhelmed by a desire to learn Chinese. In the period that
followed I worked and thought—or rather dreamed—about how to penetrate
that mysterious discipline. If only I could produce some small thing in that field I
would count myself grandson of the gods and king of kings. Like a pregnant rabbit, I collected everything in my burrow, whatever I could find to make up some
kind of dictionary and some introduction to the rules of the Chinese language and
to Chinese literature.[101]

The magically seductive appeal of an unknown and enigmatic body of
knowledge could hardly be rendered more compellingly. In the case of
Leibniz and the *Yi Jing*, I pointed out how the missionary impulse to
read ancient Chinese works from within Christian frameworks suggested the beginnings of a shift in the Western conception of the legitimacy of Chinese symbols. Once one reaches Bayer, it would seem, the
transformation is complete. For earlier English writers, the special qualities ascribed to the language evoked admiration and respect; for Bayer,
the mystery of the language—the lack of precisely identifiable qualities—provokes a rapacious desire. He takes it upon himself to fill in this
conceptual void by "penetrating" the discipline and assembling scraps
of information about it "like a pregnant rabbit." The curiously her-
maphroditic assortment of reproductive metaphors in the passage suggests an impulse to subsume the production of linguistic legitimacy
entirely within his own mastery of the language, in effect independently
to "conceive" the order he knows to be there. As seen above in the case
of other writers, notions of order in language were commonly figured in
sexual terms. In Bayer's fantasy, not only is his production of "some
small thing in that field" a sexualized process, it is one that results in an
affirmation of genealogical legitimacy and power that ultimately encompasses himself: "I would count myself grandson of the gods and king of

kings." The Chinese language here is no longer a self-contained, autonomous source of primal legitimacy, but rather a fragmented and impenetrable domain to which unity and coherence can be restored only through and in accordance with the determined interventions of the European sinologist.

Bayer derives his hypothesis of a logical order underlying the characters from Leibniz, who, as I have noted, toyed with the language as a possible model for his universal characteristic. The study of Chinese, Leibniz wrote in a letter to a Berlin orientalist who was a friend of Bayer's, "seems to me to be of utmost importance, for if we could discover the key to the Chinese characters we would find something useful for the analysis of thought." But the greatest impetus to Bayer's own quest was the confirmation by the respected Paris academician Etienne Fourmont that a system or key of the kind Leibniz had sought did in fact exist. According to an account of a lecture by Fourmont published in the *Journal de Trevoux* in 1722:

The Chinese script system is immense; there are 80,000 characters; each thing has its own character; in reality they are hieroglyphs. But according to M. Fourmont, the beautiful order the Chinese keep in composing their characters is a philosophical and a geometrical order, more analogical than that obtaining in any other language. Because of this order the difficulty felt at first in the face of the innumerable characters is considerably reduced. M. Fourmont asserts that the composition of the Chinese characters is the noblest achievement of the human race; there is no system in physics that approaches it in perfection.[102]

Once one looked beyond the grandiose claims, however, Fourmont, like Müller before him, remained exasperatingly vague about the details of the system. Bayer, undeterred and fully convinced of the truth of Fourmont's assertions, set out on his own to substantiate them. He borrowed from Mentzel the insight that the composition and arrangement of characters in dictionaries might contain some part of the secret, but whereas Mentzel had been content to describe the organizational systems he found in Chinese dictionaries, Bayer undertook to construct a new etymological dictionary of the language himself. Positing a combinatory logic applying not just to the radical components of characters but also to the individual brushstrokes of which these radicals were composed, he set out first to determine the meaning of the nine primitive elements he had identified and then to demonstrate the derivation of complex characters and their meanings from these constituent parts.

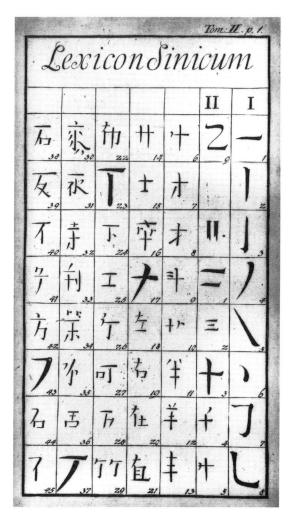

3. First page of the Chinese dictionary in T. S. Bayer's *Museum Sinicum*, 1730. Courtesy of the Annenberg Rare Book and Manuscript Library, University of Pennsylvania.

Bayer cites the hexagrams of the *Yi Jing* as evidence for the presence of a combinatory principle at the dawn of Chinese writing.

Look at the first two simple figures, the whole and the broken line. From them they make four composite ones, from those again eight more complex ones and from these complex ones they form the 64 hexagrams—that is how the *Book of Changes* is composed. This kind of thing did not belong to old popular ideas of the people, but it caught the eye and seemed to these primitive human beings to be something divine and of eternal significance. If this invention was employed by them, then I believe that the ancient people may well have used the symbols as words—even today they (the eight trigrams) are said to mean something, namely Heaven, Pools, collected in the Mountains, Fire, Thunder, Wind, Water, Mountain and Earth. . . . [It is] extremely likely that the Chinese, playing around with such combinations, went on to form simple characters, out of which came more and more complicated ones.[103]

He elaborates this hypothesis in a section of his *Museum Sinicum* called "On the nature and the analogy of the Chinese characters" that stands out among the vague conjectures of his predecessors in the clarity and precision of its claims. Here, finally, were the details of the *clavis sinica* that had been concealed from the world for so long: "First there are some very simple characters, single strokes, which, however, all mean something. From these the other characters are composed, gradually and step by step. The first simple characters, nine in all, are shown below." He proceeds to list his nine elementary strokes, providing for each a transliteration and definition, as best as he understood it. The first stroke, a horizontal line 一, meant "one." The second, a vertical line 丨, meant "a relationship between something above and something below," while the third 亅, a hooked variation on the same, meant "a hook or connection." The two diagonal strokes 丿 and 乀 signified "primordial heat" and "humidity"; a single point 丶 meant sovereignty, while the angled stroke ㄱ denoted only "a lateral sign." The eighth stroke, ㄴ, is described as "the same sign turned around," and like the previous one, escapes his understanding: "This and the one before have some meaning which I have not been informed about. I do not want to speculate about it." The final zigzag stroke 乙, signifies "one," and is taken to be a cursive variant on the first.

Characters of increasing complexity arise from combinations of these basic strokes like branches on a tree.

This is the first set of characters. Two such characters, joined together, make up the secondary set, three the tertiary, four the quaternary and so forth, but they are still called simple characters. Then all these (simple) characters . . . are combined to form other (complex) characters. . . . Thus, in this system each character is a root as well as a branch. It is the branch of a simpler character and the root of a more complex one.

The meanings of the various elements are combined and compounded at the same time, so that "in the component parts of the complex characters a certain system of analogies obtains, a subtle indication of the meaning of the character, something about the use of something, or some quality. From this you may suspect what the character means, even before the teacher tells you."[104] What the Chinese had forgotten, in other words, and Bayer thought he had rediscovered, was the fundamental principle of the language by which the meanings of characters still in use today could be shown to be grounded in the primal concepts of an ancient symbolic code. His identification of a specific point of origin for his nine elemental strokes in the hexagrams of antiquity situates his theory squarely within a framework of legitimate descent. His original contribution to this framework lies in his literal interpretation of the notion of regulated derivation that underlies it. One can almost envision Bayer laying out his thousands of character cards in precise geometrical order, each of his nine roots giving rise to a predetermined number and kind of combinatory branches sprawling in splendid symmetry across the floor of his garret. The quasi-mathematical generation of meaning that he ascribes to Chinese writing reflects a view of linguistic perfection and perfectibility unrivaled in its rationalist optimism since Bishop Wilkins's day. To the "mysterious discipline" that had so captivated him as a young man he had restored a long-forgotten order, replacing ambiguity with taxonomical clarity and the profligacy of signs with a systematic regime of regulated recombination.

Bayer was fully conscious of the potential significance of his achievement. Whereas Bacon, Webb, and even Leibniz had ventured to speculate on the fundamental nature of a language they could neither read nor speak, Bayer had studied it assiduously for more than a decade in order to produce a lexicographic method and arrangement of characters that would both reveal the underlying logic of their meanings and render obsolete what he saw as the senseless organization of existing Chinese dictionaries. Although he was aware of his own shortcomings, he never doubted that in constructing his system he was restoring to the Chinese an integral component of their language that they had lost. So when he began receiving letters from missionaries in China that seemed to undermine his central assumptions about the language, his replies conveyed both incredulity and despair. In 1735, after learning of new and damaging evidence of an ancient, variant form of the script used in engraving stone seals, he writes to his teacher Father Parrenin:

If the inventors of the Chinese characters, in defining such properties, followed some philosophical method, as it seems to me from innumerable examples that they must have done, if they have stuck to the same principle in forming the simpler characters and even in the nine elementary ones from which the others derive, what shall we say then about the ancient seal characters, the forms of which we recognize in the new ones, but not the system and the nature of them? Truly, I do not know what to say about it. Were the old ones just fortuitous forms? If no ingenuity were at work in shaping them, from whence then did the artfulness of the new ones come? Were the books of Confucius written with these chaotic characters? And before that—if it was from before—the Book of Changes? . . . All these things have the highest consequence; I beg you, Reverend Father, to explain them to me![105]

What is perhaps most notable in this passage, apart from the pathos of the author's perplexity and distress, is the catastrophic alternative Bayer imagines to the universal validity of his own theory. Stripped of the legitimacy he has labored so long to provide, the language relapses into an anarchy of unaccounted origins and arbitrary forms, a confusion of "chaotic characters" upon which a masterwork of reason and virtue could not possibly hope to stand. His own understanding of the Chinese language having evolved through the analytic hypothesis he first brought to its study, he is unable to imagine an alternative set of historical or linguistic circumstances under which the script would remain minimally viable as a representational system. With new levels of sinological expertise, in other words, comes a new precondition of linguistic legitimacy: the precise conformity of the language to the Western scholar's increasingly particularized understanding. The basic conception of the Chinese script as composed of "characters real" grounded in some higher order of truth has not changed appreciably since Bacon's time; what is new is the contingent specificity and consequent fragility of this assessment.

Bayer had set out with the dream of creating a monument of representational legitimacy that would affirm the essential order underlying the Chinese script from within a distinctly Western paradigm of taxonomic analysis. The great irony of the enterprise was that this same system, when coupled with a similarly Western moral paradigm, enabled him precisely to prefigure the condition of representational chaos that finally precipitated its own collapse. In a commentary he composed on the earliest history of China, Bayer indulges in some etymological speculation, guided by the tenets of his combinatory theory, on the original, forgotten meaning of a number of crucial characters in classical Chinese sources. The name of Fuxi's sister, Nü Kua, particularly captivated him. The character

for *nü* 女 was straightforward enough: it was a common word for female, virgin, or woman. But *kua* 媧, he realized, was "exactly the same
sound as the Hebrew word for Eve—Chaua!" Moreover, the intriguingly
complex character yielded a corroborating analysis: "The right part of
the character for Kua means bite of the mouth, but also sin. For it is composed of the following simple elements: Nui, inside, Kium, vacuity, and
Keu, mouth. Inside the hollow mouth . . . inside the mouth . . . what else
is that but the bite? Therefore, Kua means the woman who bit and also
the woman who sinned."[106] The conditions of the fall of mankind from
grace and of language from its original condition of transparency, in other
words, had been present from the outset among the scriptural vestiges of
ancient Chinese civilization. If a well-formed *clavis* from the West could
bring their deepest mysteries to light, it took only the repudiation of the
same to consummate, in Bayer's eyes, their darkest prophesy.

   The Jesuit Joseph de Prémare (1666–1736), the final interpreter of the
Chinese written language I will consider, was another master locksmith in
this mold. A student of Bouvet, he subscribed to the belief of the Jesuit
figurists that the essential truths of Christian revelation had been known
to the original founders of Chinese culture and were made manifest in
their writings and in the characters of the script itself. From this figurist
perspective, the legitimacy ascribed to the language is of a different order
from what Bayer envisioned altogether. Chinese writing remains the vehicle of a pure and originary truth, but this truth is one that emanates from
the word of God rather than from a philosophical or mathematical law.
The knowledge of its origins and hidden structure is again presumed to
have been lost by the Chinese people, but for these Jesuit philologists the
project of "restoring" this lost knowledge is explicitly subordinated to a
broader evangelical enterprise.

   The figurist approach to the Chinese classical texts derived from a tradition of speculative theology that was well established in seventeenth-
century Europe. Traces of Christian doctrine, according to such older theories as the "Prisca Theologia," could be found in every culture;
prefigurations of New Testament events, according to typological schools
of biblical exegesis, could be found everywhere throughout the Old.[107]
The group of Jesuit missionaries in China who came to be labeled—
derogatively—as figurists by their counterparts in Europe became convinced through their studies of China's philosophical and literary canon
that the writers of these books had grasped on some level the essential
tenets of Christian theology and had encoded this knowledge in their

work. The most notable members of this group, Bouvet, Prémare, and Jean-François Foucquet, set out in various ways to document their discovery through protracted analyses of ancient Chinese texts and symbols. If the modern Chinese literati could only be persuaded of the validity of the method and the significance of the divine wisdom it helped to unlock, they would have no choice but to accept the Jesuits' Christian "key."

Prémare's primary contribution to this effort was in the field of Chinese philology. According to biographer Knud Lundbaek, his linguistic expertise after thirty years of study was unparalleled: "None of the Jesuits, from the days of Matteo Ricci till now, had penetrated so deeply into the genius of the Chinese language."[108] Among his works was the first comprehensive grammar of Chinese to be written in either China or Europe, *Notitia Linguae Sinicae*, sent to Paris in 1728. A systematic presentation of both modern and classical Chinese, it attempted to elucidate the intricacies of syntax and rhetoric through literary examples provided with the express intent of fostering not only a reading and speaking but also a writing knowledge of the language. There are suggestions even in this textbook of a level of meaning to the characters beyond mere dictionary definitions, but Prémare reserved the elaboration of his theory for a separate series of polemical figurist writings (64–72). His evidence for the divine knowledge of the ancient Chinese consists largely of reflections, inspired by Bouvet, on the etymology of individual characters. The character 來, *lai*, meaning "to come," for example, appeared to both men a clear visual representation of Christ on the cross, with the two small 人, *ren*, or person, indicating the thieves who died with him. Another cross-like figure, 午, *wu*, refers to the noonday hours, and as Prémare notes, "Christ was crucified at that time of the day." An entry for 僉, *qian*, meaning "all," explains first the word's literal connotations and then expounds on its figural basis:

This character represents how all human beings that have been, that are and that will be are enclosed in two persons, 二 人 口, namely Adam and Eve. The two persons became sinners, 小 人, and drew their posterity with them into the state of sin. They and all human beings have been united under one head, the only one that was capable of pulling them out of it, and that head is Jesus Christ, this unique man, 一 人. (129–30)

As these examples suggest, the interpretation of the Chinese script that he develops differs remarkably little in its premises from the relatively amateur speculations of those who preceded him, in spite of his vastly superior training in the language and his more markedly religious outlook. It may be helpful, therefore, to preface a discussion of his views with a summary of my observations up to this point.

The Western fantasy of linguistic legitimacy I have been considering has been grounded in three mutually reinforcing suppositions, corresponding to the three distinct perspectives from which the problem has been seen. First, the moment of origin of a legitimate language is marked by the definitive authority of the source of meaning, whether natural, divine, or philosophical, from which its signs spring fully formed as from the head of an Olympian god. The temporal moment, second, is one of changelessness, of uncanny resistance to the force of history, and of the preservation of ancestral forms against the corruptions and betrayals of time. The causal link between the authority and the immutability of such a language, finally, is its internal order. The ontological moment is that which manifests the severely rational structure, hierarchical, taxonomical, or geometrical, that determines the relationships among its elements.

Prémare's account of the Chinese language stands out as the apotheosis of legitimacy so conceived. The authority he proposes for the original meanings of the characters is none less than that of God himself. In a dialogue he composed to help explain the principles of his system, Prémare has a young scholar ask his old master about the origin of the characters. The master replies, "The heavenly spirits established language by giving it to the kings. The first kings received the characters from Heaven. They passed them on to later rulers. . . . This is the meaning of the word 'characters,' and that is why I say: 'They stand for the words of Heaven'" (147). His years of intensive study of the language convinced him that its underlying system was "as old as the characters themselves" and divine in inspiration: "Even if all these books had disappeared in China, the characters themselves would suffice to show that he who invented them had been informed about all our mysteries" (142). It was this conviction that finally stood behind his entire life's work. "My ulterior motive for writing this book and my other works," he writes in a 1733 letter to Fourmont in Paris, "is to make everybody know that the Christian religion is as old as the world, and that the God-Man was certainly known to him or those who invented the hieroglyphs and composed the *Jing*" (61). How else, after all, could one account for the representations of Christ's life and teachings that they so clearly contained?

For Prémare it was self-evident that the events recounted in the

Chinese classics corresponded to Christian teachings. "It is highly proba-
ble that all the (three) *Jing* have as their sole subject a saint or holy person. His virtues, merits, benefits, his mysteries, his sacred law, his reign
and his glory are reported in these books, obscurely, no doubt, for the
Chinese, but so clearly for us to see who know Jesus Christ" (133). If the
narratives and poetry of ancient China contained a coded knowledge of
the true God, one might reasonably suppose their enigmatic characters
did as well. In his commentary on an often-quoted passage from the *Shi
Jing* about the conception and birth of the mythological hero Hou Ji,
Prémare turns to the characters for evidence in support of his Christian
nativity reading.

Let us look at the names of the mother and the son. The mother is called 姜 *Jiang*.
She is a virgin 女 *nü*, because she has conceived a God by God. She is the lamb
yang 羊, who has carried in her substance a lamb for us. She is also called 嫄 *yuan*,
because she is the source or origin of virginity. Her son is called 棄 *Qi*, the
rejected one, as if he were a worm and no man; a reproach of men, and despised
of the people. (135)

Prémare does not insist that every writer who told such stories or used
such words was necessarily conscious of precisely this allegorical dimension. His argument rests rather on a preponderance of circumstantial evidence. The fact that these particular stories were so frequently told, and
that so many of their characters were composed and used in such deeply
suggestive ways weighs in favor of a theory of a divine, if partially forgotten, origin to their meaning.

The structure Prémare identified as underlying his Christian interpretations and providing for the systematic ordering of the language as a
whole departed sharply from the relentlessly analytic taxonomies that
informed the linguistic ideals of the likes of Wilkins and Bayer. He agreed
with Bayer that Chinese characters could be broken down into simpler
meaningful components. For Prémare, however, the key lay not in deduc-
ing the significance of a set of primary elements, but rather in understanding the various means by which all characters, simple and composite, generated the meanings that they did. His thoughts on this question
derived largely from his study of the *Shuo Wen Jie Zi*, a Han dynasty dictionary known for the etymological explanations it provided for the composition of each character. Of particular interest was the assignment in
this dictionary of every character to one of six ordered classes according
to the ostensible principle of its composition.

The Chinese had, as usual, forgotten the true nature of this system. Prémare offered them his own interpretation in a dissertation of 1721 entitled *Liu Shu Shi Yi* (The true meaning of the six types of characters), which he had composed in Chinese under the pseudonym Wen Gu Zi. The names and basic explanations he provides for the six classes are given in accordance with the Chinese tradition. He correctly describes, for example, the *zhi shi* or "indicate things" characters as abstract symbols for immaterial phenomena, the *xiang xing* or "imitate form" characters as stylized pictorial representations of common objects, and the *xing sheng* or "form and sound" characters as combinations of semantic and phonetic components. The order in which he lists the classes is also borrowed from his source, but the importance he ascribes to this ordering and the justifications he offers for it are his own additions and reflect the legacy of earlier Western language theory and conceptions of Chinese. He divides the classes, for example, according to their qualities of *ti* and *yong*, philosophical terms connoting "body" or "fundamental," on the one hand, and "function" or "secondary," on the other. He accords a special status to the *ti* classes, which, according to his analysis, are comprised of characters whose components contribute in a direct and immediate way to the meaning of the word. The two *yong* classes, in contrast, seem to him derivative and arbitrary, in some sense etymologically impure, and are blamed for cluttering the lexicon with needless redundancies and ambiguities (149–57).

The most privileged category in Prémare's classificatory scheme is exemplified by the *zhi shi* or "indicate things" characters. They are pure *ti* in that their meaning is in the most immediate possible sense fully present in their forms, and they convey this meaning through a single, simple character without recourse to the more typical combinatory procedures. Taken together, these qualities would seem to approximate Prémare's highest linguistic ideal, an ideal that will be recognized as a direct descendent of Bacon's "characters real." "Oh, marvelous 'indicate-things' characters!" he expostulates in the enraptured voice of his old teacher Bayer, "They have no form, they are not images, but the myriad forms and the myriad images come from that source. . . . The supreme mystery of the science of characters, the science of the *Jing*, the science of *Li*—it is all contained in the 'indicate-things' characters" (150, 157). The absolute purity of their form is reflected in their limited number: seven altogether, simple combinations of dots and lines, in appearance and posited function not unlike the trigrams of the *Yi Jing* or Bayer's nine primary strokes.

But for Prémare their real significance lies in the abstract "things" he takes them to "indicate," and his figurist training asserts itself as he indulges in a flight of quasi-mystical speculation on the proto-Christian origins of the symbols.

According to my view, I humbly submit the following explanation. These four characters 丶, 一, 二, and 三 [literally, "point" or "small amount," "one," "two," and "three"] all indicate one thing. One cannot separate them. . . . The first is 丶, it indicates the substance of the Supreme Master. 一, 二, and 三 indicate the persons of the Supreme Master. . . . 一 is not 二 or 三, but it is the root of 二 and 三. 二 is not 一, but it is born from it. 三 is neither 一 nor 二, but it is that which was sent by them. . . . We know that the mysterious substance is not two. Its precious persons are three. Then we have one in three-one. We know that the persons are three, the substance is one, then we have three in one-three.

The lexicographic ordering system he believed he had discovered in the characters thus provided the key for Prémare to their ultimate theological legitimacy. Not only, in his reading, do the basic symbols of the script derive from an intimate understanding of the trinity, the compound symbols that they form mirror the genealogy of divine creation in the etymological structure of the language as a whole. The simple stroke 丶, denoting "the substance of the supreme master," is also "the origin of the thousand single characters and the ten thousand composed characters" (151). This one stroke, in other words, projects the creative function of the Godhead onto the lexical domain by evoking there the calligraphic genesis of the entire universe of characters.

The fundamental assumption behind the figurist excavation of such primal religious nuances was that the originary and structural legitimacy revealed in the characters was matched on the historical plane, in that the Chinese had fastidiously preserved the original forms of these characters. Not surprisingly, then, Prémare is hostile to innovations that might compromise the clarity of the ideographic window into the past. He writes with contempt, for example, of recent attempts to reform the character classification system used by Chinese dictionaries on the grounds that contemporary lexicography was undermining the etymological foundations of what was for him, after all, primarily a fossilized historical artifact (71). His fears for the continued conservation of the script are reflected as well in his characterization of the *xing sheng* or "form and sound" class of characters as a corruption within the system of its essential principles of composition. These characters, which are to this day by

far the most common type, consist of a "radical" component that provides some clue to the meaning of a character (the "water" radical, for
example, is used in the words for "river," "sea," "to drink," and "alco-
hol," among many others) combined with a "phonetic" component providing some indication, often equally imprecise, of its sound.[109] Prémare
condemns this combinatory method as a relatively recent innovation that
is neither helpful—because the semantic clues are so vague—nor necessary, as meanings can be represented adequately without it using the
methods of the other classes.[110] His denunciation of this "least important" group of characters highlights again the importance of historical
integrity in his idealization of the Chinese language, but also the degree to
which he views a certain lexical amnesia among the Chinese as a threat to
"the riches that can be extracted from so many precious remains of the
oldest times, preserved in Chinese books" (43). The charge of careless-
ness applies not just to the interpretation of individual characters and isolated passages but also to the classical canon as a whole. Referring to the
Yi Jing in a letter of 1731 Prémare writes, with scarcely veiled contempt,
"On the other hand, what benefit did the Chinese derive from having
inherited this precious text and having preserved it? They forgot its meaning ages ago. It is a treasure, but a treasure hidden to them" (160, 164).

   Some version of the amnestic hypothesis is a necessary premise of
Prémare's entire interpretive enterprise: if the Chinese had preserved the
Christian knowledge so clearly evident in the writings of their ancestors,
they would, after all, have no need for missionaries to restore it to them.
One cannot escape, however, the paradox implicit in this supposition.
Prémare succeeds in establishing the supreme legitimacy of the Chinese
script in terms of its origins, structure, and history. And yet owing to
the negligence of its recent guardians, its modern meanings, like bastard
offspring cast out from the line of succession, are bereft of their inheritance and reduced to degenerate shadows of their noble forbears.
Misreadings have multiplied into a cascade of ignorance that threatens
to overwhelm the truth-claims that were supposed to be the very essence
of Chinese writing. As Prémare laments, "A hundred schools arose, the
six kinds of characters were forgotten. The six kinds of characters gone,
the six Classics became confused. The six Classics confused, the Way of
the first kings was effaced" (149). The form of legitimacy remains, perhaps, but its substance has been erased by the very assumptions that
enabled it, leaving a language that is little more than a parodically hollow shell.

A Chinese Babel

Subsequent chapters will treat at length the implications of this inversion of the ideal of representational legitimacy for the Western encounter with other aspects of Chinese culture. But before turning from the case of the Chinese language itself, it may be helpful briefly to sketch the history of its reception in Europe in the remaining years of the eighteenth century as a means of more fully elaborating the terms in which this inversion will be played out. Between Prémare's death in 1736 and the founding of modern academic sinology with the publication of Abel Rémusat's *Elemens de la grammaire chinoise* in 1822, interest in the topic seems to have declined. What attention the language received was tinged with a marked skepticism toward the encomia it had drawn in earlier decades.[111] The cultural conditions that had favored the idealization of Chinese writing had largely passed, and the nostalgic quest for linguistic purity no longer had a place on the forward-looking agenda of a more self-assured Enlightenment rationalism. The Jesuit Louis Le Comte, whose 1696 *Nouveaux Mémoires sur l'état présent de la Chine* helped to popularize the findings—and often controversial positions—of his missionary colleagues in East Asia, set the tone for subsequent eighteenth-century attitudes toward Chinese writing. I have noted an abiding tendency to circumvent the problem of the extreme complexity of the script by either denying it outright or positing a relatively simple underlying structure by which it could be explained away. Le Comte not only called attention to the incontrovertible difficulty of the characters but also declined to acknowledge any redeeming qualities that might justify it. He regarded as an insufferable burden the necessity of "taking into one's head this frightful multitude of figures and being constantly occupied with deciphering imperfect hieroglyphics that have almost no analogy with the things they signify." The magnitude of this task, far from encouraging wisdom and virtue, was "the source of ignorance of the Chinese," in that it left scholars little time for other, more productive study. Reversing the reverential attitude of Webb, Leibniz, Bayer, and Prémare, he implied that the Chinese had more to learn from the users of alphabetic writing than the other way around.[112]

Even more influential than Le Comte's work, Jean Baptiste Du Halde's *Description géographique, historique, chronologique, politique, et physique de l'empire de la Chine* (1736) was a compendium of unpublished Jesuit reports that for the first time made the fruits of the missionaries'

intensive study of their host country widely available to the European
public. Although his chapter on the language is subtitled "Du Génie de la
Langue Chinoise" and shares none of Le Comte's dismissive contempt,
his pointed emphasis on the spoken over the written language substantially undercuts the claims of earlier accounts. Whereas Webb, for example, had glossed over dialectal differences in his devotion to the theory of
a unified, uncorrupted language, Du Halde foregrounds the linguistic
diversity of the Chinese, commenting on variations among provincial
dialects and between the language of the common people and of the
literati. Moreover, in describing the latter, official language, he remarks
on the paucity of basic syllables in its spoken form, thereby reintroducing
the theme of ambiguity in terms that recall contemporary condemnations
of European vernaculars and that sharply distinguish spoken Chinese on
any scale of legitimacy from its written counterpart.

These few syllables, however, suffice for expressing oneself on every kind of subject, because without increasing the number of words, the number of meanings is
almost infinitely multiplied by variations in accents, inflections, tones, breathing,
and other vocal changes: it is this variety of pronunciations that is a frequent
cause of equivocation for those not well versed in the language.[113]

The most striking contrast with his predecessors, however, appears in
Du Halde's explanation for the extraordinary number of Chinese characters. A generalized form of the implicit understanding of previous decades
might have gone something like this: Chinese is a "philosophical" language that provides a unique sign for every concept and thing. The vast
quantity of signs that results is, however, less cumbersome than it first
appears, as the characters are composed and arranged according to a fully
rational system. The number of characters, in this view, is an incidental
by-product of their philosophical nature and their correspondence with
the vast universe of things. For Du Halde, in contrast, it is the ideographic
basis of Chinese writing that is incidental; the multiplicity of characters is
a mere secondary consequence of the need to distinguish on paper the
equivocal sounds of the *spoken* language. "As the Chinese only have figures for expressing their thoughts, and as they lack written marks to indicate variations in pronunciation, they require as many different figures or
characters as there are different tones that give to the same word so many
divergent meanings." The problem is compounded by their preference for
highly specific single characters where combinations of more versatile
characters would seem to suffice, but once again, the characters are con-

ceived as mere secondary tokens of verbal expression, rather than, as previously, through a primary relationship to the material world:

There are, besides, characters which signify two or three words and sometimes entire phrases: for example, to write the words "Good day, Sir," instead of joining the character for "good" and that for "day" with the character for "sir," one must use a different character which alone expresses these three words, and it is this which so multiplies the number of Chinese characters.[114]

Thomas Percy, one of the few writers to take up the question of the Chinese language in the middle of the century, devotes an entire section to it in his *Miscellaneous Pieces Relating to the Chinese* of 1762. He reverts to the view of the primacy of the script and of the written characters as "immediate representatives of ideas," rather than of sounds or words. But he differs from earlier advocates of the linguistic legitimacy of Chinese in that the derivation of symbols from the nature of things suggests to him a primitive rather than exalted origin. The founders of such a language were most likely not philosophers but ignorant barbarians, for whom the patently figural hieroglyphics from which he supposes the modern script descends would have only been "the first and most obvious kind of writing," comparable to the "wild attempts of some of the savages of North America." For Percy, it is not this "first expedient of untutored man," but rather the refined and "happy art of writing by an alphabet" that is likely to have been "the invention of unassisted reason, or the result of divine instruction." The script having been continually refined and adapted from its humble origins to accommodate increasingly abstract modes of thought, its characters were, Percy acknowledges, "at length . . . formed . . . into a complete language, sufficient for all the purposes of literature." The spoken tongue, however, "having no affinity" with the written, "hath still continued in its original rude uncultivated state," namely, "barren and contracted, wholly consisting of a few undeclinable and uncompounded monosyllables."[115] Its phonemic deficiency, Percy suggests, may be owing to a characteristic deformity of the Chinese mouth. He quotes from Du Halde, "Their teeth are placed in a different manner from ours: the upper row stands out, and sometimes falls upon the under lip, or at least on the gums of the under row, which lies inward; the two gums scarce ever meet together, like those of Europeans." Whatever the cause, native speakers of the language are incapable of pronouncing the letters D, R, X, and Z, a circumstance which, Percy notes, "subjects the missionaries to great inconvenience in fitting European words to Chinese mouths." The only unfamiliar sound they offer in compensation is one whose description recalls the barbaric origins of their script:

They have still further a kind of vowel or simple sound wholly unknown to us. . . . It [is] a kind of cry fetched from the hollow of the stomach; of which it is difficult to give an exact idea in speaking only to the eyes. This sound deserves so much the more the name of a cry, as it is never joined with any other whether vowel or consonant, but is always pronounced apart.[116]

By the final quarter of the century, this degradation of what once had been the prince of languages had become commonplace. Although he had written sympathetically of the Chinese at other points in his life, in 1778, according to Boswell,

Johnson called the East-Indians barbarians. Boswell: "You will except the Chinese, Sir." Johnson: "No, Sir.". . . Boswell: "What do you say to the written characters of their language?" Johnson: "Sir, they have not an alphabet. They have not been able to form what all other nations have formed." Boswell: "There is more learning in their language than in any other, from the immense number of their characters." Johnson: "It is only more difficult from its rudeness; as there is more labour in hewing down a tree with a stone than with an axe."[117]

The collapse of the myth of exalted origins was accompanied by an equally dramatic reversal in the assessment of the internal order of the language, the logical basis in clear rules and distinctions that had seemed to justify the various claims to philosophical legitimacy made on its behalf. I have alluded briefly to the theme of ambiguity in the spoken language as one indicator of this shift. I will conclude with a passage from what is no doubt the most entertaining exposition of this complaint, a satirical letter of 1769 addressed by the fictitious China missionary P. François Bourgeois to a lady correspondent. The very tone of the passage emphatically marks the transformation of the Chinese language from an object of intense intellectual fascination to a freakish curiosity best known for its boundless confusion, a plaything for the badinage of a petulant Paris wit.

Chinese is quite difficult. . . . The same word never has more than one ending; there is nothing like that which in our declinations distinguishes the gender and number of the things of which one speaks. . . . In a word, among the Chinese the same word is noun, adjective, verb, adverb, singular, plural, masculine, feminine, etc. . . . Not only that, all the words in the spoken language can be reduced to three hundred and some, which are pronounced in so many ways as to signify eighty thousand different things that are expressed by as many characters.

And that is not all. The arrangement of all these monosyllables would seem not to follow any general rule, so that in order to know the language, after having learned all the words, one also has to learn each individual phrase. . . .

But getting back to the words. I was told that *shu* means book. I expected that every time the word *shu* appeared, it would have do to with a book. Not at all: *shu* reappears, meaning tree. So there I am, divided between *shu* book, and *shu* tree. And so it goes on: there is *shu* great heat, *shu* storyteller, *shu* dawn, *shu* rain, *shu* charity, *shu* habituated, *shu* to lose a bet, etc. I would never finish if I wanted to give all the meanings of the same word.[118]

By portraying spoken Chinese as the primary form of the language and as characterized above all by a crippling lack of rules and distinctions, the author negates the premises of earlier students of Chinese who had sought there an antidote precisely to the ambiguity and misunderstanding that seemed to plague vernacular language in the West. But of what use was this foreign model if it only magnified to an unimaginable degree those idols of the marketplace that reformers had lamented since Bacon's time? We end, then, with an abject renunciation of the claims to linguistic legitimacy with which we began. The founding sage has lapsed into savagery, a guttural howl has displaced the elegance of the hexagrams, a sublimely rational system of signs has collapsed into an entropic chaos where misbegotten meanings have multiplied until they seem to mean nothing at all.

CHAPTER TWO

The First Ancestor: Intimations of Chinese Divinity

Le malais était devenu l'Asie elle-même; l'Asie antique,
solennelle, monstreuse et compliquée comme ses temples
et ses religions; où tout . . . est fait pour confondre et
stupéfier l'esprit d'un européen.

[Malay had become Asia herself, a place as ancient,
solemn, monstrous, and intricate as her temples and her
religions, a place where everything is contrived to
confound and stupefy the spirit of the European.]

—Baudelaire, *Paradis Artif*

The Chinese script presented a multivalenced cipher to the European imagination. Not only were the characters themselves unintelligible, the means by which they conveyed or embodied ideas remained a provocative mystery. If the variety and complexity of explanatory schemes they provoked in scholarly circles suggests the depth of interest they generated, the prominence of a distinct representational ideal within these schemes points to a crucial component of this collective enterprise in cross-cultural cryptography. Generally speaking, the first response to the sign of cultural illegibility is an attempt to assimilate it within a familiar framework of established values. Reading the Chinese script through a lens of linguistic legitimacy not only situated it comfortably within the arena of lively contemporary debates on the state of language and society in Europe but also assigned it a set of specific attributes calculated to cancel precisely the threat of its obscurity. For even if the scholars who proposed these schemes could scarcely read or write the language themselves, the mastery they sought to establish over it represented a potentially far greater prize than mere linguistic competence: the *clavis sinica*, the key to the cipher, the promise of legibility according to the rules of a clearly defined and rational system.

Those few seventeenth-century Europeans—mostly Jesuit missionaries living in China—who actually succeeded in learning Chinese had little use for the ersatz mastery of the language seemingly promised by the legitimacy hypothesis. Their interest was not so much speculative or theoretical as pragmatic: competence in the native language was regarded by the founders of the mission as a prerequisite to the effective harvest of souls. Missionaries tended to approach the difficulties of the script, accordingly, as a Western business person might do today: that is, as a significant obstacle to be overcome in the pursuit of a practical objective, but certainly not a vexing conundrum to be considered in its own right and in the context of weighty political and philosophical considerations. The context of the Jesuit approach to the language was that of their evangelical mission, and in devising strategies for spreading the faith, they came to recognize the profound importance the Chinese themselves attached to their writing system and its consequent centrality to their own enterprise. On the one hand, they realized, a thorough knowledge of literary Chinese would enable them to disseminate their teachings through the highly respected and efficient medium of printed texts. On the other, it would permit them far more readily to tailor their message to the exigencies of the local context. At the level of style, this might mean adopting the established rhetorical conventions of the Chinese classics in their own writings, by buttressing their claims, for example, with liberal allusions to canonical Chinese authors. At the level of theological content, it would imply appropriating Chinese terms for divine or spiritual phenomena in order to situate the essential elements of Christian doctrine in relation to traditional Chinese systems of belief.

This latter task, as one can imagine, posed a considerable problem of translation.[1] How does one communicate with any precision the idea of a highly particularized deity within the context of an entirely alien culture sharing none of the historical patterns of thought that shape and sustain it at home? Working with approximate terms and descriptions in the host language poses the risk of conveying, at best, only the rough contours of what often are, and certainly were in the seventeenth century, endlessly intricate doctrinal truths, or at worst, a hybrid, patchwork theology hopelessly contaminated by local connotations of borrowed terminology. Obviously, the closer the match between the available religious vocabulary of the native culture and one's own, the less the danger of gross distortion on the level of basic concepts. Although a fortuitous convergence in metaphysical orientation might not guarantee the receptivity of potential converts, at the very least it would offer some assurance that one's words were not being entirely misunderstood.

The first Jesuits in China attempted to resolve this fundamental problem of theological translation by discovering, or claiming to discover, precisely such a convergence between classical Confucian texts and basic Christian doctrine. They pointed to striking correspondences between the lives and teachings of ancient Chinese sages and their own savior. Through their study of the classical canon they accumulated evidence not only that early Chinese religious philosophy presented the conditions for a monotheistic belief system, but that references to Godlike entities in Chinese texts indicated an early awareness of the true Judeo-Christian God. This knowledge had since been corrupted by the influence of foreign—and especially Buddhist—doctrines into a largely unrecognizable form, but its germ could still be detected within the central tenets of early Confucian thought.

By positing an essential compatibility between Catholic doctrine and the religious ideas of the ancient Chinese, these Jesuits constructed an interpretation of Chinese culture that was premised on a conceptual foundation closely related to that employed by their more philologically minded contemporaries back in Europe. While Webb, Wilkins, Leibniz, and Bayer grounded their understanding of China in a vision of the language as an originary and rationally ordered system, a representational medium whose structure and symbols were anchored in the incontestable truths of nature and antiquity, Matteo Ricci and his followers elaborated a reading of their host culture as one whose theological underpinnings were just as solidly grounded in an ancient knowledge of the one true God. In their projections of this ideal of primal groundedness and authority onto an alien civilization, the two groups, in other words, play an identical theme in slightly different keys. If the language theorists were concerned with validating the particular mode of symbolic expression inherent in the characters of the Chinese script, the Jesuits sought to vindicate the symbology implicit in Chinese speculations on the divine. What stands out in both cases is the persistent association of Chinese culture with a privileged form of representation, a utopian anticipation of absolute legibility in the face of inscrutable otherness.

These interpretations of Chinese writing and religion played a crucial role in opening the European imagination to the cultural wealth of East Asia in the seventeenth and eighteenth centuries. As I have shown in the previous chapter, the types of interpretation that flourished in the period were closely connected in Europe with the particular preoccupations of a specific historical moment: in the case of language, these included the rise of Baconian science and ongoing crises of legitimation in religious and political spheres. Responses to Chinese religious thought likewise arose from and contributed to a complex web of theological contexts, not least among them the tumultuous history of the Society of Jesus itself and the iconoclasm of Enlightenment challenges to orthodox religious doctrine. What remains constant through these vicissitudes, however, and through the bewildering variety of responses to Chinese spirituality that they engendered, is a powerful predisposition to imagine Chinese culture through the lens of legitimacy and to interpret its belief systems according to the model of a structured representational order that the concept implies. Whether the resulting vision suggested a history of unimpeachable piety among the Chinese or its converse, the persistence of this paradigm tended to delimit the range of European responses to China's belief systems, further reifying more broadly applicable patterns of interpretation that would persist into the early nineteenth century and beyond.

In this chapter I will trace the history of these responses through three distinct although broadly defined phases. The first phase encompasses the founding of the Jesuit mission in China by Matteo Ricci (1552–1610) and his subsequent articulation of an accommodationist policy toward ancient Confucian doctrine. The cornerstone of this policy, I will argue, was Ricci's rhetorical insistence on distilling the original essence of the early Confucian belief system from the syncretic potpourri of religious practices that he encountered in the pluralistic climate of the late Ming dynasty, and on distinguishing it in particular from the confused and disorderly tangle of doctrines that characterized Chinese Buddhism in his mind. The second phase corresponds to the long-simmering theological debate on the religious character of Confucian teachings known as the Rites Controversy. Ricci's policy of accommodation in China provoked considerable dissent both from his Jesuit successors in the China mission and among the rival mendicant orders over the central issue of doctrinal compatibility between the Confucian tradition and Catholicism. The dispute erupted into public prominence in Paris between 1696 and 1700 when the publication of Le Comte's popularization of Jesuit accounts in *Nouveaux Mémoires sur la Chine* provoked an outspoken attack by a rival religious order in a letter to the pope and a denunciation of the Jesuits before the faculty of theology at the Sorbonne. What is most striking about this affair, when considered as a crucial interpretive episode in the period's encounter between East and West, is the degree to which the conflicting views of Confucianism that fueled the debate drew upon the same conceptual dichotomy that had been developed by the early missionaries in differentiating the Confucian tradition from what they took to be its idolatrous rivals. Although the cultural standing of traditional Chinese belief systems declined precipitously at the hands of the Jesuits' detractors, its fall occurred within the framework of a familiar paradigm, reinforcing the currency of the paradigm itself in subsequent stages of the encounter.

The final stage that will be explored in this chapter is the reassessment of Chinese religion that accompanied the rise of libertinism in eighteenth-century France. For Bayle and Voltaire, in particular, the Chinese case proves crucial in the development of a rationalist critique of Christianity. In their analysis, which entails a radical reversal of the anti-Jesuit position in the Rites Controversy, China emerges as the virtuous paragon of natural religion and tolerance, while Christianity stands condemned for its vicious sectarianism, narrow-mindedness, and violence as a grotesque perversion of these "Chinese" ideals. Universal law displaces divine revelation as the transcendent source of truth in this new, enlightened vision of theological legitimacy, but the rhetorical operations of the paradigm remain intact, as the valorization of Chinese tradition and the vilification of its Western counterpart preserve the language Ricci had deployed in distinguishing rival traditions in China more than a century before.

Each of these three phases of theological activism and controversy, in other words, involves the projection onto Chinese religious culture of a conceptual framework closely resembling, in its notions of authority, derivation, and epistemological purity, that which was shaping, at the same time, European responses to the Chinese language. Just as the myriad interpretations of the Chinese script enabled writers to make sense of its characters in terms that answered to pressing personal and cultural imperatives, so the competing constructions of Chinese religious symbols and rituals likewise comprised a form of ideographic fantasy that enabled the mastery and appropriation of an inscrutably alien code. The idea of legitimacy and of its originary, historical, and structural modes once again figures centrally here. The most significant texts of this theological encounter contain familiar clusterings of metaphors that evoke the longing for universal ordering systems and the concomitant fear of unchecked forms of symbolic proliferation and corruption that so animated the writings of Bacon, Webb, Leibniz, and Bayer. Owing largely to the shaping force of these metaphors, China remained a place where meanings could exist and symbols function either in a pure, immutable form or not at all. The rhetoric of legitimacy proved a powerful and adaptable weapon in theological dispute, but more importantly, the polemical potency of its underlying constructs ultimately led to their emergence as the very condition of cultural legibility in Europe's first sustained encounter with the vast empire of the East.

From Babel to Babylon: Jesuit Readings of Chinese Religious Doctrine

That a sustained encounter took place at all is owing to the Jesuits' early recognition that it would have to be conducted on Chinese terms. The persistent threat of invasions from the north and piracy along the coasts that China faced in the sixteenth century heightened a traditional attitude of wariness toward foreign incursions of any kind, and early European merchants and missionaries alike found their persistent overtures repeatedly rejected.[2] Although limited trade privileges were granted to foreign vessels in the port of Canton after 1554, efforts to preach in the city were consistently repulsed, and offending priests sent back to the Portuguese city of Macao or sometimes jailed. After witnessing the failure of numerous petitions and official requests, the Spanish Jesuit Juan Bautista Ribeira secretly landed on the southern coast of China in 1568 with the aim, apparently, of converting the inhabitants through the sole grace of God, as he had obtained the benefit of neither the authorization of their magistrates nor any familiarity with their language. The failure of his brash attempt provoked the angry conclusion that where God's grace proved insufficient, only military might could prevail. In a letter to his superiors he wrote, "In the three years I was there [at Macao], I tried everything I could to penetrate [the continent], but nothing I could think of was of any use. . . . There is no hope of converting [the Chinese], unless one makes use of force and they bow before the soldiers."[3]

The solution his successors finally settled upon seems obvious perhaps only in retrospect, because it required a significant shift in the prevailing attitude toward the Chinese. The first successful mission was established in China in 1583 by two Italian Jesuits, Michele Ruggieri and Matteo

Ricci, who had, at the behest of their superior and predecessor in Macao, Alessandro Valignano, committed themselves to learning the language and mores of the "great and worthy people" of whom he had spoken so highly.[4] Their efforts at linguistic and social adaptation no doubt conveyed a flattering respect for Chinese institutions and helped to placate the concerns of those mandarins who had been troubled by the barbarian brazenness of Ribeira and those like him. The newcomers had obviously learned from their earlier mistakes: "At the beginning," Ruggieri writes, "it is necessary to proceed very gently with this people and not to act with indiscreet fervor, for it would be very easy to lose this opportunity, which we might not have again."[5]

If prudence in the face of pronounced xenophobia dictated the missionaries' submission to the study of Chinese and strict observance of local manners, it clearly required deference to prevailing dress codes as well. The most appropriate models for the Jesuits' role as religious teachers appeared at first to be Buddhist monks, who, like their Christian counterparts, wore full-length robes, took vows of poverty and chastity, and chanted music resembling plainsong in their temple services. The Jesuits accordingly adopted names and attire befitting men of that order and set about their work. "If only Your Reverence could see me as I am now: I have made myself a Chinaman," Ricci wrote in a letter of 1585. "Indeed, in our dress, our looks, our manners, and in everything external we have made ourselves Chinese."[6] The Jesuits' willingness initially to present themselves within familiar social categories was clearly calculated to minimize the hostility and suspicion with which the Chinese greeted barbarian visitors who flaunted their foreignness; in this respect it proved a successful strategy. On two other counts, however, it later appeared to be a misguided decision. To begin with, as the Jesuits soon discovered, men of the cloth in China were not accorded nearly the same degree of respect and authority that they enjoyed in Europe. Without such social status, Christian missionaries would be unlikely to achieve widespread acceptance of their teachings and had little hope of gaining access to the ruling class of officials and literati whose endorsement would ultimately be crucial to their enterprise. Their vows, in particular, seemed to backfire: the exalted, Christlike virtue signified by religious self-denial in the European context were lost on a Chinese audience for whom the perpetuation and enrichment of the family line counted as preeminent moral duties. A modest display of wealth, by contrast, brought unmistakable credit to the mis-

4. Matteo Ricci, portrait by unknown Chinese artist included in Giulio Aleni's
Ta-hsi Hsi-t'ai Li hsien-sheng hsing-chi, ca. 1616. Courtesy of the Vatican Library
(Borg. Cin. 350, fasc. 3).

sion in higher social circles: "It was necessary for our people to wear a
proper silk garment for the visits of magistrates and other important persons who came on visits to the house in their ceremonial dress and head-
piece." The success of the mission took precedence over doctrinal purity,
and if associating with the lower orders of society brought the missionar-

ies contempt rather than admiration and respect, Ricci realized, they would have to change their ways. In a letter of 1592 he writes:

To give ourselves more dignity we do not walk the streets on foot, but have ourselves carried in chairs, on men's shoulders, in the manner of persons of rank here. We have great need for such authority in these parts, as without it our efforts would bear no fruit among these gentiles: for the name of foreigners and priests is so vile in China that we need this and other such stratagems to show them that we are not priests as vile as their own.[7]

Of even greater concern for Ricci than the social stigma of being associated with a vile and degraded band of friars, however, was the very real risk that the missionaries' Christian doctrine might be confused for a new variety of Buddhism, and their savior consigned to some lowly, if quaintly exotic office in the sprawling pantheon of local saints and deities.[8] Much to Ricci's chagrin, there were, in fact, striking resemblances between the two traditions that could not, unfortunately, be discarded as easily as the borrowed robes of Buddhist monks. In addition to their foreign origin and a formal priesthood given to monastic vows and ceremonial chants, Buddhism and Christianity shared an emphasis on the virtues of charity, compassion, and the suppression of passions, a prominent doctrine of salvation and eternal life, a calendar of popular religious festivals, and an assortment of spiritual accoutrements including incense, sacred images, and saintly relics. Such similarities must have seemed reassuring to the Chinese who gathered to hear the Jesuits speak and to examine the religious materials they brought with them. The Jesuits, in any case, were warmly welcomed, wined and dined, and initially flattered by the attention they received and the respect their deity seemed to command. Antonio Almeida writes of the reception he and two other Jesuits enjoyed when they arrived, still clad in their Buddhist robes, in northern Guangdong Province: "We are surrounded on all sides by monks who treat us in a friendly manner and every evening come to hear about the things of God; . . . there has been no way to protect ourselves from the multitude which gathers to see us; we show our altar to the most important of them and they do reverence to the image of the Savior."[9]

Such hospitality would have qualified as a miracle itself in many a foreign missionary field. Yet it soon became evident that the Jesuits' conscientious attempts at cultural assimilation were succeeding all too well: the generous treatment they had interpreted as a mark of particular respect was nothing more than the polite welcome customarily accorded itinerant monks, wealthy donors, and government officials.[10] Christian missionaries stood little chance of distinguishing their creed in the context of a popular religious culture characterized by the accommodating, utilitarian attitude that Marcel Granet has referred to as "syncretic pragmatism," in which the practical ends of worship entirely justified the means. In late Ming China, one faced no imputation of inconstancy in paying reverence to any plausible idol that came one's way; indeed, if one found one's prayers answered more efficaciously by a new deity than the old, one would be perfectly justified in shifting one's allegiance accordingly.[11] But a Chinese worshipper who approached a Christian altar with only a provisional devotion and a reserve of local gods waiting in the wings was not the kind of "convert" the European fathers had in mind. Even if he could be persuaded to accept the supremacy of the Christian God, it proved impossible from within the Buddhist framework to establish the jealous exclusivity of this god's relationship to men. Niccolò Longobardi, who succeeded Ricci as the head of the Jesuit mission, explained the difficulty of weaning potential converts from their accustomed practices:

For although it is very easy to persuade the Chinese to worship God, the Lord of Heaven, as the sovereign deity, conversely it is just as difficult to get them to tear down all their idols from their thrones and no longer honour them at all. For they cannot bear these images not even to be included among the ranks of the ministers of God or that they be refused the honour that we accord to our saints.[12]

The outward similarities between the two religions, then, combined with the confounding expansiveness of the Buddhist pantheon, created the prospect of a religious synthesis on terms the early Jesuits were not prepared to accept. After witnessing the failure of Ribeira's battering-ram approach to the salvation of the Chinese, the Jesuits had resolved on an assimilationist paradigm in rethinking the terms of the encounter: it would be necessary, they realized, to sinicize themselves to some degree in order to achieve a modicum of credibility and acceptance within Chinese society. But the transformation of their god into a Buddhist idol, even a supremely powerful one, was another matter altogether. Buddhist beliefs were too deeply entrenched in Ming society to be displaced by a rival sect, especially when that rival could so easily be accommodated within the framework of existing practices.

Unwilling to give up entirely on the assimilationist strategy after this first failed attempt, the Jesuits finally exchanged their Buddhist robes and weary limbs for the silks and sedan chairs of the literati. Associating with this elite class of scholars and officials not only promised increased status and prestige but also avoided the danger of Christianity in China being subsumed into an idolatrous cult. The Confucian philosophy of the scholar class, after all, was not so much a religious system as a practical moral code and political ideology. While the practical virtues that it advocated were largely compatible with their Christian counterparts—Confucius taught a version of Jesus' golden rule—it possessed fewer of the overtly religious trappings or rituals of worship that in the Buddhist case had tended to mislead potential converts in their interpretation of Christian teachings.[13] The attraction for Ricci of his new scholar allies was precisely the secular and hence theologically uncompromised basis of their moral code:

As they neither command nor prohibit anything of what is to be believed concerning the afterlife, and many of them follow, along with this one, the two other sects, we might conclude that this is not a fixed law, but strictly speaking only an academy, instituted for the good governance of the republic. And so they can certainly be of this academy and also become Christian, since in its essential part it contains nothing contrary to the essence of the Catholic faith, nor does the Catholic faith prohibit anything that its books advocate, but on the contrary it contributes greatly to the peace and quiet of the kingdom.[14]

Confucianism, then, seemed to offer an ideal social and ethical foundation for Christian faith in China while, as a largely materialist philosophy, presenting a minimum of doctrinal interference. There was little reason to challenge it, therefore, and given its absolute centrality to the established political and social order, even less hope of doing so successfully. In his approach to Confucianism, which he developed and elaborated over the rest of his life in China, Ricci chose a path, rather, of creative accommodation. Just as the early growth of Christianity had required introducing the gospels to pagan communities on their own terms, so the conversion of the Chinese, Ricci recognized, would have to proceed from their own cultural starting point.[15] The beneficiaries of a complex and fully formed tradition that had served them well for thousands of years, they would never accept a rigid alternative doctrine imposed on them from the outside. They might, however, be persuaded that a foreign teaching was essentially compatible with their own and that its metaphysical conclusions, however unfamiliar, were consistent with their own premises. This was, of course, precisely the hope that would later animate the Leibniz-Bouvet exchange on the significance of the *Yi Jing*. As late as 1697, Bouvet claimed that there was nothing "in the world more likely to dispose the minds and hearts of the Chinese to embrace our holy Religion than showing them how closely it conforms with the principles of their own ancient and legitimate philosophy."[16]

The story of the Jesuits in China in the seventeenth century is largely the story of the evolution and consequences of this policy of accommodation toward the native Confucian tradition. Historians of the mission have written exhaustively about the personalities and conflicts that enliven this period; I will make no attempt to duplicate their efforts here.[17] I will focus instead in the remainder of this first section on the strategic responses Ricci and his followers formulated to the two principal sets of teachings they encountered in China and the relationship between them, responses notable for both their sheer rhetorical force and their particular metaphorical resonances. Buddhism, on the one hand, emerges in Jesuit writings as a threat far more pernicious than a mere cult of misguided idolaters; the status of Confucianism, on the other, far surpasses that of a convenient stepping-stone to grace. These writings reveal a rigidly dualistic paradigm as the cognitive precondition for the European interpretation of Chinese religious culture in this period, a conceptual framework in which a vision of theological legitimacy was distilled from and juxtaposed against its opposite, a dystopian vision of spiritual dissolution and chaos. Elements of this paradigm were borrowed from the Chinese themselves, who since the introduction of Buddhism during the Han dynasty (206 BCE–220 CE) had been no strangers to doctrinal rivalry and conflict on this score. The Jesuits, of course, brought their own history with them as well, and their language is deeply inflected with the schismatic violence that attended the Protestant Reformation in Europe. The specific genealogies of Jesuit tropes, however, will be of less concern to me here than the continuity of their applications in the myriad responses to Chinese religious culture over the course of the following century. Here as in the case of the enigmatic Chinese script, a schema rooted in a transcendent ideal of purified representation permitted European interpreters to project a reassuring order on a vast and unwieldy alien universe of signs that threatened, otherwise, to unsettle their own. Although the Jesuit mission ultimately failed in its aims, the images of the Confucian sage and idolatrous bonze that resulted from these projections took their place alongside Rousseau's noble savage as among the most compelling and ubiquitous emblems of foreignness in eighteenth-century Europe.[18] Lionel Jensen, in *Manufacturing Confucianism*, argues that the modern idea of "Confucius" is largely an early Jesuit creation, and one that has profoundly affected subsequent attitudes toward Chinese culture among not only Westerners but also the Chinese themselves. Whether or not crucial components of this idea predated the Jesuits' arrival, it is clear that the missionaries brought their own distinctive purposes and paradigms to bear on their representations of the historical figure of Kongzi and his teachings. My own interest here is in teasing out the recurring patterns of interpretation that are woven through these readings and responses and in highlighting their suggestive resonance within other contemporary spheres of the encounter.

The cornerstone of Ricci's interpretive strategy was his insistence on the need for clear distinctions and hierarchies in the face of the religious syncretism of the late Ming dynasty (1368–1644). The stormy religious climate of sixteenth-century Europe was one in which the Truth was often taken to lie concealed among a baffling array of imitations and impostures and in which any claim to doctrinal authority entailed the meticulous differentiation of competing beliefs and the merciless unmasking of error. Ricci, who had studied for seventeen years under Jesuit masters at the height of the Counter Reformation, was well versed in techniques for combating heresy and applied them vigorously to the tangled morass he saw in the belief systems of the Chinese. As noted above, ordinary Chinese had historically seen little need to draw sharp demarcations between various systems of belief, so that the religious outlook of a given individual typically combined elements from two or more traditions. Indeed, for Gernet, "The very idea of belonging to one particular religion is inapplicable [in China]."[19] Even those neo-Confucian literati who, from the Song dynasty (960–1279) onward, premised their revival of the Confucian tradition on the repudiation of the "alien dross" of Buddhism could never entirely escape its pervasive influence and regularly appropriated Buddhist concepts in their own writings. Toward the end of the Ming dynasty, however, these syncretic impulses became much more pronounced, and there were conspicuous efforts to merge the three primary schools—Confucianism, Buddhism, and Taoism—into a loose amalgam of the whole known as *sanjiao*, or three teachings.[20] Such an accommodating approach, however, could hardly find favor with a Christian observer accustomed to a unitary and exclusivist conception of religious truth. Ricci scarcely veils his scorn:

The most common opinion today among those who consider themselves the most wise is that all three of these sects are one and the same thing and can all be observed together. In this they deceive themselves and others, causing great confusion, since it seems to them that in religious matters, the more ways there are of saying something, the better for the kingdom. In the end, everything comes out contrary to what they expect, as in attempting to follow all three laws they remain without any, since they do not truly believe any one of them in their hearts.[21]

A pluralistic compromise that in the Chinese context might appear as a pragmatic response to an historical reality for the sake of social harmony offended Jesuit sensibilities as an invitation to doctrinal anarchy and moral confusion, with consequences not only for Chinese society but also for its very intelligibility in European eyes.

In the previous chapter I suggested that the Chinese script appeared as a provocation to the Western philological imagination, a vast field of illegible ciphers, a "mysterious discipline" that would yield up its secrets only to the possessor of a rationalist "key." Müller's *clavis sinica* and every other attempt to penetrate the mystery of the characters served both as a response to pressing contemporary problems in the philosophy of language and, at the most basic level, as an interpretive hypothesis for making sense of an otherwise baffling representational system. Central to many of these efforts was a taxonomic paradigm whereby the formless profusion of illegible marks could be analyzed, classified, and systematized according to their proper place within a hierarchically ordered scheme. Ricci's confrontation with religious syncretism in China bears close comparison with these early European readings of the Chinese script. Ricci, like Bayer and Prémare, was initially baffled by his first encounter with an alien symbolic code, a code whose confusing proliferation of signs was rendered largely illegible precisely by the lack of clear rules of distinction among them. Just as a cognizance of principles of difference is a prerequisite to finding meaning in language, so theological insight is premised on the demarcation of religious ideas. If Ricci seems especially hostile to the religious "tolerance" of the literati, it is because their willingness to accommodate heterogeneous approaches to questions of observance and belief subverts the epistemological foundation of what is, for him, the supreme symbolic order. If there can be no speech, for a structuralist, without the differentiation of phonemes, then there can be no God, for a Jesuit, without clear distinctions between truth and heresy. The success of the mission depended on the Jesuits' ability to find a place for their god within the Chinese belief system, to make sense of this system in familiar terms in order to respond effectively to it on the ground and to justify their audacious approach in the eyes of an often skeptical church establishment.

In the catechism he composed in Chinese for native initiates to the Christian faith, Ricci introduces a vivid metaphor to illustrate the dangers attending the doctrinal confusion he finds around him.

Formerly, in your esteemed country, each of its three religions had its own image. In recent times a monster has appeared from I know not where: it has one body and three heads and is called the Religion of the Three in One. The common people ought to have been frightened of it, and the lofty scholars should have attacked it with all speed; in fact, however, they have prostrated themselves in worship before it and made it their master. Will this not corrupt men's minds even further?[22]

It is not the ugliness of the monster's three heads that repulses Ricci in this passage, but the simple fact that there are three of them. He seems willing, for now, to admit the possibility of the individual merit of any one or even all of these three; it is the grafting of the three heads onto a single body that renders the creature monstrous and the attempt at syncretic faith logically incoherent.

First, the Three Religions are either all true and complete or they are all false and incomplete; or one of them is true and complete and the other two are false and incomplete. If each of [them] is true and complete then it is enough to believe one of them; why should one have to practice the other two? If they are all false and incomplete then they ought all to be rejected. Of what use is it to embrace all three of them?[23]

Certain of Ricci's successors in the years that followed would advocate slaying the beast outright and replacing it with an imported and thoroughly domesticated Christian species. Ricci, a more diplomatic hero than St. George, preferred a selective, surgical approach. The Chinese dragon might be tamed if it could be satisfied with a single head at least nominally receptive to Christian influences. He focused his efforts, therefore, on undoing the confusion that syncretism had wrought by insisting, first, on a sharp differentiation between Confucianism and its rivals and by then further distilling the teachings of this favored school into a pure and rarefied form that would ultimately admit of an unproblematic comparison and fusion with Christianity.

This process of differentiation would require that Buddhist, Taoist, and even modern neo-Confucian accretions on an idealized core doctrine of ur-Confucianism be hacked away without mercy. While the teachings of ancient sages would be upheld as the originary sources of truth and virtue in the Chinese tradition, Buddhism would be condemned as a foreign imposter and as a merely derivative imitation of Christianity. The rational and moral purity of Confucian doctrine would be contrasted with the corruption and depravity of rival sects. And on the level of the texts themselves, the apparent coherence and unity of the classical canon would find its antithesis in the fragmentary nature of Buddhist and Taoist writings and a scattered proliferation of widely variant teachings that defied any quest for orthodoxy. The Jesuit response to Chinese religion, in other words, would employ a conceptual paradigm and rhetorical repertoire strikingly similar to those employed by European philologists in coming to terms with the Chinese language in the same period. The linguists compiled lexical keys, the missionaries catechisms; both were efforts to define and establish a sound and reliable basis for meaning within an indomitably foreign system of signs.

The Chinese writing system was esteemed for its seemingly ageless antiquity and was favored as a result with hypotheses crediting it with divine origins, or at least with unimpeachably rational underpinnings. The Jesuit policy of accommodation with Confucianism required that it boast a similarly legitimizing pedigree. In the thumbnail introduction to Chinese religions that he provides at one point in his journals, Ricci takes pains to argue the essential compatibility of Confucianism with Catholic doctrine. The Confucian belief system that he champions, however, is not that of the neo-Confucians of the Song dynasty, nor even the ethical system preached by Confucius (551–479 BCE) himself and recorded in the *Analects* after his death, but rather the religious and political world view embodied in the Zhou dynasty documents of several centuries before upon which Confucius based his teachings and which later came to be identified as the Confucian classics. It is the very antiquity of these most ancient of Chinese writings that seems largely to validate the comparison.

Of all the gentiles who have come to our attention in Europe, I know of none that made fewer errors concerning matters of religion than did the Chinese in their earliest antiquity. Thus I find in their books that they have always worshipped a supreme deity which they call the Lord of Heaven or of heaven and earth.[24]

This reverence for Chinese antiquity and the attribution of a legitimating authority to cultural artifacts on the basis of this antiquity is a phenomenon that has appeared before. Both Webb and Prémare, and especially Leibniz and Bouvet, were captivated by the Chinese writing system precisely because its ancient origins served to promise a representational authenticity and access to forms of truth that modern, degraded languages could no longer provide. In both cases, too, there is a paradoxical tension implicit in European projections of such ideals onto the symbolic systems of ancient China. On the one hand, Chinese antiquity evoked the compelling image of an incorruptible origin, a perfect state of prelapsarian purity, a golden age predating any and all history of degeneration and decline. On the other, the surviving artifacts of these systems exercised a powerfully seductive appeal in that the very distance of their origin rendered their meaning so ambiguous that they could be called upon to support even the most extravagant foreign hypothesis. Antiquity lends a patina of authenticity, but what was finally authenticated, in both cases, was not so much an "original" meaning at all (if, indeed, one can even conceive of such a thing) as a historically contingent and deeply motivated interpretation.

Like their writing system, then, the divine knowledge of the Chinese dated, in the Jesuit view, back to "the very beginning of their history." Its own originary status seems, for Ricci, almost to overshadow its happy congruence with Western monotheism, as it promises access to the essential core of truth at the very heart of Chinese culture. The political and cultural authority of the literati, the ruling class of scholar officials, derives from their adherence to this originary, native philosophy: "[The law] of the Literati is the most ancient in China, and accordingly they have always had and today still have the governance of China in their hands. For this reason it is the one that flourishes best, has the most books, and is the most respected." The tradition is preserved from one generation of scholars to the next through a system of classical education founded upon its precepts. "They do not choose this law, but rather through the study of letters they drink it in, and no graduate nor magistrate neglects to profess it. Its author or restorer and head is Confucius."[25] This method of transmission has not been without flaw, and elements of the original teachings have been distorted in the several millennia that have passed since they were first recorded. The truth, however, is still preserved in the most ancient of the Chinese classics, texts whose originary status for Ricci guarantees the validity of his lifelong effort to redeem their misguided modern inheritors: "I have noted many passages [in the classical texts] that favor aspects of our faith, such as the unity of God, the immortality of the soul, the glory of the blessed, etc. . . . Those books of the literati of the greatest antiquity and authority offer reverence only to heaven and earth and the Lord of them both."[26] In positing a distinction between the pure, ancient meaning of classical texts and degraded modern interpretations, Ricci draws upon a well-established Chinese tradition. As David Mungello points out, "The history of Confucianism is the history of Chinese attempting to recapture the original and *true* meaning of the classics and expressing this meaning through the writing of annotated editions of the classics."[27] Ricci inflects this tradition with both an evangelical zeal and a predisposition to discover "true meanings" that bore some resemblance to a Christian cosmology.

If the Chinese classics served as an idealized textual point of origin, their monotheistic resonances encouraged Ricci to seek in them evidence, as well, of a belief in a transcendent point of origin in the metaphysical realm. But although Ricci is able to cite numerous passages suggesting an ancient Chinese belief in a lord of the heavens, he uncovers less direct evidence in the classics for a Chinese doctrine of divine creation and is left to deduce it from the traditional emphasis on values of order and obedience. His persistent and often ingenious attempts to foist upon a dimly visible Chinese deity the creative powers of the God of Genesis and to realign Chinese conceptions of universal history in accordance with biblical metaphysics underscore the centrality of the trope of origination to his interpretive paradigm. The legibility of Chinese religious culture is premised, for Ricci, on the primal legitimacy of its textual sources; the viability of the deity that he discovers there depends, likewise, on its originary stature as a unique and all-powerful creator.

This creative potentiality is precisely the godly attribute that anchors Ricci's vision of Christianity in the catechism he prepared for his Chinese readers, *The True Meaning of the Lord of Heaven* (Tianzhu shiyi, 1603). The introduction to the work begins with a systematic derivation of the doctrine of creationism from native Confucian principles and the bitter lessons of Chinese political history.

1. All doctrines about making the whole world peaceful and governing a country rightly are focussed on the principle of uniqueness. Therefore, worthies and sages have always advised the ministers to be loyal, that is not to have a second [lord in their mind]. . . .

2. In ancient times, whenever a large number of heroes disunited [the country] and fought against each other in times of anarchy, and when it was still uncertain who would be the rightful lord, every just man examined carefully who could be the legitimate lord and then [decided to fight for him and even] to die for him. This decision was irrevocable.

5. "Cum Fu Çu sive Confucius," portrait by unknown Western artist included in Philippe Couplet et al., *Confucius Sinarum Philosophus*, 1687. Courtesy of the Special Collections Library, University of Michigan.

3. Every state or country has [its own] lord; is it possible that only the universe does not have a lord? A country must be united under only one [lord]; is it possible that the universe has two lords? Therefore, a superior man cannot but know the source of the universe and the creator of all creatures, and then raise his mind [to Him].[28]

Having spent several years in the guise of a Buddhist monk, Ricci was painfully aware of the foreignness of principles of devotional fidelity to Chinese religious practice. He calculated, however, that a long history of devastating civil wars might render the Chinese considerably more receptive to a doctrine modeled on values of unity and loyalty to an all-powerful sovereign. While serving the clear pragmatic purpose of translating Christian monotheism into a Chinese idiom in the interest of winning converts, Ricci's analogy contributed as well to his own ongoing personal struggle to make sense of a complex, obscure, and culturally alien set of teachings in reassuringly familiar terms.

A second, even more striking analogy Ricci offers in the same work affirms his remarkable versatility in reconciling his own interpretive requirements with those of his Chinese audience. Within a society that seemed to revere, if not to worship, lines of ancestors reaching countless generations into the past, what better means of conveying the respect due the Christian God of creation than through a genealogical metaphor? At the same time, where could one seek a more compelling affirmation of the legitimacy of a hybrid deity than through analogy with a first ancestor, a kind of great-great grandfather of them all?

The way that we respect and admire the supremely honored one is not only by burning incense and worshiping Him, but also by often meditating upon the great achievement of the first Father who is the creator of all things. . . . Since wombs, eggs, and seeds are themselves things, we must ask what first produced them so that they in turn could produce other things. We must trace every kind of thing back to its first ancestor; and since nothing is capable of producing itself, there must be Someone who is both original and unique who is the creator of every kind of thing and object.[29]

Ricci's sino-Christian god, in his primal originality and reproductive potency, maps onto the world of Chinese cosmology a set of ideals and aspirations that when applied later in the century to another equally inscrutable universe of signs would give rise to the ideographic fantasies of European philology. The first ancestor and the *clavis sinica*, as readings of the East, are of the same imaginative cloth, kindred productions of a specific interpretive paradigm serving a Western desire for recognition and mastery in a first encounter with an inscrutably foreign cultural code.

What Ricci offers his novitiate readers, in the end, is a catechism conforming to the contours of both the dominant religious culture in China and an imported epistemic framework. His emphasis on the role of authorizing creators, both philosophical and divine, in his mediation of this encounter will provide him with the necessary rhetorical leverage to set Confucianism clearly above and apart from its myriad sectarian rivals within the religious mosaic of the late Ming dynasty. Securing a sound foundation for Catholicism in China would require, after all, not only the repudiation of syncretic tendencies among the literati and the identification of the Chinese Lord of Heaven with the Christian God, but also a decisive assault on any creed that might threaten the ascendancy of this vulnerable new god. Not surprisingly, then, once he had completed his own initial "conversion" to the sect of the literati, Ricci became an implacably hostile foe of the Buddhist teachings he had left behind.

The reasons for this violent renunciation were many and complex. In addition to the pragmatic considerations in favor of Confucianism discussed above and the natural disdain of the Christian missionary for seemingly idolatrous sects of all kinds, they most likely entailed a combination of jealous resentment at the manifest popularity of Buddhism and an anxious recognition of the enduring resemblances between the two religions.[30] Ricci was no doubt inspired as well by a long history of Chinese attacks on what Confucian scholars often viewed as dangerous foreign idolatry. Going back at least as far as the Tang dynasty (618–907), memorialists such as the eminent philosopher Han Yu condemned Buddhist teachings on the grounds of their barbarian (that is, Indian) origin, their neglect of the importance of hierarchical social relationships, and their weakening effect both on rulers and on local economies burdened with the construction and maintenance of extravagant temples and monasteries.[31]

What is certain, however, is that while Ricci drew on these native Chinese critiques to inform his arguments, and while certain of the charges he levels against the Buddhists have parallels, as well, in contemporary anti-Protestant diatribes in Catholic Europe, the language of his attacks preserves a striking paradigmatic continuity in its representation of Buddhism through a precise rhetorical inversion of the foundations he had established for Confucian legitimacy. It does not suffice Ricci to dismiss the Buddhists as a misguided sect of heathen idolaters, even as a particularly pernicious one. The charges against them are far more specific, in that they arise from within precisely the same conceptual and metaphorical framework that informed his reading of the Confucian classics. Whereas Confucianism was dignified by its association with an ancient scriptural pedigree and a doctrine of divine first ancestry, Ricci derides Buddhism as effectively an orphan sect, a parasite on society without any claim to legitimate origins in either the historical or theological sense. If Confucius was the founding prince of Chinese philosophy, then the Buddha, for Ricci, was its bastard son.

In strictly pragmatic terms, depicting Buddhism as a perfect negative image of Confucian worthiness was an effective means of both dramatizing the contrast between them and reinforcing Confucianism's identification with those virtues that Buddhism lacked. But the metaphorical continuity in Ricci's presentation of the two rival creeds simultaneously served his own interpretive imperatives, in enabling him to name and to account for a theological perspective that he could neither accept nor fully comprehend. Ricci seems at best to have achieved a limited understanding of the object of his contempt, but in a civilization that once had glimpsed the divine meaning of the Sovereign on High perhaps a greater penetration was unnecessary: Buddhist teachings were, to Ricci's mind, superfluous, a clamorous din that distracted his audience from their recovery of the one true way. It was necessary, however, for the integrity of his vision, to situate himself in relation to this clamor, to place it firmly within his own interpretive schema as the very token of alien resistance to rigid schematization.

In sharp contrast to Confucianism, firmly rooted in an ancient corpus of written texts, Buddhism, for Ricci, is without any sound historical foundation whatsoever. The teachings of the original Buddha, the Indian prince Gautama Sakyamuni (ca. 563–483 BCE) appear to him, rather, as the fanciful deceptions of a religious charlatan, based largely on an imported Greek theory concerning the transmigration of souls.

After the death of Pythagoras . . . the teaching somehow leaked out and found its way to other countries. This was at the time when Sakyamuni happened to be planning to establish a new religion in India. He accepted this theory of reincarnation and added to it the teaching concerning the Six Directions, together with a hundred other lies, editing it all to form books which he called canonical writings. Many years later some Chinese went to India and transmitted the Buddhist religion to China. There is no genuine record of the history of this religion in which one can put one's faith, or any real principle upon which one can rely.

A view of the Buddhist scriptures as a pack of outrageous lies offers a convenient explanation for the troubling parallels with Christianity that they present: Ricci surmises that Sakyamuni, like a clever Protestant evangelist, intentionally inserted "two or three elements of [Christian] orthodoxy" into his teaching in order to promote it, for "otherwise no one [would] believe him.[32] A tragic irony, for Ricci, lies in the possibility that the Chinese legates to India might have been deceived by these Christian borrowings into mistaking Buddhism for the Christian gospel that was the real object of their quest. Buddhism arrived in China, he claims, at the time of the Apostles, rumors of whom might well have inspired the Chinese to seek out their teachings in the West. Unfortunately for the Chinese, they "brought back this false doctrine in place of the Gospel."[33] In contrast to the pure, ennobling pedigree provided by the Confucian classics, then, the historian of Buddhism could expect to find only a trail of mistaken borrowings and distortions that had been formed together into a vile parody of the truth.

What was crucially lacking, in Ricci's view, from this "false doctrine" was any notion of a unique and transcendent first cause to give meaning and order to the universe. The historical illegitimacy of Buddhism (and to a lesser extent Taoism as well) was matched by its metaphysical groundlessness, the complacent emptiness it seemed to offer in the place of a powerfully creative divine. Ricci paraphrases the Buddha on the subject of creation with the words: "The visible world emerges from voidness"; he credits Lao Tzu, the founder of Taoism, with the claim that "things are produced from nothing." For one who had seen fit, in the Chinese context, to emphasize the role of God as the first ancestor of all things, the glaring absence of any agent of generation in such teachings must have appeared a travesty akin to a castration of the divine, or at best an insinuation of godly impotence.

When we come to speak of the source of all phenomena we are clearly speaking of that, the value of which is beyond all comparison. How, then, can one employ despicable [words like] "voidness" and "nothingness" to represent it? . . . How can things which are essentially nothing or void employ their voidness and nothingness to cause all things to come into being and to continue in existence?[34]

Ricci presents the reader of his catechism with a stark choice between two contrasting visions of universal creation that correspond in their epistemic outlines with the two competing paradigms of the history and development of language I presented in the previous chapter. The coming into being of the world, like that of language, can be imagined either as an authorized, regulated, and consciously controlled process, or, alternatively, as one that is more spontaneous, prolific, and unconstrained. The presence of an omnipotent will guarantees the legitimacy of language and of God; its absence entails the collapse of moral order in the linguistic as in the worldly realm.

Ricci's depiction of the moral standing of the rival religions in China is fraught with imagery that reinforces the parallel between the linguistic and theological realms. Just as the philosophical system that seemed to underlie the Chinese script promised a means of checking the shameless bastardization of language and boundless proliferation of its signs, so Confucianism appeared to Ricci as a refuge of rationality and restraint in a sea of treacherous ambiguity and uncontained licentiousness. In reality, as I have noted, the demarcations among belief systems in Ming China was never as sharp as Ricci tended to imply. Rather, his rendering of the moral divide within Chinese religious culture reinforced his efforts to distill the essence of Chinese ethical thought under the banner of Confucianism, while relegating the messy and opaque doctrinal residue that remained to a contemptible second-class status.

The paramount function of this idealized ethical system was, for Ricci, to strengthen the coherence of the social fabric by instilling an unwavering deference to absolute authority and the social structures that sustained it. Ignatius de Loyola, the founder of the Society of Jesus, had famously emphasized the value of obedience and strictly graded hierarchies to the effective government of the Society, and Ricci drew upon the "orderly, medieval, and wholly theocentric worldview" he had absorbed in the course of his training in making sense of the Chinese context.[35] The ultimate law-giver, the "supreme deity which they call the Lord of Heaven," was a unique and consummate master who brooked no rivals. "This law admits no idols, but offers reverence only to heaven and earth or to the Lord of Heaven," Ricci writes of the belief system of the literati. "It recognizes other spirits, but does not give them as much power as is given the Lord of Heaven." Unlike other ancient civilizations, the Chinese had resisted the degeneration of their conception of the divine, just as they had resisted, in the European view, the corruption of their written language. "They never believed such disgraceful things of the Lord of Heaven and his other spirits and ministers as those which our Romans, the Greeks, the Egyptians, and other foreign nations believed." His continued supremacy, moreover, was assured by his association with "the dictates of reason . . .

received from heaven," which the Confucians "made a great effort to follow in all their works."[36]

The sanctity of the Lord of Heaven was preserved in part by his strict
isolation from the corrupting tendencies of common people through the
person of the emperor, who, like the Catholic priest, reserved for himself
the exclusive privilege of transacting directly with the divine. For ordinary citizens, the expression of piety took the form of strict observances
of respect within a prescribed set of clearly defined relationships that constituted the social order.

The ultimate purpose of this law of the literati is the peace and quiet of the kingdom and the good government of the home and of private citizens, for which they
give very good advice. . . . They make much of the five social relationships that
they view as common to all men, namely those between father and son, husband
and wife, master and servant, older and younger brother, and between friends. . . .
They greatly emphasize the obedience of children to parents and the fidelity of
servants to masters and superiors.[37]

As in the theological domain, a strict precept of singularity preserved the
integrity of the hierarchical structure of these social relations as well:
"The good woman is not a wife of two men, and the good vassal does
not serve two masters." To these restrictions were added an annual ritual
in honor of one's ancestors, which Ricci interprets as a measure for reinforcing the spirit of filial piety by extending it beyond the temporal limits
of the flesh. Although the religious significance of these rites would
become the subject of heated controversy after Ricci's death, he had
implied that they were primarily civil observances serving to strengthen
social bonds, a means of "showing respect to their departed relatives, that
is 'to serve them in death as if they were alive.'"[38]

The respect for reason, social stability, and clear hierarchical structures
that Ricci took to be the essence of Confucian virtue found its antithesis,
in his view, in China's rival cults. Buddhist teachings, in particular, had
corrupted the purity of this ancient legacy behind an ever-expanding
cloud of irrationality and moral anarchy. The dangerously syncretic tendencies in contemporary religious thought were one clear sign of this
process, but even taken by themselves, Buddhist writings suggested to
Ricci a habitual sloppiness of thought, a glaring contempt for conceptual
clarity and consistency, and an exasperating tendency to muddle distinctions, ignore contradictions, and dismiss out of hand the rules and categories of logical reasoning.

Buddhist teachings, for Ricci, consist of nonsensical precepts their adherents scarcely can grasp themselves. The very number and variety of their writings has resulted in "a Babylon of doctrines so intricate that there is no one who can fully understand or explain it." They confuse even such basic oppositions as "heaven and earth, paradise and hell, teaching that souls remain eternally in neither one nor the other, but are rather reborn after many years into other worlds, where they are able to amend past sins."[39] The most disturbing of these rational lapses, however, is the Buddhist tendency to confound material and transcendental substance, to collapse the boundaries structuring the metaphysical hierarchy so central to Ricci's Catholic-Confucian synthesis. This doctrine, known within Buddhist writings as the *dharma-dhātu* or the order of interbeing, asserts, in Ricci's words,

that this entire world is composed of a single substance, and that its creator, together with the sky and the earth, men and beasts, trees and grasses, and with the four elements, all comprise a continuous body and are all members of this body; and from this unity of substance they derive not only the charity with which we are meant to treat each other, but also the belief that all men can become like unto God for being of the same substance as Him.

Within Ricci's tradition, built upon the strict separation between God and matter posited by Aquinas, to claim an identity between creature and creator could only appear as "an arrogant declaration of the devil Lucifer."[40] The passion that inflames Ricci's denunciation of this doctrine of universal causation stems in part, no doubt, from its uncanny resemblance to some of the materialist peasant heresies confronted by the Roman Inquisition in late-sixteenth-century Italy.[41] But Ricci is writing here as an apostle of accommodationism, not a judge of the Holy Office. Buddhist heterodoxy alarms him principally as a menace not to the unity and authority of the church, but to the stratified taxonomy of the Confucian cosmology on which he has staked the success of the mission and his reading of the Chinese religious landscape. In their irrational perversity, their stubborn resistance to the imperatives of order and differentiation that constitute the legitimacy of the original Confucian doctrine, Buddhism assumes a role for Ricci as a heresy as indispensable as it is intransigent, in that the perfect symbolic negation of Confucian first principles that he finds in its doctrines enables him, finally, to subsume the entirety of Chinese religious culture within a single totalizing framework.

The most insidious site of diabolical confusion and dissolution of crucial boundaries within this framework, however, is not the pagan temple but the adjoining boudoir, where, as in the Calvinist bacchanalia of Catholic fantasy, unbridled desire undermines any semblance of priestly propriety, social decorum, or even stable gender boundaries. Ricci's choice of metaphors in describing Buddhist teachings as "a Babylon of doctrines" resonates deeply, as it turns out, with his view of the Buddhist monks' sexual morality. In spite of their vows of chastity, they admit women into their temples and enjoy their company with a gusto unmitigated by threats of whipping, imprisonment, or even death at the hands of the local magistrates. Their affinity for transgression and the perverse comingling of separate spheres is reflected in their popular following, which "for the most part are women and eunuchs and coarse commoners."[42] Like Swift, who a century later would imagine a revolt against the rationalized language of the Lagado Academy led by "the women in conjunction with the vulgar and illiterate," Ricci associates illegitimate representation—ungrounded, irrational, prolix—with those marginalized groups whose interests were most likely to be ignored by the dominant social order, and whose self-presentation was hence most likely to appear as transgressive within it. Swift's outcasts are condemned for their adherence to a fallen vernacular, Ricci's for allegiance to a degenerate sect, but both are ultimately reduced to symbolic placeholders in an exclusionary paradigm that is premised on their condemnation.

Just as Ricci credits Confucianism with all the virtues of the Chinese, so he lays the vices of the populace at large at the feet of its sectarian rivals. If he does not blame the Buddhists directly for what he regards as the lamentable moral state of the Chinese masses, his depiction of public depravity certainly suggests the pervasive influence of the monks' licentious ways. Ricci tellingly invokes the same biblical metaphor he had applied to the Buddhist scriptures in describing life in the capital: "Thus has this city become a true Babylon of confusion, overflowing with every kind of sin, without a glimmer of justice or piety in anyone, nor any desire for personal salvation."[43] The citizens seem to take after the monks and their followers in being "an effeminate and hedonistic people." Adultery is rampant, adolescent boys so weaken themselves with sexual adventures that they are unable to father children as adults, and forty thousand prostitutes walk the streets of Peking. If Buddhist teachings appear to Ricci as a haze of mendacities "obscuring all the light . . . of truth," then his references to eunuchs and prostitutes and effeminate men represent a transposition of this notion of doctrinal imposture onto the sexual sphere. In his most vituperative account of the Chinese proclivity for perversion and deceit, Ricci provides what may also be the clearest antithesis to his conception of Confucian virtue as embedded in a system of rigidly hierarchical categories.

> But that which is saddest and which best reveals the misery of this people is that no less than the natural lusts is exercised among them the unnatural and preposterous [la libidine . . . contrannaturale e prepostera], which is neither prohibited by law nor seen as illicit nor shameful. And so it is talked about openly and practiced everywhere, without any impediment. And in some cities . . . there are public streets full of children acting like prostitutes along with people who buy these children and teach them to play, sing, and dance; and being very gallantly dressed and made up with rouge like women they inflame poor men to this ignominious vice.

Like the citizens of Geneva in the Catholic imagination, the populace of China had been seduced by a religious heresy into a state of depraved licentiousness, a preposterous inversion of natural law that ultimately threatened the integrity of the entire social order.[44]

If the missionaries were cognizant of the danger of doctrinal confusion blurring the boundaries between Buddhism and Christianity, they were wary, too, of the risk of being carried along, in popular perception anyway, by the carnivalesque tide that had swamped their Chinese Babylon. The Jesuits themselves, Spence notes, faced a constant torrent of rumors and "disquieting charges of sexual misconduct" as a result of the fathers' nonobservance of Chinese rules of decorum in their interactions with local women.[45] Sacred icons had to be guarded against equally scandalous misinterpretations: Ricci describes how the Virgin Mary lost her place on a Jesuit altar to an image of her son, because "the Chinese were spreading the rumor that the God whom we worshipped was a woman." Such compromising misreadings became so commonplace that the priests on occasion willingly endured the indignity of one seeming imposture if only to avoid another more shameful one. According to Ricci's compatriot Trigault, certain Jesuits submitted to the "horrible womanish coiffures" in fashion among Chinese men in order to avoid being mistaken for the bare-headed Buddhist monks.[46] An outward appearance of effeminacy, apparently, could never be so damning a charge as a false identification with those whose beliefs and lifestyles seemed to promote it.

For language theorists from Bacon to Johnson, the risk of deception and confusion associated with illegitimate uses of speech and writing stemmed largely from an uncontrolled, unregulated proliferation of signs. The attraction of a real character, an historically grounded dictionary, or the Chinese writing system was that they each promised to stem the multiplication of false usages by providing for the regular, systematic correspondence of words and ideas. In China, the missionary response to religious heterodoxy likewise emphasized its unruly abundance of symbols and icons. In contrast to the consistent, self-contained unity of Confucian doctrine, Buddhism in particular appeared to Ricci and his followers as an inchoate, sprawling mass of fragmented and even conflicting teachings. But the Jesuits' disdain for the rival tradition's amorphous forms and porous boundaries was matched by their revulsion at its sheer symbolic fecundity, its shameless and irreverent propagation of inassimilable and hence apparently hollow meanings.

The arguments ascribed to Ricci's Buddhist adversary in a famous theological debate in Nanjing are marked, in the Jesuit account, by just this kind of unmanageable rhetorical excess. After responding to an initial query with a supercilious grin, the monk "began to cite a flood of authorities on the doctrine of the idols, in which he was well versed." When Ricci insisted on drawing arguments only from reason rather than authority, his opponent, instead of taking up the argument, "did nothing but escape behind various sharp *sententia* of his language, managing always to show that he was the victor, and finally concluding that God was neither good nor evil, in the hopes of proving that a thing which could be good could also be bad."[47] The noisome prolixity of Buddhist speech extends as well to the written works of the sect, which Ricci condemns in similar terms. Although the cult of the idols "has had mixed success, flourishing and declining at various times like the ebb and flow of the sea, . . . it was always increasing in its books," which, whether imported from abroad or written by the Chinese themselves, contributed to their "always feeding this flame and never being able to dampen it."[48] In both their spoken and written forms, Buddhist uses of language appear as monstrously prolix and yet also somehow strangely, almost sensuously seductive. The symbolic excess they represent is echoed, finally, in Buddhist iconography: Ricci often finds the staggering number of religious statues alone enough to overwhelm him. Spilling over from their gilded temples into every corner of the kingdom, they seem in their infinite variety to crowd out the very conceptual possibility of a uniquely legitimate divine.

What is difficult to believe is the multitude of idols that are in this kingdom, not only in the temples, which are full of them, sometimes to the number of several thousand, but also in private homes, where there are great numbers kept in a specially dedicated place; in the plazas, in streets, on mountains, on ships and in public buildings, one sees nothing but these abominations.[49]

But as in the case of the Buddhist's sonorous hallucinations, the allure of such opulence is no more than a shallow superfice, a representational mirage concealing a crass parody of rational and authentic religious faith. The idols would seem to prevail through their very omnipresence, yet the worship they enjoy is nothing better, in Ricci's view, than hypocritical opportunism. "Few people actually believe what is said about [these idols]," he writes, "and think only that if they do no good, at least it can do no harm to venerate them outwardly." By his account, even high priests of the Buddhist order shared something of his cynicism. He reports that the prior of one temple he visited in Guangdong Province admitted "that idols were not worthy of worship, but [that] our masters, seeing that the people of the south were rather barbaric and incapable of sustaining religious belief in the absence of outward images, created idols for them."[50] Legitimacy falters in signs without substance, and no coherent moral order can be established on the foundation of fractured meanings they provide. For Ricci, the danger of Buddhist falsehoods is not so much that they encourage self-deception, as that their horizontal proliferation erodes the capacity for true faith by obscuring the vertical structuring of authority that sustains the social fabric in a monotheistic universe. The Western scholar in Ricci's *True Meaning of the Lord of Heaven* implicates modern Chinese philosophers in the disastrous fragmentation of an imagined primal, unitary, and authoritative truth.

[They] have divided men's minds into three schools of thought, and other meddlesome people have established further sects, inventing new teachings, so that before long the three schools will be divided into three thousand schools at least. Although each calls itself the correct Way, the more ways there are the more strange and confused they become.

The dissipation of divine authority leads, in turn, to the anarchic inversion of the moral order that Ricci sees afflicting the Chinese society of his day.

The superior insult the inferior, and the inferior profane the superior. The father behaves violently and the son wilfully. Sovereign and ministers are suspicious of each other, and brothers murder each other. Husbands and wives divorce, and friends cheat each other. Mankind is filled with deceit, flattery, arrogance, and lies and is devoid of sincerity.[51]

In this despairing vision, Ricci returns implicitly to his Babylonian metaphor of social chaos and confusion. He returns, that is, to an imported Western—and specifically Counter-Reformation—paradigm for making sense of a multiplicity of religious beliefs and practices that would otherwise threaten to defy comprehension altogether. Having designated an idealized proto-Confucianism as the sole legitimate analogue of Christian orthodoxy in China and thereby invested it with unique claims to authority and truth, he is obliged to differentiate it sharply from the mutant forms and rival sects with which it has become entangled and to dismiss these latter as illegitimate heresies: polymorphous, grounded in falsehoods, and disruptive of established hierarchies. While Ricci devotes little effort in these writings to grappling with the complexities beneath the surface of Buddhist texts, the dualistic framework that arose through his encounter with Chinese religious thought rendered Buddhism sufficiently legible to serve him as a vividly contrasting backdrop to his accommodationist enterprise.

The Rites Controversy

Ricci's interpretation of the religious situation in China went largely unchallenged up until his death in Peking in 1610 and continued to inform the policies of the Jesuit mission in China well into the eighteenth century. As Europe increasingly turned its eyes eastward during this period, his sharply bifurcated conception of Chinese religious thought, relentlessly promoted by writers affiliated with the Society of Jesus in Europe, played a definitive role in the mapping of Chinese culture in the imaginations of their readers. As Lionel Jensen observes, the Enlightenment fascination with Confucius, in particular, can be traced back to Ricci's construction of the ancient sage as a primal wellspring of reason in the service of virtue and the public good. The Jesuit strategy of erecting a doctrinal edifice in China upon supposedly native Confucian foundations, however, invited dissent from those within the Catholic Church who saw in such a gesture of accommodation a needless and even heretical compromising of the Christian faith. Not surprisingly, the prospect of somehow sharing the mantle of theological authority with a completely alien religious or philosophical tradition troubled those observers whose own *mappa mundi* was generally coterminous with the doctrinal reach of the papal see. In order to justify his rapprochement with the Confucian establishment and to differentiate an idealized vision of early Confucianism from the sectarian detritus that later encumbered it, Ricci—and later certain of his followers—glorified the early sages and their teachings to the point where they seemed to rival the stature of the first apostles themselves.

Ricci had condemned religious syncretism in China on the grounds of its doctrinal monstrosity. The irony of the Rites Controversy, as the ensuing debates over the theological status of Confucianism came to be called, is that the Jesuits, in their seemingly divided sympathies and hybrid ecclesiology, could be accused of breeding similarly monstrous heterodoxies themselves. If the classical Chinese sages were, after all, as venerable, wise, and thoroughly imbued with proto-Christian virtue as they were often made out to be, then on what grounds could Christian revelation establish its unique authenticity? In the first phase of the early modern encounter with Chinese religion, the paradigm of legitimacy served the cause of cultural legibility in enabling the Jesuits to distinguish along familiar lines among the various strands of Chinese thought. Such an analogical interpretation, however, entailed a logical paradox that ultimately destroyed it: by claiming for Confucianism a theological authority modeled on that of Christian doctrine, in effect proposing a comparison to the incomparable, the Jesuits appeared to undermine the unique exclusivity that formed the basis of their own faith. In the Rites Controversy, the Jesuits found their own paradigm turned against them. Their opponents, determined to reestablish the fundamental distinctions between the Eastern and Western terms of the Jesuits' earlier analogy, sought emphatically to subordinate the alien Confucian doctrine the Jesuits had first rendered intelligible to the teachings of the Catholic Church. This drastic reversal in the assessment of Confucianism, however, left the Jesuits' interpretive framework intact. If the Jesuits' rivals in the controversy condemned the Chinese literati as atheists, they were atheists in precisely the same mold of Chinese illegitimacy as the Buddhists of Ricci's earlier accounts. The dogged persistence of this figural construct suggests a degree of indispensability, as if contemporary China watchers, whatever their sympathies, found some version of its essentializing perspective a necessary precondition for recognizing any meaning at all in the cultural artifacts they encountered.

The critique of the Jesuit reading of Confucianism comprised two complementary claims. The first concerned a matter of terminology. Ricci had suggested that certain Chinese words denoting "heaven" or the "heavenly master" in the classical canon referred to a deity analogous, if not identical, to the God of the Judeo-Christian tradition. His opponents within the church argued, to the contrary, that such terms referred only to the material heavens, the Chinese language lacking any conception of purely spiritual substance. The rituals traditionally practiced by the Chinese in honor of their ancestors were the second target of attack: while Ricci had maintained that these were purely secular manifestations of a profound sense of filial piety, others saw in them the idolatrous worship of ancestral spirits.[52]

Both of these anti-accommodationist counterclaims represent direct challenges to Ricci's construction of a viable Chinese basis for Christianity. The idea of legitimacy that seventeenth-century writers ascribed to Chinese writing and religious practice requires at the outset a concept of originary purity, a transcendent starting point capable of grounding the manifold meanings that follow from it; Ricci thought he had discovered such traits in the ancient figure of the "Lord of Heaven" he had so laboriously extracted from classical Chinese texts. The contrary assertion, that such terms refer instead to a merely material, immanent phenomenon, undermines the claim to legitimacy by denying not so much the point of origin itself as its necessary transcendence. Likewise, in Ricci's view, the ancestral rites reinforced divine authority by helping to maintain a social hierarchy descending through the generations from "the first ancestor." To interpret these rites as a form of worship, as Ricci's detractors resolutely did, implied, on the contrary, a fragmentation of spiritual power, from which inevitably would follow social as well as spiritual confusion and decay.

In the decades following Ricci's death, the attacks on his interpretation of Confucianism came primarily from three quarters: dissenting Jesuits within the China mission, rival missionary orders within the church, and Jansenist groups in France, who were to engage the Jesuits in tendentious disputes over the relative importance of divine grace and free will in achieving spiritual salvation. As a new order within the church that had quickly risen to become the single most powerful force in the Counter Reformation, the Society of Jesus had amassed no shortage of enemies in the century since its founding in 1540. Quite apart from the Protestants and other heretics who were the despised objects of the Jesuit crusade, the more established rival orders of the Franciscans and Dominicans resented the Jesuits' extraordinary success at monopolizing control of schools, colleges, foreign missions, and the confessionals of the rich and powerful. Spurred on by Pascal's withering satire on Jesuit casuistry in his

Provincial Letters (1656–1657), those who had been left behind in the competition for souls and political influence increasingly revolted against the doctrinal flexibility and moral pragmatism that seemed to be the cornerstones of the Jesuit enterprise both in Europe and overseas.[53]

The rearguard challenge to Jesuit supremacy in the nascent Chinese church reached a climax in the year 1700, when for two full months the Faculty of Theology at the Sorbonne deliberated the question of China's relationship to the divine. According to a contemporary report on the proceedings, no fewer than thirty assemblies were held on the subject, "in which one hundred sixty Doctors spoke their minds, and several among them with much eloquence and erudition."[54] The tracts that had arrested the attention of this august body were two popular accounts of Chinese culture and the role of the Jesuit mission that had been recently published in Paris, *Nouveaux Mémoires sur l'état present de la Chine* by Father Louis Le Comte (1696), and *L'Histoire de l'édit de l'empereur de la Chine* (1698) by Father Charles Le Gobien. The evident purpose of these openly polemical works was to build support for the Jesuits' apostolic methods among the Society's potential friends in Europe. Unfortunately for the authors, their writings had caught the eyes of the directors of the Congregation des Missions Etrangères, a staunchly anti-Jesuit rival order within the French church, who had condemned the books in a letter to the pope and called the matter to the attention of the Sorbonne faculty, urging the body to censure a number of particularly troublesome propositions they contained.

The first alleged heresy to be considered was drawn from Le Comte's work. Extrapolating perhaps rather too boldly from Ricci's own conclusions, the Jesuit popularizer had written, "The people of China have preserved for nearly two thousand years a knowledge of the true God, and have honored him in a manner that might serve as an instructive example even to Christians."[55] A more modest version of this claim was, as I have suggested, a cornerstone of Ricci's doctrine, most clearly conveyed in his interpretation of the Chinese terms for heaven or heavenly ruler as denoting the biblical God. Ricci's immediate successor as head of the mission, however, Father Niccolò Longobardi, had held a more skeptical view of the theological significance of these terms, and the Jesuits' opponents seized on these doubts in discrediting the accommodationist position at the Sorbonne and in the vicious pamphlet war that accompanied the proceedings.

Longobardi acknowledges a Chinese concept of a seemingly transcen-

dent first cause, but he denies it the animated, sentient qualities under-
pinning the divine authority of the Christian God, thereby reducing it to
a "merely" natural phenomenon. In his *Traité sur quelques points de la
religion des chinois*, he writes:

> There was one cause that preceded all the others, and that constituted their prin-
> ciple and their origin; they gave to this cause the name of Li, that is to say reason
> or foundation of all nature; they conceived that this cause was an infinite and
> incorruptible entity, without principle and without end. . . . This great and uni-
> versal cause, according to their view, possessed neither life, nor knowledge, nor
> any authority.[56]

The term *li* refers to the central concept in neo-Confucian philosophy of
an abstract and eternal principle or law of which things are the material
embodiment, a notion roughly analogous to Platonic form or essence.
The development of the concept by Cheng Yi (1033–1108) had precipitated a great controversy, comparable, in turn, to that between Platonic
realists and Kantian idealists over the metaphysical status of *li* and the
question of whether its laws were immanent in nature or legislated by the
mind.[57] Over the next several pages, Longobardi aligns himself with an
uncompromisingly materialist understanding of *li* by rendering it successively as "chaos," "infinite matter," and "infinite chaos." A primary
cause that fails to transcend nature can only subsist diffused chaotically
within it, collapsing the very idea of an origin into all that has followed
from it. One of the central precepts of Chinese thought, Longobardi
stresses, is that "all things are of the same substance," an error from the
Christian standpoint noted previously in Ricci's account of Buddhist doctrine. If the Buddhist blindness to crucial distinctions damned the sect in
Ricci's eyes, it is a similar failure of demarcation that, ironically, condemns the Confucians themselves as godless atheists for his successor. In
the passage that most succinctly encapsulates the polemical core of his
argument Longobardi writes, "It is consistently clear that the Chinese did
not recognize any spiritual as distinct from material substance, such as
God, angels, and the rational soul."[58]

The necessary corollary to transcendent origin in establishing the legitimacy of a linguistic or theological signifier is a process of controlled and
orderly generation. Ricci complained of the seemingly boundless proliferation of Buddhist writings and idols in China; Longobardi's account of
the process of creation associated with *li* conveys a similar sense of root-
less and anarchic disarray. The Chinese ignorance of spiritual substance

that he has just asserted "is confirmed again in that they had no knowledge of creation from nothing by an infinite power." Rather than pro-
ceeding from the hand of God, "the creation of heaven and earth
occurred by chance, in a completely natural manner, without deliberation
and without guidance." The accidental and impersonal nature of this
process freeing it from any ordering constraint, its consequence is a
chaotic proliferation not of idols but of entire worlds. At the end of our
own existence, "the Li will begin to produce another world, which having
expired in its turn will be followed by another, and so on to infinity."[59]

But it is not only in its laissez-faire metaphysics that Chinese divinity
falls short in the anti-accommodationist view. Its textual basis, for
Longobardi, is equally flawed, and in remarkably similar ways. Not only
the First Principle but also the passages that describe it in classical texts
turn out to be nothing more than superficial materialities, ungrounded in
originary truth, and therefore capable of bringing forth only an anarchic
profusion of worlds and words. In the first two sections of his treatise,
Longobardi reviews the scope and status of the classical canon as it per-
tains to religious matters and then turns to the problem of their interpretation. The Jesuits, he rightly maintains, have consistently favored going
back to the original sources in order to recover and restore what, in the
Jesuit view, was an ancient Chinese doctrine of the true God. Their rivals
in the missionary field, however, along with many Chinese, looked to the
long tradition of learned commentaries on the classics for help in unraveling their often obscure meanings. Longobardi favors the latter
approach, and his justification for the choice reveals a radical skepticism
toward the very possibility of locating a legitimate origin—theological or
rhetorical—at the heart of the Chinese tradition.

The books of the Ancients are generally obscure, and in many places there are
errors in the Texts, owing either to an abundance of superfluous words or an
absence of necessary ones, as the literati themselves agree. Moreover, the Ancients
often employ Enigmas and Parables to conceal the mysteries of their
Philosophy. . . . It is for this reason that if, in this obscurity, one does not take as
a guide and a torch the Commentaries of the Interpreters, one will understand
nothing, or at least one will be likely to fall into great errors.[60]

It is not that these foundational texts do not seem to point to the existence of a heavenly divine—he acknowledges that at times they do—but
rather that they *only* point, through ambiguous circumlocutions and
rhetorical games, without definitively establishing anything at all. The

originary doctrine of the Jesuits' quest is an illusion, he seems to imply, in a flash of deconstructionist insight. "Les nécessaires y manques": there is no bottom to these texts, no epistemological core, no revelation of the divine, but only the ceaseless play of shamelessly profligate words.

In his letter to the pope condemning Le Comte's claim that the Chinese had knowledge of the true God, Charles de Brisacier, chief director of the Congregation des Missions Etrangères, seizes on Longobardi's reading. For Brisacier, the rhetorical instability of these classical sources critically undermines not only the accommodationist gloss of the Chinese term for "heaven" but also the entire underlying methodology of seeking proto-Christian meanings in the most ancient Chinese words and texts. Like Longobardi, he finds in the very antiquity of the classics a more likely source of fatal ambiguity than of divine truth and a more pressing cause for doctrinal vigilance than for blindly accommodating faith. The textual origins that for Ricci, in other words, guaranteed the theological viability of the Confucian belief system, become for his enemies damning evidence for precisely the contrary claim.

The Fathers are . . . obliged to accept that the term [heaven] is equivocal, metaphorical, dangerous, and capable of introducing error. . . . It is figural and metaphorical, as it does not apply to God in a proper sense, in that the passages in the classics by which the Fathers would authorize their invention, are . . . nothing but metaphors and figural manners of speaking. It is dangerous, finally, specious and capable of introducing error, in that the first thought of Chinese who see the inscription, "Worship heaven," is that we worship as they do the heavens that pass over our heads.

The figurative richness of such a term is no merely incidental flaw in Brisacier's eyes. Religion, he recognizes, whatever its origin, is ultimately transcribed in language and therefore depends upon a stable linguistic foundation. To attempt to build the temple of God on an ephemeral Chinese metaphor could bring only disaster. "Could one choose, to signify the object of Christian worship and, as a consequence, the foundation of all religion, a term subject to such great misapprehension, and better suited to destroy than to establish it?"[61]

If the Chinese had failed, in their understanding of the Creator, to transcend the categories of unguided natural phenomena, they had not, in the anti-accommodationist view, neglected religion altogether. The conceptual barrier to transcendence had, rather, forced them to project and diffuse the idea of divinity onto a multitude of lowly objects undeserving of the name. Having no knowledge of the true God, they conjured myriad

earthly spirits and worshipped in particular those of long-departed ancestors. Such, anyway, was the second charge leveled against the Chinese and
their Jesuit champions in the period of controversy surrounding the
Sorbonne investigation. Simply stated, the dispute concerned the question
of whether traditional ritual observances to ancestors in China were civil
or religious in nature. Those Jesuits who, following Ricci, upheld the
legitimacy of the ancient Confucian belief system insisted that these were
mere civil observances, innocuous expressions of respect and gratitude
modeled after those offered to living state officials and dignitaries. Their
rivals, however, smelled idolatry in the often elaborate ceremonies of
"prayer" and "sacrifice" that the rites entailed, and they accused the
Jesuits of compromising the faith in their tolerance for practices so clearly
incompatible with true monotheistic faith.

More was at stake here, clearly, than simple semantic hair splitting.
The European disputants in the Rites Controversy wrestled over competing paradigms for approaching a phenomenon that both sides placed
squarely at the heart of the Chinese cultural tradition. The Jesuits who
accepted Ricci's interpretation of the Rites not only defended them
against charges of idolatry but also presented them as pillars of the
Confucian social order, integral to the preservation of the seamless structure of hierarchical authority they envisioned as descending, pyramid-
like, from the mandate of the Lord of Heaven through the emperor and
his officials to fathers in their households in a model of political harmony
and stability. Their descriptions of the Rites, accordingly, make the case
for their usefulness by placing them alongside more familiar instances of
well-regulated vertical social relations and by stressing the simple humil-
ity of these gestures of respect.[62] Charles Le Gobien, one of the two Jesuit
writers attacked by Brisacier and examined by the Sorbonne, describes
the "purely civil honors" offered in memory of one's ancestors in a passage particularly notable for its reassuring clarity and deferential tone.

All the relations assemble in this room twice each year, in the spring and in the
autumn. The wealthiest lay out meats, rice, fruits, fragrances, wine, and candles
on the table with the same compliments and more or less the same ceremonies
that one employs in making such presents to officials when they take office, to
mandarins of the first rank on their birthdays, and to persons one wishes to honor
with a ceremonial meal.[63]

The ancestral rites, in other words, are not just innocuous from a religious standpoint, they have a salutary effect on a well-ordered civil society in that they reinforce those sentiments of respect and deference by

天明五年
八月初三日

天龍八部鬼神女等

which it is maintained. They are nothing more, for Le Gobien, than straightforward expressions of filial piety, that cardinal virtue among the Chinese from which respect for all forms of authority must ultimately arise. Their ultimate purpose, simply stated, is "to inspire in children a profound respect and tender piety towards their elders."[64]

But the Jesuits' detractors discovered meanings considerably more troublesome in the same ritual observances and described their findings in terms that, as in the dispute over Chinese notions of the divine, turned the Jesuit ideal of Confucian legitimacy on its head. Where the Jesuits saw in the rites a laudable manifestation of the rigidly vertical ordering of Chinese society, their adversaries found signs of a reckless leveling of rank among the higher orders of God's kingdom and a proliferation of false pretenders to honors due God alone. Where the Jesuits had described simple expressions of selfless respect and deference, their rivals portrayed extravagant rituals of self-serving solicitation. The image of China that emerges in these hostile accounts of the ancestral rites mirrors in many respects the vision of religious anarchy that Matteo Ricci had conveyed in his depiction of the corrupting influence of Buddhism: a society in a state of decadent disarray, spawning countless false gods in the service of hedonistic self-absorption, oblivious to the very idea of a higher good. The Franciscan friar Antoine de Caballero (also known from his writings as Antoine de Sainte-Marie, 1602–1669) doesn't pause to equivocate in the refutation of Jesuit claims he published in a treatise of 1701: "The cult which consists of making sacrifices to ancestors is by no means civil in the minds of those who make the sacrifices, but religious, since they believe that these sacrifices are not addressed to mortal men, but to spirits that they place at the rank of gods, and that they associate with the supreme being." By elevating ancestral spirits to the level of the divine, the Chinese, in this view, undermine any claim to divine legitimacy such a being might have had by obviating any remnant of its unique, originary authority, and by substituting for a regulated hierarchy descending from a supreme creator an undifferentiated hoi polloi of derelict demigods, "a crowd of false deities . . . [a] multitude of spirits that they worship as their gods."[65]

6. (*opposite*) *The Eight Hosts of Celestial Nagas and Yakshis*. Hanging scroll, 1454. Ink and color on silk, 141 × 79.2 cm. China, Ming Dynasty. © The Cleveland Museum of Art, 2000. John Severance Fund, 73.71.

The most convincing proof, for Sainte-Marie, that the Chinese worship their ancestors as gods is that they regularly ask them for favors. But because the collapse of true divinity into "a crowd of false gods" has entailed among the Chinese an erosion of their capacity to aspire to a higher, transcendent good, their prayers rarely reach beyond the vain desire for worldly prosperity. Their scale of values is flattened into the same confused homogeneity as their pantheon of spirits, so that there is no order or direction to their lives, only an aimless accumulation of offspring and wealth, a veritable orgy, in other words, of unregulated and hence illegitimate production. Among the rewards for faithful service to one's ancestors, Sainte-Marie discovers, are "a lush and abundant harvest, a fertile lineage . . . in a word, all the advantages that best satisfy men's desires." Having reviewed the prayers offered to ancestral spirits in the course of a typical ceremony, he confirms their transcendental vacuity. "I have transcribed them; there is not a single one that doesn't set out to obtain the benefits of earthly prosperity."[66]

Sainte-Marie heightens this aura of vain extravagance in his description of the ceremonies themselves. One recognizes in his account a ritual nearly identical in its outlines to that so respectfully described by Le Gobien, but in contrast to the almost austere simplicity of the earlier rendition, this one exudes a baroque luxuriance and aesthetic self-indulgence that will ultimately emerge, as I argue in the next chapter, as the hallmark of the chinoiserie style in the decorative arts.

For the cult honoring the Cicu ancestors, that is, making sacrifices to them, the most wealthy have temples that they call *Miao*. . . . The sacrifice that I saw and that I will describe took place in a large, superbly ornamented chapel. . . . This chapel contained five altars bearing lighted candles, braziers, and flowers. Among the five altars, each one with its vase, rose the master altar, accompanied by two others . . . one saw there a painted image representing a most ancient, majestic personage, dressed in long, ample robes of a reddish hue.

The author's insistence on the notion of a sacrifice, the plurality of altars, and the presence of a graven image evoke a scene of depraved idolatry—one almost expects to see a golden calf peering out from behind a porcelain vase. But the construction of the very idea of depravity in this scene presumes a comparison with an implicit Christian model of religious sanctity. How much less depraved the ceremony would appear to Christian eyes if Sainte-Marie, like Le Gobien, had refrained from introducing culturally incongruous terms like "chapel," "altar," and later in the passage "ministers" and "orison." He employs these terms, of course, precisely in order to render his description of a thoroughly alien phenomenon powerfully meaningful—and meaningfully repugnant—to his Western audience; its very legibility depends upon its inscription within a familiar paradigm. He acknowledges as much in a rhetorically self-conscious gesture in which he seeks to excuse his conspicuous and jarring use of terms saturated with Christian ritual significance: "Our manner of speaking will make my thoughts more readily understood."[67] Without familiar words like "chapel" and "altar," he implies, his description of what he observed at this ceremony would be largely impenetrable to a European reader. Stripped of his interpretive framework, in other words, the ceremonies in themselves are essentially meaningless, unfathomable, absurd. Like the classical sources on which they are based, they present a collection of radically ambiguous signifiers, a mirage of superficial figures and ungrounded metaphors, hollow at the core. The condition of legibility of both these artifacts is the acknowledgment of this essential vacuity, the source of a semantic illegitimacy that can be contained but never fully controlled.

Brisacier, who, as I have noted, condemned the Confucian classics for their irredeemable figurality, finds that the ancestral rites stand on equally unstable ground. "Putting aside their names, it is clear that the very substance of the ceremonies is corrupt, that their foundation comes to nothing, and that everything bears the taint of a profane and superstitious cult." Jesuit attempts to establish the acceptability of the rites through an appeal to their primitive form are doomed, he maintains, for the corruption reaches to the "empoisoned" source.[68] The implications for the church are clear, and Sainte-Marie concludes his treatise with a strident repudiation of the accommodationist vision in terms that emphasize again the intrinsic—and dangerous—groundlessness of Chinese religious representation.

Let us not, then, be caught up by the attractive appearance of Chinese doctrine. Let not our desire to see our faith embraced by the literati and the great men of the kingdom in the hope that they will draw the populace along with them lead us to accept their reasoning, which tends to blend their ancient ceremonies with the faith that we preach. The statue of superstition would remain standing. The Chinese church would be founded not on solid rock, but on the shifting sands of Chinese vanity.[69]

If the imagery of false appearances and shifting sands contributes powerfully to the stigma of illegitimacy evoked by this passage, so too, finally, does the threat of theological confusion, the suggestion that Christianity in China might simply vanish into a sea of all-assimilating sophistries. It was this underlying fear that largely animated the specific complaints directed against Jesuit interpretations of Chinese terms and rituals and that, when stated explicitly, provided what was perhaps ultimately the most compelling argument leveled against the Jesuits during the controversy. One might, indeed, have expected Ricci to have foreseen a charge so closely analogous to his own denunciation of the three-headed beast of *sanjiao* religious syncretism. The primacy of a belief system, he realized, had to be unique and uncontested if its justifying claims to originary authority were to be sustained. But by promoting ancient Confucianism as the paramount system in China, he set the stage for conflict with fellow Christians who inevitably recognized in Ricci's claims for this alien cult a threat to the unique authority of the Catholic Church. The urgency of his detractors' attempts to slay this new rival fully matched Ricci's own zeal in dispatching Buddhism in China. The devil had changed his guise, but the interpretive arsenal arrayed against him remained essentially unchanged.

Whatever its specific theological errors, Confucianism had by necessity to be considered an illegitimate, idolatrous religion if only because the integrity of the church depended on it. Sacred doctrine provided for only one chosen people, one law, one source of revelation. How could the China Jesuits now proclaim that there were two? Brisacier shudders at the implications of their position:

> If they [the Jesuits] speak the truth and if their findings are correct, what becomes of the entire foundation and plan of the Christian religion, brought to its perfection by Jesus Christ, preserved in a slightly less perfect state by the Jewish people, and carried to this people from the time of Adam through the posterity of Seth? . . . What becomes of the choice of a cherished people, and its famous separation from all other nations of the earth? . . . What becomes of the consistent distinction and difference between Jew and Gentile, who remained separate until Jesus Christ broke in his beloved flesh the wall of separation that divided them?
>
> Where will the Jesuits place this third people that is neither Jew nor Gentile?[70]

Indeed, looking back at the set of condemned propositions with which I began this discussion, the issue that seems most to have occupied the faculty of the Sorbonne was neither the precise nuances of Chinese terms for the divine, nor the significance of their ancestral observances, but rather the challenge the Chinese represented in these Jesuit texts to the exclusive hegemony of Christian doctrine. The harshest censure of the faculty was reserved for the first article, which, as noted above, brazenly suggested not only that the Chinese had known the true God but also that the purity and historical duration of their knowledge may well have surpassed that of even Christians. This claim, which made the mistake of promoting Confucian doctrine at the expense of Christianity, was condemned as "false, reckless, scandalous, erroneous, injurious to the Holy Christian religion." The second proposition, which fared little better with the faculty, extended the claim of antiquity for Chinese knowledge of the divine into an assertion of outright primacy: "It is no small glory for China to have sacrificed to the Creator in the most ancient temple in the universe." Most revealing, however, was the response to the third proposition, which maintained "that moral purity, the sanctity of custom, faith, . . . &, if I dare to say it, the spirit of God were once sustained in China for over two thousand years." According to the examiners, not only was such a doctrine false, scandalous, impious, contrary to the word of God and heretical, not only did it "overturn Christian faith and religion," it also made this faith superfluous in that it "rendered useless the passion & death of J.C."[71] As Ricci had attested in China, religious truth could have only a single origin. But by making this claim of unique legitimacy for Confucianism against its local rivals, he unwittingly precipitated a backlash a century later against the doubts such a claim seemed to cast upon the relevance of the Messiah himself.

Ricci believed he had found a firm foundation for the church in the ancient theology of the Chinese. A later generation of Catholics, buffeted by the schismatic turmoil of the Counter Reformation and increasingly desperate to preserve the viability of their own faith, sought to prove him wrong by unraveling his meticulously wrought doctrine into a tangle of rhetorical illusions, a shifting and chimerical bundle of confusion on the model of the Babylonian Buddhism he had so despised. Their wholesale dismissal of the entire religious culture of the Chinese was meant not only to remove a thorn in the side of the church but also to clear the stage in China for the arrival of a pure, uncompromised Christianity that would redeem the natives from both their own idolatries and Jesuit errors. The long-term effects of this act of repudiation, however, and of the public controversy that raged around it, were far more widely felt, paradoxically, in Europe than in China, and profoundly shaped the religious and aesthetic landscapes and battlefields of the eighteenth century.

China and the Rise of Libertinism in France

By September of 1702, Pope Clement XI had not yet reached a final verdict on the dispute that had consumed the faculty of the Sorbonne two years before. In response to growing impatience on the part of the Missions Etrangères, on the one hand, for a papal pronouncement, and to the efforts of Louis XIV's Jesuit confessor Father La Chaise to rally French bishops to the defense of the Society, on the other, the renowned writer and theologian François Fénelon (1651–1715) wrote a letter to La Chaise defending the pope's caution in evaluating a matter of such importance. Fénelon, although an archbishop, a friend of the Jesuits, and a one-time spiritual leader in the royal court, had been a voice of moderation in the aftermath of the king's revocation of the Edict of Nantes in 1685 and had himself recently suffered the consequences of rash papal censure for his public defense of Quietism. His letter, which reflects both his commitment to toleration and bold independence of mind, is perhaps the earliest assessment of the Rites Controversy to recognize the fundamental problem of cross-cultural interpretation behind the heated polemics that it had generated over the course of the previous century. There was no question but that the decision facing the pope was a painfully daunting one. To rule against the Jesuits, after all, would mean not only overturning a papal decree explicitly condoning their activities issued by his predecessor Alexander VII, but also condemning several generations of zealous and often brilliant missionaries as dupes to idolatry and putting at risk the fragile edifice of Christianity they had painstakingly erected in China over the past hundred years. To rule in their favor, however, would be to alienate their equally powerful opponents and to make of the Jesuits' generous accommodation of non-Christian beliefs a precedent that would inevitably weaken the role of the Holy See as the final arbiter of orthodoxy. In principle, according to Fénelon, the entire controversy could be reduced to "a pure question of fact," but establishing the facts of the matter was itself a complex interpretive problem.

Some say a certain Chinese word signifies the material heavens; others respond that it also signifies the God of the heavens. Some say, there is a temple, an altar, a sacrifice; others respond, no, that is nothing, to the mind of the Chinese, but a room, a table, and an honor accorded simple men, without any expectation of gain.

One's conclusions concerning such "facts," in other words, might finally depend on the perspective one brought to them. The signs and symbols used by various peoples in religious activities were by no means universal in their significance, but rather both historically and culturally contingent.

The manners and ideas of these people, concerning demonstrations of respect, are infinitely far removed from our own. We know from our own experience, besides, that the signs used in expressing religious devotion can vary with time and the customs of each nation. The same incense which expresses the supreme faith when one offers it to the Eucharist, no longer signifies the same belief, though in the same temple and the same ceremony, when one offers it to the entire congregation, or even to the bodies of the deceased. . . . It is thus clear . . . that the tokens of belief are in themselves arbitrary, equivocal, and subject to variation within each country: how much more reason for them to be equivocal between nations whose manners and prejudices are at such a remove from one another!

The difficulty in pinning down the precise meaning of such signs as used in a foreign culture was a compelling reason, Fénelon found, to refrain from passing hasty judgment on them, and the pope was well advised to take all the time he needed in his deliberations.[72]

Fénelon himself, recognizing the impossibility of reaching a sufficiently qualified conclusion from any single vantage point, declines to take sides in the dispute. However, in its conspicuous refusal to leap to judgment and its eloquent apology for equivocation, his letter marks a significant shift in China's relationship to her European interpreters. All of the readings of Chinese religious culture reviewed up to this point have implicitly invoked a paradigm of legitimacy as a framework for assimilating alien systems of belief into a familiar cultural context. Its clear and powerfully resonant dichotomies of authority and anarchy, transcendent origin and monstrous proliferation, provided Ricci and the disputants in the Rites Controversy with an effectual hermeneutic tool for sorting through the bewildering babel of sectarian tongues in China and for defining them in relation to one another and to Christianity. Although Europeans disagreed over the image of China that appeared through the interpretive lens it provided, their disputes finally concerned the nature of the object under view rather than the construction or orientation of the lens itself. Only from a perspective at some remove from the fray could the terms of the debate themselves be held up for scrutiny; it is just such a perspective that the archbishop provided. By stepping back from the contested processes of cultural interpretation, he was able, for the first time, to bring them into focus in their own right and to reveal their precarious position among the myriad blind spots of a relativist universe. The interpretive gaze becomes, from this vantage point, much less rigidly unidirectional. The primary objective remains a true understanding of Chinese religious culture, but the mechanisms for achieving such an understanding now appear by necessity far more complex. The subject position, to begin with, has become radically self-reflexive—the European no longer simply looks upon the Chinese, but looks upon himself looking and criticizes what he sees. The imperative of reflexivity in turn opens the imaginative possibility of turning the gaze of the Chinese back upon their European visitors. Fénelon, exasperated by his countrymen's blindness to the arbitrariness of their own rituals, discovers the rhetorical power of imagining a reversal of subject and object positions and of attributing critical cross-cultural judgment for the first time to foreign eyes: "What Chinese would not be mistaken, if he came to examine our ceremonies?"[73]

The question was one that the Rites Controversy had itself, ironically, provoked. The polemical zeal of the disputants on both sides and the repeated comparisons between largely incongruous elements of Christian and Confucian belief must have had the effect of defamiliarizing the Europeans' own common ground and rendering their religious tradition something of an exotic curiosity in its own right. How else can one account, in Louis XIV's France, for the apparently serious warning that the teachings of an itinerant Chinese sage might somehow render superfluous the suffering of the Savior? And yet the arguments raised by the Jesuits' rivals had equally perplexing implications. If China was, in fact, as thoroughly and incorrigibly godless as Brisacier and company seemed to imply, how was it that their civilization was so consistently vaunted for its superior moral virtue? Taken to its logical conclusion, such a separation of religion and morality could lead only, as Le Comte pointed out in a later defense of his position, to yet another kind of superfluity for the divine.[74] The polemics on either side could be taken to unsettling extremes that invited alienation and skepticism, and it was in the wake of this discovery that the ancient religion of China found its way into the European Enlightenment.

Pierre Bayle (1647–1706) and Voltaire (1694–1778), in particular, offer responses to Fénelon's rhetorical question that are very much in this spirit. Like Fénelon, they were jarred by the spectacle of the Rites Controversy into stepping back from Christian orthodoxy to bring it into a single, relativizing perspective with its Chinese counterpart, and like Fénelon they both experiment in their writings with imaginary Chinese subject positions as a means of embodying this self-alienated viewpoint. Whereas the archbishop, however, was constrained by his position within

the church hierarchy, his earlier censure, and his own moderating disposition to defer to the judgment of the pope, neither Bayle nor Voltaire recognized, nor thought fit to recognize, any master beyond himself on points
of religion. Both, consequently, were able to explore the more radical
implications of Chinese belief systems for a newly relativized Christianity.
Their writings on the topic are necessarily less well informed than those of
their missionary predecessors, and their interest in Chinese culture at
times seems limited to its utility as a foil in the service of their critiques of
Christian practice and doctrine. Although the collapse of Christianity as
the necessary starting point for any evaluation of a foreign religious system lessens their reliance on the authorizing model that accompanied it,
China occupies a privileged place in their analyses of religious culture and
is invoked with an authority that suggests that the formal structure of the
Riccian conception of Chinese legitimacy remains very much intact. The
context within which they invoke it, of course, has been radically revised:
while Ricci had employed an integrative, accommodationist framework
for his construction of a theologically acceptable Confucianism, Bayle
and Voltaire adopt a relativist platform that serves to validate Chinese
culture by virtue precisely of its exteriority to the Christian tradition. The
subject position of the oriental outsider becomes fetishized in their writings as a new kind of transcendent origin and ultimate arbiter of truth,
symbolizing in its very distance and difference the unencumbered standpoint of objective, unflinching rationality. The idea of legitimacy remains
a condition for the apprehension of Chinese otherness, but this apprehension no longer serves the purposes of proselytization and cultural mastery, but rather of an abject self-reflexivity. The ideographic impulse to
impose a hierarchical hermeneutic on an unfamiliar world of signs turns
in upon itself, seizing upon the foreign as an Archimedean point from
which to unsettle an all-too-familiar hierarchical order at home.

Bayle, two-time apostate and author of the iconoclastic *Dictionnaire
historique et critique* (1697–1702), first sketches the outlines of this
approach in his early treatise on religious toleration, the *Commentaire
philosophique* (1686). Drawing on a range of historical material, Bayle
argues here against a literal interpretation of the apparent biblical mandate for forceful conversion, "compel them to come in."[75] The example of
China comes up in a chapter concerned not with Chinese religion per se,
but with the higher law that might justify a Chinese emperor in banishing
Christian missionaries from his kingdom. The author imagines a hypothetical encounter between the emperor and a small group of papal emis-

saries sent to China to preach the gospel, and who, crucially, "are sufficiently sincere to respond candidly to the questions put to them." After
enquiring as to the purpose of their voyage, the emperor's counselors ask
the missionaries how they have been instructed to treat Chinese subjects
who, having heard their sermons, decline to convert to their faith. The
visitors, endowed with more candor than discretion, go on to describe the
alternative means of persuasion authorized by their scriptures:

> As a consequence of this order, our conscience obliges us . . . to chase down, rod
> in hand, all Chinese idolaters in Christian churches, to imprison them, reduce
> them to beggary, and to make an example of several by taking away their children
> and abandoning them to the mercy of the soldier, along with their women and
> property. If you have any doubts, here is the gospel, here is the commandment
> plain and clear, "Compel them to come in"; that is to say, employ whatever vio-
> lence is appropriate in overcoming the obstinate resistance of men.[76]

What, Bayle asks, would be the proper response of a Chinese ruler to such
a provocation? Not surprisingly, the emperor's counselors advise him to
rid the kingdom immediately and permanently of this "public menace,"
and voice, in the process, a scathing critique of Christian intolerance from
the hypothetical viewpoint of its foreign victims. Proffering such a critique from the Chinese perspective serves to heighten the sense of indig-
nation and absurdity that Bayle regards as an appropriate reaction to
excessive evangelical zeal. But beyond its emotional impact, his rhetorical
strategy associates the Chinese position with an image of implicit legitimacy that substantially magnifies its polemical force. Bayle's foreign
observer, after all, is no ordinary Chinese, but a rightful sovereign whose
own authority stands to be severely undermined by the alien presence in
the kingdom. If he refused to convert, then these missionaries and their
converts would "summon the Crusades from the West to seize his crown
and establish on the throne a loyal child of the church," replacing the
Chinese legal code with "the law of Christianity," which would "legitimate theft, murder, and rebellion when they are useful to Religion."
Given its destructive nature, the emperor would be fully justified in rejecting such a law, even if it meant he "would remain eternally in the false
religion."

But the emperor's justification, and the validity Bayle ultimately
ascribes to the Chinese position, derive from a higher law than that of
mere self-preservation. Bayle delights in demonstrating the moral as well
as the political necessity, in this hypothetical case, of the Chinese rejection

of the missionaries' faith. The emperor is called upon not only by practical expedience but also by the "necessary and immutable" moral order of natural religion to expel from the kingdom all those who, like the Christians, "come to subvert the boundaries that separate vice and virtue, and to convert the most abominable deeds into acts of piety."[77] The dichotomy Bayle constructs here, between an immutable and transcendent source of moral order, on the one hand, and the anarchic blurring of moral boundaries, on the other, resembles Ricci's paradigm for distinguishing Confucian and Buddhist strands of Chinese philosophical and religious thought. But while the status Ricci accords to Confucianism within this framework reflects his own personal engagement with classical Chinese scholarship, Bayle's exaltation of the Chinese position is much less specifically Chinese. The Chinese court provides a uniquely appropriate setting for Bayle's vignette, but its moral stature is largely the product of Bayle's own relativizing framework, rather than any specific claims about the righteousness of its customs and beliefs. For Christianity to be regarded critically, as he prescribes, it must be regarded from afar, and China presents a convenient space within which to imagine such a perspective. The legitimacy of the Chinese position, then, arises not so much from its intrinsic nature as from the critical distance that it affords. For Ricci, the paradigm of Confucian legitimacy had presumed an essential compatibility with church doctrine and was intended to serve the missionary aim of establishing the church in China. A century later, the paradigm remained as a familiar lens through which to contemplate the East, but it had now been transformed into a weapon against the church. The special status it ascribed to China derived no longer from a bold presumption of essential similarity but from an acknowledgment of irreconcilable difference.

This fundamental transformation in the European conception of China is rendered complete in the writings of Voltaire, the French Enlightenment's most avid sinophile and most prolific popularizer of the antiquity and myriad virtues of Chinese civilization. Between 1722 and 1778, Voltaire mentions China in no fewer than fifty-nine works, including at least eight that treat Chinese themes at length. Most frequently discussed are perhaps his adaptation in 1755 of a Yuan dynasty music drama, *Orphelin de la Chine*, which had been translated in a Jesuit account, and the lengthy eulogy of Chinese history and culture with which he opens *Essai sur les moeurs* (1769).[78] Voltaire, who was educated in Jesuit schools and clearly had assimilated the Society's high regard for traditional Chinese civilization, nonetheless conceives the relationship between

Europe and China in a fundamentally different light than had the
founders of the China mission. Like Bayle, he finds in China a secure
exterior vantage point from which to refute Western hegemonic claims.
But while Bayle is content to qualify this Chinese exteriority as a viable
alternative to Christianity, Voltaire portrays it as possessing an exclusive
monopoly on a Deist religious truth of which the myriad Christian sects,
and especially Jesuit Catholicism, are but sadly degraded variants. In
doing so, he appropriates the original Jesuit model Ricci had constructed
to distinguish Confucianism from its rivals as a vehicle for satirizing the
universalist pretensions of the church that first had authorized it. The
consequence of Chinese religious legitimacy for Voltaire, in other words,
is the corresponding illegitimacy of Western religious orthodoxy.

I will limit my remarks to a single representative work by Voltaire, his
Relation du bannissement des Jésuites, a fictional dialogue between a
Jesuit missionary and the Chinese emperor first published in 1768. Like
Bayle in the *Commentaire philosophique*, Voltaire sets out here to imagine the reactions of a powerful non-Christian sovereign to the frank reve-
lations of a Catholic enthusiast regarding certain of the less immediately
fathomable tenets of his religious doctrine. Whereas Bayle derived the
legitimacy of Chinese disbelief from political necessity and an abstract
conception of a higher moral law, Voltaire grounds it from the outset in a
Riccian conception of an originary Chinese monotheism, set against the
background of a civilization as ancient as it is glorious. The encomium
with which he begins the piece typifies his attitude toward the Eastern
empire. "China," he writes, "once entirely unknown, for a long time
thereafter disfigured in our eyes, and finally better known among us than
many provinces of Europe, is the most populated, flourishing, and ancient
empire in the world." Extrapolating rather loosely from Jesuit accounts
of early Chinese religion, he then attributes to the modern emperors the
same clairvoyance with regard to the divine that Ricci had pointed to in
the canonical texts.

The religion there is simple, which is incontestable proof of its antiquity. For more
than four thousand years, the emperors of China have been the first pontiffs of the
empire; they worship a unique God, and offer the first fruits of the harvest from
a field they have worked with their own hands. The emperor Kangxi composed
and had engraved over the entrance to his temple these very words: "Shangdi is
without beginning and without end; it created everything; it governs everything; it
is infinitely good and infinitely just.". . . The emperor's religion . . . is all the more
beautiful in that it is not sullied by any superstition.

Although one already detects in Voltaire's emphasis on simplicity something of a Deist cast to this description, the Riccian ideal persists in the elements of purity, uniqueness, authority, hierarchy, and the creative potency of the deity. Recalling the opposite pole in Ricci's dichotomy, it comes as no surprise that Voltaire views the Buddhist monks, or bonzes, with considerably less sympathy. Just as in Ricci's writings, these are the illegitimate misfits: monstrous, profligate, strangely seductive.

All the wisdom of the government could not prevent the bonzes being introduced into the empire; just as all the attention of an innkeeper cannot prevent rats from slipping into his cellars and storerooms.

The spirit of tolerance, which imbued the character of all the Asian nations, enabled the bonzes to seduce the people; but . . . they were not permitted to govern them. They were treated as one treats charlatans: they are allowed to peddle their orvietan in public places; but if they incite the people, they are hanged.[79]

While Ricci would no doubt have approved Voltaire's characterization of his Buddhist nemeses as rats and charlatans, he would have been taken aback by the subtle shifts in nuance that one and a half centuries had wrought. To begin with, contemporary readers of Voltaire would have recognized in his treacherously insinuating bonzes an allusion to Bayle's caricature of Catholic missionaries as subversive aliens and a public menace. The unsettling resemblances between Buddhism and Christianity that Ricci so valiantly struggled to suppress erupted with a vengeance in the Enlightenment's arsenal of anticlerical barbs, among which was the commonplace substitution in satire of the despised figure of the bonze for the Catholic priest.

More disturbing still to an early China Jesuit would have been Voltaire's insistence that Buddhism was recognized as a fraudulent creed that thrived in the kingdom only at the emperor's pleasure. Ricci had faulted the Chinese literati for being unable or unwilling to distinguish the three principal teachings that constituted their body of religious belief, and he denounced the three-headed monster that resulted as a harbinger of religious and ultimately civil anarchy. For Voltaire, their peaceful coexistence suggests, rather, a laudable "spirit of tolerance," an imperial magnanimity toward religious dissenters that only confirms the wisdom and security of the official creed. The projection of this new Enlightenment idea of tolerance onto the Chinese scene marks a fundamental shift in the function of the old Jesuit paradigm. Accommodationism had encouraged interpretations of Chinese culture deriving from European models. Voltaire's revisionist account, in contrast, elevates China to a model for Europe. Like Bayle, he appropriates the idealized image of China bequeathed by the Jesuits and reframes it as a foreign stage on which to enact scathing critiques of the European church, an alien exemplar of virtue and truth next to which Europe can only appear contemptible by comparison.

The denigrated status of the Westerners in Voltaire's imaginary dialogue is apparent from the moment they appear on the scene. The emperor receives them precisely as Ricci had always most feared being received: as yet another nondescript sect of Buddhist bonzes from the West. Their religion is tolerated, just as the others have been, but it soon falls into disrepute among the Chinese owing to the incessant sectarian squabbling among the missionaries themselves. "The high-minded quarrels among the missionaries soon rendered the new sect unbearable. The Chinese, who are sensible people, were surprised and indignant that European bonzes dared to propagate in their empire opinions on which they could not agree among themselves." In Voltaire's account, in other words, the Jesuit missionaries occupy the same position of illegitimacy relative to ancient Chinese truth that the Buddhists had for Ricci. He refers to them explicitly as "bonzes," a class of beings he has just ranked on the order of sewer rats. He characterizes their doctrines as hopelessly multifarious and confused. One might argue, stretching the point only slightly, that he faults them implicitly as well for a Buddhist-like proliferation of false idols. Their religion, as it turns out, is accepted and tolerated for no merits of its own, but rather "out of admiration for the armillary spheres, barometers, thermometers, and lenses that they had brought from Europe" (218–19). The tools of science are no more than implements of seduction, as chimerical and insidious as the rhetorical webs of illusion spun by the Buddhist priests of Ricci's Chinese Babylon.

The dialogue between the emperor and the Jesuit Brother Rigolet that makes up most of the narrative is a satirical tour de force. Here, drawing copiously on the example of Montesquieu's *Lettres Persanes* (1721), Voltaire realizes the full power of the foreign observer device, as he imagines all the unbounded sagacity of the East gazing down with an air of bemused incredulity on the foolish foibles of a visiting Western friar. The tenets of Catholic orthodoxy appear throughout in the most ridiculous possible light, but at the same time their comic deflation is clearly "Chinese" in its rhetorical origin. The "Relation" is not merely a generic anti-Catholic satire that happens to be set in China, but a cleverly constructed caricature based on the familiar paradigms underlying Jesuit accounts of the Chinese religious universe. The emperor appears as the paragon of the ancient Confucian wisdom of Ricci's model, while the Christians are reduced to so many scampering bonzes whose doctrines invite the same contemptuous dismissal as that afforded the Buddhist followers of *Fo*.

To begin with, their god, much like the Buddha in Ricci's eyes, is of relatively recent and rather dubious origins: "born in a stable, seventeen hundred twenty three years ago, between a cow and an ass." The peculiar circumstances precipitating his birth recall the Buddhist reputation for transgressive sexuality and cast further doubts on his legitimacy. To the emperor's perplexed query, "God slept with his mother, then, in order to be born of her?" Brother Rigolet replies, "That's correct, your Sacred Majesty, grace is working upon you already." This god has, furthermore, no just pretensions to universality, his followers being "confined to a small corner of Europe," and his teachings having been transcribed by forty followers whose accounts "all contradict one another" (220–26). Religious artifacts, however, abound, and in a grotesque mimicry of Ricci's account of the proliferation of Buddhist statues, Rigolet boasts, "We put gallows in our temples, in our houses, in our intersections, and on our roadways." Much like Ricci's Buddhist scholars, these visitors are, finally, incapable of drawing the most basic categorical distinctions: the emperor mocks Rigolet's account of the mysteries of transubstantiation with an irreverent insinuation to which the Jesuit, thankfully, is too dim-witted to take offense. "'But my dear friend,' said the emperor, 'you have eaten and drunk of your god: what becomes of him when you have need of a chamber pot?'" (230–31). The absurdity that Ricci saw in the Buddhist doctrine positing the unity of all matter finds its match in the unfathomable logic of the eucharist, as Voltaire turns the interpretive framework the Jesuits had developed back upon themselves and asks them to consider how their own doctrine would stand up to the scrutiny of their idealized Confucian sage.

But the Christian fanaticism that blinds the novice to the import of the Chinese emperor's barb portends political as well as doctrinal illegitimacy, in that it threatens to undermine the security of the crown and the serenity of the kingdom. The emperor's secretary of state ominously warns his patron of the unhappy fate of dissenting monarchs in European history—twenty assassinated and thirty stripped of their thrones—and concludes with a metaphor that nods to Ricci while consigning him to the darkest circle of his own hell. "There have never been more dangerous monsters on the face of the earth, nor has God ever had more deadly enemies." The emperor is persuaded by this speech and asks the missionaries to leave in order to preserve "our ancient, unchanging religion" from the "poison that consumes you" (228–33). Many contemporary French readers no doubt found it persuasive as well, and while not all would have become converts to Voltaire's cause, they surely would have acknowledged the efficacy of a satirical inversion that seized upon the established image of Chinese cultural legitimacy as a fulcrum from which to destabilize the very ideology that had created it.

Voltaire's closing image of an essential Chinese religious purity dating back to antiquity echoes not only Ricci, of course, but also the conceptions of a transcendent and incorruptible basis to the Chinese language I elaborated in the first chapter. What I have tried to demonstrate in this second chapter is the remarkable tenacity with which this common paradigm also shaped European interpretations of Chinese religious culture throughout the tumultuous period of the Counter Reformation and Enlightenment. Introduced by Ricci in the first years of the seventeenth century, this model facilitated the clear distinctions among the interwoven strands of religious teaching in China that underpinned the Jesuits' accommodationist dream. During the Rites Controversy, the Jesuit reading ultimately backfired. Ricci's successors in the mission projected an idealized vision of Chinese religion so bold that it seemed to emerge from the shadows of the Catholic Church with the stature of a now necessarily illegitimate rival and usurper. But the anti-accommodationist denunciations only reinforced, through their simple negations, the terms of the old paradigm, and ultimately provided eighteenth-century critics of the church with a secure outside platform from which to launch and finally to legitimate their own attacks on the Catholic establishment. The once urgent struggle to make sense of the Chinese cipher was eclipsed, in the end, by its appropriation as a symbol in the service of more pressing domestic ends, a subordination of interpretation to spectacle as the dominant mode in the Western encounter with China that would find its fullest expression in the aesthetic playground of chinoiserie.

CHAPTER THREE

Chinoiserie and the Aesthetics of Illegitimacy

Plates and tea wares have made us better acquainted with
the Chinese than we are with any other distant people.
—Robert Southey, *Letters from England*, 1807

The rhetorical posturing of its participants notwithstanding, the Rites
Controversy was less a clash between Eastern and Western cultural values
than between conflicting European interpretations of Chinese cosmology.
The fact that such a seemingly esoteric matter could be debated at such
length and with such passion in turn-of-the-century Paris is testimony to
the success of the intrepid emissaries of the Jesuit order in their archaeological pursuit of a Chinese conception of the divine. Spurred on by the
dream of establishing a foundation for the Catholic Church in China,
Ricci and his followers had excavated the bewildering morass of Chinese
religious history and practice in search of epistemological underpinnings
that would ground the extraordinary theological alliance on which they
staked their mission. On reaching Europe, their discoveries provoked a
vigorous denunciation of their accommodationist methods, but even the
attempts to censure their position constituted a form of cross-cultural
interpretation: that the opposing parties to this dispute arrived at such
markedly different conclusions, in other words, should not obscure the
common enterprise of discovery in which they were engaged. Although
the Jansenist or the Franciscan approached the problem of the fundamental nature of Chinese belief systems with an objective sharply at odds
with that of his Jesuit peer, the two sides shared a sense of the urgency of
the debate and of its significance for the future of the church. Like the
European philosophers of language who struggled to grasp the full significance of the Chinese script, the participants in the Rites Controversy

set out to distill an abstracted essence of a single, reified component of Chinese culture that would permit a systematic comparison with its counterpart in their own.

Beyond the walls of the church and the academy, however, the period's encounter with the East proceeded under conditions of considerably less gravity. For those who did not share an overriding theological stake in its outcome, the meeting of cultures provided an occasion rather more for lighthearted pleasure than for philosophical angst. A second wave of interest in things Chinese, this time focused primarily on the aesthetic offerings and consumer goods of East Asia, overlapped with the final years of the Rites Controversy and continued through most of the eighteenth century. Imports of Chinese porcelains, lacquerware, furniture, silks, and wall hangings had risen steadily since the mid-seventeenth century, and the new, strikingly exotic design motifs they brought with them stimulated the growth not only of domestic porcelain manufactures but also of an entire industry of designers and producers of chinoiserie from the Beauvais tapestries to Chippendale furniture and the "Chinese" temples and pagodas of the English landscape garden. In England especially, the "Chinese taste" reached remarkable heights of popularity. Extravagant spectacles featuring Chinese costumes and ornaments drew crowds to the theaters. Chinese plays were adapted and widely performed. A craze for chinoiserie furnishings and architecture transformed sitting rooms and gardens across the country and fueled the flames of classicist satire on the degradation of contemporary taste.[1]

The collectors and consumers of these vast quantities of Chinese and Chinese-inspired goods remained generally oblivious of the ambitions of a Ricci, a Bayer, or a Brisacier to "know" China, to render legible its vast universe of endlessly perplexing signs. Rather than approaching China as a cultural terrain to be mapped and mastered through a paroxysm of heroic hermeneutics, the majority were content simply to enjoy a delicious surrender to the unremitting exoticism of total illegibility. To luxuriate in a flow of unmeaning Eastern signs, to bask in the glow of one's own projected fantasies, such were the pleasures afforded by China's arrival in the marketplace of contemporary taste.

Chinoiserie, in other words, was an aesthetic of the ineluctably foreign, a glamorization of the unknown and unknowable for its own sake. If the Jesuits had taken an archaeological approach to religious culture in China, excavating the classical canon in search of primitive origins and the deep structure of Confucian monotheism, the consumerist response

to the Chinese taste in housewares and garden architecture was a celebration of superfice, a fixation on the glossy sheen of the porcelain vase
and the surface play of patterns in the willow-pattern worlds it conjured
up for the viewer's eye. China became in chinoiserie a flimsy fantasy of
doll-like lovers, children, monkeys, and fishermen lolling about in pleasure gardens graced by eternal spring. There was no substance to such a
vision and indeed no desire for substance: the entire movement represented an explicit rejection, in the aesthetic domain, of the very principle
of substantiality that had been ascribed to China by those who had
sought there a privileged site of linguistic or theological legitimacy.

If the cross-cultural gaze of chinoiserie was entranced by oriental surfaces, it discovered among these exotic veneers a mode of representation
that subverted earlier readings of Eastern sign systems as premised on a
supremely rational and authoritative ground for meaning. The vision of
China as a semiotic universe dominated by hierarchy, historical rooted-
ness, stability, and control gradually gave way to a hedonistic conception
of a mythical Cathay detached from time or place and given over to an
anarchic abundance of disjointed images and delightfully meaningless
signs. Such a conception, however radical its implications for prevailing
standards of taste, was not, as I have pointed out, without precedent.
Reading records relating to the China mission alongside contemporary
descriptions of chinoiserie, one is struck by congruities suggesting that the
principles of chaos, licentiousness, and proliferation that the Jesuits had
so violently denounced in Buddhism and Taoism were transformed in chinoiserie into the precepts of a new aesthetic outlook. In both the productions of chinoiserie and in the classicist backlash that it provoked, the predominant motifs and aesthetic values that characterized the new style
bore an unmistakable relation to the widely accepted characterizations of
Confucianism's rival cults as corrupt, irrational, and finally absurd. In the
decorative arts of the period and the lavish "Chinese" spectacles of the
French and English stage, in the manifestos that shaped the movement
and the satires that lampooned it, chinoiserie emerged as a bold celebration of disorder and meaninglessness, of artifice and profusion, an exuberant surrender to all that remained unassimilated by rationalist science
and classical symmetries. Like the renegade religions that so provoked the
Jesuits' ire, it was described by its critics in terms of monstrosity, anarchic
proliferation, and doctrinal confusion, terms suggesting a semiotic system
that, like Ricci's Buddhism, mockingly defies the very preconditions of
legitimate representation.[2]

My purpose in this chapter is to consider how the European production and reception of chinoiserie might be interpreted as a form of cross-cultural representation and to compare the images of China that informed and in turn were elaborated by chinoiserie with those conceptions evoked by the linguistic and theological discourses described in the two preceding chapters. When viewed within the context of these other discourses, I argue, chinoiserie represents far more than a mere exotic twist on the rococo style that emerged in tandem with it, or, for that matter, on the Burkean sublime it came to resemble in some of its later manifestations. Rather, it suggests an alternative interpretive model—an ideography—based on a dramatic reversal of those tropes and assumptions that had largely defined European ideas of China over the preceding century. Both the Chinese written language and the Confucian belief system had been venerated as emblems of stable, legitimate forms of representational authority. Chinoiserie, by aestheticizing the idea of this authority, effectively eviscerated it, transforming symbols of awe-inspiring cultural achievement into a motley collection of exotic ornamental motifs. Subsequent sections of this chapter will trace the aesthetic deflation of the cultural authority of the Chinese in the realms of politics, religion, nature, and sexuality, drawing on representative examples both of chinoiserie and of the impassioned responses it provoked among English writers of the mid-eighteenth century.

I use the term "chinoiserie" loosely throughout to refer to objects, whether of European or Chinese manufacture, that an eighteenth-century viewer would have recognized as "Chinese" in style. Eighteenth-century consumers do not seem to have concerned themselves, on the whole, with the actual provenance of "exotic" decorative goods, so long as they fulfilled their desired aesthetic purpose. Certainly there does not seem to have been a significant a priori difference, in contemporary eyes, between the aesthetic value or cultural meaning of a Chinese import and a domestic imitation. The constant flow of decorative patterns and stylistic influences between European and Chinese workshops from the late seventeenth century onward makes a meaningful distinction, in any case, difficult to sustain.[3] In selecting the works I will discuss here, I have set out neither to provide an historical survey of the development of the chinoiserie style, nor a comparative analysis of its trajectory in different parts of Europe. My aim, rather, has been to consider how chinoiserie as a generalized aesthetic phenomenon might usefully be compared with other types of responses to Chinese culture during this period. I have cho-

sen examples, then, that are both broadly representative and richly resonant in their particulars with the recurring topoi of this encounter.

As the bulk of what follows concerns the vision of Chinese culture
implicit in chinoiserie, two clarifying remarks on the nature of the paradigm shift represented by this new vision may be in order. First, the transformation in prevailing attitudes toward China is a gradual one, occurring
over the course of several decades during which there is a certain degree of
overlap. A characteristically eighteenth-century literary treatment of
Chinese porcelain, for example, occurs as early as 1675 in Wycherley's
The Country Wife, while quasi-mystical interpretations of the Chinese language persist until the death of the Jesuit figurist Joseph de Prémare in
1736. The new view, in other words, does not so much actively repudiate
the old as progressively supersede it as the image of China comes to be
deployed for an altogether different set of cultural purposes.

Second, the shift in attitudes corresponds to a shift in the prevailing
genres of representation from scholarly writings to the decorative arts.
One might argue that a comparison between a Jesuit tract and a porcelain
vase would inevitably yield conflicting representations of their foreign
other simply as a result of this generic incongruity, and indeed my argument would falter were the two genres historically coterminous. But in
fact they are not: the comparison is meaningful not only because the two
types of "texts" are the products of distinguishable historical periods
(roughly 1600–1740 in the first case and 1675–1775 in the second), but
also that they typify the predominant ways in which China was imagined
and represented in their respective periods. This shift in the prevailing
modes of representation of China from the scholarly to the aesthetic is
itself an essential component of the transformation I describe, and one
that justifies my premise that the decorative arts can legitimately be read
in such a context as a site of cultural representation. While the early-nineteenth-century poet laureate Robert Southey's remark that "plates and tea
wares have made us better acquainted with the Chinese than we are with
any other distant people" may not reflect favorably on the depth of this
acquaintance, it does suggest the degree to which such objects were perceived as being "about" the place to which, however reductively, they
referred.[4]

A tradition of significant allusions to chinoiserie runs through English
literature of the Restoration and eighteenth century, from Wycherley to
Pope, John Gay to William Beckford. The literary work, however, that
most fully captures the spirit of chinoiserie as a cultural phenomenon is

Oliver Goldsmith's *Citizen of the World*, a text that in spite of its relative obscurity Wayne Booth regarded as its author's most important achievement.[5] First published serially as *Letters from a Chinese Philosopher* in the *Public Ledger* beginning in 1760, Goldsmith's satire deploys Montesquieu's well-worn device of a foreigner resident in a European city to comment on local customs and mores. Prominent among these are the contemporary fashion for all things Chinese and the propensity of the English to flatten the accompanying idea of Chineseness into a merely aesthetic arena for the surface play of insubstantial signs. Indeed, the stubborn illiteracy of the English when it comes to cross-cultural encounters makes for one of the longest-running jokes throughout the letters and provides a recurrent target for Goldsmith's unrelenting irony. Those London acquaintances of the Chinese visitor Lien Chi Altangi who have any reaction at all to his "Chineseness" not only fail to understand what such a cultural difference might mean but also seem to insist on their prerogative to ignorance. As Charles Knight and others have observed, Goldsmith himself is somewhat equivocal in his presentation of Lien Chi's "Chinese" identity, at times stressing it emphatically and at others dropping it altogether. Whether or not one accepts Christopher Brooks's conclusion that the work as a whole is an elaborate fabric of orientalist impostures, the idea of "China" clearly remains for Lien Chi's interlocutors a luxuriously empty slate for their own exotic fantasies and musings; to color it with the kind of "real" knowledge of the place that Lien Chi tirelessly proffers would be to corrupt its function as the imagination's carte blanche.[6]

Not surprisingly, then, colorful *mis*conceptions about the Chinese abound throughout the letters. Invited for a meal, Lien Chi is offered a cushion in lieu of a chair, and a choice of bear's claws or bird's nests as an entrée. When he objects that he is unacquainted with these dishes and would prefer roast beef instead, he is rebuked with the assertion, "The Chinese never eat beef." His hosts helpfully inform him, in the course of the evening's conversation, that the "true Eastern sense" consists of nothing more than "sublimity" and "lay it down as a maxim, that every person who comes from thence must express himself in metaphor; swear by Alla, rail against wine, and behave, and talk and write like a Turk or Persian."[7]

But the most striking among the fantastic notions and interpretive fallacies unmasked by Goldsmith's satire are those that deny Chineseness any meaningful content at all. A lady of distinction who has invited Lien

Chi for an interview remarks on first seeing him, "What an unusual share of *somethingness* in his whole appearance," and seems to value the knick-knacks in her Chinese porcelain collection only in so far as she believes them to be "of no use in the world." A certain "grave gentleman," after discoursing learnedly on the use of chopsticks and Chinese geography, finally sums up the appeal of the Orient as that place "where all is great, obscure, magnificent, and unintelligible," while a connoisseur of the popular genre of Eastern tales explains that the authenticity of their style lies in the privileging of sound over sense: "[They] should always be sonorous, lofty, musical, and unmeaning." Finally, a little beau praises "Asiatic beauties" as "the most convenient women alive," on the grounds that "they have no souls."[8] The English sinophiles' insistence on the vacuity of their object of admiration constitutes precisely the kind of "flattening" of cultural value that is the hallmark, I argue, of chinoiserie. Confronted with a potentially disruptive surfeit of foreign meanings, these admirers of the Chinese exotic consistently dissolve it into a glimmering spectacle of "somethingness," "uselessness," or plain "unintelligibility." Although Goldsmith himself clearly delights at times in his own narrative renditions of the chinoiserie aesthetic and so might be said to exploit the fashion he parodies, such moments of indulgence are so saturated with self-irony as to reinforce the predominant gesture of playfully exposing the foibles of his countrymen, of which the intellectual insipidity of their response to foreignness is but one particularly vexing example.[9]

Goldsmith dramatizes this systematic negation of Chinese "meanings" through recurrent images of the literal degradation of Chinese artifacts. Silk cloth, perhaps the most widespread and historically significant of Chinese imports, appears three times in association with processes of corruption and decay: in the old military banners of tattered silk that strike Lien Chi as a pathetic emblem of English honor, in a noose purportedly used to hang a criminal of the nobility, and in the absurdly long trains that fashionable ladies have taken to trailing behind them in the muck as a sign of their importance and majesty, but with the result that the fabric has to be replaced ten times in a season.[10] When Lien Chi's society hostess offers him a tour of her Chinese rooms to show off her collection of "sprawling dragons, squatting pagods, and clumsy mandarines," she is inspired to descant on neither what the objects might represent nor why she admires them but on their essential ephemerality. "Three weeks ago, a careless servant snapped off the head of a favourite mandarine . . . [then] a monkey broke a beautiful jar; . . . yesterday crash went half a dozen dragons upon the marble hearth stone; and yet I live; I survive it all." While her melodramatic litany serves to deflate her own claims to good taste and social importance, it simultaneously degrades the cultural standing of China in its metonymic and typographical reduction of an empire to a gaudy display of decidedly lowercase china and chinoiserie. Long-forgotten in the English china closet that it indirectly inspired is the rapt admiration of an earlier generation of sinophiles, the bearers of an interpretive tradition fundamentally at odds with the narrow-minded self-absorption of the fashion-conscious collector.[11]

But the most blatant and painful form of negation is that suffered by Lien Chi himself at the hands of his professed admirers. Although he is portrayed as occasionally dull, tendentious, and naive, there is no perceptible irony in his characterization as a good, honest philosopher, a man of considerable learning and indisputable taste, and a representative of a culture that surpasses Britain's in the magnificence of its history and achievement. As a reviewer observed in 1762, "All his observations are marked with good sense, genius frequently breaks the fetters of restraint, and humour is sometimes successfully employed to enforce the dictates of reason."[12] And yet English society regards him as little more than a curiosity to be gaped and wondered at, in which role, as he points out, a rhinoceros would do just as well. Once he aims to appear "rather a reasonable creature, than an outlandish idiot," however, the interest of his hosts begins to wane and he finds himself dismissed with a yawn as either an imposter or a bore. To the extent that the otherness of Altangi's Chinese "reality" is rejected and finally superseded by his hosts' exotic expectations, Lien Chi appears, as Brooks has suggested, as the "'original victim' of orientalism," a figure whose "essence is only marginal to his expectation-laden appearance."[13]

Both Brooks's invocation of Said's notion of orientalism in this context and the repeated conflation in the minds of Goldsmith's English characters of the cultures of Near and Far East into a generic "orient" raise the question of the degree to which chinoiserie more generally can be read as being specifically and distinctly "about" China at all. Part of the contemporary fascination with the style, without a doubt, partook of a generalized interest in the exotic, a category in itself inherently inimical to nuanced distinctions among points of origin. Furthermore, chinoiserie appears, in many of its incarnations, to owe as much to European as to "oriental" stylistic influences. The chinoiserie designs of Watteau and Pillement, for example, might easily be classed as quaintly exotic variations on rococo themes; across the Channel, architectural design books published in England in the 1750s regularly intermingled Chinese and Gothic motifs.[14]

The undeniable hybridity of the chinoiserie style does not, however, detract from its legibility as an emblem of contemporary responses to Chinese culture. In the case of the Goldsmith letters cited above, I would argue, the conflation of cultures does not so much efface the difference of Chineseness as attach the principle of cultural effacement as a quality particular to it. The interchangeability of "Eastern" or "Asiatic" cultural attributes, in other words, reinforces the notion that Lien Chi's culture is characterized by an essential quality of indeterminacy that echoes the indescribable air of "somethingness" about his own appearance. The myriad artistic currents that contributed to the development of the chinoiserie style in Europe can, likewise, themselves be read as emblematic of the domestic reception of a foreign cultural influence. To recognize the rococo elements in a Watteau chinoiserie is not to deny the Chineseness of the inspiration behind the theme, but rather to acknowledge an inevitable process of stylistic translation between two very different cultural milieux. In interpreting such an artifact, then, the rococo cast that emerges from this process of translation can in itself be read as one component of the inherently ephemeral vision of China implicit in the work.

Goldsmith's *Letters* appeared at the height of a classicist backlash against the Chinese taste in the mid-eighteenth century. As one of many satires against the shallow extravagance of the virtuoso and the connoisseur in their reception of a newly exoticized East the letters hit their mark: the faddish tearoom prate of Lien Chi's London seems a world apart from the urgent controversies over the language and religions of China of only a half century before. But it is the content of these newly flattened images of China and the nature of the reaction to them that provides the most striking contrast with the paradigm of legitimacy pursued by the missionaries and philologists of an earlier age. In its relation to themes of authority, nature, and sexuality, chinoiserie overturned the dominant conceptions of the sinophilic intelligentsia to replace them with a modern aesthetic vision exalting the very principles of semiotic chaos and illegitimacy Jesuits and language projectors alike had so deplored. In rejecting the imperative of legibility in their reception of the foreign, the purveyors and consumers of the Chinese fashion discovered a mode of encounter and of "reading" that prized irreverent laughter over mastery and that reveled in the playfully anarchic fantasies of an unintelligible world.

In part, no doubt, this shift represented an inevitable reaction against the earnest and often reverential attitude toward Chinese culture that had dominated the previous century's writings on the topic. The more interesting explanation, however, revolves around the changing demographic and historical context of the encounter. Early Jesuit missionary writings on China, however widely read by contemporary standards, ultimately addressed only a relatively small, intellectual elite. This readership, by necessity preoccupied with the crises and upheavals—political, religious, linguistic—that defined their worldview, interpreted Chinese culture through the lens most readily available to them and applied their interpretations, in turn, to addressing the pressing concerns of their age. The audience for chinoiserie objects, in contrast, was both vast and increasingly materialist in orientation. The effective popularization of the Western awareness of China through the medium of fashionable commodities that began in the late seventeenth century necessarily diverted attention from the arcane speculations of missionaries and philologists and encouraged more readily accessible modes of response. The development of commercial societies, new rationalist paradigms, and the heightened sense of enlightened self-assurance that accompanied both meant, furthermore, that these new modes of response emerged within a correspondingly modern matrix of cultural fantasies and desires. Prosperous eighteenth-century consumers were no longer drawn to China in search of a reassuring image of order and stability; they were enticed, rather, by the promise of fresh inspiration for their imaginative fancy and novel vehicles for aesthetic innovation and social display. They turned to East Asia for a different purpose than had their scholarly predecessors, and they took away, not surprisingly, a vision that answered to their needs.

A formal analysis of this phenomenon, however, may prove as revealing as a diachronic one. What ultimately intrigues me more than the historical reasons behind the shift in attitudes toward China is the mirror-image quality of the reversal, the remarkable continuity, that is, in the face of dramatic changes in the cultural context of perception, of the basic conceptual framework underlying each period's characteristic response. The final section of Chapter 2 traced the peculiar persistence of the Jesuits' interpretive paradigm even within openly anticlerical libertine writings. This chapter will document its continuing vitality and influence within an aesthetic domain equally inimical to an earlier, idealized vision of Chinese civilization.

Authority

As I have argued in the two preceding chapters, analytic responses to the foreignness of Chinese culture typically entailed the projection of highly structured models of authority on the unruly confusion of Eastern linguistic and religious signs. These hierarchical systems, legitimated in the European view by their ancient historical derivation, provided a crucial interpretive foundation for the work of early protosinologists. Both the rationalist linguistics of language philosophers and the accommodationist precepts of the China Jesuits presumed an absolute authority on the part of the earliest founders of Chinese civilization that guaranteed its intelligibility to—and eventual mastery by—its Western interpreters.

The creators and connoisseurs of chinoiserie, in contrast, put aside the will to interpretive mastery in their response to the provocation of radical foreignness. Viewed through the kaleidoscopic refractions of the porcelain vase, the once-venerated emblems of Chinese authority disintegrated into a parodic pastiche of gaudy and insubstantial fragments. In the tapestries, drawings, and architectural plans that set the tone of the Chinese rage in the decorative arts, "Chinese" temples, palaces, and even the emperor himself succumbed to the trivializing exigencies of ornamental design. There was little space on a teacup to evoke four millennia of cultural achievement, let alone the respectful awe that such a prospect had once inspired. With the reduction of an empire into a series of miniaturized motifs and the aestheticization of the very concept of the foreign into an excuse for decorative extravagance, the ideal of a deep-rooted epistemological authority native to Chinese culture degenerated into brazen self-parody. No longer the home of ancient and universal truths, China became in these images the site of capriciousness, folly, and illusion, its philosopher's stone nothing more than a glittering shard of pottery.

The process by which the idea of Chinese authority was progressively eviscerated and, ultimately, delegitimized entirely in chinoiserie stands out most clearly in the depictions of the Chinese emperor that were especially popular in turn-of-the-century France. As a symbol of that oriental despotism that Montesquieu would so passionately condemn and as a paramount link in the Confucian chain of being that Ricci had so admired, the person of the emperor embodied in the political arena precisely those qualities of Chinese culture—authority, stability, tradition—that Europeans had long sought to discover in Chinese language and religion.

7. Frontispiece to Johan Nieuhof's *Embassy to China*, 1669. Courtesy of the University of Michigan Libraries.

Western visitors tended to accept the Chinese view that the absolute power and legitimacy of their sovereign was incontestably grounded in both heavenly mandate and a patrilineal line of descent. According to Johan Nieuhof, a member of the Dutch East India Company's embassy to Peking of 1655:

> The King or Emperour of China, commands the Lives and Estates of all his Subjects, he alone being the Supream Head and Governour; so that the Chinese Government, as we have said, is absolutely Monarchical, the Crown descending from Father to Son. . . . Their Emperour is commonly called Thienfu, which signifies the Son of Heaven; and this name is given them . . . because they Adore and Worship Heaven for the highest Deity; so that when they name the Son of Heaven, 'Tis as much as if they said the Son of God.[15]

In the portrait of the emperor that serves as the frontispiece to Nieuhof's published account of the expedition, the Son of Heaven cuts an awesome figure well in keeping with this description (see figure 7). Seated erect upon a raised throne, his arm extended nonchalantly across a large globe at his side, he gazes out at the viewer with an air of imposing majesty. Gathered close around him are a sizable troop of fierce-looking guards (numbering 112 on each side, according to the text) armed conspicuously with all manner of weaponry, while kneeling at his feet are a number of abject supplicants in chains and a supine monk with his head locked in a wooden stock. The emperor is shaded by a parasol held over his head, but apart from this there are few concessions to regal opulence in the decor: the image conveys all the strength and self-assurance of an ambitious Manchu warrior-king. Both here and in Nieuhof's descriptions of the imperial court and state bureaucracy, what seems most to impress the members of the embassy is the sheer power of the sovereign and the ordered efficiency of his administration: a political system, in other words, that in its enviably stable grounding and closely regulated hierarchies appeared in perfect harmony with European visions of the philosophical writing system and ancient Confucian cosmology of the Chinese.

Nieuhof's lavishly illustrated account first appeared in Dutch in 1665 and was quickly translated into Latin, French, and English. Along with Athanasius Kircher's *China Monumentis*, it provided one of the most influential descriptions of China through the end of the seventeenth century, and its more than one hundred engravings provided a rich source of imaginative inspiration to the first creators of European chinoiseries.[16] The best-known adaptations of the imperial portrait appeared in a series

of ten wool-and-silk tapestries produced by the royal workshop in Beauvais in the early eighteenth century. Based on cartoons painted by several well-known French artists under the principal guidance of Guy-Louis Vernansal (1648–1729), the often-reproduced series came to be known as the first *Tenture chinoise*.[17] Small details in the Beauvais artists' rendering of the emperor himself—the identical position of the hand upon the waist, the same long pearl necklace, cocked head, and drooping moustache—establish the influence of the Nieuhof frontispiece. But the resemblance ends here: in their stylistic reconception of the ambience of the imperial court, these later images convey a radically different response to the very authority of the Chinese monarch than did the stoic severity of the Nieuhof model. The shift in context from a Dutch commercial embassy to a decadent French court no doubt accounts for some part of the difference, but this shift is itself emblematic, as I have suggested, of a larger shift in the dominant mode of perception vis-à-vis Chinese civilization from an intellectual concern with principles of order and hierarchy to a materialist concern with aesthetic pleasure. By mapping the transformation of images across this divide, one can better understand not only the specific content of the chinoiserie "vision" of China but also its formal continuities with the seemingly unrelated conceptions that preceded it.

The most famous tapestry of the series and the one most closely comparable to the original engraving in its setting is *The Audience of the Emperor* (see figure 8). Once again the emperor is seated on a raised throne with supplicants prostrate at his feet and attendants standing behind him. One's first impression on seeing the image, however, is less that of a counsel of state than of a sumptuously appointed menagerie. Winged dragons and peacock feathers adorn the intricately carved throne, while a large elephant glares out menacingly from behind it. A stork struts across the foreground, a peacock looks on attentively, and a dozen exotic birds flutter conspicuously overhead. The soldiers that crowded the Nieuhof drawing, in contrast, have retreated into the background. A single languid guard stands at the emperor's side, his shield resting on the ground, his banner sagging beside his drooping head. A second attendant

8. (*opposite*) *The Audience of the Emperor*, tapestry from *The Story of the Emperor of China* series, France (Beauvais), before 1732. Designed by Guy Louis de Vernansal I, Jean Baptiste Belin de Fontenay, and, probably, Jean-Baptiste Monnoyer. Wool and silk, 3.18 m × 5.03 m. Courtesy of the Fine Arts Museums of San Francisco. Roscoe and Margaret Oakes Collection, 59.49.1.

glances distractedly off to the side as he holds the elephant's rein. Several other soldiers in clownish caps joke among themselves as they peer around a curtain from behind the main platform. Overhead stands an extravagantly ornamented canopy on spindly columns, while a luxurious oriental carpet spills sumptuously down the steps before the throne.

The emperor seated amidst all this baroque magnificence still strikes an impressive pose, but the overwhelming decadence of the decor ultimately detracts from his own glory. Not only do the animals and attendants appear oblivious to the ostensible gravity of the moment, the viewer, too, is invited to wander intrepidly about the scene, sharing in the audacity of the strutting stork and the hilarity of the royal guards. The emperor continues to occupy the focal point of the image as is his due, but he occupies a much smaller center than in the Nieuhof portrait relative to the image as a whole and consequently has some difficulty sustaining the air of dignity that it should confer. The opulence and activity that surround him seem rather to reduce him to the status of just another curio in the pastiche of exotic fantasy that the scene presents. His once absolute authority degraded into parodic decadence, the majesty of his court into sheer spectacle, the Chinese sovereign has been reduced under the weaver's loom to the ruler of a large, lavishly illustrated wall hanging—and no more.

One final detail in the tapestry that has no counterpart in Nieuhof's original engraving is a panel of pseudo-Chinese characters set into the back of the throne behind the emperor's head. Clearly meant to represent an inscription exalting, in one way or another, the ruler's power and majesty, these marks implicitly invoke the mystique of antiquity and philosophical potency once associated with the Chinese script in affirming the status of the monarch who sits beneath them. And yet this implicit allusion to an ancient tradition of cultural achievement, like the trope of vast imperial power in the figure of the emperor himself, wavers on the edge of irony. The inscribed panel is framed by incidental details that defy any attempt to contemplate it with the reverence it would seem otherwise to invite. The elephant's gigantic ear flaps irritably on one side and the lethargic guard nods off on the other, while immediately above a pudgy batlike creature with gaping beak and furrowed brow glares down from a perch crowned by a plume of peacock feathers. The incongruity and gratuitous exoticism of these elements captivate the viewer's eye with their restless play, but by the same token discourage lingering reflection or any impulse to read the noble wisdom of a Confucian sage into the wild scrawls above the emperor's head. The visual context of the inscription reduces it, rather, to yet another decorative element amidst the rich surface patterning of the scene. The depth of meaning once ascribed to the Chinese writing system is nowhere to be found: the ancient script functions here as mere ornament, as ungrounded and intentionally meaningless as the floral patterns on the oriental rug.

A second tapestry in the same Beauvais series, *The Emperor on a Journey* (see figure 9), repeats similar motifs. The emperor, seated in much the same pose, occupies center stage once again, only now he is being carried in a dragon-crowned palanquin through a rich garden landscape in the company of several standard-bearing horsemen. The luxuriance of flora and fauna, emphasized by the presence of a servant sprinkling flowers before the emperor's path, the flock of curious-looking fowl fluttering overhead, and the pagodas in the distant background, contribute to the predominant feeling of quaint exoticism about the scene. Nonsensical "Chinese" characters make an appearance here as well, this time on one of the banners carried by a guard. As in the first tapestry, familiar tokens of Chinese legitimacy are aestheticized by the artists of Beauvais into so many decorative elements in a resplendent mirage. But this time Chinese writing and imperial rule do not bear the burden of the slight alone. On the left side of the image, symmetrically opposite the aforementioned banner, is an open temple revealing an idol seated upon a thronelike altar. Monks belonging to the temple flank the idol on either side, incense offerings burn before it, and a cross-legged Buddha surveys the scene from a precarious rooftop perch. If it is not clear precisely who or what the two seated figures might represent, this hardly seems to matter: the temple is a site of idol worship and as such falls into that undifferentiated category of illegitimate "other" sects that both Ricci and his subsequent detractors had so despised. A viewer needs no knowledge of Eastern rites to recognize that the posture of the lower idol mimics that of the emperor passing before him, or that the architecture of his temple echoes that of the emperor's palanquin. Whether these resemblances foretell a scene of royal ancestor worship or suggest the sovereign's patronage of local gods, their allusion to Chinese religious practices that had so recently been the object of such vehement public denunciations could only contribute to the further deflation of his status in a contemporary Western observer's eyes. The heathen idol and the decadent prince, joined visually not only by their similarity in appearance but also by the staircase that bridges the space between them, represent respectively the degraded

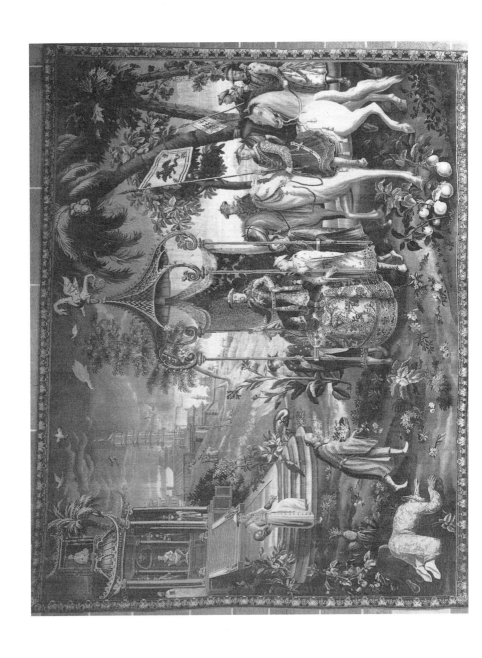

antithesis of legitimate authority in the religious and political spheres. The distinctive aesthetic of these two tapestries, the manner in which in their flattening of perspective they privilege surface over depth, in itself recalls the dismissive, trivializing terms China's missionary writers used in describing heterodox systems of belief. Proliferation, impenetrable confusion, and a kind of monstrous fecundity were all that Ricci and others saw in their superficial glance over non-Confucian religious culture in China; it fell to the artists and craftsmen of Beauvais to recognize the rich aesthetic possibilities in such a vision and to transpose its degenerate exoticism onto the ideally suited medium of their tapestries.

The Western observer implied by both these images makes a cameo appearance in the *Journey* tapestry in the bearded figure of the Jesuit Adam Schall, shown at the bottom of the steps leading to the temple holding a compass and a globe. The historical Schall, an accomplished astronomer and mathematician, won over two Chinese emperors and their courts to the Jesuit cause through his scientific teachings and was ultimately appointed director of the Bureau of Astronomy in 1644 and granted an honorary title of the first rank in the imperial bureaucracy a decade later.[18] His presence in the tapestry, nonetheless, seems at first strangely incongruous. His long plain robe and simple cap contrast sharply with the bejeweled finery of the imperial procession, not to mention the colorful plumage of the tropical birds that stand beside him. Even the tools of his trade, signaling a coolly rationalist approach to the natural world, seem out of place within a landscape whose luxurious abundance defies quantification or taxonomic analysis.

This foreign priest is an outsider, then, in every respect, yet one whose gaze over the passing entourage commands an unexpected power. The austerity of his dress marks him as a detached observer of the processional scene before him, a scene that is transformed through his very presence into a microcosmic spectacle within the overall image itself. But Schall is no passive spectator. The most plausible explanation for his conspicuous placement at the foot of a pagan temple is that he intends, by means of his Jesuitical admonitions, literally to stand between the emperor and his idolatrous double. By obstructing the ruler's passage up the temple stairway, the figure of the foreigner intervenes dramatically within the internal spec-

9. *(opposite) The Emperor on a Journey*, tapestry, France (Beauvais), 1720–1730. Courtesy of the Württembergisches Landesmuseum Stuttgart.

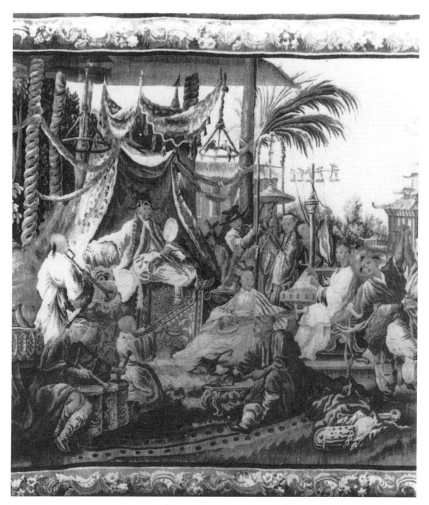

10. *Musicians Entertaining Ruler*, tapestry, France (Aubusson), 1750–1775. 58 × 111 in. Courtesy of the Baltimore Museum of Art. The Mary Frick Jacobs Collection, BMA, 1940.143.

tacle that his presence has evoked. But the most decisive indicator of his determinative role within the image is the large globe he carries under his right arm. A symbol not only of his astronomical vocation but also of a masterful, godlike vision of the world seen from afar, it connotes a new, scientific foundation for legitimate knowledge of the East on the part of its Western visitors. In the original Nieuhof engraving, it will be recalled, a similar globe suggested the boundless power and ambition of a mighty warrior-king. By transferring this emblem of universal domination from the emperor's hand to that of a Western missionary, the designers of this tapestry signal a discernable shift in the perceived balance of power within the history of the encounter. China, once the fount of privileged and universal forms of knowledge, has succumbed to the greater epistemological power of the Western scientific gaze. Deprived of its philosophical underpinnings, the image of China flattens into a dazzling play of surfaces, a cornucopia of exotic images within which even an emperor's rule extends only as far as the picture frame.

The progressive delegitimization of Chinese imperial power—and of its linguistic and religious corollaries—can be traced in the subsequent history of the chinoiserie style. A second *Tenture chinoise*, comprising six tapestries after designs by François Boucher, was produced in twelve sets at Beauvais in the mid-eighteenth century.[19] The style here is considerably less formal and more voluptuous, as crowds of mingling bodies, sensuously draped, replace the staid and stylized figures and garden ornaments of the earlier series. The thematic focus has shifted correspondingly as well: from carefully posed, stately scenes from the emperor's life to the spontaneous, nearly carnivalesque leisure activities of the court and town. The emperor has been banished entirely from most of these scenes, which is telling in itself; when he does appear it is as a shadow of his former self. In the tapestry *Musicians Entertaining Ruler*, the once haughty Son of Heaven lounges dreamily on a canopied platform as his entertainers crowd around him (see figure 10). Whereas in the earlier series, as noted above, suggestions of the emperor's dignity seemed to waver on the edge of irony, here any pretense of imperial stature has been abandoned altogether. Carelessly attired in oversized robes and crowned with a clownish cap with wispy tufts protruding above the ears, he seems lost in a blissful reverie, oblivious to the viewer's gaze. Stripped of his guards, his composure, even his self-assertive mien, he drifts among the strains of music as an entertainer among entertainers, a comic parody of the authority that his title would imply.

An emperor-like figure—although perhaps now he has been reduced to a local official—appears again in *The Chinese Fair* (see figure 11). Standing above the busy crowd of peddlers and their wares, he is conspicuous as the only figure to return the viewer's gaze. But it is a look this time that conveys not self-assurance but resignation and perhaps a hint of silent despair. With the exception of a prancing mountebank

11. *The Chinese Fair*, tapestry, France. Designed by François Boucher (1703–1770), cartoon by Jean Joseph Dumons (1687–1779), manufactured at Beauvais, period of Louis XV (possibly 1758, 1759, or 1767). Tapestry weave; silk and wool weft, cotton warp, 332.6 × 312.4 cm. © The Cleveland Museum of Art, 2000. The Elisabeth Severance Prentiss Collection, 1944.134.

intent on pressing a snake upon his hat, no one in the crowd pays him any heed. Occupied with their own business they look steadfastly away, the centripetal force of their wayward glances isolating him in his shame, leaving him to ponder with the viewer the degradation of his name. He presides over the scene from the height not of a throne but of an auction block. Like the porcelain dish poised precariously beside him he stands on display before an indifferent sea of eyes, a fragile and finally meaningless commodity, mute testimony to the triumph of an aestheticizing Western gaze.

Eventually, the eviscerated token of Chinese legitimacy that was the emperor vanishes from the scene altogether. In the remaining tapestries of this second series, as I have mentioned, he doesn't appear at all, while in the other representational media favored by chinoiserie his iconic status is evoked only rarely. What remains of Chinese imperial majesty in these works is typically little more than a hollowed-out architectural shell. Indeed, the design books for furniture and garden structures "in the Chinese taste" that were popular in England in the midcentury are full of fanciful illustrations of "royal" garden seats, "triumphal" arches, and even an "Imperial Retreat for Angling."[20] The royal personage implied by such titles, of course, persists as only a vague fantasy: these designs represent the final stage in the distillation of an aestheticized aura of Chinese imperial authority begun by the weavers of Beauvais. Paul Decker's plan for a "Royal Garden Seat," for example, is pure ornamental context, a throne without a king, a sanitized setting for play and leisure intended for the pleasure gardens of the rich (see figure 12). Any vestige of that legitimacy to which the artist whimsically alludes has evaporated entirely from the scene, leaving only decorative latticework, layers of exotically bowed awnings, and the quaint little bells that hang from their corners, jangling in the wind. A triumphal arch that in China, according to Nieuhof, would have been "made of Stone or Marble, with great Art, Cost, and Ingenuity" and "erected in honour of some famous Act, Thing, or Person . . . to eternize their Memory" similarly becomes in English garden architecture a flimsy wooden structure that serves only as "a proper Termination of a grand avenue leading from a Gentleman's seat to a road or navigable river."[21] The English gentleman in his country seat has replaced the Chinese emperor on his throne and, in the process, reduced the honor of his rival to an incidental ornament in a panoramic view.

The vaunted moral authority of Confucius proved every bit as vulnerable as emblems of Chinese imperial power to the whimsical fancy of chinoiserie. Alongside plans for the famous Great Pagoda and a generic Chinese Pavilion, the catalog of Kew Gardens' structures prepared by royal architect William Chambers for Princess Augusta in 1763 includes the design for a "House of Confucius" with intricate latticework and rooftop bells that proclaim its kinship with Decker's "Royal Garden Seat." Although this structure occasionally appears alone in later reproductions, Chambers's own depiction of its garden setting leaves no doubt as to its

12. Paul Decker, *Royal Garden Seat*. Engraving in *Chinese Architecture, Civil and Ornamental*, 1759. Courtesy of the University of Michigan Libraries.

merely incidental function there. Grandly entitled *A View of the Lake and Island, with the Orangerie, the Temples of Eolus and Bellona, and the House of Confucius*, his engraving depicts the gardener's salute to the Eastern sage sandwiched awkwardly between a Chinese bridge and an artificial mound capped by a temple to the Greek god of winds, and within a stone's throw, one might surmise, of the Gothic cathedral and Turkish mosque pictured in nearby plates (see figure 13).[22] In the Jesuit pantheon, Confucius once stood Christlike and alone, but for the eighteenth-century garden architect he is but one heathen god among many, his temple just another quaint attraction in the theme park of a princess.

The free-ranging iconoclasm of Kew Gardens was exceptional in striking so close to the philosophical heart of the contemporary China craze. More commonly, allusions to Chinese religion in European art and design followed the lead of the *Emperor on a Journey* tapestry in seizing upon the generally discredited "idolatrous" sects of the Chinese as a more suitable and less potentially conflicted source of purely exotic imagery.

13. William Chambers, *A View of the Lake and Island, with the Orangerie, the Temples of Eolus and Bellona, and the House of Confucius.* Engraving in *Gardens and Buildings at Kew*, 1763.

Thanks largely to the Jesuits' efforts, the figure of Confucius—like that of the Chinese emperor—was still likely to evoke a modicum of respect and admiration for some European viewers. In a medium that prized levity above all things, therefore, artists could not casually employ such a figure without taking measures of the kind seen above to banish every trace of legitimate authority from its appearance. The obvious advantage of the rival sects, in this regard, was that the missionaries had definitively settled the question of their theological status in advance. Uniformly condemned by writers from Ricci onward as a breeder of proliferate idols and meaningless doctrines, the multiheaded beast of popular religion in China provided an ideal trope for the new oriental aesthetic in Europe, for which meaningless abundance and a cast of inscrutable exoticism were, after all, the very source of its appeal.

The French painter Antoine Watteau (1684–1721) drew upon the rich imaginative possibilities of an idol-worship motif in his several influential chinoiserie designs.[23] The drawing *Divinité Chinoise* shows an open-air temple set within a frame of florid rococo decoration (see figure 14). An idol in a broad-rimmed hat sits cross-legged on a dais, while a number of

14. *Divinité Chinoise*, 1729–1730. Gabriel Huquier (1695–1772), after Antoine Watteau. Black chalk, brush and gray ink on cream laid paper, lined, 260 × 380 mm. Courtesy of Cooper-Hewitt, National Design Museum, Smithsonian Institution/Art Resource, N.Y. Gift of the Council, 1911-28-295.

avid worshippers, arms outstretched, climb the flanking stairs to approach him and finally to bow prostrate at his feet. The seamless blending of the lush woodland setting into the intricate rocaille ornamentation that fills the spaces above and below the temple obliterates any clear distinction between the two: the stairways serve as the backbones to a pair of symmetrical floral scrolls, while a bell-shaped bauble suspended weightlessly over the center of the scene doubles as a parasol shading the placid god beneath it. Although this figure represents an object of religious devotion within the scene, it serves a purely formal function in the outside viewer's eye, its solid, stable mass centering the perfectly balanced tableau. The gaze of aesthetic admiration both mocks and displaces the scene of pious reverence represented in the drawing, transforming an emblem of Chinese religious authority into a fetish of rococo taste.

A similar transformation occurs in *Idole de la Déesse Ki Mao Sao*, one of Watteau's paintings for the Cabinet du Roi in the Château de la Muette (see figure 15). Here again one finds a blending of setting and ornament,

15. *Idole de la Déesse Ki Mao Sao*, ca. 1729. Jean Aubert, after Antoine Watteau. Courtesy of Metropolitan Museum of Art. Gift of Mr. and Mrs. Herbert N. Straus, 1928.

a formally balanced structure, and a central divine figure who commands both the viewer's gaze and the humble reverence of a pair of kneeling worshippers. This time, however, the deity is no stone-faced idol but a beautiful Paris *salonière* transplanted from one of the artist's *fêtes galantes* paintings and armed with a parasol and a curious long-handled feathered implement for the requisite touch of local color.[24] Watteau here does away with the pretense of native Chinese divinity altogether. It is the European, after all, who finally takes pride of place in chinoiserie and rules over the fairy-tale landscapes of its exotic dreams. As the Chinese devotees, in drooping moustache and comically pointed hat, reach out to kiss the feet of their new Parisian goddess, the older fantasy of Chinese legitimacy evaporates into the mist of sparkling irony that envelops the scene.

Out on the grounds, meanwhile, one finds not only that the generic "Chinese temple" rivaled the royal garden seat as a favorite theme of the architects and designers of the period, but that it, too, was treated in a similar spirit of uncompromising levity. Along with a drawing of such a temple, the architectural designers William and John Halfpenny (whose surname, as one critic drily notes, provides a fair comment on their merit) published a plan for a hybrid structure "in the Chinese taste" that might serve equally well, they averred, as "an open temple or garden seat." Robert Sayer offered an engraving of a "Summer Dwelling of a Chief Bonzee or Priest," complete with thatched roof and a pair of gardeners. In the text accompanying his famous furniture designs, Thomas Chippendale suggests that a set of his Chinese chairs "are very proper for a Lady's dressing-room," adding, however, that "they will likewise suit Chinese Tempels."[25] The interchangeability of two such seemingly incongruous settings from an interior design point of view is striking, but viewed against the background of Jesuit writings on China, hardly unexpected. For Ricci, Buddhist temples had become metonymic extensions of the nests of doctrinal and even sexual instability and confusion they contained; Chippendale's caption, I am suggesting, represents the transposition of the received Jesuit reading of such a space into a decorative domain.

One can distinguish in these design books two distinct but complementary ways in which contemporary treatments of Chinese architectural motifs delegitimize the idea of Chinese cultural authority. On the most immediate level of content, they present icons of royal and religious prerogative in China as so many inconsequential "toys in architecture," as William Chambers called them, valued solely, "as toys are sometimes, on account of their oddity, prettyness, or neatness of workmanship."[26] On the level of style, meanwhile, they deny the architectural authority of the very models from which they presume to work. What does it mean to suggest that a Chinese temple can be furnished in the same manner as a lady's dressing room, to propose that a temple will serve the purpose of a garden seat, or to design a summer house or temple "partly in the Chinese Taste"?[27] The integrity of a respected stylistic model—the Palladian, for example—typically precluded such extremes of hybridization. Chinese architecture, however, commanded no such respect. In contrast to the studied efforts to codify the design principles underlying classical and renaissance models, little effort was made in most of these books to discern, let alone reproduce, the Chinese draftsman's modus operandi; the available models and descriptions, rather, were taken as an incoherent corpus, a fragmentary assemblage of unconnected design elements that could be endlessly adapted and recombined.

The prevailing perception of Chinese architecture as fundamentally unintelligible was corroborated and encouraged by the influential first-hand accounts of recent visitors to China. In "A Particular Account of the Emperor of China's Gardens near Pekin" (trans. 1752), the Jesuit Jean-Denis Attiret writes admiringly of the emperor's pleasure houses but finds ultimately that their very strangeness defies accurate accounting: "I should be very glad, if I could make such a Description of these, as would give you any just Idea of them; but that is almost impossible; because there is nothing in the whole, which has any Likeness to our Manner of Building, or our Rules of Architecture."[28] The total absence of familiar design elements in these buildings rendered them as opaque to Attiret's understanding as ever the doctrine of a Buddhist sutra appeared in Matteo Ricci's eyes. And in both cases, the experience of opacity generated a presumption of irrationality on the part of the Chinese creators of the offending artifact. For Chinese architects, it turns out, flout not just classical rules of proportion, but the very principle of regularity itself. "In their Pleasure-houses," Attiret adds in a later passage, "they rather choose a beautiful disorder, and a Wandering as far as possible from all the Rules of Art. . . . I have not yet observed any Two of the little Palaces in all the grand Inclosure which are alike." The presumed authority of the written language and ancient religion of China derived from the ability of European observers to assimilate and rationalize these initially unfamiliar systems within their own conceptual categories. In the case of Chinese garden architecture, Attiret seems to imply, no adequate conceptual framework is available to the Western—or indeed any—viewer. "The only way to conceive what [these buildings] are," he remarks, "is to see them."[29] He promises, accordingly, to send drawings at a later date, but one can speculate that his superficially self-effacing words, reprinted repeatedly over the space of two decades, themselves contributed substantially to reinforcing the idea of a Chinese aesthetic as one fundamentally better suited to the fleeting pleasures of the eye than to the studied comprehension of the rational mind.

Attiret's English contemporary William Chambers, whose work on Kew Gardens had been inspired in part by a trip to Canton in his youth, noted a similar lack of uniformity in his firsthand account of Chinese religious architecture, but he found considerably less to admire in the prevailing spirit of innovation. To begin with, the resulting absence of clearly discernable rules and patterns frustrated his draftsman's impulse to specify precise and standard measures for the types of structures he set out to describe and illustrate. Having completed a considerable inventory of temples and pagodas in the city, he was able to generalize the rough layout of their courts and pavilions, but their principles of proportionality eluded him. In the opening pages of his *Designs of Chinese Buildings* (1757), he writes:

The most common form used in temples is that represented in Plate II, which is almost an exact copy from one in the Cochin-China Pagoda, in the eastern suburb. I have measured several of this sort, and found so much difference in their proportions, that I believe they do not work by any certain rule; but that every artist varies his measures at pleasure.

To make matters worse, a so-called temple was not always what it seemed. The design elements associated with the temple form, it appeared, were more generic architectural motifs than reliable indicators of bona fide religious significance. Like the architectural conception behind them, they proved exasperatingly chameleonic cultural signifiers.

The Chinese have not, as the antients had, certain forms of building appropriated to sacred purposes. The particular kind of structure which they call *Ting*, or *Kong*, is used indifferently in all sorts of edifices. We meet with it in almost every temple, in all their palaces, over the gates of cities, and in all buildings where magnificence is aimed at.

Here, as in Attiret's account, Chinese architecture proves stubbornly resistant to a Western viewer's attempt to reduce it to a fixed and stable paradigm. For Attiret, it was the absence of any discernible "rule of art" that confounded him; for Chambers it is the lack of both standard proportions and of a reliable correspondence between form and function. Despite his fastidious attempts to rationalize the architectural principles of temple design through his plates and figures and exacting descriptions ("the diameter of the second order of columns is about four fifths of that of the first; and the columns are six and a half diameters high, without bases . . ."), the Chinese temple remains for him a troubling conundrum that eludes both rigid definition and assimilation into a Western mold. A fitting symbol for the doctrinal anarchy in China that had so vexed Matteo Ricci, the temple spurns, in Chambers's account, even the basic distinctions and demarcations through which, in a Western model, religious legitimacy is sustained: not only are nominally religious motifs casually employed for secular purposes, even in temple burial grounds, "priests and animals are promiscuously interred, both being equally honoured with monuments and inscriptions."[30] As an aesthetic principle for garden architecture in eighteenth-century Europe, promiscuity, as noted above, tended to prevail over chaste simplicity. The moral overtones of such a choice, however, did not go unnoticed, and indeed it was the critics of chinoiserie who most explicitly repudiated an earlier generation's conception of the cultural authority of the Chinese.

At first glance, such a claim might appear paradoxical. It was the creators of chinoiserie, after all, who in their fanciful and irreverent designs reduced the emperor and gods of China to an endlessly adaptable series of quaint decorative motifs; one might expect the critics of such a transformation to lament the dignity of the "authentic" cultural value that had been lost in the process. On the contrary, those who railed against the movement found no quarrel with its tawdry aestheticization of Chinese authority. What alarmed and rankled these critics, rather, was the challenge posed by the resulting chinoiserie style to their own authority as arbiters of public taste and guardians of the nation's moral and aesthetic sensibility. The Earl of Shaftesbury and countless popular essayists denounced the new style as a frivolous and effeminate foreign fetish that threatened to turn men's gaze from the proper objects of their regard, the Herculean statuary and symmetrical facades of Augustan England's classical patrimony. China, viewed through the now prevailing lens of chinoiserie, appeared to them a breeding ground for grotesque and barbarous forms that in their flagrant disregard for timeless precepts of measured simplicity and grace threatened to corrupt the untrained eye and with it the moral fiber of the nation. By denouncing the rival Chinese taste as, in effect, an illegitimate usurper of the public gaze, the style's critics concluded the reassessment of the idea of Chinese authority that the *tapissiers* of Beauvais had begun. If the aesthetic of chinoiserie stripped Chinese culture of its aura of dignity in the name of exotic charm, its critics compounded the disgrace by vilifying the aesthetic, in turn, as a sign of complete cultural degradation.

François Fénelon, who had attempted to dampen the polemical flames of the Rites Controversy with his measured reflections on religious alterity in 1702, turned his attention to the excesses of artistic sinomania in the imagined encounter between Socrates and Confucius included in his *Dialogues des Morts* (1712–1730). Although the lopsided exchange between the two philosophers presents a range of targets for the Greek's vituperation that reaches far beyond chinoiserie, the specific rhetorical gesture that underlies his sweeping condemnation of Chinese culture set the tone for the more narrowly directed classicist satire of later decades. For Fénelon's Socrates, the fatal flaw of Eastern civilization lies in its superficiality and hence, essential falseness. The text's most explicit and literal elaboration of this theme occurs in Socrates's scathing critique of the Chinese arts. After dismissing Chinese achievements in porcelain as owing more to a fortuitous pedological accident than native artistic talent, he turns to the other most familiar examples of Chinese aesthetic sensibility:

> Your architecture shows no sense of proportion: all is low and flattened out, all is confused and weighed down with little ornaments that are neither noble nor natural. Your painting has life and a certain kind of grace, but it is correct neither in drawing, layout, the nobility of its figures, nor the truth of its representations; one sees neither natural landscapes, historical scenes, nor evidence of reasonable and coherent thought; one is only dazzled by the beauty of the colors and polish.[31]

What passes for beauty in China, in other words, is nothing more than deformed, deceptive, and ultimately meaningless surface clutter; there can be no lofty striving for truth and nobility of form where "all is low and flattened out." But the curse extends beyond the arts to the realm of religion and philosophy, so that Socrates finds a corresponding lack of depth in the much-vaunted wisdom and virtue of the Chinese. "This is a people that has devoted all of its wisdom to the preservation of its laws without daring to examine their merit, . . . [they are] rigid observers of the outward form of their ancient customs, without seeking in them justice, sincerity, and other internal virtues."[32] Chinese laws, as they are observed by the Chinese, carry no legitimate authority in the eyes of the Western philosopher for the same reason Chinese paintings could never please the trained Western eye: they have no roots in the rational pursuit of truth. If Chinese manners present the appearance of virtue, this is owing to a surface illusion very much like the striking but superficial beauty of Chinese art, for these manners are mere "virtues of habit and opinion . . . founded upon the custom and prejudices of a people," rather than products of that true moral reflection that is the exclusive domain of the Western philosopher. The very prevalence of such superficial virtues suggests a moral authority tainted by the accessibility of its principles to the untrained mind. For Fénelon's Socrates, the difficulty of grasping a moral idea is a reasonable first measure of its truth: "I persist in believing that the whole of a people is incapable of rising to the principles of true wisdom."[33] The legendary wisdom of the Chinese must be rejected as false, then, if only on the grounds that it is far too common.

Fénelon's forward-looking relativism in the religious sphere notwithstanding, his Greek spokesman declares the essential aesthetic and philosophical superficiality of Chinese culture markedly inferior to the considered profundity of both aesthetic judgment and moral reasoning in the West. On the basis of the class bias evident in his remarks, one might infer that Fénelon himself detects in the disturbingly democratic flattening of both taste and virtue in China an implicit challenge to those cultural and class hierarchies in Europe that the very ideal of such narrowly exclusive discourses helped to sustain. The irony here, of course, is that Fénelon's diagnosis of an excessively populist strain within Chinese philosophy and art entirely ignores the historical role of Confucianism and a system of imperial and aristocratic patronage of the arts in reinforcing a rigidly hierarchical social order within China. His blindness in these passages to the political contexts of the traditions he so excoriates in itself testifies to the remarkable efficacy of the chinoiserie craze in subverting those conceptions of China that had tended to privilege the legitimacy of its representational authority.

One of the earliest influential critics of chinoiserie on the other side of the Channel, meanwhile, was undoubtedly that stalwart champion of aristocratic values and a beleaguered classical taste, the Whig philosopher Anthony Ashley Cooper, Third Earl of Shaftesbury. Shaftesbury wastes few words denouncing the Chinese style per se as a specific instance of aesthetic depravity, preferring, like Lien Chi's hosts in *Citizen of the World*, to lump it together with those other varieties of gaudy and grotesque foreign extravagance that seemed to exercise a particular fascination for his contemporaries.[34] His remarks on the subject are sufficient to suggest, however, that like Fénelon he drew a parallel between the aesthetic and moral values of the Far East and perceived on both counts a Chinese threat to established forms of cultural authority at home.

Shaftesbury's great contribution to contemporary discussions on matters of taste was his contention, following upon his unequivocal equation of beauty and truth, that the faculties of aesthetic and moral judgment were inextricably linked. By conscientiously training one's eye in the appreciation of the most exemplary paragons of classical beauty, "right models of perfection" that, in the course of a continental tour might include, for example, "the truest pieces of architecture, the best remains of statues, the best paintings of a Raphael or a Caraccio," one might learn properly to distinguish "merit and virtue" from "deformity and blemish" and thereby aspire to "the character of a man of breeding and politeness." Examples of false taste, by the same token, were to be studiously avoided if one was not to bear the imprint of their deformity upon oneself.[35]

The art of the East clearly falls into this latter category. Like Fénelon, Shaftesbury acknowledges the seductive charm of its surface splendor. Yet to linger among superficial charms is to cloud one's appreciation of true and lasting beauty and, by implication, of moral truth. He offers a hypothetical case that, in its associational clustering within an oriental context of glossy paint, the corruption of taste, and the transgression of sexual norms echoes Matteo Ricci's excoriation of the preposterous proclivities of Buddhist monks and their popular following in China.

Effeminacy pleases me. The Indian figures, the Japan work, the enamel strikes my eye. The luscious colours and glossy paint gain upon my fancy. . . . But what ensues? . . . Do I not for ever forfeit my good relish? How is it possible I should thus come to taste the beauties of an Italian master, or of a hand happily formed on nature and the ancients?[36]

Eighteenth-century aesthetic discourse revived a long-standing classical and civic humanist tradition that associated "luxury" with a notion of male effeminacy detrimental to both public and private virtue. Men who indulged a taste for unmanly luxuries, as Livy's famous account of the causes of Rome's decline had made clear, were unlikely to devote themselves with requisite zeal to the most basic civic responsibilities, let alone the defense of the nation. Shaftesbury invokes these fears in his suggestion that the softening of masculine virtue before the gaudy spectacles of exotic wares might entail a permanent emasculation of the highest faculties of aesthetic and moral judgment, and a consequent threat to what Burke would later call the "manly, moral regulated liberty" of the English.[37] If the lack of depth and verisimilitude in Chinese art reflected for Fénelon the philosophical standing of the Confucian notion of virtue, it fell to Shaftesbury to posit a causal connection between the aesthetic and ethical domains and to implicate the oriental taste directly in the corruption of moral authority and civic virtue among its elite Western consumers. In doing so, he set the stage for a critical onslaught against chinoiserie that would challenge not only the questionable aesthetic standards that it embodied but also the frightening vision of social, political, and religious anarchy that it seemed to portend. China had been transformed, for these critics, from an unassailable seat of cultural legitimacy to a wellspring of depravity that threatened to unravel the very fabric of a well-ordered society, one enchanted viewer at a time.

Very much like the Jesuit attacks on Buddhist understandings of the divine, the satirical backlash against the alien style that crested in the

1750s relied heavily on images suggesting the usurpation or degradation of established icons of cultural authority. In his review of a contemporary Drury Lane production of Arthur Murphy's adapted tragedy, *The Orphan of China*, Goldsmith scolds contemporary leaders of fashion for succumbing to the foolish whimsies of the "Asiatic" taste:

The refined European has, of late, had recourse even to China, in order to diversify the amusements of the day. We have seen gardens laid out in the Eastern manner; houses ornamented in front by zig-zag lines, and rooms stuck round with Chinese vases, and Indian pagods. If such whimsies prevail among those who conduct the pleasures of the times, and consequently lead the fashion, is it to be wondered, if even poetry itself should conform, and the public be presented with a piece formed upon Chinese manners?[38]

With the sinification of English poetry and European standards of refinement, there was nothing to prevent even houses of worship from falling victim to the mania for Eastern novelty. "The Chinese taste, which has already taken possession of our gardens, our buildings and our furniture," predicted a contributor to *The Connoisseur* in 1755, "will also soon find its way into our churches: and how elegant must a monument appear, which is erected in the *Chinese* Taste, and embellished with dragons, bells, Pagods and Mandarins!" And in case oriental theatre and dragon-topped steeples were not enough to inculcate the new aesthetic orthodoxy among young men of means, the Grand Tour might be modified, as an anonymous writer in *The World* facetiously suggested, to permit the substitution of Peking for Paris on the standard itinerary.[39]

The playwright William Whitehead, who succeeded Colley Cibber as poet laureate and was a frequent contributor to *The World*, perhaps best captures the prevailing sense of alarm among classicist critics in a colorful essay of 1755. Having warned in general terms that the fashion for chinoiserie threatened "the ruin of that simplicity which distinguished the Greek and Roman arts as eternally superior to those of every other nation," he hammers his point home with a poignant illustration of the kind of calamity that lay in store. A certain Lady Fiddlefaddle, he ominously reports, who had inherited a collection of Italian masterpieces from her grandfather, cast them out to make room for Indian paintings, "and the beautiful vases, busts, and statues, which he brought from Italy, are flung into the garret as lumber, to make room for great-bellied Chinese pagods, red dragons, and the representation of the ugliest monsters that ever, or rather never, existed."[40] By conflating the figure of the forsaken patriarch with the neglected ideals of classical beauty in his critique of the Chinese menace, Whitehead invokes, with a parodic twist, the well-worn trope of Chinese ancestral authority. Only now, the legitimacy of the ancestors is on the European side, and the ancient, originary truths of the Chinese sages have collapsed into a motley assortment of absurd phantasms and abominable representations of, as it turns out, nothing at all. Whitehead's displacement of an earlier notion of Chinese plenitude with a highly stylized but ultimately vacuous play of images restages the subversion of the emperor's majesty observed in the Beauvais tapestries. For the satirist, however, this displacement is only a starting point, setting the scene for a definitive coup de grace against the now gasping dragon of the European sinophiles. This final blow, of course, is left to the cultivated reader, as Whitehead holds up the disemboweled "Chinese" aesthetic of chinoiserie for ridicule next to the unassailable supremacy of Rome.

Lest the specter of pagodas popping up in country courtyards or aristocratic grandfathers turning in their graves should seem too remote to be taken seriously, the enemies of chinoiserie could cast their crusade in starker political terms. The established principles of good taste were connected not only, as Shaftesbury had argued, with the moral foundations of sound character but also with the stability of the social order. The feckless hankering after novelty that stimulated fashionable collectors and trend setters in their pursuit of the exotic and the bizarre was a symptom of restless changeability, which in turn, as Beverly Allen observes, was widely associated with political and religious unrest. The spread of the luxurious taste represented by chinoiserie, moreover, could only serve to exacerbate the often-noted weakening of social distinctions between aristocratic and merchant wealth, between persons of quality and the maddening hoards of climbers, imitators, and parvenus forever nipping at their heels. Novelty as an aesthetic principle, after all, was far more readily accessible to the middling sort than the "severe art" and "rigid rules" of the classical masters. Chinoiserie, in particular, as Christopher Brooks has noted, "was essentially not class exclusive and so allowed the troublesome class movement . . . to take place."[41] From a marketing perspective, this presented obvious advantages: the Halfpennys, promoting their second collection of designs for Chinese architecture, claim to have "laid down several Objects in the Chinese manner hitherto unknown, yet made easy to the meanest capacity." From the loftier viewpoint assumed by the

lawyer and politician Sir James Marriott, however, the political implications of chinoiserie's mass appeal were unmistakable:

The present vogue of Chinese and Gothic architecture has, besides its novelty,
another cause of its good reception; which is, that there is no difficulty in being
merely whimsical. A spirit capable of entering into all the beauties of antique simplicity is the portion of minds used to reflection, and the result of a corrected judgment; but here all men are equal. A manner confined to no rules cannot fail of
having the crowd of imitators in its party, where novelty is the sole criterion of
elegance.[42]

A half century before the murder of a queen prompted Burke's fiery
denunciation of the red-capped revolutionaries in France, the figurative
dissolution of the Chinese monarchy by the tapissiers of Beauvais set the
stage for another kind of antiforeign backlash, a concerted rejection of
the aesthetic jacobinism of chinoiserie on the grounds that it flattened distinctions of rank and merit and elevated the politically charged notion of
novelty for its own sake to an unprecedented pride of place among the
pleasures of the imagination.

   Just as Fénelon's Socrates accused Confucius of having promulgated a
superficial understanding of virtue that was ultimately reflected in the
shallow showiness of Chinese art, so too, for the English classicists, the
careless whimsies of chinoiserie cheapened the noble ideals of Art and
Beauty by distorting them into conformity with popular taste. For critics
on both sides of the Channel, then, Chinese culture presented an excessively populist model of artistic pleasure that threatened to undermine
existing structures of aesthetic, moral, and even political authority. In
what can only be seen as a perfect inversion of the paradigm of a previous
generation, China now appeared, in its stubborn unassimilability, an
impossibly anarchic cultural landscape inimical to legitimate hierarchies
of taste and judgment and dangerously oblivious to the universal standards it was their business to enforce.

Nature

The cultural topographies of chinoiserie, however unruly, made their
most conspicuous and lasting impact among the compliant hills and dales
of the English landscape garden. While the degree to which Chinese ideas
on gardening—or Western interpretations thereof—actually shaped the

course of British gardeners' revolt against the prevailing formality of the French style remains open to debate, the popular interest in these ideas and the vigor of the controversy surrounding them would have left few innovators unaware of at least a partial debt to Eastern models. Triumphal arches, temples, and pleasure houses "in the Chinese taste" imparted a quaintly exotic flavor to the hilltops and lakesides of country estates even as they trivialized those forms of authority to which they playfully alluded. It was in the representation of nature itself, however, rather than in these stylized symbols of exotic religions and royal courts, that chinoiserie revolutionized the very idea of the garden, and, in doing so, set forth a radically altered conception of the nature of the Chinese sign. The doctrine of legitimacy that had informed early research on the written language of China from Bacon onward presumed an absolute, originary grounding of the meaning of its "characters real" in the true nature of things in themselves. The special qualities ascribed to the script derived, ultimately, from this philosophical foundation. With the proliferation of treatises on Chinese gardening in the eighteenth century, however, this notion of a privileged basis for Chinese representation began to unravel. While tapestries, porcelain pagods, and an army of satirists were conspicuously subverting icons of Chinese cultural authority, theorists of landscaping design quietly undermined the corollary principle of semiotic legitimacy by asserting an essential incompatibility between Chinese constructions of nature and their presumptive basis in the true nature of things.

A Chinese written character had appealed to the likes of Wilkins, Leibniz, and Swift because it was guaranteed to mean something, and because that meaning appeared stable, unambiguous, and reliably grounded. In contrast to the words of European vernaculars, constantly subject to the vagaries of careless usage and relentlessly shifting meanings, an ideograph embodied etymological purity, historical continuity, and a sense of rational, philosophical truth. The modes of representation that prevailed in chinoiserie, however, presented a entirely different scenario, and not simply owing to a lack of naturalistic verisimilitude. Nature in this novel, highly stylized aesthetic appeared little more than a vehicle for the most extravagant flights of imagination, exercises in pure fantasy that seemed to repudiate the grounds of reliable, rational representation altogether. If nature had once served as an original, unshakable foundation for the language and philosophy of the Chinese, it emerged now in their art in the very negation of that role, a purely aesthetic principle that rejected mimesis altogether in the name of a new conception of exotic beauty.

The advocates of the imported style made no effort to conceal its glaring disregard for the precepts of natural law. The fantastic scenes that enlivened chinoiserie designs openly alluded to nature even as they defied its mastery: this was the source of their appeal. As Robert Sayer explained in *The Ladies Amusement; Or, the Whole Art of Japanning Made Easy*, "With Indian and Chinese subjects greater Liberties may be taken, because Luxuriance of Fancy recommends their Productions more than Propriety, for in them is often seen a Butterfly supporting an Elephant, or Things equally absurd; yet from their gay Colouring and airy Disposition seldom fail to please."[43] The primary sense of "propriety" here is simply that of accuracy, or conformity to the "proper or particular character, . . . nature, [or] essence" of a thing. In contrast to its philosophically grounded written language, in other words, the arts of China could not be trusted to convey a faithful representation of the natural world. But two additional connotations of the term further illuminate the consequences of chinoiserie's "greater liberties" and "luxuriance of fancy." The most familiar is that of "conformity with good manners or polite usage; correctness of behavior or morals," a definition that recalls in this context Shaftesbury's conflation of aesthetic and moral virtue. A more archaic but equally illuminating meaning of "propriety" is "the proper, strict, or literal sense of a word, strictness of meaning, literalness."[44] The "luxuriance of fancy" that distinguishes chinoiserie productions thus implies a potentially untoward freedom from the strictures of literal meaning, a figural exuberance that obliterates the presumption of any correct or natural "truth" in art.

Critics, predictably, denounced the rejection of nature and propriety they saw in chinoiserie with the same vigor that they had used to condemn its implicit subversion of established cultural authority. As the lawyer James Marriott, taking his cue from Fénelon, railed in *The World* of March 27, 1755, Chinese

> paintings, which, like the architecture, continually revolt against the truth of things, as little surely deserve the name of elegant. False lights, false shadows, false perspective and proportions, gay colours . . . , in short, every incoherent combination of forms in nature, without expression and without meaning, are the essentials of Chinese painting.[45]

The standard against which chinoiserie appears as false, incoherent, and meaningless is an idealized conception of classical simplicity, a pure, universalizing mode of representation that captures the beauty of nature without distortion or adornment. "Simplicity," wrote the critic and poet Joseph Warton in the same periodical, "is with justice esteemed a supreme excellence in all the performances of art, because by this quality, they more nearly resemble the productions of nature." His contempt for collectors of chinoiserie stems from their perverse predilection for disfigured forms that undermine the very precept of natural resemblance and the precondition of aesthetic legitimacy.

If these observations are rightly founded, what shall we say of the taste and judgment of those who spend their lives and fortunes in collecting pieces, where neither perspective nor proportion, nor conformity to nature are observed; I mean the extravagant lovers and purchasers of China, and Indian screens. I saw a sensible foreigner astonished at a late auction, with the exorbitant prices given for these splendid deformities, as he called them, while an exquisite painting of Guido passed unnoticed, and was set aside as unfashionable lumber. . . . No genuine beauty is to be found in whimsical and grotesque figures, the monstrous offspring of wild imagination, undirected by nature and truth.[46]

Given its resonance with the prominent reproductive metaphors in contemporary discussions of language and religion, Warton's invocation of the imagery of monstrous birth seems by no means fortuitous here. Indeed, the bastard child of unshackled fantasy that was chinoiserie could seem sufficiently disruptive of the familiar representational order so as to suggest an explicit parallel with grotesque distortion in the biological sphere. Alluding to the tradition that held fetuses to be affected by images that inflamed their mothers' imaginations, the surgeon and political writer John Shebbeare railed against "walls covered with Chinese paper fill'd with figures which resemble nothing of God's creation, and which a prudent nation would prohibit for the sake of pregnant women."[47] Art inspired by divine creation, like a healthy child, suggests a process of faithful, legitimate reproduction of natural meaning that serves to further God's plan; a disruption of the code of resemblance, on the contrary, can lead only to monstrous progeny or—as in this case—bad art. Much like Buddhism's complex and multivalenced representations of the divine, the representation of nature in chinoiserie lacks sufficient grounding in a stable, unitary source of coherent meaning to assimilate readily into Western structures of knowledge. This did not preclude a certain image of China taking shape around these conceptions just the same. Robert Southey was presumably not alone in attributing to Chinese imported wares his countrymen's unprecedented familiarity with the "distant people" that had created them. But such an "image" could consist of little more than a tincture of ineluctable foreignness, an exotic veneer that, once the initial gasps of wonder and accompanying collectors' mania had passed, would leave many viewers with a sense of only irritation and contempt.

The "unnaturalness" of Chinese renderings of nature continued to excite impassioned responses among both trendsetters and traditionalists as the style's distorted scenes spread from porcelain plates to the planted terraces of country estates. Gardening, as Lovejoy suggests, "was perhaps the eighteenth-century art *par excellence*," and its regular acknowledgment in both theory and practice of widely known principles of Chinese garden design gave rise to the notion of *le goût anglo-chinois*. The diplomat and essayist Sir William Temple, who is generally credited with having first introduced these ideas to Europe, was a figure of sufficient literary reputation to ensure their continued prominence throughout the eighteenth century.[48] His presentation of the Chinese garden aesthetic confirms both its continuity with the chinoiserie style in the decorative arts and its origins in a similarly anarchic conception of natural beauty. In his essay *Upon the Gardens of Epicurus* (1692), Temple claims that the Chinese scorn English gardeners' rigid adherence to "some certain Proportions, Symmetries, or Uniformities" in their planting as a sign of a woeful lack of inspiration, saying that any "Boy, that can tell an Hundred, may plant Walks of Trees in straight Lines." The Chinese, in contrast, employ the

greatest Reach of Imagination . . . in contriving Figures, where the Beauty shall be great, and strike the Eye, but without any Order or Disposition of Parts, that shall be commonly or easily observ'd. And though we have hardly any Notion of this Sort of Beauty, yet they have a particular Word to express it; and, where they find it hit their Eye at first Sight, they say the *Sharawadgi* is fine or is admirable, or any such Expression of Esteem. And whoever observes the Work upon the best *Indian* gowns, or the Painting upon their best Skreens or Purcellans, will find their Beauty is all of this Kind (that is) without Order.[49]

A number of commentators in the early eighteenth century, including Mason, Addison, and Pope, took up and elaborated this new creed as English gardeners began to move away from the now-outmoded symmetrical style.[50] But because the discovery of the Chinese garden coincided with a widespread movement away from the prevailing formalism of Le Nôtre, it was and remains difficult to isolate the degree of Chinese influence on the general trend toward a more "naturalistic" appearance in garden landscapes. It ultimately fell to Sir William Chambers to restore the mark of exotic difference to the Chinese approach. He distinguished it from the English style into which it had been assimilated by reinterpreting Temple's *sharawadgi* as a provocative new variation on the familiar motifs of eighteenth-century chinoiserie and, in doing so, elaborated the idea of the Chinese garden into a full-blown cultural fantasy.

An English gardener with an francophobic axe to grind was likely to take "beauty without order" as a slogan justifying his use of serpentine pathways and rolling meadows in place of the gridlike symmetries of the Versailles paradigm. He would have read "order" as the forced conformity of nature to a rigidly rationalist model. Chambers, in contrast, influenced no doubt by the "monstrous" and "unnatural" forms of traditional chinoiserie, equated "order" with the classicist precepts of "simplicity" and close conformity with "nature and truth." His rendition of "beauty without order," then, rejected both the slavish French adherence to regular straight lines and the equally slavish and forced "naturalness" of the English in the name of a Chinese aesthetic based on the principles of variety and surprise and on a conception of the garden as an artfully contrived panoply of heightened sensation.

Temple had warned his countrymen early on against casual attempts to recreate in their own gardens the effect of disorderly beauty he admired in those of the Chinese: "They are Adventures of too hard Achievement for any common Hands." On first exploring the topic in the Preface to his *Designs of Chinese Buildings* (1757), Chambers seems equally determined to stave off smug complacency in readers who might otherwise have fancied themselves already well versed in the essentials of the Chinese style. "The Chinese excell in the art of laying out gardens," he remarks pointedly. "Their taste in that is good, and what we have for some time past been aiming at in England, though not always with success." Having thus baited his audience, he finally reveals the misunderstood principles of this newly exoticized taste in a concluding section of his text entitled "Of the Art of Laying Out Gardens among the Chinese." The first principle he introduces here would have seemed familiar enough to any reader of Temple's work: "Nature is their pattern, and their aim is to imitate her in all her beautiful irregularities." The Chinese approach to achieving this aim, however, must have surprised readers accustomed to the graceful and subdued irregularity of English country estates. According to Chambers, the Chinese gardener sets out to contrive a variety of powerfully affecting

scenes, "pleasing, horrid, and enchanted," which by means of clever artifice and an endless succession of visual contrasts and sublime effects work
an irresistible magic on the imagination of the spectator.[51]

So tantalizing an account by an architect of such eminence could not
pass unnoticed, and Chambers's essay was subsequently reprinted both
in the *Gentleman's Magazine* and Bishop Percy's *Miscellaneous Pieces
Relating to the Chinese*. He followed up this early success and the triumph of his Grand Pagoda at Kew with the remarkable and controversial
Dissertation on Oriental Gardening in 1772. Building on the principles of
Chinese garden design he had introduced in his brief essay of some twenty
years before, he developed in this lengthy treatise an elaborate composite
of horticultural theory, satirical polemic, and extravagant chinoiserie fantasy. The burden of the argument is that the prevailing style in garden
design, the literalist naturalism of Lancelot "Capability" Brown with its
predictably undulating walks and hills, had fallen into dullness and insipidity. The Chinese approach, with its emphasis on variety, surprise, and
an active engagement of the viewer's imagination, supplied, in Chambers's view, the perfect remedy. The bulk of the essay is devoted to a fanciful and rather far-fetched description of an elaborate Chinese garden
that in its obvious hyperbolic excess seems intended to mock the bucolic
blandness of the English country estate. At every turn in the garden path
there are horrid and enchanted scenes replete with imported tigers and
elephants, implements of torture and bolts of artificial lightning, thun-
dering cataracts, and Tartarian damsels in diaphanous gowns. Such imaginative immoderation proved an irresistible temptation to Brown's
Whiggish allies and quickly provoked a satirical rebuke from the poet
William Mason in the form of a *Heroic Epistle to Sir William Chambers*,
a small masterpiece of pugnacious political pasquinade that went through
fourteen editions in five years, much to the detriment of Chambers's credibility.[52] To his second edition of the *Dissertation*, then, Chambers felt
compelled to add *An Explanatory Discourse* in the assumed voice of a
recent Cantonese visitor to England, Tan Chetqua. Here he set out to clarify points that had been misunderstood in the earlier work, while expanding on his grandiose dream of transforming all of England into a vast garden *à la chinoise*.

The common thread in all three of Chambers's published writings on
the subject is an extravagant vision of the Chinese garden as a vast pleas-
ure-house of the senses. Chambers ascribes to the Chinese a wildly hedonistic conception of nature that turns classicist pieties on their head and

celebrates the irreverence toward ideals of verisimilitude that characterized so much chinoiserie. But if he offers a richly imaginative exposition
of the Chinese taste in landscapes, he also constructs a compelling allegory to account for the pleasures of chinoiserie as a space of fantasy
where the exotic and erotic mingle among the mysterious sensualities of
unknown desire. Chambers expands the flattened splendor of the
Beauvais tapestries into a three-dimensional virtual world that engulfs the
entire body of the spectator within its glittering surfaces. The superficial
becomes all-consuming, representation becomes reality, the ungrounded
vacuity of the Chinese sign is transformed into a universe of rarified perception, unmediated and unrestrained.

These transformations begin with Chambers's presentation of the very
idea of nature in the Chinese garden. The Chinese, like the English classicists, hold up nature as a model for their art. But where the classicists venerate nature as a fount of ordered grace and simplicity and the touchstone
of a highly cultivated sense of beauty, Chinese gardeners relish its unpre-
dictability and the rich variety of sensations it can engender as a consequence, regarding it not as an immutable standard of truth but as an endlessly variegated source of stimuli. This utilitarian approach to natural
beauty frees the Chinese artist from the representational constraints that
shaped the work of his classical counterpart. Nature is no longer an idealized paradigm to be revered and imitated, but rather a medium to be
shaped and arranged by art so as to maximize its impact on the senses
and imagination of the viewer.

From the outset of the *Dissertation*, Chambers posits this freedom
with regard to nature as the central axiom of Chinese gardening. He reiterates his assertion from the *Designs* essay that the Chinese take nature as
their pattern and aim "to imitate all her beautiful irregularities." But this
time he substantially qualifies the notions of "pattern" and "imitation."
"Though the Chinese artists have nature for their general model, yet are
they not so attached to her as to exclude all appearance of art; on the contrary, they think it, on many occasions, necessary to make an ostentatious
show of their labour. Nature, say they, affords us but few materials to
work with," so that the gardener's art is called upon to "supply the scant-
iness of nature." He rejects the fetishization of unadorned nature that has
taken hold in English landscape gardens as an uninspired product of a
worn-out classicist creed. "Inanimate, simple nature," he maintains, "is
too insipid for our purposes."[53] He goes on to amplify the charge in the
Explanatory Discourse with a stinging riposte to Shaftesbury and his ilk:

If I must tell you my mind freely, Gentlemen, both your artists and connoisseurs seem to lay too much stress on nature and simplicity; they are the constant cry of every half-witted dabbler, the burthen of every song, the tune by which you are insensibly lulled into dullness and insipidity. If resemblance to nature were the measure of perfection, the waxen figures in Fleet-street, would be superior to all the works of the divine Buonarotti.[54]

In order to excite the "powerful sensations" that have replaced Shaftesbury's studied appreciation of "hidden graces and perfections" as the essence of the aesthetic experience, nature requires the assistance of an art capable of transforming it beyond the familiar limits of the merely natural.

Chinese gardening, according to Chambers, is just such an art. Replacing the tired doctrine of imitation with the aims of variety, surprise, contrast, and intense psychological effects of every kind, it liberates the Chinese artist from precisely those constraints of representational legitimacy that had, in the European view, shaped the formation of his written language and state religion. Although the successful gardener requires a strong intellect, judgment, experience, and "a thorough knowledge of the human mind," he finally aspires not to the wisdom of the philosopher or the sage but to the genius of the poet: "Gardeners, like poets, should give a loose to their imagination, and even fly beyond the bounds of truth, whenever it is necessary to elevate, to embellish, to enliven, or to add novelty to their subject."[55]

Although recent English writers—Dryden, Addison, and Johnson among them—had noted the aesthetic value of novelty and celebrated the imaginative emancipation underlying true genius, as a sympathetic reading of Chinese cultural activity this is unlike any encountered previously. Chambers credits the Chinese with the creation of a new species of aesthetic pleasure that subverts prevailing categories of beauty in the visual arts. Their gardeners traffic in representational forms that share with Buddhist idols—and the Chinese arts more generally—the mantle of symbolic illegitimacy in their groundlessness, sensuality, and unbounded proliferation. But Chambers breaks from Ricci and his rationalist counterparts among the critics of chinoiserie in celebrating the achievement. Drawing liberally on contemporary aesthetic discourses celebrating the pleasures of variety and the sublime, he overturns the long-standing paradigm that had stigmatized the polytheistic, bacchanalian tendencies Westerners had long denounced in Chinese culture, elevating them instead into an art form that at its best, in his view, rivaled "the great productions of the human understanding."[56]

In doing so, Chambers rewrites the script of the European encounter with the foreignness of the Far East. The mark of the foreign, whether in the impenetrable cipher of a Chinese character or the convoluted doctrines of a Buddhist scroll, had hitherto provoked a sense of frustration and unease, leading philologists and missionaries to neutralize the perception of difference through either admiring gestures of interpretive accommodation or contemptuous shrugs of disdain. Chambers is the first significant writer in this period to exalt the experience of cultural estrangement as a worthy and even commendable end in itself. He was the only respected commentator on the Chinese arts to have actually traveled to China; perhaps the thrilling memory of his own youthful adventures in Canton prompted him, in his later years, to redeem the much-abused chinoiserie style by ascribing to it an intoxicating aesthetic of sublime alienation. His bold reconfiguration of the script of encounter captures something of the spirit of a first foreign voyage: it immerses the Western visitor in a landscape calculated to mislead and confound, but also, ultimately, to enrapture and delight. The Chinese garden and, by extension, China itself is no longer a terrain to be subdued by rationalist cartographies but one in which to luxuriate in the sensual allure of foreignness and to take respite from the dullness and insipidity of the everyday.

The *Dissertation*, in particular, provides an alternative mapping of the experience of the foreign through a formal structure suggestive of an allegorical narrative of voyage and discovery. The visitor who makes his way among the Chinese garden's seemingly endless labyrinthine passages is referred to as a "traveller" or "passenger," and the magnificence of the landscapes he encounters fully justifies the use of such terms. These are not the quaint backyard arrangements of rock gardens and goldfish ponds that the reader expects, but seemingly full-scale renditions of sublime natural wonders that transport the unsuspecting "visitor" into a compellingly "real" virtual world.

Sometimes the traveller, after having wandered in the dusk of the forest, finds himself on the edge of precipices, in the glare of day-light, with cataracts falling from the mountains around, and torrents raging in the depths beneath him; or at the foot of impending rocks, in gloomy vallies, overhung with woods, on the banks of dull moving rivers, whose shores are covered with sepulchral monuments, under the shade of willows, laurels, and other plants, sacred to Manchew, the genius of sorrow.[57]

While this and other such "enchanted" scenes would seem designed to evoke a specific and well-defined emotional response, as a rule Chambers seems far more intent on conveying—and delighting in—the uncertainty and confusion that attend the visitor's encounter with the unfamiliar. The appearance of new and unexpected objects "which present themselves at every change of direction" on the pathway occasions not only the imaginative pleasure Addison identified in surprise but also a less obviously agreeable "incertitude of the mind" and "anxiety," all of which "very strong impressions [prevent] that state of languor into which the mind naturally sinks by dwelling long on the same objects." Equally salutary are the arrangements of garden structures that, "by their whimsical combinations" when they are gathered into a single view, exhibit "the most magnificent confusion imaginable." Sharp contrasts and striking oppositions are employed throughout the grounds to stave off complacent familiarity and to sustain the experience of boundless variety, a variety more easily attained if the planter himself be a traveler able to duplicate for his visitors the "thousand beautiful effects along the common roads of the countries through which he has passed." To the sequestered European reader implied by Chambers's *Dissertation*, the Chinese garden, in other words, could open a door to an entire unexplored world beyond his or her view, an endlessly variegated landscape of pure sensation, unpredictable and unrefined, where "nothing is forgot that can either exhilarate the mind, gratify the senses, or give a spur to the imagination."[58]

If Chambers reconfigures the encounter with Chinese foreignness through an aesthetic remapping of cultural anxiety, he simultaneously transforms that foreignness from a site of intellectual assimilation and mastery to the object of a less ethereal form of desire. The landscape garden, like other forms of chinoiserie, renders the signs of unmanageable difference into a delicious exotic spectacle. Where the garden's potent combination of mystery and sensuality exceeds the bounds of more traditional aesthetic categories, it spills readily over into the domain of erotic fantasy. Drawing on the well-established genre of seraglio tales that had flourished in France and England following the translation of the *Arabian Nights* at the beginning of the century, Chambers seeds his Chinese garden with pornographic possibilities, titillating vignettes that promise the reader, like the wide-eyed traveler of the text, a taste of those pleasures that can only accompany a thorough submission to the unknown.

The very description of the grounds frequently calls to mind a well-constructed erotic narrative, with its emphasis on suspense, concealment, voyeurism, and variety and its masterful modulation of curiosity and the

progressive revelation of the object of desire. The art of Chinese gardening, for Chambers, would seem at times more closely to resemble the arts
of seduction than those of porcelain painting or lacquerware carving:

Another of their artifices is to hide some part of a composition by trees, or other
intermediate objects. This naturally excites the curiosity of the spectator to take a
nearer view; when he is surprised by some unexpected scene, or some representation totally opposite to the thing he looked for. The termination of their lakes they
always hide, leaving room for the imagination to work; and the same rule they
observe in other compositions, wherever it can be put in practice.[59]

The centrality of these pleasures to the ethos of the garden is mirrored
in its very topography. "In the center of these summer plantations,"
Chambers writes, "there is generally a large tract of ground set aside for
more secret and voluptuous enjoyments." Artful concealment once again
enhances the pleasures of discovery: the tract "is laid out in a great number of close walks, colonnades and passages, turned with many intricate
windings, so as to confuse and lead the passenger astray." Hidden among
the thickets between these paths are "many secret recesses," each one
containing "an elegant pavilion" inhabited by the owner's "fairest and
most accomplished concubines." Should the traveler's wanderings lead
him to the enchanted scenes in another corner of the garden, he will find
himself soothed not only by "the singing of birds, the harmony of flutes,
and all kinds of soft instrumental music" but also by a variation on the
voluptuous theme better suited to this ambiance:

Sometimes, in this romantic excursion, the passenger finds himself in extensive
recesses, surrounded with arbors of jessamine, vine and roses, where beauteous
Tartarean damsels, in loose transparent robes, that flutter in the air, present him
with rich wines, mangostans, ananas, and fruits of Quangsi; crown him with gar-
lands of flowers, and invite him to taste the sweets of retirement, on Persian car-
pets, and beds of camusath skin down.[60]

If the Chinese garden provides Chambers an occasion to fantasize on the
luxuriant sensuality of a Turkish sultan's court, it is no less "Chinese" for
this indulgence. The aesthetic of the Chinese garden, for Chambers, consists in the unfettered indulgence of the most extravagant pleasures of the
body and mind, a cornucopia of sensation that can only be supplied by
subsuming within the idea of "Chinese" the more generalized experience
of exquisite foreignness. Although he borrows elements of his vision from
the contemporary topoi of the sublime and the oriental seraglio, he weaves
these elements into a novel interpretation of chinoiserie that restores to an

aging fashion trend the psychological intensity of cross-cultural encounter. What the China of the Chinese garden finally represents for Chambers, in other words, is an essence of radical otherness distilled into an aesthetic *frisson.*

Sexuality

Chambers's erotic twist on the exotic motifs of chinoiserie frames the issue of their representational status in a language of excess familiar from earlier writings on Chinese writing and religion. The "monstrous forms" of chinoiserie, I have argued, in their departure from classicist definitions of artistic merit, violated implicit codes governing legitimate representation. The Chinese taste bore the stigma of illegitimacy insofar as it flaunted a seemingly anarchic contempt for standards of derivation from a universalized "nature." Brazenly ungrounded, absurdly meaningless, and yet dangerously popular, they threatened an established hierarchical order of taste with their shameless extravagance.

But the leisurely, playful, almost hedonistic spirit that animates many of the creations of chinoiserie from the Beauvais tapestries to Chambers's three-part manifesto on the pleasures of Chinese gardening raised another kind of concern for their classicist critics: namely, the incompatibility between the disinterested experience of true beauty and merely sensual delight. "Grotesque and monstrous figures often please," Shaftesbury admonished his readers, "but is this pleasure right?" The discerning viewer turns his eye from all that is "gaudy, luscious, and of a false taste," having realized that "'tis not by wantonness and humour that I shall attain my end and arrive at the enjoyment I propose," but rather by submission to the rigid rules of art.[61] Chinoiserie is suspect not only because it deviates from nature but also for the simple reason that it is too much fun, too "wanton" in its invitation to immediate gratification and its frustration of virtuous restraint.

The skillful concubines and Tartarean damsels that inhabit the Chinese garden of an Englishman's dreams embody the logical culmination of this forbidden aesthetic of wanton sensuality in its most explicitly realized form. The pleasures they proffer are as boundless and sublime as the plunging cataracts outside their abodes and entirely alien to reasoned, rational modes of representation. Although Chambers was unusual in his polemicized presentation and sympathetic rendering of this fantasy, he draws upon a long-established tradition of sexualized representations of chinoiserie. The midcentury critic James Cawthorn, in his attack on the prevailing "luxury of taste" in contemporary English cuisine, gardening, and architecture, condemns the reigning mode of church building as "loose and lascivious," and, like Shaftesbury, attributes the decline of the "august and manly" style of the ancients in part to an insidious Eastern influence.

> Of late, 'tis true, quite sick of Rome and Greece,
> We fetch our models from the wise Chinese:
> European artists are too cool and chaste,
> For Mand'rin only is the man of taste.

The Chinese artist, by implication, tends toward a feverish licentiousness. He lays out his gardens "without the shackles or of rules or lines"; as the contagion of his designs spreads to Europe and "our farms and seats begin / To match the boasted villas of Pekin," so too must his idolatry and moral laxity invade the English sitting room.

> On ev'ry shelf a joss divinely stares,
> Nymphs laid on chintzes sprawl upon our chairs;
> While o'er our cabinets Confucius nods,
> Midst porcelain elephants and china gods.[62]

These sprawling nymphs, close cousins of Chambers's sylvan concubines, can be read, surely, as the symbolic progenitors of "the monstrous offspring of wild imagination" that Joseph Warton had decried. The unbridled sensuality of chinoiserie comes to be coded, in other words, as an aesthetic analogue of illegitimacy in the sexual sphere. Signaled by a proliferation of bastard forms, ungrounded in nature and truth, chinoiserie overturns the immaculate genealogies ascribed to the Chinese script in an orgy of antirepresentational exuberance.

The earliest and surely the best-known literary antecedent for these sexualized constructions of chinoiserie is William Wycherley's *The Country Wife* (1675), in which the young libertine Mr. Horner gains access to the married women of the town by passing himself off as a eunuch. The erotic climax of the play draws upon a curious metaphor:

(Enter Lady Fidget with a piece of china in her hand, and Horner following.)

Lady Fidget. And I have been toiling and moiling, for the prettiest piece of china, my dear.

Horner. Nay she has been too hard for me, do what I could.

Mrs. Squeamish. Oh Lord I'll have some china too, good Mr. Horner, don't think
 to give other people china, and me none, come in with me too.

Horner. Upon my honour I have none left now.

Mrs. Squeamish. Nay, nay I have known you deny your china before now, but
 you shan't put me off so, come—[63]

While the steamy innuendo of this exchange is typical of Restoration
comedy, its talismanic emblem prefigures a characteristically eighteenth-
century trope. Just as the Tartarean damsels and sprawling nymphs of the
Chambers and Cawthorn texts conveyed a sense of generalized licentiousness, so a Chinese artifact appears in this exchange as a symbol of
extravagant and illegitimate sexuality, a porcelain priapus evoking a vivid
scene of rampant cuckoldry and voracious female desire. The ladies'
newly horned husbands, after all, are not the only losers here: Horner
himself, whose transformation from a eunuch to a man hangs on the
invocation of a metaphor, finds himself figuratively emasculated again as
the scene begins. The "hard" Lady Fidget possesses the china now, and
her apparent delight in its acquisition gives one ample cause to believe his
self-ironic claim—uttered, one presumes, in a high-pitched whine—to
"have none left." Horner's dual role in itself suggests a fundamental instability of gender positions within the play. As Derek Cohen suggests, there
are other moments when female characters' "aggressive self-confidence"
tends to "efface Horner's normally robust presence," leaving him, as in
this scene, "that impotent and useless object which the world publicly recognizes him to be."[64] Lady Fidget's pleasure in this exchange effectively
consummates Horner's symbolic—if only temporary—unmanning as the
piece of china that passes between them sheds its mantle of phallic
authority for a shudder of pure *jouissance*.

 This transformation from potency into pleasure echoes the threatened
displacement of Mr. Fidget's legitimate paternity at the hands of his wife's
illegitimate desire. At the same time, it prefigures a later critique of chinoiserie as a site where firmly grounded, established forms of aesthetic
knowledge are undermined in the pursuit of passing sensual delights.
Hostile critics, as I have noted, repeatedly decried the china closet's monstrous proliferation of illegitimate forms and concomitant corruption of
the moral and aesthetic codes of artistic reproduction, calamities following upon the style's overt, unregulated, and often eroticized sensuality.
The Wycherley scene, in turn, suggests that the critical gloss of "Chinese"

sensuality in terms of sexual transgression is by no means fortuitous: the mechanism of illegitimate reproduction, whether of bastard sons or mis-shapen porcelain idols, is one in which pleasure triumphs over knowledge and phallic certainty succumbs to the vagaries of illicit—and generally female—desire. Chinoiserie emerges over the course of the century spanned by Wycherley and Chambers as a token of an emasculating feminine libido that strips art of its classical patrimony in the service of an aesthetic of immediate and irreverent sensual appeal.

Literary and artistic allusions to chinoiserie throughout the first half of the eighteenth century corroborate such a reading. The narrative climax of Pope's *The Rape of the Lock*, for example, turns on a piece of porcelain that establishes Belinda as a direct descendent of Wycherley's Lady Fidget. The image of the China jar, as Cleanth Brooks points out, appears three times in the poem, each time drawing upon well-established metaphorical associations to comment on the fragility of female chastity and honor. Elizabeth Kowaleski-Wallace, working from Laura Brown's reading of the poem as a "locus classicus" of themes of commercialization and imperialist expansion, complicates this equation by reminding us of Belinda's own role as a consumer in the mercantile emporium Pope so lavishly evokes and of her own "keen appreciation for the very commodity that acts as a metaphor for her condition."[65] In her relationship to porcelain, in other words, Belinda appears as a powerful, desiring agent, not simply the hapless victim of male violence and hypocritical social codes. The complexity of this position emerges in her immediate reaction to the Baron's assault:

> Then flash'd the living Lightning from her Eyes,
> And Screams of Horror rend th' affrighted Skies.
> Not louder Shrieks to pitying Heav'n are cast,
> When Husbands or when Lap-dogs breathe their last,
> Or when rich *China* Vessels, fal'n from high,
> In glittring Dust and painted Fragments lie![66]

The image of the shattered porcelain clearly functions on one level to dramatize Belinda's fall from innocence. But it works simultaneously on another level as part of a satirical deflation of a husband's standing in an ungrateful lady's eyes: his demise, after all, appears of no more consequence than that of an amusing pet or a showy vase. All three are contemptible and ultimately interchangeable objects of vanity and sources of fleeting and superficial pleasures. In what can be read as an opening salvo of the epic battle of the sexes that follows in Canto V and a prelude to the million murders that will be attributed to this fierce virago's killing eyes, Belinda avenges her violation at the hands of a brazen male through a rhetorical riposte that repeats Lady Fidget's figural transformation of phallic authority into an aestheticized and insubstantial fragment.[67] Although it is the Baron who wields the scissors, in Pope's rendering of her scream it is Belinda who does the cutting, reducing, if only for a brief ironic moment, the vigorous *virtus* of emboldened manhood into the glittering dust of a collector's virtu.

Eight years later, in 1725, John Gay once again invokes a piece of china as an object of female desire and a male lover's rival in the poem "To a Lady on her Passion for Old China." Although the poem satirizes a woman's misplaced affections—along with the follies of the virtuoso more generally—the lovesick speaker is no disinterested observer.

> What ecstasies her bosom fire!
> How her eyes languish with desire!
> How blessed, how happy should I be,
> Were that fond glance bestowed on me!
> New doubts and fears within me war:
> What rival's near? A China jar.

The lover addresses his coy mistress with all the frenzied passion of an Andrew Marvell ("Love, Laura, love, while youth is warm"), but her "coyness," mediated through her own all-consuming passion for chinoiserie, renders her oblivious to his impassioned appeals. The workings of this mediation are suggested by the lover's own accolade to antique jars later in the poem, in which he compares them in their purity, polish, and fragile beauty to "the types of womankind." The simile suggests a sufficient motive for female coyness, for as he concedes, "She who before was highest prized,/Is for a crack or flaw despised." As in Belinda's case, in other words, china serves as a trope both of feminine virtue and of the materialist vanity of commodity culture. He finds himself excluded from her affections by her identification with an immaculate, untouchable form of beauty and the pleasure she takes in contemplating fine porcelain rather than "the strong earthen vessel" of "courser stuff" that is the male of the species. Whether her preference for a china jar over a male suitor is a token of narcissistic virtue or homoeroticism, it represents a troublesome libidinal self-determination that threatens not only to "break a faithful heart" but also to subvert the sexual economy that sustains its hopes. A woman in possession of china, these last three works imply, has little need for a man. Encompassing the iconography of both unsullied virgin and insatiable whore, chinoiserie represents for their female characters an emancipation of pleasure from the confines of patrilineal legitimacy. If, as an aesthetic, chinoiserie privileges surface play over a firm basis in nature and truth, as a sexual metaphor it proclaims the freedom of desire from the dictates of both the law of the father and of the pining lover's laments.[68]

The violation of these dictates is, then, from a masculine perspective the source of both sexual and aesthetic illegitimacy. Chinoiserie is typically described as a fundamentally transgressive and anarchic perversion of true taste. In a venomous diatribe against the Chinese taste published in *The World* in 1753, William Whitehead insists that "Taste, in my opinion, ought to be applied to nothing but what has as strict rules annexed to it. . . . People may have whims, freaks, caprices, persuasions, and even second-sights if they please; but they can have no Taste which has not its foundation in nature, and which, consequently, may be accounted for."[69] Chinoiserie, by disregarding classical rules prescribing for art the natural foundation that can alone provide a legitimate basis for representation, gives rise to a profusion of fatherless forms and foolish pleasures that defy any genealogical accounting. To the extent that maleness or at least masculine authority, in a broadly symbolic sense, is premised on the enforcement and enforceability of the rules of taste and of representational and biological descent, their flagrant disavowal in the wanton fantasies of chinoiserie suggests a boldly emasculating gesture. The rampant cuckoldry effected by a piece of china and the ironic suggestions of male impotence occasioned by its surrender in *The Country Wife* are literary renditions of such a gesture, as are the rhetorical humiliation of the archetypal husband in *The Rape of the Lock* and the lover's frustration in Gay's poem.

The many allusions to chinoiserie motifs in the popular arts of the period provide visual corollaries to these literary scenes. Hogarth, in particular, repeatedly creates visual juxtapositions linking the extravagant excesses of chinoiserie with a figural unmanning of male characters. He evokes the libidinous spirit of Lady Fidget most overtly, perhaps, in the second plate of *A Harlot's Progress*, which depicts a bare-breasted Moll deliberately upsetting a tea table to distract her wealthy keeper while her young paramour slips out the door behind them (see figure 16). Her startled companion, a cup and saucer poised precariously in one hand, tries to stabilize the table with the other as the rest of the porcelain tea set goes crashing to the floor in front of him. Like her predecessor in Wycherley's

16. William Hogarth, *A Harlot's Progress*, Plate II, 1732. Engraving. © Copyright The British Museum.

play, Moll consummates her adulterous deception through the mediation of a piece of china. Although the shattered fragments, as in Pope's haircutting scene, may reflect on her fallen virtue, like the rocaille horns that seem to sprout from the Jew's head they simultaneously remind the viewer of the cuckold's humiliation, a plight rendered all the more poignant by his vain efforts to avert the spill. As both an exotic commodity—like the vaguely orientalized black servant boy—and a marker of the fragility of female virtue, china emblematizes the danger to a male-centered order of Moll's voracious appetites in both the economic and sexual spheres. The servant boy himself, carrying a kettle to refill Moll's china teapot, serves both as a further, racialized symbol of emasculation and as a reminder of the increasingly interconnected global ramifications of fashionable domestic consumption. Chinese tea appealed to the British palate, after all, only after being sweetened with Caribbean sugar harvested by the servant boy's enslaved kin.[70]

A similar commentary on the dangers of foreign—and in particular Eastern—luxury occurs in the second plate of *Marriage à la Mode* (see figure 17). Exhausted and disheveled after a night of wild partying, husband and wife repose amidst the cluttered disarray of an elegant sitting room. The decor would suggest that, among their other troubles, the couple has fallen victim to the corruptions of the Chinese taste. As if to mock the stately elegance of the palladian architectural motifs, a Chinese fire screen stands against the wall, a porcelain tea set adorns the table, and over the fireplace a motley assortment of squatting pagods and clumsy mandarines jostle for space in a clutter anticipating the accounts of china collections in Goldsmith's *Letters* and the satirical essays of *The World*. In typical Hogarth fashion, these ornaments reflect the moral tone of the scene, in this case one of generalized debauchery. The wife stretches out her foot enticingly from under the tea setting in a pose reminiscent both of Cawthorn's sprawling nymphs and of the reclining nude in the curtained-off painting in the next room. On the fire screen, meanwhile, a woman with a Chinese parasol peers out suggestively from behind the husband's chair while the family dog sniffs out the telltale bonnet in his coat pocket. In spite of his recent conquests, however, the young gallant conveys an air of abject defeat. In contrast to his wife, who seems game for another frolic, he stares listlessly at the floor, oblivious to the remonstrances of a steward come to collect on a sheaf of unpaid bills and, most crucially, to the shameful spectacle of a sword lying broken at his feet. Like Horner before him, he has sacrificed his manhood at the altar of a porcelain fantasy. Unable to pay his debts, win his quarrels, or even respond to his wife's advances, he slumps dejectedly in his chair, while over his head "Confucius nods, midst porcelain elephants and china gods."

These transplanted china gods found plenty of new worshippers among the English eunuchs they created. In *Taste in High Life*, Hogarth depicts a foppishly long-lashed beau who seems every bit as entranced by a dainty cup and saucer pair as his dowdy female companion (see figure 18). For the editor of *The Connoisseur*, such foppery and an appreciation for fine porcelain went hand in hand. Responding to a letter from one "W.

17. (*opposite*) *Marriage à la Mode*, Plate II, 1745. Bernard Baron (1696–1762), after William Hogarth (1697–1764). Etching and engraving, 38 × 46.6 cm. © The Cleveland Museum of Art, 2000. Gift of Mr. and Mrs. Milton Curtiss Rose, 1959.312.

18. *Taste in High Life*, 1746, after William Hogarth (1697–1764). Etching, 19.4 × 26.3 cm. © The Cleveland Museum of Art, 2000. The Mr. and Mrs. Charles G. Prasse Collection, 1954.331.

Manly" lamenting the neglect of a "vigorous constitution" among the "pretty fellows" of the land, Mr. Town affirms that many of "our fine gentlemen . . . affect the softness and delicacy of the fair sex" and may spend hours repairing their battered countenances at a fully appointed toilette. On a visit to the dressing room of a "Very Pretty Fellow," he loses no time in discerning the aesthetic predilections of "that ape of female foppery, call'd a Beau." His host had not yet risen from bed when he arrived.

I was accordingly shewn into a neat little chamber, hung round with *India* paper, and adorned with several little images of Pagods and Bramins, and vessels of *Chelsea China*, in which were set various-coloured sprigs of artificial flowers. But the Toilette most excited my admiration; where I found every thing was intended to be agreeable to the *Chinese* taste. A looking-glass, enclosed in a whimsical frame of *Chinese* paling, stood upon a *Japan* table, over which was spread a coverlid of the finest chints.

Alongside these exotic ornaments he discovers perfumes, powder puffs, ladies' makeup implements, and a small ivory comb intended, as the valet informs him, "for the eye-brows." Mr. Town speculates at some length on the question of how a man might wind up with "such a delicate make and silky constitution" as to require the aid of an eyebrow comb in keeping up his appearance, concluding that he was most likely deprived as a youth from the improving influences of study, exercise, and the occasional flogging. But what he finds most disturbing about "these equivocal half-men," as he calls them, "these neuter somethings between male and female," is the sheer incongruity of their emasculated natures. "What indeed can be more absurd, than to see an huge fellow with the make of a porter, and fit to mount the stage as a champion at *Broughton's* Amphitheatre, sitting to varnish his broad face with paint and Benjamin-wash?"[71] If chinoiserie is not directly responsible for the unmanning of such men, as a dominant aesthetic backdrop to tropes of gender transgression in the period it clearly, as Shaftesbury anticipated, is an accomplice to the crime. Certainly Matteo Ricci, given his own sensitivity to the preposterous perversion of gender roles among his Buddhist counterparts and their countrymen, would have shared Mr. Town's concern and joined him in pointing an accusing finger at anarchic Chinese modes of representation as the analogue, if not the origin, of such unnatural abominations.

The luxurious extravagance of which the Chinese style was an all-too-visible sign had financial repercussions that often mirrored its perceived moral and aesthetic effects. Hogarth's young Squanderfield has not only a broken sword to show for his wife's love affair with chinoiserie but also a growing mountain of unpaid debts. Debtors, then, increasingly joined the sorry assembly of cuckolds, eunuchs, and fops that seemed to be all that remained of British manhood in the wake of the China craze. In the following chapter I examine the role of commerce and trade narratives in the formation of British attitudes toward things Chinese. I will close here with a final, telling anecdote from *The World* that, in recapitulating the themes I have developed in this chapter also points to the perceived economic consequences of female indulgence of the chinoiserie craze.[72] The torrents of materialist desire that the style unleashed unmanned not only those who, like Horner and Hogarth's Jew, gave up their precious china in the flood but also those whose pocketbooks sustained the fashion on the open marketplace. The issue of September 20, 1753, recounts the woeful tale of a man who, having married a "woman of taste," watches on as she redecorates his home under the guidance of a Chinese upholsterer by the name of Mr. Kifang. By the end of several months, he finds his house

entirely new furnished; but so disguised & altered, that I hardly knew it again. . . . The upper apartments . . . which were before handsomely wainscotted, are now hung with the richest Chinese & Indian paper, where all the powers of fancy are exhausted in a thousand fantastic figures of birds, beasts & fishes, which never had existence. And what adds to the curiosity is, that the fishes are seen flying in the air or perching upon the trees. . . .

The chimney piece also (and indeed every one in the house) is covered with immense quantities of china of various figures; among which are Talapoins & Bonzes, and all the religious orders of the east.

As my furniture increases, my acres diminish, and a new fashion never fails of producing a fresh mortgage.[73]

Even as the undifferentiated profusion of kitsch on the mantelpiece mocks the once-vaunted religious authority of the Chinese, and as the wallpaper degrades nature from a wellspring of truth and beauty to a handmaiden of monstrous deceit, the meaningless abundance of hollow images that characterizes the new decor enacts a radical subversion of an implicit ideal of legitimacy in representation. The reckless fantasy of a woman of taste spawns an uncontrolled proliferation of groundless signs that drag their nearest referent, China, with them into a swamp of aesthetic, moral, and finally cultural illegibility. The husband gains a mortgage in the process, but what, after all, is a mortgage if not a gaping void where his patrimony should be, a eunuch's scar patched over with a glimmering illusion.

CHAPTER FOUR

Commercialist Legitimacy and the China Trade

Mony and blood in this agree,
When they're in Circulation free,
A Healthful Corps and Purse ensues,
But both are sick when both we lose.

—Richard Ames, "Lawyerus Bootatus
   and Spurratus," 1691

The proliferation of Chinese garden pavilions and porcelain buddhas notwithstanding, by far the most conspicuous Chinese commodity in English households during the eighteenth century was not a form of chinoiserie at all, but rather the newly fashionable beverage known as tea. The earliest printed reference to "that excellent and by all Physicians approved drink called by the Chineans Tcha" appeared in an advertisement for a London coffeehouse in 1658.[1] By 1701, annual East India Company sales of the dry leaf had increased from a slow trickle to 65,000 pounds. By 1780 this figure had ballooned to close to 5 million pounds, reflecting the rapid transformation of tea from the status of an exotic luxury to that of an indispensable necessity of daily life, from a precious commodity suitable as a gift to the king to a significant source of royal tax revenue.[2] With the soaring popularity of tea came a heightened demand for the porcelain accessories that accompanied it to the tea table. Much of the interest, indeed, in Chinese designs addressed in the previous chapter stemmed from a burgeoning market in fashionable tea settings.

It comes as no surprise, then, that the rituals of the tea table, laden with Chinese-inspired porcelain and Chinese tea, evoked in some observers a cluster of associations comparable to those generally attached, by midcentury, to chinoiserie. As Elizabeth Kowaleski-Wallace argues, the consumption of tea was not only gendered feminine in the literary discourse of the eighteenth century but also linked frequently to a dangerously insubordinate femininity. In Simon Mason's *The Good and Bad Effects of Tea Considered* (1701) she finds "a world 'turned upside down,' one in which [tea-drinking] women have seized the initiative and conspired to emasculate men by stripping them of their power," through their irreverent gossip rendering them impotent, tame, submissive, and obedient.[3] If, as noted in the previous chapter, a new wife's passion for the Chinese taste could threaten the economic ruin of the patriarch, the idle chatter of women around the tea table might augur his social undoing.

Another eighteenth-century treatise on the subject of this insidious new drink, Jonas Hanway's *An Essay on Tea*, corroborates the gender politics of such a reading. The Chinese, who are the greatest sippers of tea, are also, one learns here, "some of the most effeminate people on the face of the whole earth," in contrast to the "wise, active, and warlike" English. For Hanway, however, the dangers of adopting this custom reach far beyond the hapless victims of teatime chatter. If Mason detects in the tea-drinking craze a conspiracy for the emasculation of overbearing husbands, Hanway warns of the enslavement of the nation. Comparing the ascendancy of tea among the English to that of opium among the Turks, he asks, "Will the sons and daughters of this happy isle, this reputed abode of sense and liberty, for ever submit to the bondage of so tyranni-cal a custom as drinking tea?"[4]

Tea, Hanway maintains, is "very injurious to health," but its most per-nicious effects, and those that most endanger the "sense and liberty" of the nation, are rather with regard to domestic industry and labor. Offer-ing calculations of the vast quantities of time and wealth that are annually squandered on the ceremonies of the tearoom, he concludes that this "idle custom [and] absurd expense" occasioned not only "laziness and fruit-less discourse" but ultimately, as the habits of effeminate tea-sipping fops insinuated the ranks of the armed forces, a weakening of the nation's mil-itary preparedness as well. Gone were the glorious golden days of invin-cible English *virtus*, eclipsed by the seductive pleasures of an imported foreign drug. "He who should be able to drive three Frenchmen before him, or she who might be a breeder of such a race of men, are to be seen sipping their tea! . . . Were they the sons of tea-sippers, who won the fields of Cressy and Agincourt, or dyed the Danube's streams with Gallic blood?"[5]

To those who denigrated tea drinking as a pernicious social custom, then, it appeared an extravagant luxury that promoted waste and idleness and obstructed the native industry that was the basis of England's wealth and power. As with chinoiserie, its charms came to be associated with a potentially subversive femininity. But here the two discourses diverge. Both the appeal and the critique of the Chinese style in the arts involved what were essentially aesthetic responses. Although they portrayed themselves as guardians of the moral order of society, classicist critics concerned themselves primarily with questions of taste and beauty and defined their conception of a legitimate moral order along these lines. Hanway's excoriation of Chinese tea, in contrast, introduces a competing conception of cultural legitimacy figured in economic terms. The fable of the chinoiserie-induced mortgage cited at the end of the last chapter pointed in this direction: one could see how the illegitimacy of a whimsical woman's taste was compounded by the consequent erosion of her husband's financial standing. The feminine pursuit of idle luxury produced an emasculating insolvency that marked her fashionable excess as flawed and dangerous on economic as well as aesthetic grounds.

The implicit ideal that she undermines, of course, is the Protestant ethic of material salvation, the belief that, in Hanway's words, "virtuous and useful industry is the true foundation of riches." A nation becomes opulent, he argues, by trading in "useful articles of commerce" that promote the employment of the idle and provide for the necessities of life. Importing such useless commodities as tea, on the contrary, must ultimately impoverish the state, because they encourage habits of idle consumption that hamper industry and sap the economic vitality of the nation.[6] The metaphor of economic enervation would have had powerful resonances for contemporary readers familiar with recent debates on the foreign trade and its impact on the nation's gold and silver reserves. The disappointing failure of British export products—primarily woolens, lead, and tin—to capture the interest of Chinese merchants in Canton forced the East India Company to finance its massive tea purchases primarily with silver bullion. The resulting trade deficit alarmed bullionist critics like Hanway, who saw the lifeblood of the burgeoning commercial economy being drained away through the shortsighted folly of domestic tea sippers. Conflating the economic vitality of the nation with the physical vitality of its citizens, he asserts that it would be a lesser evil to purchase wrought silks for domestic use "than thus to consume our strength in tea, by which we can possibly make no profit, except upon ourselves, whilst it sucks up our very blood; and, by exhausting our treasure, weakens the nerves of the state."[7]

Hanway depicts the agent of all this mischief in strikingly familiar terms. Although tea itself is the nominal object of his wrath, his bullionist position leads him inevitably to demonize its foreign source: if our blood is being sucked, it follows that someone is doing the sucking and profiting at our expense. The culprit is not hard to find:

It is generally apprehended, that India and China are such gainers on their trade with Europe, that they draw away, by sensible degrees, all the gold and silver . . . in this quarter of the globe. . . . Thus you see how we lay the burthen of enriching China, from whose friendship or alliance we can expect no kind of succour in time of danger, upon our own shoulders, and make ourselves the dupes of our own folly!

In a moment of metaphorical lucidity informed by a century and a half of angst-ridden encounters with the powerful and yet inscrutable empire of the East, he gives a vivid shape to his arch-nemesis: "Be assured," he addresses his readers, "it is in your power to destroy this many-headed monster, which devours so great a part of the best fruits of this land."[8] Matteo Ricci, for whom a unified, coherent religious system stood as the paramount ideal, had envisioned the tangled doctrines of competing Chinese sects in the form of just such a beast. The critic Joseph Warton, speaking from a classicist pulpit, was not far off when he decried the proliferation of "whimsical and grotesque figures" in chinoiserie as "the monstrous offspring of wild imagination." For Hanway, however, the Chinese monster represents not a religious or aesthetic abomination but an economic one. Chinese cultural illegitimacy, once envisioned as a threat to a Catholic/Confucianist synthesis in China and the hegemony of classical taste in England, appears now as the enemy of capitalist wealth and prosperity. The monstrous, in all three cases, is an emblem of the transgressive potential of difference, the irreducible core of foreignness produced and revealed by every act of cross-cultural interpretation. Unlike "ideographic" Chinese characters and Confucian epigrams, which could be assimilated within preexisting hierarchical frameworks, Buddhist scriptures, porcelain idols, and, ultimately, Chinese trade practices all stubbornly refused to conform to Western rules and categories of understanding, presenting instead an illegible cipher, a grotesque and darkly subversive "other" to familiar modes of representation.

This commercialist reincarnation of the Chinese menace bears obvious resemblances—in its very monstrosity and in its strength-sapping, emasculating powers—to its chinoiserie cousin, and, I would argue, arises in tandem with it. But whereas both the cult and critique of chinoiserie emerged within Europe as a local response to imported products and aesthetic ideas, the conception of China as an uncooperative and potentially dangerous trading partner that took shape during the same period was formed in large measure by those European—and in the eighteenth century, predominantly British—merchants who actually visited Chinese port cities and experienced firsthand the conditions that prevailed there. In 1699, just one year before the faculty of the Sorbonne denounced the accommodationist creed of the China Jesuits, the British ship *Macclesfield* anchored at Macao, marking the foundation of the permanent East India Company trade at Canton.[9] The subsequent expansion of the China trade and its written record corresponded, as a result, to a decline in both the Jesuits' presence in China and the authority their accounts enjoyed in Europe. The gradual displacement of glowing missionary texts by the more skeptical writings of British merchants, sailors, and ambassadors as the predominant source of firsthand knowledge of China largely contributed to the reversal of China's fortunes in the public imagination over the course of the eighteenth century.

Hanway's attack on tea and the tea trade reflects, in part, a widespread hostility toward the East India Company and its operations that had been in evidence since the company's incorporation in the early seventeenth century and that was particularly pronounced during the protectionist controversies of its final decades.[10] But his characterization of China, and in particular Chinese tea, as a blood-sucking beast that threatened to cripple British industry and enslave the nation also reflects more specifically, I will suggest, an emerging set of attitudes toward Chinese trade policy and the conditions of trade at Canton among British visitors of the period. The Chinese, who showed little interest in European products or in securing foreign markets for their own, seemed to tolerate the presence of European merchant ships largely out of deference to the customs revenue they generated for the throne. Chinese laws promulgated over the course of the century restricted the foreign trade to the single port of Canton and imposed numerous other regulations that Europeans, not surprisingly, perceived as arbitrary, humiliating, and contrary to the commercial and diplomatic principles they increasingly took for granted. Foreigners were forbidden to study Chinese with native speakers, bring their wives to their factories on shore, trade with Chinese merchants outside the officially sanctioned monopoly trade group (the infamous Cohong), or petition officials directly regarding their accumulated grievances. Substantial bribes, presents, and fees were an inescapable part of doing business, and these, combined with the artificially low prices for British woolens and inflated prices for teas and silks established by the Cohong monopoly, squeezed profit margins to a point where the continued viability of the Canton trade fell frequently into doubt.[11]

If tea and its country of origin could be held responsible, as Hanway charged, for the enervation of British manhood, their life-draining force derived ultimately from China's economic obstructionism. British traders and diplomats, working within a model of cultural legitimacy that privileged circulation over stasis, discovered plentiful analogues to this obstructionism in every sphere of Chinese life. Among the most frequently recurring tropes in their firsthand accounts are images of artificial impediments not only to the natural flow of wealth but also of language, knowledge, and sentiment. The degree of restriction and constraint that seemed to define the most basic human interactions in China offended the sensibilities of English visitors and contributed to a widespread view of the empire's moral and political culture as backward, corrupt, and tyrannical. The systematic degradation of the once sacrosanct idea of Chinese authority in these writings, together with its simultaneous deflation in the frivolities of chinoiserie, contributed to the patronizing and imperious attitude toward China that took root at the turn of the nineteenth century and that ultimately set the stage for the Opium Wars.

The Legitimacy of Commerce

The ideal of free circulation that functions as the implicit standard of cultural legitimacy in these British accounts derived from an established tradition, dating back to at least the late sixteenth century, that proposed the vitality of trade as the paramount measure of a society's greatness.[12] By the eighteenth century, this commercial ideal had achieved broad cultural acceptance, becoming something of a literary commonplace in well-known writings of the period. Although they lacked the sophistication of an Adam Smith, ideological predecessors including Addison, Defoe, and Lillo advanced the premises of his analysis in their passionate advocacy of mercantile activity as an a priori social good.[13] In their enthusiastic depictions of trade, these writers delineate a system of cultural value that closely resembles the idealized notions of linguistic, religious, and aesthetic legitimacy described in previous chapters and that, I will argue, provided a similar kind of conceptual framework for making sense of the vexing enigmas China posed in the commercial sphere.

The central defining feature of this new commercialist literature is the degree to which it not only foregrounds trade but accords it a foundational, axiomatic status with respect to civilized society. Like a philosophically grounded ideograph, an ancient moral precept, or a balanced and harmonious artistic form, the principles of trade originate in a divinely given natural order of things. In an issue of his *Review* of 1713, for example, Defoe proposes "a kind of divinity in the original of trade." God himself has ordained trade as part of "the order of nature," has accordingly "prepared the world for commerce," and "seems to expect trade should be preserved, encouraged, and extended by all honest and prudent methods."[14] The prosperous merchant Thorowgood in George Lillo's *The London Merchant* (1731) concurs with such a view when he advises his young admirer Trueman that "the method of merchandise" is more than just a means for acquiring wealth. " 'Twill be well worth your pains to study it as a science, see how it is founded in reason and the nature of things."[15] And in his overview of European economic history in Book III of *The Wealth of Nations*, Adam Smith relies repeatedly on phrases such as "the nature of things," "the natural course of things," and the "natural order of things" to establish his central dichotomy between "unnatural" feudal institutions and the "natural" inclination toward commercial activity that they thwarted for so long.[16] Defoe, Lillo, and Smith, in other words, assert a legitimacy for trade based on its derivation from originary, transhistorical principles of human nature and society.

A second common element in the legitimizing myths discussed up to this point is the claim to universality. The Chinese written language fascinated European observers in large part because of its apparent ability to transcend linguistic barriers and serve as a universal symbology among China's neighbors. Similarly, the underlying premise of Ricci's accommodationist enterprise was that certain forms of religious representation retained their significance across cultural boundaries. Even the classicist critics of chinoiserie, although less tolerant than the China Jesuits in the promulgation of their creed, similarly pretended to its universal validity, admitting no relativist accommodation of Chinese differences in taste. There could be only one true standard of aesthetic merit, and those unfortunate artists in nations beyond the reach of Roman influence were damned, like Dante's pagans, through their own blameless ignorance.

The most common argument in defense of foreign trade similarly invokes the universal validity of its principles. Commerce emerges as the universal language of the mercantile age, with its promises of reciprocal advantage for trading partners smoothing over the potential for conflict in much the same way that the schemes for a lingua franca tirelessly promoted by seventeenth-century language projectors were to have defused religious discord in Europe. Thorowgood's paean to trade in *The London Merchant*, to take but one prominent example, invokes Addison's famous description of the Royal Exchange in its glowing evocation of this mercantile *pax humana*. Trade "has promoted humanity as it has opened and yet keeps up an intercourse between nations far remote from one another in situation, customs, and religion; promoting arts, industry, peace, and plenty; by mutual benefits diffusing mutual love from pole to pole."[17]

Although Adam Smith, recognizing the potential for its abuse, is somewhat more circumspect in his approval of foreign trade, he, too, acknowledges the universality of its appeal. "That trade which, without force or constraint, is naturally and regularly carried on between any two places, is always advantageous, though not always equally so, to both." Even in the contrary case of colonialist outrages, Smith anticipates Marx in suggesting that an increase in foreign commerce presents the most likely remedy for the sufferings of a weaker nation on the grounds that its benefits, even if deferred, will eventually extend to its original victims. For brutalized colonies to earn the respect of the stronger European nations would require a strength on par with their colonizers, and "nothing seems more likely to establish this equality of force than that mutual communication of knowledge and of all sorts of improvements which an extensive commerce from all countries to all countries naturally, or rather necessarily, carries along with it."[18]

Finally, eighteenth-century advocates of commerce affirm its role as a guarantor of social order and stability. Those essentially conservative principles, geared to the preservation of authority and privilege, that Ricci admired in Confucianist social hierarchies and the classicists attached to hierarchies of taste, trade writers recognized as grounded in property rights and the commercial activity that flowed from them. For Defoe, the right of subjects to honest labor and the honest possession of what they have earned "is the foundation of what we call law, liberty, and property, . . . [and] the true foundation of order in the world," and he paints a grim picture of the social anarchy that would follow upon a cessation of trade in England. "The poor would eat up the rich; the land would not feed the multitude; your rich trading and encroaching neighbours would hire and entertain all your youth, who would fly to them for bread, and being armed by them, would come back and conquer you."[19] A contemporary tract on the importance of the East India trade provides the historical con-text for such a prognosis. The barbarity of the Britons of Caesar's day, the anonymous author reminds his readers, was owing to their being strangers to trade; if the modern trade were ever to fail, England would follow the rest of the world and "return to our primitive State of Ignorance, Poverty, and Barbarism."[20]

Such visions of social devolution imply that although trade contributes, in this paradigm, to maintaining certain aspects of the political status quo, its historical impetus is fundamentally progressive. Linguistic, religious, and aesthetic ideals of legitimacy, as I have argued, hearkened back to an originary moment of representational purity that, far from being in need of improvement, required a never-ending struggle to preserve or restore. Their advocates, as a result, were essentially conservative in outlook and hostile to the prospect of change: one need only think of Ricci's rejection of the modern tradition of Confucianist exegesis, Johnson's reaction to recent depredations upon the English language, or Shaftesbury's repudiation of fashionable trends in the decorative arts. The defenders of trade, on the contrary, celebrate its role as an indefatigable instrument of progress and one that has propelled modern nations on the trajectory from barbarism to civilized prosperity. Although the first principles of trade may be grounded in a transcendent "natural order of things," the crucial point of historical reference to the mercantile mind is in the future rather than in the past. For Smith, "the great purpose" of a society's economic activity is "the progress of the society towards real wealth and greatness."[21] The best measure of the legitimacy of an economic system, then, is its effectiveness in driving a society toward that aim.

The great motor of this economic progress, the principle by which wealth is perpetually multiplied and the continued growth of a national economy is assured, is the circulation of capital and of knowledge, fashion, and ideas. Again, while this is not an idea that is new to the eighteenth century—Dryden refers to the circular flow of trade in his *Annus Mirabilis* of 1667—the conflation of economic and physiological usages of the term reaches an apotheosis in this period. Prior to the first English translation of William Harvey's treatise on the circulation of blood in 1653, according to the *OED*, the verb "to circulate" referred primarily to processes of rotation and distillation. The expanded sense of circular movement through a complex system was invoked increasingly with reference to both blood and money in the following decades, and by 1691 the relationship between these two forms of "circulation," as the lines quoted in the epigraph make clear, was explicit.[22] Defoe devotes an entire issue of his *Review* to the topic of "Circulation in Trade" and a vigorous defense of the proposition that "circulation is the life of general commerce." Like blood flowing through the body, the perpetual motion of trade goods over England's highways sustains and enriches the nation. By way of example he famously describes the production of a single suit of clothes and the labor of the hundred families of farmers, staplers, clothiers, shalloon-makers, spinners, weavers, shippers, merchants, carriers, and various middlemen that earn part of their subsistence thereby. "The circulation of trade in England," he concludes, "is the life and being of all our home trade. By this means one man employs a thousand—and all the thousand employs him."[23]

Defoe's amalgamation of financial and biological metaphors is complicated further still by the anonymous author of the East India trade tract cited earlier. In a spirited defense of the East India Company against the widespread charge that its exotic imports promoted luxurious extravagance and moral corruption, he adapts the notion of a healthy and productive process of transformative exchange underlying Defoe's model to the world of taste and fashion. Taking his cue from Mandeville, he argues that the importation of exotic goods is a necessary consequence of economic prosperity and indeed a condition of its continuation.

Men's Tastes, like all other Parts of Nature, require Variety and Change; the very Air we live by would be fatal, without a fresh Succession, and a new Circulation. No Part of the World can vie with the East-Indies, in the Variety and Goodness of its Product, and consequently no Trade can so well humour and satisfy the Pleasures of every Man's arbitrary state. Fashion and Custom, and indeed the Nature of Things, having fix'd and set a Value on the East-India Goods, they are become necessary to all the nations of Europe; and Men can be no more restrain'd from them, than they can from their Food and Raiment.[24]

If the new consumerist demand for constant variety and change is grounded in the nature of things, so too, apparently, is the role of East Asia in supplying this demand. As I will suggest below, it is China's steadfast refusal to conform to this "natural" role and to accommodate Western notions of free circulation that gives rise to the commercialist denigration of Chinese cultural institutions over the course of the eighteenth century.

At the same time, however, the period's belief in the universal appeal of trade sustained an implicit hope and even expectation that China might eventually recognize the benefits of joining in the "mutual Intercourse and Traffick among Mankind" according to the commonly accepted rules. The forceful means of opening China's doors to foreign trade that would eventually prevail in the nineteenth century received little serious consideration prior to the Amherst embassy of 1816. This was partly owing to self-interested strategic concerns: British officials feared that military coercion "would not only miscarry, but be productive of the most fatal Consequences" for existing trade.[25] But a patient optimism also contributed to their restraint: as Lord Macartney wrote during his own embassy of 1793–1794, "Our present interests, our reason, and our humanity equally forbid the thoughts of any offensive measures with regard to the Chinese, whilst a ray of hope remains for succeeding by gentle ones."[26] The gentler measures of earlier decades had entailed adapting as best as possible to existing Chinese regulations while at the same time vigorously proselytizing on behalf of a Western circulatory creed.

British advocates of an expanded overseas commerce believed, indeed, with a nearly missionary zeal in the mutual benefits that would accrue to equal partners in foreign trade and were as baffled as many a religious missionary has been since by the apparent inability of the Chinese to recognize their own best interest in the matter.[27] Although it was a lesson the Dutch had learned much earlier, the British didn't fully grasp until the end of the eighteenth century that exasperated foreigners pounding on the gates of Canton were unlikely to prove the most effective advocates of European mercantile interests. The three formal embassies to the Chinese emperor sponsored by the British Crown between 1787 and 1816 signaled a belated recognition that for the merchants' case to be heard at all, it would have to be presented in a time, place, and manner dictated by Chinese ceremonial usage.[28] All three embassies ultimately failed in their mission, but the Crown's very persistence in pursuing them suggests the depth of their promoters' faith in the rational appeal of their commercialist creed. If only the proper channels of communication could be found, they assumed, the Chinese would awaken to the providential reason that stood behind the tradesman's mantra of commerce, circulation, and progress.

The frontispiece to Sir George Staunton's exhaustive account of the Macartney embassy evokes something of the evangelical optimism that inspired the expedition (see figure 19). According to an explanatory note,

19. Frontispiece to George Staunton's *Historical Account of the Embassy to the Emperor of China*, 1797. Courtesy of the University of Michigan Libraries.

the plate represents "the Earl of Macartney's Entrance into China, introduced by a Mandarine. In the back ground are Cities, Canals, &c. The three Figures, between the Mandarine and the Female representing Commerce, are Soldiers of the Emperor."[29] As Commerce pulls back a drape to reveal the prosperous landscape beyond the portal, the Chinese official, having apparently been won over by British diplomatic tact, beckons the ambassador to step into the scene and partake of its offerings. To judge from the landscape that opens before him, the ambassador has no further need for the lengthy disquisition on the virtues of economic circulation he has undoubtedly prepared for the occasion: he would be preaching to the converted. The two prominent waterways that divide the scene are filled with vessels of every size and description, while the sturdy bridge crossing the canal at its center provides a link between the prosperous city and the fertile farmland surrounding it. Two towering pagodas identify the setting as unmistakably Chinese, while at the same time, in their ironic allusion to Chambers's contribution to the Royal Gardens at Kew, recalling Britain's reliance on the circulation of exotic fashions to sustain the vitality of trade.

King George III himself, in the preparations for Macartney's embassy, indulged a similarly optimistic fantasy concerning the possibilities of Chinese commerce. In his letter to the ambassador conveying the king's commands, Home Secretary Henry Dundas makes clear that His Majesty's purpose in undertaking the embassy is to further the commercial interests of British merchants and, by extension, the greater interests of the kingdom. The rhetoric of mutuality, however, within which he frames these interests situates the embassy squarely within the discursive framework of commercialist legitimacy observed in Defoe, Lillo, and Smith. In his conversations with the emperor, the Crown's ambassador is to avoid delicate political subjects and to stress instead "the mutual benefits to be derived from a trade between the two nations." In the unlikely case that he encounters resistance stemming from "jealousy" on the part of the Chinese, he is instructed

to obviate it by declarations the most free and unqualified, that in seeking to improve our connections with China, we have no views but the general interests of humanity, the mutual benefit of both nations, and the protection of our Commerce under the Chinese Government . . . upon a permanent principle equally beneficial to the subjects of both countries.[30]

The ideal of circulation and exchange that informs this letter extends beyond the immediate goal of a more favorable trade relationship to encompass the transmission of scientific and cultural knowledge. The king intends the embassy to China in the spirit of a voyage of reciprocal discovery and hopes it will begin both "to communicate and receive the benefits which must result from an unreserved and friendly intercourse between that Country and his own."[31] As a means of encouraging the mutuality of this exchange, the king proposes to send with the embassy experimental instruments and "models of the latest inventions" that "cannot fail to gratify a curious and ingenious people." Technological marvels had long been a favorite device of the Jesuits for enhancing the reputation of European learning among the Chinese; like the missionaries who preceded them, the king's diplomats hoped through their displays of scientific and technical mastery to promote the acceptance of Western ideas by the Chinese court. But by its very nature, the doctrine imported by these later visitors promised a degree of reciprocality that the Jesuits could never have countenanced. As much as Ricci and his peers might have respected Confucian learning and accommodated elements of it within their presentation of Christianity, their ultimate purpose in China was the conversion of the emperor and his subjects to Roman Catholicism. The king's catechism, in contrast, and the ethos of free circulation that it embodied, suggested a commerce of goods and knowledge that would enrich and transform both parties to the exchange. "So liberal a procedure," Dundas writes, "may probably obtain in return, a free inspection, as well as models of their numerous inventions, together with accounts and descriptions of their most valuable arts and Manufactures and Specimens of their most useful productions."[32]

Such language, in another context, might well evoke the specter of imperialist exploitation, and, indeed, as James Hevia points out, "Macartney was an exemplary representative of British imperial ambitions" who would fantasize during his embassy about the British conquest of the Chinese navy. At the end of the eighteenth century, however, the imperialist found little encouragement for his ambitions here: China remained a formidable adversary in the minds of British strategists and an unlikely arena for a restaging of recent South Indian exploits.[33] There was certainly no question of condescending to the Chinese emperor. The more pressing concern for the British was how to present their barbarian monarch as worthy of being considered his equal in Chinese eyes. Rather than read it teleologically as a euphemistic conceit in the service of veiled expansionist designs, then, it seems more useful to read the pervasive language of free communication and mutuality in the embassy documents as a reflection, above all, of the preeminence of the circulatory ideal within the basic interpretive framework that conditioned this stage in the encounter.[34] Just as a paradigm of linguistic legitimacy shaped European responses to the Chinese script, so too a version of this commercialist ideal, I would argue, informs the vast majority of trade-related accounts of China published in England over the course of the eighteenth century. Viewed through this lens, Chinese attitudes and social institutions appear cramped, constrained, and in every respect inimical to the unquestioned values of a modern mercantile society. The reaction of individual English visitors typically combines frustration, puzzlement, boredom, and even contempt. But China's stubborn unassimilability within an interpretive model privileging the free circulation of cultural commodities had a larger consequence: a growing consensus that Chinese illegitimacy in the religious and aesthetic spheres was fatally mirrored in the economic, social, and political as well.

Chinese Trade Policy

Signs of consternation temper the optimism of the Macartney embassy from the outset. The phalanx of armored foot soldiers guarding the entrance to the Chinese scene in the Staunton frontispiece casts a shadow of doubt over the wondrous commercial prospect that is displayed before the ambassador's eyes. Although the Chinese official seems to invite him forward to inspect the scene, the soldiers stand directly blocking his path and appear markedly less welcoming in their mien than the obliging Lady Commerce and her cherubs. The artist seems to have taken a hint from the same bleak reports on the foreign-trade situation in China that had suggested the need for an embassy in the first place. The official reason, after all, that the king hoped to "cultivate a friendship and increase the communication with China" was that the relationship had proven so unsatisfactory in the past. As Dundas notes in his letter to Macartney,

Hitherto . . . Great Britain has been obliged to pursue the Trade with [China] under circumstances the most discouraging, hazardous to its Agents employed in conducting it and precarious to the various interests involved in it. The only place where His Majesty's Subjects have the privilege of a Factory, is Canton. The fair competition of the market is there destroyed by Associations of the Chinese — Our Supercargoes are denied open access to the Tribunals of the Country, and to the equal execution of its Laws, and are kept altogether in a most arbitrary state of depression, ill suited to the importance of the concerns, which are entrusted to their care, and scarcely compatible with the regulations of Civilized Society.[35]

The limitation of the British trade to Canton, its control by the local merchant monopoly, and restricted access to legal redress constituted formi-

20. *The Western Factories at Canton*, Chinese artist, 1790s. Gouache, 17 ¼ × 23 in. Courtesy of Martyn Gregory Gallery, London.

dable impediments to the principle of free circulation that alone could provide a legitimate basis, in the British view, for a "civilized" commercial relationship. Although the embassy approached China with a clear mandate to foster "full and free communication" between the two nations, it did so in the knowledge that China had proven consistently hostile to an "unreserved and friendly intercourse" in the past. This had been amply demonstrated by the cold reception afforded earlier Dutch and Portuguese embassies to China and the dashing of their unrealistically high expectations for establishing profitable trade partnerships there.[36]

The issue of trading privileges had long been the primary point of dispute. Although the East India Company was itself a monopoly trade association protected by British law against unregulated competition, its agents insisted that the existence of a counterpart organization at Canton constituted an unfair restriction on their freedom to trade with whomever they pleased. As early as 1704, English supercargoes were complaining about the Chinese regulation of international commerce. In doing so, they evoke a by-now-familiar figure of foreign illegitimacy:

A new monster [has] sprung up at Canton called an Emperor's Merchant, who having given 42,000 Tales at Court for his employment is invested with authority to ingross the whole Trade with the Europeans, and that no China Merchant shall presume to interfere with him, unless for a valuable consideration he shall admit him to partnership . . . it may be hop'd this new Monster in trade may be kept from doing us a Prejudice this Season.[37]

The monstrous, once again, is an emblem of the inassimilable alien. The "monstrosity" of the emperor's merchant stems from his unaccountable ability to interfere so brazenly with the legitimate pursuits of Western traders and the profitability of the company's enterprise. He is a close cousin, in this respect, of the economically rapacious, many-headed monster Hanway would see some fifty years later in Chinese tea. They are related both to one another and to the monsters of Jesuit and classicist diatribes by their defiance of the founding premises of a dominant cultural discourse and, of course, by their association with China, a site of imaginative projection that increasingly takes on the role in the eighteenth century of a universal nemesis in opposition to which such discourses come to be defined.

Contemporary commentators on Chinese trade practices typically account for the frustration of British merchants by pointing to Chinese departures from the three tenets of the commercialist creed outlined above: conformity with natural law, universality, and social authority. In a chapter on agricultural economy in *The Wealth of Nations*, Adam Smith presents China as an example of a nation whose economic policies, unlike those of modern European states, favor agriculture over manufactures and foreign trade. "The Chinese," he writes, "have little respect for foreign trade," and have been known to dismiss it as "Your beggarly commerce!" in talks with Western envoys. While he concedes that China may actually have little need for foreign products, his teleological view of economic progress as the great purpose of every society leads him to consider artificial constraints on foreign trade, whatever their origin, as an unnatural and illegitimate imposition. "Foreign trade, therefore, is, in China, every way *confined* within a much narrower circle than that to which it would *naturally* extend itself, if more freedom was allowed to it" (emphasis added).[38] The degree of freedom allowed the naturally expansive impulse to pursue wealth through trade, in other words, provides a measure of the legitimacy of a nation's economic policy, a measure by which China must fall miserably short.

If Chinese policy gives insufficient leeway to economic instinct, it also fails properly to appreciate the universality of the advantages attending a more liberal attitude toward trade. Sir George Staunton, a member of the Macartney embassy, speculates that Chinese hostility to foreign trade may be rooted in "ancient prejudices to strangers" and the need to "prevent the contaminating powers of bad examples among their own people." In terms that might seem familiar to modern soccer fans, he points in particular to a long-standing Chinese prejudice against John Bull stemming from "those unrestrained emanations of liberty and independence too frequently indulged in by the natives of Britain." Such displays no doubt reinforced the moral condescension of Chinese officials toward Western merchants, whom, according to Staunton, they were advised to indulge "only from motives of humanity and benevolence, not from necessity or inclination on their part, nor any mutual benefit to be derived."[39] As long as the Chinese merely tolerated foreign trade as an act of charity toward pitiable barbarians, they could hardly be expected to pursue it with the zest and zeal of a nation that properly appreciated the reciprocal advantages a "mutual traffic and intercourse among mankind" might entail.

The economic and moral barriers to an expanded trade with China identified by Smith and Staunton were widely seen to be reinforced by a third, political source of obstruction in the nature of the Chinese government itself. In England, the ideal of a healthy, unobstructed commerce derived its aura of legitimacy in large measure from its perceived association with existing political structures and ideals; it followed that the state, in turn, had an obligation to protect and encourage commerce. In China, the dynamics of this relationship appeared, in British eyes, to be inverted. Here, the state interfered with trade, and the disruption of natural processes of economic circulation undermined the credibility and, ultimately, the stability of political institutions. A parliamentary committee on the East India Trade, concerned to repudiate the suggestion that difficulties in China were to "be entirely attributed to the Want of Ability and Exertion of the Traders themselves," places the blame instead on state interference and "the Nature of the Chinese Government, which is the most corrupt in the Universe."[40] Whatever the reason behind the government's restrictive policies, it was obvious to the committee that Chinese consumers and producers both stood to gain from access to foreign trade at a northern port and that the government's obstinacy in prohibiting such access evinced an unaccountable and inexcusable indifference to the economic well-being of the nation.

Obstructionism in Chinese Society

As I will argue later in this chapter, the perception of this indifference con- tributed to the progressive delegitimization of Chinese political authority in the eyes of British observers. But the more immediate consequence of British frustration with Chinese policies was its transformative effect on visitors' reactions to other aspects of Chinese society. In the accounts of traders and diplomats of the late eighteenth century, the economic metaphors of circulation and blockage are systematically transposed from the commercial context to intellectual, social, and linguistic spheres. Like Smith's image of the confinement in China of a potentially vital foreign trade to an unnaturally narrow circle or the parliamentary committee's evocation of the "cramped and humiliated" conditions under which it took place, the descriptions of daily life in China that one finds in these accounts convey a uniform sense of stifling oppressiveness and the unhealthy constraint of natural impulses. The governing standard of "naturalness" underlying such judgments was, obviously, as contingent a product of historical circumstance as the ideal of commercial legitimacy it helped to underwrite and was shaped by some of the same fundamental trends in English society: the development of a modern trade economy, the emergence of the bourgeois public sphere, and the ever-expanding currency of Enlightenment ideas of progress. From within such a cultural framework, China's seeming hostility to the circulatory impulse in the economic domain contributed to its consistent association in others with potent imagery of obstruction, languor, and tedious monotony. China, rather than moving forward on the wheels of innovation and trade, appeared trapped by a complacent sense of its own superiority in an increasingly irrelevant past.

John Barrow, the private secretary to Lord Macartney during his embassy to China in 1793, wrote on his return what is perhaps the most vivid and personal of the several accounts that appeared following the expedition. Where Staunton had concerned himself primarily with the "incidents and transactions" of the embassy itself, Barrow announces his intention to put aside Jesuit encomiums on Confucian cultural achieve- ment and "to shew this extraordinary people in their proper colours, not as their own moral maxims would represent them, but as they really are."[41] Not surprisingly, one of the first intimations of what this essential nature might be occurs in a discussion of commercial navigation. For

Barrow, the notorious indifference to foreign commerce among the Chinese was less a product of the economic, moral, and political considerations cited by earlier commentators than a simple matter of the inadequacy of their maritime technology and navigational skills. "Long voyages are never undertaken where they can be avoided," he notes, and the devastatingly high frequency of shipwrecks assures that "when a ship leaves [Canton] on a foreign voyage, it is considered as an equal chance that she will never return."[42]

A crucial factor contributing to these disappointing odds, in Barrow's mind, was the ironic failure of the Chinese fully to capitalize on their early invention of the compass. Whereas English voyages, as the king liked to boast, were graced with an aura of scientific legitimacy, Chinese navigational methods remained mired in "their most ancient and favourite mythology" (42). With every change in the weather, according to Barrow, Chinese sailors made offerings of incense to the magnetic needle of the ship's compass in a small temple set aside for the purpose. He describes with ironic relish the "compendium of . . . astronomical (perhaps more properly speaking) astrological knowledge" contained in concentric circles of characters surrounding the compass needle in its case (see figure 21). The second circle, for example, reveals "eight mystical characters denoting the first principles of matter, said to be invented by *Fo-shee*, the founder of the monarchy," the tenth contains "characters denoting the 28 signs of the Zodiac," while the twenty-forth and twenty-fifth are so obscure as to be "inexplicable even by the Chinese" (62–63). Like the nonsensical "ideographic" characters in the early Beauvais tapestries, Barrow's derisive treatment of Chinese written symbols both mocks and effectively subverts the legitimatizing reading of seventeenth-century sinophiles. Whereas Leibniz, Bayer, and others had struggled heroically to establish the systematic legibility of the *Yi Jing* and the ideographic etymology of Chinese characters, Barrow dismisses out of hand the very presumption of significant meaning in a text that so flagrantly violates the commercialist telos of its context.

Barrow is happy to concede the original invention of the compass to the Chinese and, indeed, takes some pains to reassert their claim in a footnote. But by thus emphasizing the blindness of the modern Chinese to the value of their early discovery, he only reinforces the impression of intellectual inertia he seeks to convey. That the compass languished for so many centuries in China as the untarnished idol of "long established superstitions" rather than evolving into a practical instrument of naviga-

21. Chinese geomantic compass, eighteenth century. Courtesy of the Whipple Museum of the History of Science, Cambridge University.

tion is no mere historical curiosity, but rather crucial evidence in Barrow's indictment of the Chinese character. A potent symbol, in the West, of ever-widening spheres of knowledge and commercial enterprise, the compass in China remains encased, along with the Chinese mind itself, within the rigid circles of half-forgotten myth.

The failure of inventions to bear fruit and of ships to return to port is mirrored by instances of blockage and stagnation on a more quotidian level. Even those forms of circulation essential to basic health and hygiene seem to be lacking. The "monstrous fashion" of foot binding is objectionable not only because it impedes a woman's own movement, robbing her "of one of the greatest pleasures and blessings of life," but also on sanitary grounds. "The interior wrappers of the ladies' feet are said to be seldom changed, remaining, sometimes, until they can no longer hold together; a custom that conveys no very favorable idea of Chinese cleanliness . . . they are what Swift would call a *frowzy* people" (76). From here matters only get worse, as Barrow indulges in a gratuitous elaboration of the essential frowziness that lurks beneath the polished surfaces of Confucian refinement.

> The comfort of clean linen, or frequent change of under-garments, is equally unknown to the Sovereign and to the peasant. . . . [Their] vestments are more rarely removed for the purpose of washing than for that of being replaced with new ones; and the consequence of such neglect or economy is, as might naturally be supposed, an abundant increase of those vermin to whose production filthiness is found to be most favourable. The highest officers of state made no hesitation of calling their attendants in public to seek in their necks for those troublesome animals, which, when caught, they very composedly put between their teeth. (76–77)

As in his systematic exposition of the symbology of a Chinese compass housing, Barrow here adopts a pose of objective description in order to ridicule the backwardness of Chinese society. The ironic juxtaposition of the high official and the lowly louse corresponds to that between the historical genius of the inventors of the compass and the travesty of its modern use; both pairings effect an abrupt deflation of the presumptive claim to cultural accomplishment and dignity that the compass and official would seem to assert. And in both cases, the backwardness evoked by shipwrecks and lice seems to stem from a pervasive triumph of the static over the dynamic, a fundamental failure of Chinese civilization to accommodate movement and change. If superstition in China has never given way to science and personal habits have never benefited from the use of soap, the root cause would seem to be a glaring absence of that principle of circulation—whether of ships, ideas, clothing, or commerce—that sustains the superior rank of civilization in the West.

Although Barrow allows occasional exceptions to the rule, it is only in the service of this kind of deflationary parody. The one prized article that does circulate with notable efficiency is human waste. But the author's seeming praise for the resourcefulness and frugality of the Chinese in their management of manure is tempered by the substantial irony in the elevation of filth to the status of circulating commodity.

Although Pekin cannot boast, like ancient Rome, or modern London, of the conveniences of common sewers to carry off the dirt and dregs that must necessarily accumulate in large cities, yet it enjoys one important advantage, which is rarely found in capitals out of England. . . . Each family has a large earthen jar, into which is carefully collected every thing that may be used as manure; when the jar is full, there is no difficulty of converting its contents into money, or of exchanging them for vegetables.

The absence of the healthy, civilized forms of circulation promoted by sewers and proper hygiene has left the Chinese stagnating in their own excrement for so long that it has become the currency of a perversely thriving secondary economy in its own right. Although a form of free-market circulation thus flourishes in the gutters of China, the payoff for the larger social body has come in the form not of prosperity but a pestilential stench (98–99).

Even when commerce climbs out of the gutter it remains tainted with the imagery of death. Had it only been set in London, the lively market scene that Barrow describes inside the city gate of Peking might well have evoked reflections more consistent with Defoe's rhapsodic rendering of economic circulation as a life-sustaining natural process. He finds shops and warehouses lining both sides of a wide street, colorfully decorated signposts, and houses "not less brilliant in the several colours with which they were painted, consisting generally of sky blue or green mixed with gold." But the seemingly vibrant spirit of the marketplace is unstrung by a dissonant chord. "What appeared to us singular enough, the articles for sale that made the greatest show were coffins for dead" (94–95). Like fecal currency or a state minister's lice, a thriving market in coffins presents a jarring incongruity that radically unsettles the implicit legitimacy of its context. Where circulation has degenerated into a monstrous parody of itself, a social stagnation follows in which only the dead can thrive.

In a country where the state of hygiene and commerce converge in the figure of the coffin, the mind could hardly be expected to soar. At the four principal intersections of the city, according to Barrow, "were erected those singular buildings, sometimes of stone, but generally of wood, which have been called triumphal arches" (95). These are the same monuments, it will be recalled, whose implicit homage to political legitimacy was so playfully subverted by English garden architects. Barrow com-

pounds their degradation through his judgment that there is little suggestion of triumph, political, aesthetic, or otherwise, in their execution, but
only a deadly dullness. "They are neither objects of grandeur nor ornament, having a much closer resemblance to a gallows than to triumphal
arches, as the missionaries, for what reason I know not, have thought fit
to call them" (328).

The gallows analogy, besides resonating with the coffins in the marketplace, suggests an essential depravity of design familiar from earlier
characterizations of chinoiserie. Indeed, Barrow's description of other
instances of Chinese sculpture as "grotesque images of ideal beings, and
monstrous distortions of nature" could have been lifted from any of a
number of classicist diatribes. But his assessment of the arches' singular
lack of grandeur and ornament, along with his claim that the empire contained "not a statue, a hewn pillar, or a column that deserves to be mentioned," points to a strikingly different basis for Barrow's contempt.
From the perspective of Fénelon, Shaftesbury, or indeed of William
Chambers, it was precisely the exuberant disregard for naturalistic representation that characterized the aesthetic method of Chinese and Chinese-
inspired arts. Barrow, in contrast, has no quarrel with Chinese standards
of verisimilitude. Chinese painters, he writes, are such "scrupulous copy-
ists" that "it is impossible to imitate the brilliant colours of nature more
closely." Rather, it is precisely in this imitative acuity that they fail in their
art and reveal an insidious form of blockage afflicting the Chinese spirit.
In creating their works, Chinese artists

exercise no judgment of their own. Every defect and blemish, original or accidental, they are sure to copy, being mere servile imitators, and not in the least feeling
the force or the beauty of any specimen of the arts that may come before them; for
the same person who is one day employed in copying a beautiful European print,
will sit down the next to a Chinese drawing replete with absurdity. (327–28)

It is not the absurdity per se of such a drawing that repulses him so much
as the lack of originality in its rendering of the absurd. Without the vigorous circulation of artistic ideas that sustains innovation and experiment, Barrow seems to imply, aesthetic judgment winds up swinging from
the gallows of conformity.

The obstruction of the creative faculties in China is not limited to the
visual arts. In his own personal journal of the embassy, Lord Macartney
points to systematic constraints on the free flow of invention and ingenuity arising from an excessive deference for tradition and firmly reinforced

by mandates from the highest levels of society. The emperor himself, Macartney discovers in the course of negotiations, is strictly observant of the invariable laws and usages of China and perpetually "upon his guard against the slightest appearance of innovation." In practical matters as well, it was "the policy of the present government to discourage all novelties," so that when a Chinese merchant commissioned the construction of a ship based on English models, local officials "not only forced him to relinquish his project but made him pay a considerable fine for his delinquency in presuming to depart from the ancient established modes of the Empire."[43]

Neither Macartney's famed negotiating skills nor the king's technological marvels succeeded, in the face of such attitudes, in igniting Chinese interest in the "unreserved and friendly intercourse" that the British so desperately sought. They tried once again with an embassy headed by Lord Amherst in 1816. But Henry Ellis, third commissioner and chronicler of this final attempt to bring China into the fold of international commerce by peaceful means, largely corroborates the findings of his predecessors on the crippling burden of Chinese tradition. "The influence of established usage," he writes, is so numbingly omnipotent that even "the despotism of the sovereign is subordinate to the despotism of manner." Like Barrow, he finds that this rigid adherence to custom has had a devastating effect on the Chinese imagination, an effect he describes by extending Adam Smith's diagnosis of the constricted state of foreign commerce in China to the intellectual sphere. "The mind would seem to be treated here like the feet of the women, cramped by the bandages of habit and education, till it acquires an unnatural littleness."[44] The vast and once awe-inspiring edifice of Chinese cultural achievement becomes in this view a stifling crypt impervious to the light of progress. The greatest "obstacle to intellectual improvement" is an "inordinate respect for remote antiquity," especially as embodied in the classical canon. Referring to a notorious book-burning episode in Chinese history, Ellis speculates that "if Tsin-chi-hoang-ti, the Chinese Omar, had succeeded in destroying all the books in his empire, posterity would have had [no] reason to regret it. Chinese literature still remains a cumbrous curiosity, and a melancholy instance of the unprofitable employment of the human mind for a series of ages."[45] One envisions a mountain of musty tomes bearing down with crushing weight on a hapless Chinese scholar, his mind's natural instincts toward profitable employment subdued into a dull and obsequious passivity. The cumbrous curiosity of old books stands for Ellis in the same relation to the potential for circulation and profit as does Chinese tea for Jonas Hanway. Whether it is the industry of the English worker or the intellectual vitality of the Confucian savant that is at stake, the influence of Chinese culture seems uniformly to be one of stifling the universally expansive strivings of an essentially self-interested human spirit.

The effects of this cramping and constriction cast their pallor over the entire face of Chinese society. Although there are isolated sights and customs that capture each traveler's interest, the overall impression left by the legendary land of Marco Polo and the Kubla Khan on the minds of late-eighteenth-century English visitors is, rather remarkably, one of drab and tedious monotony. Tourism, like commerce, might be viewed as a form of circulation sustained by a taste for variety and difference. But where cultural mores have suppressed such a taste, the traveler's interest, too, must falter before the numbing prospects of conformity. China seems to bore its visitors by means of the same pervasive anticirculatory inertia that stifles the energies of its own artists and scholars. According to Barrow:

> The expectations of the man of science, the artist, or the naturalist, might perhaps be rather disappointed, than their curiosity be gratified, in travelling through this extensive country. . . . In China every city is nearly the same: a quadrangular space of ground is enclosed with walls of stone, of brick, or of earth, all built upon the same plan. . . . The temples are, nearly, all alike. . . . The manners, the dress, the amusements of the people, are nearly the same.[46]

William Chambers had condemned urban temple architecture in China for its lack of adherence to any discernable norm; Barrow, in contrast, finds fault here with its excessive uniformity. It seems unlikely that Chinese temple builders had dramatically altered their practices in the intervening decades. What the difference between the two men reveals, rather, is a shift in the conventions of cultural legitimacy that condition what they see. Chambers, the budding neoclassicist, observed a sorry disregard for "universal" principles of proportion and regularity. Barrow, the free-trade advocate, deplores the absence of that spirit of innovation so dear to the commercialist ethos. Chinese architecture is condemned in both cases as a flawed representational system that, like a Buddhist sutra or the fantastic figures enlivening a porcelain vase, flouts that projected standard on which cross-cultural legibility, at each historical moment, ultimately depends.

The great northern capital of Peking succeeds no better at captivating Barrow's interest. He spends two hours traversing the city by cart, but sees "little to engage the attention after the first five minutes. Indeed, a single walk through one of the broad streets is quite sufficient to give a stranger a competent idea of the whole city." Beyond the city walls, even the productions of nature and geography are vulnerable to this contagion of conformity. In the fifteen ancient provinces "the surface of the country . . . is subject to little variation," and Barrow himself observes "no very great variety nor number of subjects . . . in the department of natural history."[47] Henry Ellis, who had read Barrow's work, generalizes from Barrow's observations to describe a palpable social malaise afflicting the nation as a whole.

China, vast in its extent, produce, and population, wants energy and variety; the chill of uniformity pervades and deadens the whole: for my own part, I had rather again undergo fatigue and privations among the Bedouins of Arabia, or the Eeliats of Persia, than sail along, as we may expect, in unchanging comfort on the placid waters of the imperial canal.

By the end of his journey he has found his own "mind and spirit influenced by the surrounding atmosphere of dulness and constraint" and concludes his account with a dismissal of China as a "peculiar but uninteresting nation."[48] This radical reversal of the prevailing tropes of eighteenth-century exoticism denies China any claim to the widespread fascination with cultural difference that underpinned the entire genre of travel writing, transforming Marco Polo's extravagant tapestry of imperial grandeur and Jesuit monuments to the triumphs of Confucian civilization into a dreary panorama of unrelenting sameness. Patricia Meyer Spacks argues that the evolution of the idea and the experience of boredom has roots in the heightened expectations for variety and diversion engendered by the rapidly expanding capitalist economy of eighteenth-century Britain.[49] But if capitalism, by encouraging the desire for novelty, conditions the experience of Barrow's boredom in China, its constitutive metaphors provide the framework of cross-cultural interpretation suggested by such an experience. China could only appear uninteresting, that is, in the light of the same dream of free-flowing and mutually enriching commerce that had sanctified the expansion of the new economy for the readers of Defoe's *Review* and that had inspired England's embassies to China in the first place. The deadening chill that Ellis notes, the placid waters, the constrained atmosphere all suggest a breakdown in those "natural" processes of circulation that increasingly formed the basis of a society's legitimacy and worth.

Ellis attributes the "monotony" of the Chinese cultural landscape to the discrepancy in the pace of historical change in China and the West: "As centuries have produced less change in China than a generation in Europe, variety is not now to be expected."[50] Lord Macartney, pressing the matter further, attributes this lack of change not to an intrinsic failure or absence of the progressive impulse in China, but to an illegitimate and ultimately doomed attempt to obstruct an inexorable force of nature. Reflecting on the lack of interest in the embassy's scientific apparatuses, Macartney remains decidedly optimistic. The natural force of curiosity that would tend to favor technological exchange, he predicts, will eventually overcome the impediments of misguided policy and pride. "It is . . . in vain to attempt arresting the progress of human knowledge. The human mind is of a soaring nature and having once gained the lower steps of the ascent, struggles incessantly against every difficulty to reach the highest." In a footnote to this passage, he reaffirms with Popean certainty the deterministic logic of his position. "Whatever ought to be will be. The resistance of the adamant is insufficient to defeat the insinuation of a fibre. Time is the great wonder worker of our world, the exterminator of prejudice and the touchstone of truth. It is endless to oppose it."[51] The soaring aspirations of the human mind, combined with the relentless forces of history, come to guarantee, for Macartney, the universal validity of a commercialist standard of legitimacy and China's eventual acquiescence in its underlying ideals.

Macartney's vivid metaphor encapsulates the transformation in the prevailing view of China that accompanied this new standard. To an earlier generation of China watchers, situated in a more tumultuous era, it was not the flow of time but precisely the adamant-like qualities of Chinese culture, its historical inertia and social stability, that had appeared as an enviable touchstone of truth. In the eyes of a Matteo Ricci or a John Webb, it was the very antiquity of Chinese cultural institutions and their extraordinary resistance to the vagaries of historical change that had defined their seeming legitimacy. Their more progressively minded successors, in displacing the primacy of origins with the principle of circulation and the virtues of continuity with those of continual change, evolved a new standard of cultural legitimacy within which the peculiar notion of passing time as a stonelike emblem of enduring truth would appear not as a paradox, but as an article of faith.

The contrast between these two modes of response appears most plainly, perhaps, in the realm of language itself. At the end of the first chapter, I touched briefly upon eighteenth-century characterizations of Chinese speech that inverted the idealized terms in which the writing system had long been understood. Within the context of commercial and diplomatic encounters, the satirical critique of the soundness and reliability of the Chinese *parole* evolves into a condemnation of Chinese cultural norms as fundamentally at odds with the commercialist ideal of a free and transparent flow of information. Western visitors may have felt oppressed by an atmosphere of "dulness and constraint" in China, but they did not suffer its consequences directly: their own minds, if so inspired, might continue in their lofty flights. When it came to interacting with the Chinese people, however, in order to establish the "free communication" and promote the "acquisition and diffusion of knowledge" that their king desired, the authors of these accounts repeatedly found that the same oppressive inertia that thwarted the strivings of the Chinese spirit frustrated their communicative efforts as well. Not only was knowledge in China prevented from advancing, it was barred from freely circulating even in its current, sadly atrophied state. Official government policies played some role here, but unofficial recalcitrance, apparent dishonesty, and even the nature of the language itself contributed to a widely shared perception that by its very nature, Chinese society was implacably hostile to those forms of discursive freedom that would be the cornerstone of improved commercial relations.

Linguistic barriers, not surprisingly, posed the first obstacle to the English in making themselves understood. Although short-term visitors faced the greatest frustrations, even agents of the company who stayed on in Canton from season to season and traders who returned repeatedly were apt to be confounded in even the most conscientious attempt to overcome this initial barrier, for Chinese law prohibited native Chinese from instructing foreign barbarians in their language. Lord Macartney considered this a sufficiently serious impediment to British trade interests that he proposed a specific remedy among a list of requests to the viceroy of Canton in 1793: "That it be allowed to a Chinese to instruct the English Merchants, in the Chinese Language, a knowledge of which may enable them to conform more exactly to the Laws and Customs of China."[52] Macartney obviously hoped, as well, that basic competence in the language might enhance the efficacy of the perennial petitions and complaints directed by the English merchants to local Chinese officials.

Without it, foreigners were forced to depend on the notoriously unreliable native Chinese interpreters known as linguists. The trouble with these intermediaries was not so much incompetence as fear, and fear in particular of the Chinese officials to whom they were charged with conveying the barbarians' brazen and presumptuous appeals. Exasperated by their employees' rectitude, English supercargoes occasionally dispensed with their services altogether, calling on Chinese officials in person to present written statements of their demands. As they explained on one such occasion, "By this method we cannot be so lyable to be imposed upon as by conversing with him by a Linguist, They standing in such Awe of these great Mandareens they dare not tell them our true Sentiments, for fear it should be thought they instruct us." The interpreters' reticence was not entirely without grounds: it was not unknown for Chinese accused of translating offensive foreign petitions to be summarily beheaded for their pains.[53]

Troublesome as it was to communicate grievances to Chinese officials, the obstructions to the flow of information in the reverse direction were equally daunting. Its diplomatic circumspection notwithstanding, Macartney's claim that English merchants aspired to conform more closely to the letter of Chinese law contains an element of truth in its admission of a degree of perplexity in this regard. The failure of repeated attempts to clarify their legal rights and obligations proved a continual source of frustration for the English in Canton. Even the supercargoes who remained on site for years at a time expressed an almost Kafkaesque sense of confoundedness before the inscrutable face of Chinese authority:

> The Mandareens issue out their Chops or regulations for the Europeans, to which they expect obedience, altho' these remain unknown to them, either from inability of the Linguists, the selfish views or negligence of the Merchants, and thus it was the English were unacquainted with the Prohibition to lend Money in the Edict of the Year 1759, on which circumstance now depends the justice or impropriety of the claim to a debt that amounts to a million sterling.[54]

The parliamentary committee charged with reporting on the condition of the Eastern export trade in 1791 complained of a similar dearth of essential information. Two centuries of regular contact between China and Europe and the publication of innumerable descriptions of that empire had led the committee initially to suppose "that the fullest Information existed with regard to the internal Commerce of that Country." And yet, inexplicably, the requisite economic data proved wanting. "That vast Kingdom, with regard to its internal Commerce, is yet unknown to Europeans. . . . Whatever Gratification the Philosopher or the Antiquary may find in the Publications respecting this famous Empire, the Merchant can derive no Assistance from them." Whether China's opacity to European merchants was owing to their continued confinement to Canton or to the ignorance and restricted flow of information even among the Chinese traders who were their chief informants, the result was the utter failure of the committee to accomplish its mandate. "Your Committee cannot therefore obtain any particular Information upon which they can rely, relative to the various Situations and Descriptions of People in China who either do, or are likely to consume British Produce and Manufacture."[55] To the extent that the circulation of goods for profit, then as now, was premised on the free flow of market data, any systematic barrier to the transmission of reliable information inevitably undermined the legitimacy of the affected commercial arena.

One might argue that the committee's complaint, in this instance, simply reflected the reality of the vast geographical and cultural distance separating London parliamentary chambers and Chinese market squares. And yet it conforms with what is an incontestably larger pattern within English interpretations of Chinese society. According to Staunton, the Chinese merchants on whom the British relied for trade information were by no means the only citizens who were kept in the dark: "The government of China has not established any mode of conveying letters of correspondence for the conveniency of the people. . . . Information is conveyed to, or withheld from the body of the people, just as the government may deem it expedient."[56] Even more tellingly, perhaps, the same phenomenon extends in firsthand accounts to the level of individual encounters, suggesting that in the minds of their authors this information blockage is a real and intrinsic feature of the Chinese representational landscape. On occasion, it takes the form of simple conversational evasiveness, a rhetorical privileging of ornament over substance reminiscent of the extravagant flourishes of chinoiserie. Macartney recounts that after attending the emperor's anniversary festival, he took a long walk with the Grand Secretary Ho-shen through the imperial gardens in the hope of finding an opportunity to broach the official purpose of his embassy. Just as William Chambers might have predicted, however, the extravagant setting of the Chinese garden seems to have fulfilled its purpose by utterly confounding Macartney's own:

I could not help admiring the address with which the Minister parried all my attempts to speak with him on business this day, and how artfully he evaded every opportunity that offered for any particular conversation with me, endeavouring to engage our attention solely by the objects around us, directing our eyes to the prospects, and explaining the various beauties of the park and buildings.

Macartney's detailed description of these horticultural diversions suggests that they held considerable interest for him as well, and his writing in these descriptive passages occasionally rivals, in its vivid voluptuousness, the style of Chambers's *Dissertation*. The obstruction of commercialist circulation in such a setting, in other words, is not at all fortuitous. The Chinese garden not only distracts the gaze of its visitors with its stunning display—in Macartney's words—of "all the sublimer beauties of nature," it devours the very basis of legitimate business concerns in the obscure, irrational depths of the "gloomy pool and yawning chasm."[57]

Even beyond the walls of their enchanted gardens, a general hostility to reason among the Chinese appears a consistent obstacle to the forms of free communication the English visitors claim so to revere. According to Ellis:

The Chinese are so illiberal in their principles of action, and so unblushingly false in their assertions, that the soundest arguments are thrown away upon them. Denying both your general principles and your facts ad libitum, the Chinese defies all attempt at refutation; yet, though aware that duplicity and deceit are with him habitual and invariable, he has no hesitation in assuming the language of offended integrity when concealment is used by others.[58]

The charge of unblushing duplicity goes back a long way. Walter and Robins, in detailing Anson's misadventures at Canton, had first brought to public notice the notorious reputation of the native merchants for devious trade practices. "It were endless to recount," they write, "all the artifices, extortions and frauds which were practised on the Commodore and his people, by this interested race." They recount a number of them just the same, and after relating the discovery of live ducks stuffed with stones and pigs pumped full of water, they seem justified in their claim that "the tricks made use of by the Chinese to encrease the weight of the provision they sold to the [British man-of-war] Centurion, were almost incredible."[59] Macartney confirms that they "are not very scrupulous in regard to veracity, saying and unsaying without hesitation what seems to answer the purpose of the moment." Like their conversational evasiveness and their penchant for secrecy, the alleged dishonesty of the Chinese interferes with the natural processes of verbal circulation and exchange that sustain the commercialist ideal in the semiotic domain.[60]

More exactly than these other two sources of blockage, however, the charge of brazen mendacity inverts the earlier, idealized conception of the Chinese sign. Where the ideograph was held to be an originary and immutable symbol at once comprising and conveying the philosophical essence of a thing, the word of Chinese merchants and mandarins in these accounts is slippery, chameleonic, with no basis at all beyond that of immediate self-interest. But if such inconstant words imply a travesty of philosophical groundedness, they fail also as a medium of representational exchange. A business negotiation, while less exacting in its demands for linguistic stability than the earlier ideographic ideal, does require that individual signifiers retain a reasonably constant value through the course of any given transaction. The perceived dishonesty of the Chinese, in other words, violates both linguistic and commercialist standards of legitimacy. The anarchic representational universe it implies, like the wildest extravagances of the chinoiserie style, comes to stand in for the monstrosity of Chinese culture at the nadir of its fortunes in the public imagination of the West.

The motif of falseness as an obstruction to natural and legitimate forms of circulation applies not just to Chinese dealings with foreigners but also, and more disturbingly, to their most intimate interactions among themselves. The motive here is no longer intentional deception, but rather submission to what Ellis calls the "despotism of manner," the rigid regimen of ceremony and ritual that regulates even ordinary conversation and stifles the free expression of feeling at every level of Chinese society. For Western observers, not surprisingly, these two forms of falseness are closely linked. Although the Chinese had been praised for "the affected evenness of their demeanor, and their constant attention to suppress all symptoms of passion and violence," the systematic suppression of natural sentiments, according to Walter and Robins, encouraged habits of hypocrisy that led, in turn, to more blatant forms of deception.[61] Barrow, for his part, is less concerned with unmasking the essential moral laxity lurking behind the appearance of virtue than with lamenting the effects of constraining social conventions on the natural and salubrious circulation of sentiment and fellow feeling. Taking his cue from the eighteenth-century novel of sensibility, he sheds a compassionate tear over the segregation of husband and wife and even brothers and sisters in the typical Chinese household, surmising that "the feelings of affection, . . . the offspring of frequent intercourse and of a mutual communication of their little wants and pleasures, are nipped in the very bud of dawning sentiment. A cold and ceremonious conduct must be observed on all occasions between the members of the same family." But if the Chinese emperor's perplexing failure to reciprocate King George's desire for "an unreserved and friendly intercourse" between the two countries hearkens back to the deprivation of sisterly affection he suffered as a child, his indifference to trade may stem from an equally crippling atrophy of the enterprising spirit. "Boys, it is true, sometimes mix together in schools, but the stiff and ceremonious behaviour, which constitutes no inconsiderable part of their education, throws a restraint on all the little playful actions incident to their time of life and completely subdues all spirit of activity and enterprize."[62] Barrow rationalizes the failure of the embassy, in other words, by positing a deep-rooted social pathology as thoroughly implicated in China's economic backwardness as its overly restrictive trade policies.

The most damning consequence, though, of this system of social regulation was its effect on the public sphere, or, rather, on that space where a public sphere might have thrived were the circulatory impulse required to sustain it not so woefully impaired. In England, a lively "spirit of activity and enterprize" famously animated urban clubs, coffeehouses, and, as noted earlier, women's tea tables, both facilitating and embodying in the social domain the commercialist ideals of free interaction and exchange. The contrast with China is complete:

If all the little acts of kindness and silent attentions, that create mutual endearments, be wanting among the members of the same family, living under the same roof, it will be in vain to expect to find them in the enlarged sphere of public life. In fact, they have no kind of friendly societies nor meetings to talk over the transactions and the news of the day. . . . A Chinese having finished his daily employment retires to his solitary apartment. There are, it is true, a sort of public houses where the lower orders of people sometimes resort for their cup of tea or of *seau-tchoo* . . . but such houses are seldom, if at all, frequented for the sake of company.[63]

This apparent blindness to the pleasures of sociability, however incomprehensible to an English reader, is fully consistent with the sense of blockage and constraint that seemingly pervades, in these accounts, every aspect of Chinese society. A culture that systematically obstructs the circulation not only of ships and goods, linens and waste, but also of innovative ideas, information, and rational, reliable meanings in language could hardly be expected to encourage the public expression of the freewheeling passions of the mind and heart.

The Illegitimacy of Chinese Authority

Barrow plainly avails himself of such passages as these in part to advertise the liveliness in his own breast of those worthy sentiments he finds so sorely wanting in the Chinese. But his observations regarding Chinese social mores are by no means irrelevant to the purpose of Macartney's embassy, motivated as it was by his king's often-stated desire to extend the hand of fraternal affection to his Chinese counterpart. Not only does King George express his wish for an "unreserved and amicable intercourse" and "firm and lasting friendship" in his own letter to the emperor, he closes on a note of presumptive familiarity: "As We are Brethren in Sovereignty, so may a Brotherly affection ever subsist between Us . . . Vester bonus frater et Amicus Georgius R."[64] The letter of instructions Dundas prepared for Lord Macartney suggests a hope that the rhetorical promise of this salutation might actually be approached in deed:

> You will then assume the character and public appearance of His Majesty's Ambassador Extraordinary, and proceed with as much ceremony as can be admitted, . . . [conform] to all ceremonials of that Court which may not commit the honor of your Sovereign . . . [and] take care to express the high esteem which His Majesty has conceived for the Emperor from the wisdom and virtue with which his career has been distinguished.

Having addressed these necessary formalities, Dundas goes on, remarkably, to anticipate the possibility of a more intimate exchange: "It is not unlikely that the emperor's curiosity may lead to a degree of familiarity with you in conversing upon the manners or circumstances of Europe and other countries."[65] But in spite of an apparently earnest desire to encourage a constructive rapport with their Chinese counterparts, respectful friendship, let alone familiarity, turned out in practice to be a considerably more elusive goal than either Dundas or the king seem to have imagined. The primary hurdle was a misapprehension of the significance of the embassy from a Chinese perspective. Traditionally, foreign ambassadors appeared at the Chinese court as humble bearers of tribute from neighboring kingdoms. Dundas's vainglorious vision of Englishmen strutting before the dragon throne as the exalted emissaries of "brethren in sovereignty" could only appear within this context as the most preposterous presumption. A typical audience with the emperor consisted of a carefully scripted series of elaborate kowtow and gift-exchange rituals

and presented no opportunity for the "familiar" discussion of foreign policy issues that the English had counted on. For the Chinese, indeed, to
broach such matters was to violate the hierarchical order within which
the meaning of the embassy was construed.[66]

Both Staunton and Ellis report extensively on various attempts to
resolve the quandary in which their miscalculation had left the British.
For both embassies, the conflict came to a head over the issue of the kowtow, the Chinese insisting that the visitors conform precisely to the usages
of the Qing court as a condition of their reception, while the English
protested that prostrating themselves before a foreign monarch would be
unacceptably to compromise the dignity of their own. In Macartney's
case, tortured negotiations finally led to a compromise whereby the
English agreed to kneel upon one knee in the presence of the emperor.
Amherst didn't fare so well, however, and sharp disagreements over such
questions as what constituted an appropriately deferential posture before
the throne led to the abrupt dismissal of his embassy shortly after its
arrival at the Summer Palace.[67]

Both embassies set out to establish a basis for commercial and diplomatic circulation on a model of mutual accommodation and respect. Both
found themselves thwarted, to varying degrees, by the Chinese insistence
on a gesture of ritualized submission that seemed, to the British, directly
to undermine this effort. To begin with, Chinese tenacity on this point
suggested a stubborn traditionalism and resistance to innovation that in
itself ran contrary to the commercialist ideal. But more importantly, it
implied that the Chinese were complete strangers to the very notion of
mutuality in foreign relations. The emperor would never reciprocate the
British king's overtures of "brotherly affection" for the simple reason that
he could never accept the premise of their being "brethren in sovereignty." In order to appreciate the mutual advantages of communication
and commerce with the kingdom of the red-haired barbarians, he would
have to admit them as equal partners in any such exchange. But, as the
English rightly judged from his unrelenting demand that they knock their
heads on the ground nine times before his throne, this proved a conces-
sion he was unprepared to make.

The emperor's rejection, on both these counts, of the circulatory principle critically undermined, in the eyes of the embassy writers, the very
basis of his political authority. If commercialist doctrine celebrated trade
as the engine of economic prosperity, it also implied, as I have argued, a
more general link between circulation, social order, and political stability.

According to earlier, Jesuit-inspired accounts, Chinese political legitimacy was guaranteed by the very continuity of the state and its hierarchical structure across dynasties and over thousands of years. But by the late eighteenth century, the progressive impetus of the ever-advancing present had, in Macartney's terms, replaced historical continuity as the touchstone of truth, and fluid dynamism had replaced stasis and stability as the hallmark of legitimacy in every cultural sphere. A state, however venerable, that refused to accommodate the exigencies of this new world order, that rejected the mutuality of commerce and remained aloof from international affairs, would only be left behind to crumble under its own now insupportable weight.

Having condemned the blockage of circulation that afflicted every other aspect of life in China, in other words, these writers turned their sights on its political institutions, where the debacle over the kowtow ritual, in particular, resulted in an ominous portrayal of Chinese governing institutions as illegitimate in their authority and ultimately doomed. Not surprisingly, the English reacted with visceral repugnance to the very idea of the kowtow as insulting to their sovereign's dignity and their own. Staunton describes the ritual as an unambiguous exercise in self-humiliation:

> Believing the Majesty of the Emperor to be ubiquitary, [the Chinese] sacrifice to him when absent; it cannot, therefore, be surprising they should adore him when present. The adoration, or Koteou, consists in nine prostrations of the body, the forehead being made each time to touch the floor; which is not only a mark of the deepest humility and submission, but also implies a conviction of the omnipotence of him towards whom this veneration is made. . . . These abject prosternations are required not only from the subjects and tributary princes of the empire, but also from all strangers, however exalted.[68]

He refers to it later in his account as a "sacrifice of dignity," while Ellis quotes him as describing the ceremony as "incompatible . . . with personal and national respectability" and refers himself to a "possibility of personal or national degradation from performing the ceremony." And if this weren't enough, the example of an earlier Dutch embassy provided a poignant lesson on the dangers of a pragmatic capitulation. The Dutch, according to Barrow, had "meanly submitted to every degrading ceremony in the hope of obtaining profitable commercial advantages," only to complain afterward of "being treated with neglect, and of being dismissed without experiencing the smallest mark of favor."[69] Both British ambassadors, then, were determined not only to preserve national dignity

in negotiating a compromise solution but, more importantly, to insist on a degree of respect crucial to their vision of mutuality.

Their resolve, however, found its match in the emperor's propaganda machine. The English could do little, finally, to prevent their visit from being construed in the manner the Chinese found most fitting, and Macartney prudently kept his silence on discovering that the banners announcing his approach to the capital proclaimed him an "ambassador bearing tribute from the country of England." He could, however, negotiate the details of his own performance in court ceremonies. In one of the countless meetings with court officials prior to the day of the audience, he attempts to introduce a measure of mutuality in his insistence that

there must either be a reciprocity of ceremony, or that some striking characteristic should be established whereby to distinguish between a *compliment* paid on the part of a great INDEPENDENT SOVEREIGN, and the *homage* performed by TRIBUTARY princes; especially as already it had been endeavoured to confound them by giving the name of *tribute* to the British presents, as appeared by the inscriptions placed upon them by the Chinese.[70]

Lord Amherst, finding himself in similar circumstances some twenty years later, likewise proposed a symbolic gesture of reciprocity in order to emphasize the mutual basis of the exchange sought by the British king. He agreed to perform the kowtow ceremony on the condition that either a Chinese official of equivalent rank perform the same observances before a portrait of King George, or that the emperor agree to send a Chinese embassy to the British court. "The object of these conditions," according to the ambassador, "was, to prevent the proposed ceremony being construed into an act of homage from a dependent prince."[71] Such an interpretation would only reinforce existing barriers to free communication between the two courts; if the ritual could only be recontextualized as a neutral gesture of respect, the precedent might open the door to more profitable forms of circulation in the future.

As if the Qing court's rejection of the principle of mutuality were not enough, its "pride and haughty insolence" contributed in a second way to

22. (*opposite*) William Alexander, *The Emperor Ch'ien-lung being carried in procession to the Imperial audience tent at Jehol on 14 September 1793*. Color-wash drawing after a sketch taken on the spot by Lieutenant Henry W. Parish. © Copyright The British Museum.

undermining its legitimacy in English eyes. The court's extravagant displays of pomp, while they evoke admiring descriptions in some of the embassy accounts, do not simply fail to dispel their authors' views of the underlying stagnation of Chinese society, they actually tend to reinforce it. If healthy circulation, within the commercialist paradigm, brings wealth and prosperity, then its endemic obstruction could be held responsible for the myriad woes afflicting the minds and bodies of the Chinese people. If economic prosperity, to complete the equation, was the sine qua non of political stability, the Chinese state, it followed, could be perched on only the most feeble of foundations, namely, the enforced adherence of its subjects to degrading rituals of obeisance. On the basis of his experience at the Chinese court, Macartney ventured a damning explanation for the long-standing puzzle as to why the Chinese chose to limit the foreign trade to Canton. Their chief motive, he writes, "is their apprehension lest too great a communication with Strangers should interfere with that profound tranquility and that awful submission among all Classes of Men the maintenance of which is in truth the ever-present and only inalterable maxim of this government."[72] For the English to comply with the prescribed ceremonies in such a context would only serve to buttress, then, what they increasingly disdained as an illegitimate political authority. Both embassies had set out with a mandate to promote the circulation of goods and cultural capital between China and England. They paradoxically risked, however, reinforcing the existing barriers to such circulation by providing the government, through the example of their submission, with a further means of compensating for the absence of a legitimate basis for its rule.

The efforts of Macartney's predecessors, including the ill-fated Dutch embassies of the previous century, appear to Barrow to have backfired in just this way. In reviewing their uniform failure humbly to coax, charm, or cajole the Chinese court into granting their requests for trade privileges, he concludes: "It may, perhaps, be rather laid down as a certain consequence, that a tone of submission, and a tame and passive obedience to the degrading demands of this haughty court, serve only to feed its pride, and add to the absurd notions of its own vast importance."[73] It was a measure of the degree to which, in Barrow's view, the state not only thrived but also depended on this ritual submission of foreigners that the undaunted resistance of a stout-hearted Englishman should send it into paroxysms of morbid self-doubt. Two days after the emperor's birthday, he encountered an unusual scene in a courtyard of the palace.

On going as usual in the morning to the hall of audience, I found the doors shut and the old eunuch, who kept the keys, walking about in so sullen a mood that I could not get from him a single word. Different groupes of officers were assembled in the court-yard, all looking as if something very dreadful either had occurred, or was about to happen. Nobody would speak to me, nor could I get the least explanation of this extraordinary conduct, till at length our friend [the resident missionary] Deodato appeared with a countenance no less woeful than those of the officers of government, and the old eunuch. I asked him what was the matter? His answer was, We are all lost, ruined, and undone!

Intelligence had arrived from the emperor's summer residence at Gehol (present-day Chengde) that Lord Macartney, who was attending him there, had refused to comply with the usual kowtow ceremony in the absence of a reciprocal gesture on the part of the Chinese, and

that rather than do this they had accepted his offer to perform the same ceremony of respect to the Emperor as to his own sovereign. That although little was thought of this affair at Gehol, the great officers of state in the tribunal or department of ceremonies in Pekin were mortified, and perplexed, and alarmed; and that, in short, it was impossible to say what might be the consequence of an event unprecedented in the annals of the empire.[74]

For Barrow, the Chinese attachment to the rigid forms of ritualized diplomacy bespeaks a fundamental brittleness to Chinese political authority. Macartney's insistence on a degree of suppleness and accommodation as a first principle of diplomatic exchange exposes, in his secretary's view, the flawed premises of state power concealed behind the glory of the imperial throne.

Ellis elaborates Barrow's view of the court ceremonies as a form of hollow symbolism propping up a decrepit political edifice. "The great support of [the emperor's] authority," he affirms, "is the despotism of manner" that regulates its ritual reaffirmation. The strict observance of the kowtow ceremony on the part of foreign ambassadors in particular has a "direct . . . tendency to maintain his dignity in the eyes of his own subjects." The importance of this function of reinforcement becomes especially pronounced as the cracks in the dynastic edifice begin to show in the first decades of the nineteenth century. Referring, perhaps, to the anti-Manchu uprising led by religious sectarian Lin Qing in 1813, Ellis speculates that "the late civil commotions, which endangered not only the safety of his throne, but of his life, may render him averse to dispense with" the kowtow ceremony on the occasion of Amherst's embassy, in

that they make necessary "a more strict adherence on every point connected with the personality of the Sovereign than would be necessary in
more tranquil times."[75] The reason, the English came to surmise, that they
encountered such stubborn resistance to their proposals for modifying the
ceremony was that the symbolism of their embassy has been appropriated to buttress a faltering regime.

But if a more flexible policy regarding court ceremonials risked compromising the dynasty's claim to the absolute devotion of its subjects, its
failure to recognize and accommodate the natural strivings of these same
subjects posed an equally dangerous threat, in Macartney's view, to its
very survival. In a continuation of the passage, quoted earlier, in which he
exalts the soaring nature of the human mind, he ventures a bold predic-
tion premised on the indomitable power of the circulatory impulse.

> I am indeed very much mistaken if all the authority and all the address of the
> Tartar [Qing] Government will be able much longer to stifle the energies of their
> Chinese subjects. Scarcely a year now passes without an insurrection in some of
> the provinces. It is true they are usually soon suppressed, but their frequency is a
> strong symptom of the fever within. The paroxysm is repelled, but the disease is
> not cured.[76]

Macartney calls attention to the foreignness of the Qing Dynasty in
accounting for its current troubles: its rulers are not, properly speaking,
"Chinese" at all but Manchu or "Tartar." The racial division between the
rulers and the ruled clearly raises the specter of political illegitimacy. But
for Macartney the inevitability of the dynasty's demise stems more immediately from its attempts unnaturally to "stifle the energies" of its subjects. The phrase, taken in the context of his preceding remarks about the
universal strivings of the human mind, and indeed in the context of the
entire corpus of embassy accounts, calls to mind not so much revolution-
ary plots as the full range of intellectual, scientific, economic, and social
impulses that the English found systematically obstructed in China.

In an accompanying footnote, he elaborates his judgment of the government's policies of restriction and constraint. Following upon his reference, cited above, to time as "the great wonder worker of our world" and
"the touchstone of truth," he develops a second, equally intriguing
metaphor:

> The tyranny or specter of a state may stalk abroad in all its terrors and for a while
> may force a base currency on the timorous multitude, but in spite of those terrors
> there is always a certain counteraction fearlessly working in the mind of common

sense, industriously refining the ore and imperceptibly issuing or emitting a standard metal whose intrinsic value soon degrades and baffles every artifice of impure coinage.[77]

The base currency of a tyrannical state inhibits legitimate circulation in that it denies the authenticity of historical progress as the standard metal of cultural value. If time is the genuine touchstone of truth, policies grounded in and tending to enforce rigid conformity to custom appear as false, a counterfeit coin. If free circulation is the cornerstone of legitimate state power, a government that obstructs it by means of such artifices of impure coinage must eventually give way before the solid commercialist virtues of industry and common sense.

The portrayal of the Chinese government that emerges in these accounts as a proud, extravagant and finally unsound structure supported on a flimsy framework of ceremony and artifice inevitably recalls the trivializing allusions to imperial authority so common in chinoiserie. The Beauvais tapestries and the designs for royal garden seats and triumphal arches to adorn country estates transformed, as I have suggested, the political power of a foreign potentate into an ornamental trope through an aesthetic that privileged superfice over substance, whimsical fantasy over a solid grounding in nature and truth. The diplomat and the artist appear to concur, in other words, in their representations of Chinese authority as insubstantial, almost ephemeral, an empty sheath where the emperor's sword should be. While the depictions of Chinese political illegitimacy in these diplomatic accounts reflect the commercialist concern with forms of cultural blockage, their underlying metaphors hearken back to the equally familiar tropes of chinoiserie. The commercialist paradigm enables these writers to diagnose the cultural malaise afflicting China—not to mention the difficulties of conducting trade there—in terms of an unnatural stifling of the creative and communicative energies of its citizens. The stylistic clichés of chinoiserie, meanwhile, its glittering superficialities and extravagant displays, provide them with a familiar symbolic framework within which to cast the more visible outward symptoms of the disease.

First among these symptoms for Barrow is the ubiquity, in China, of the shimmering façade. His opening resolution to show the Chinese people "in their proper colours" requires first and foremost that he "divest the court of the tinsel and the tawdry varnish with which, like the palaces of the emperor, the missionaries have found it expedient to cover it in their writings." But the missionaries have only perpetuated Chinese self-delusions: the false colors in which the Chinese have previously appeared derive, after all, from their own moral maxims. And the real palaces themselves display a coat of tawdry varnish that Barrow takes evident delight in stripping away. "The very dwelling of the emperor and the grand hall in which he gives audience, when divested of the gilding and the gaudy colours with which they are daubed, are little superior, and much less solid, than the barns of a substantial English farmer." If this deflation of Chinese architectural grandeur resembles in spirit the fanciful designs of a Halfpenny or a Chippendale, Barrow's pithy summary of the current state of Chinese civilization might have been lifted verbatim from a classicist assessment of the Chinese contribution to the arts in 1750s Britain: "At this moment, compared with Europe, they can only be said to be great in trifles, whilst they are really trifling in every thing that is great."[78]

I have already noted how Lord Macartney associated the rhetorical dexterity of the Chinese with the enchanting illusions of their pleasure gardens. It comes as no surprise, then, that in describing their moral character, he, like Barrow, draws upon a set of metaphors that calls to mind the reception of the Chinese style in Europe. In observing "the effects resulting from the refined polity and principles of the government, which are meant to restrain and direct" its subjects, he "often perceived the ground to be hollow under a vast superstructure." His vision of Chinese moral hypocrisy resonates with the aesthetic model implicit in the literally groundless chinoiserie fantasies of Watteau or Pillement and the accompanying excoriations of "monstrous offspring of wild imagination, undirected by nature and truth." The aesthetic conditioning of Macartney's perspective is even more readily apparent in a subsequent characterization of Chinese morality as "in general of a very flimsy texture. . . . The tincture is more relished than the essence; the frame is more looked at than the picture; the parade of duty almost stifles duty itself."[79]

The outward signs of state power in China appear equally flimsy and ornamental to English observers: their descriptions evoke the placid soldiers of the Beauvais tapestries rather than the fearsome imperial guards of the Nieuhof frontispiece. The parade of duty in the military context, as in the moral, shows more concern for tincture than essence. "Exterior appearance," Ellis writes, "is so exclusively the object of attention, that the axes carried before police officers are merely painted wood: indeed, the whole paraphernalia of magistracy resemble gingerbread ornaments, or masquerade decoration."[80] A Chinese show of military force for the benefit of Anson's passing ships likewise dissolves, in Walter and Robins's account, into pathetic self-parody.

> And on this occasion I must observe, that the Chinese had taken care to man the two forts, on each side of that passage, with as many men as they could well contain, the greatest part of them armed with pikes and match-lock musquets. These garrisons affected to shew themselves as much as possible to the ships, and were doubtless intended to induce Mr Anson to think more reverently than he had hitherto done of the Chinese military power: For this purpose they were equipped with much parade, having a great number of colours exposed to view; and on the castle in particular there were laid considerable heaps of large stones; and a soldier of unusual size, dressed in very sightly armour, stalkt about on the parapet with a battle-ax in his hand, endeavouring to put on as important and martial an air as possible, though some of the observers on board the Centurion shrewdly suspected, from the appearance of his armour, that instead of steel, it was composed only of a particular kind of glittering paper.[81]

As in the case of the kowtow dispute, the Chinese emphasis on the display over the substance of power connotes a political illegitimacy that can only augur the eventual demise of the state.

It is no doubt fitting that the century's most forceful advocate of the principle of circulation should also become the sternest prophet of the consequences of its neglect. Daniel Defoe never ventured to China, and his brief fictional account of that country in *The Farther Adventures of Robinson Crusoe* predates by nearly thirty years the earliest of the first-hand descriptions I have been considering here.[82] Crusoe's story, with its frequent references to trade and measures of economic prosperity, echoes the commercialist orientation Defoe had developed in the *Review* ten years before. And yet the themes that emerge in the passages on China also anticipate with uncanny precision those of the real-life travelers who would follow Defoe's intrepid wanderer. Although he devotes only sixteen pages to China, these pages usefully highlight the contours of the bridge between economic theory and narrative praxis that this chapter set out to illuminate.

From the very outset, Crusoe leaves no doubt that his perspective on China will be framed by commercialist concerns. After a series of misadventures at sea, he finds himself stranded in China without a ship or any other means of returning home. The first plan that occurs to him juxtaposes this initial sense of blockage with a circulatory remedy derived from the universal panacea of trade. He resolves to wait four months until the

time of the next fair, whereupon, he surmises, "We might be able to purchase all sorts of the Manufactures of the Country, and withal, might possibly find some *Chinese* Jonks or Vessels from *Tonquin*, that would be to
be sold, and would carry us and our Goods, whither we pleased." In the
meantime, he and his company divert themselves with a journey to the
city of Nanquin (present-day Nanjing), where Crusoe discovers that
China falls far short of the thriving market society he seems to have envisioned. The land is inhabited by a "miserable people" whose fabrics,
manner of living, wealth, and so-called glory are scarcely worth mention-
ing, and whose misery stems from the fact that the conditions of commercial circulation are wanting.

What [is] their Trade, to the universal Commerce of *England, Holland, France*
and *Spain*? What are their Cities to ours, for Wealth, Strength, Gaiety of Apparel,
rich Furniture, and an infinite Variety? What are their Ports, supply'd with a few
Jonks and Barks, to our Navigation, our Merchant Fleets, our large and powerful
Navys? Our City of *London* has more Trade than all their mighty Empire.[83]

If China had simply been poor and weak, Crusoe might have dismissed
it as a hopelessly backward nation and left the matter at that. Certainly he
would have had little reason to press the damning comparison with modern European nations. His rhetorical virulence is clearly aimed in part at
debunking what he takes to be the exaggerated claims of his Jesuit predecessors. But something in the very nature of the Chinese character also
contributes to provoking his ire. The other accounts I have examined here
stress repeatedly the glaring discrepancy or disproportion between the
outward appearances of pride, polished manners, and cultural achievement in China and a rankling inner stagnation. Crusoe likewise takes
offense not at poverty per se but at the self-delusion that envelopes it.
"The Pride of these People is infinitely great," he writes, "and exceeded
by nothing, but their Poverty . . . nothing was more aukward to me, than
to see such a haughty, imperious, insolent People, in the midst of the
grossest Simplicity and Ignorance, for all their fam'd Ingenuity is no
more." His memorable encounter with a blindly narcissistic country
gentleman reminds him of Don Quixote in his "mixture of Pomp and
Poverty," but it might easily have served as a model in its own right for
Barrow's lice-infested officials at the Chinese court or for the paper-
armored soldier who would strut his stuff for Anson's passing ships.[84]

I have argued that the standard measure of legitimacy of Chinese cultural products in this period, whether in the realm of language, religion,

or art, is the degree to which their representations are perceived to be grounded in some originary, unified substratum of coherent meaning. The commercialist paradigm introduced in this chapter, with its emphasis on the vitalizing role of circulation, reconceives this static substratum as a dynamic historical impetus. The characterization of cultural forms that seem to defy these conditions of legibility remains, however, remarkably constant. From the guttural howls of Chinese speech to the babylonian travesties of Buddhist doctrine, from the monstrous phantasms of the chinoiserie style to the absurd posturing of the imperial court, the inassimilable excess that increasingly comes to dominate the conception of China in the West evokes a disquieting vision of semiotic chaos in the proliferation of illegitimate signs.

As Crusoe finally prepares to leave China in the company of a trade caravan bound for Moscow, he finds an occasion to comment on two architectural marvels. The first is a country house and garden constructed entirely of fine porcelain. His guide predicts that "after all the ill-humor'd things [Crusoe] had said" of China, he would surely admire this, "the greatest Rarity in all the Country," and indeed he does, dallying so long to examine its particulars that the caravan leader fines him three shillings for the delay. And yet one senses a Barrowesque irony in Crusoe's admiration for such a wondrous consummation of triviality and superficial splendor: he quips on first hearing of the porcelain house that he will buy it if he can carry it in a box upon his camel. If Crusoe can allow the Chinese to excel in the art of chinaware, it is only as an art that for him captures perfectly the spirit of the nation in its relentless transmutation of grounded substance into fragile, ephemeral form.

For Crusoe, the essential vacuity of Chinese civilization runs so deep that there remains no possibility of solid ground. A house built of chinaware cannot be so unusual, he suggests with mock perplexity, as "the Materials of their Building [are] the Product of their own Country; and so it is all *China* Ware, is it not?" If the architectural ware of China is all fragile chinaware, then any attempt to convey true legitimacy in this medium could only crumble, in Crusoe's eyes, into a glittering heap of absurdity. The last monument he encounters as he ventures out of China might well pass for such an attempt. "The great *China* Wall," as he calls it, "was a most excellent thing to keep off the *Tartars*," but it might as well be built of porcelain were it ever to face a real test of its strength in a battalion of Englishmen. "Well," he asks his overly credulous guide, "do you think it would stand out an Army of our Country People, with a good Train of Artillery; or our Engineers, with two Companies of Miners; would not they batter it down in ten Days, that an Army might enter in Battalia, or blow it up in the Air, Foundation and all, that there should be no Sign of it left?" Crusoe's incendiary vision seems ultimately to get the better of him, and he closes the China chapter of his tale with a final, contemptuous nod to "this mighty *Nothing* call'd a Wall."[85] With this dramatic gesture of erasure, Crusoe blithely obliterates what was perhaps the most potent and enduring symbol of China's epistemological foundations. As the dream of legitimacy succumbs to the depredations that would follow, the image of China is cast adrift toward the nineteenth century in a mist of tragicomic absurdity, a bastard nation with neither past nor future, and one that Hegel would later place outside the world's history as a stranger to the driving forces of modernity.[86] One can only wonder if the flames that engulfed the Imperial Gardens in Beijing at the hands of Lord Elgin's troops in 1860 were not fueled in part by a steadily emerging contempt toward the ephemerality of porcelain fantasies in a modern world for which the only legitimacy lay in progress.

Epilogue

If Descartes's famous pronouncement on the *cogito* of 1619 marks a symbolic point of origin for modern Western epistemology, a contemporaneous milestone in the history of travel writing serves as a reminder that the myriad forms of self-knowledge that emerged over the subsequent two hundred years reflected not only a new rationalist subjectivity but also an unprecedented cultural engagement with East Asia. The decade 1615 to 1625 witnessed the translation—first into Latin, and then into German, French, Spanish, and English—of the journals of Matteo Ricci, documenting the first successful Jesuit mission in China and making available to a rapidly transfixed European audience the extraordinary learning acquired during his nearly thirty years of residence there. One of the aims of this book has been to demonstrate how the Western knowledge of China conveyed by the Jesuits and endlessly elaborated and contested by the generations that followed invariably emerged through a Cartesian projection of familiar categories of understanding onto the cryptic ciphers of inassimilable alterity. From Bacon's passing speculations on the "character real" of the Chinese script to Barrow's unforgiving diagnosis of a thoroughgoing cultural constipation afflicting Britain's unwilling partner in trade, early modern constructions of China in Europe reveal a consistent predisposition to interpret and evaluate the emblems of Chinese culture on the basis of their conformity with a particular set of representational ideals. The persistence of these interpretive paradigms largely accounts for the seemingly paradoxical transmutation of the tropes underlying early assertions of Chinese cultural legitimacy into catalysts of mounting skepticism and, finally, undisguised imperialist disdain.

But a second, equally important purpose of these four chapters has been to suggest how the imaginative constructions they document not only reflected emergent forms of self-consciousness but participated in transforming them as well. By this I mean neither simply to reiterate the incontrovertible claim that Chinese ideas profoundly influenced Western thought during this period, nor merely to reaffirm the more general truism that societies tend to define themselves in opposition to variously constituted others, but rather to recall the more nuanced and less predictable inflections in cultural self-awareness effected by the local particularities of a sustained cross-cultural gaze. The publication of Ricci's journals inaugurated a period of two centuries in European history where significant developments in linguistics, theology, the arts, and economic thought were invariably refracted through an ever-expanding awareness of a rival civilization on the other side of the world. To contemplate China, as Gibbon discovered in his meditations on genealogical legitimacy, increasingly entailed adjusting one's own sense of origin and purpose to accommodate the implications of the very cognitive apparatus that made such contemplation possible. In each of the preceding chapters, I have pointed to individual instances where variations on the ideographic fantasy have engendered not only exotic visions of the East but also reassessments of established ways of thinking within the West. One might recall, for example, Gottfried Bayer's reaction to the devastating prospect of the absence of any underlying system to the Chinese script, or the iconoclastic parody of Brownian landscape design William Chambers achieved through the fanciful elaboration of chinoiserie motifs.

As a closing gesture, I would like to return briefly to each of the four spaces of encounter I have traversed to speculate on some of the more enduring consequences of the interpretive self-reflexivity that the omnipresent fascination with China provoked. One of the lessons of postcolonialism has been that the dialogical legacy of even historically distant contacts extends to the present day and often expresses itself in unexpected ways. Given the phenomenal expenditure of cultural energy on the act of interpreting Chinese culture in the seventeenth and eighteenth centuries, it would be surprising if the very intensity of this gaze did not in itself produce identifiable effects at home, whether by contributing to existing historical trends in literary and artistic self-expression, for example, or by inaugurating new ones.

In the realm of language, Bayer's despair at contemplating philological anarchy where he had fervently hoped and expected to discover a miraculously ordered system would seem a poignant emblem of the cultural costs of the sustained interpretive enterprise of which he was a part. To apply the paradigm of representational legitimacy to the Chinese written language, as Bayer and so many others did, was to reinforce both the expectation of the perfectibility of language and the corresponding conception of European vernaculars as falling short of that ideal. If these projectors had occupied a parallel universe within which the perfect linguistic systems of their dreams were realizable goals, then their proposals to fix and purify the basic tools of human thought and expression might have been carried out, and we might be reading the novels of Austen and Flaubert in an orderly philosophical language modeled on Chinese. The failure, for better or for worse, of the projectors to achieve this outcome contributed inevitably to the dissipation of their guiding ideal and to the acceptance of the condition of language as necessarily dynamic and imperfect. These in themselves were significant developments that arguably would not have occurred at the time or in the manner they did in the absence of the deeply engaging theoretical stimulus and experimental test case provided by the Chinese. There may be an echo, in other words, of Gottfried Bayer's lament in the attitude of resigned pragmatism with which Samuel Johnson ultimately regarded his own pathbreaking lexicographic enterprise. Even the emergence of the eighteenth-century novel, with its resolute and triumphant flaunting of the transience, effusiveness, and temporality—in short, the illegitimacy—of common language, might trace a wayward root or two to the collapse of the ideographic dream.

In the religious domain, the most strikingly ironic consequence of the naturalization of the Jesuits' accommodationist paradigm was its subsequent appropriation by libertine philosophers in their attacks on the Catholic Church. It is worth stressing again that the scathing satires Bayle and Voltaire set in China reflect not so much an inherited image of China or the influence of Confucianism on their own thought as a well-developed interpretive reflex conditioned by decades of Jesuit writing. No Jesuit would have countenanced a portrayal of a Chinese emperor ridiculing the creed of a novice confessor; what Jesuit accounts undoubtedly did provide, however, was a perceptual apparatus that, by casting the figure of the Chinese sage as an emblem of theological legitimacy, unwittingly provided a critical vantage point that could be turned against the Jesuits themselves.

A second, equally paradoxical effect of Ricci's paradigm was to create and flesh out, in his rendering of Chinese Buddhism, a new species of religious illegitimacy in the Western imagination. Christianity had never faced a shortage of heresies and idolatries to oppose and condemn, but the living example of a rich and highly developed creed with such marked similarities to itself and with such a long and illustrious history posed an unusual challenge in the allure of its sheer exoticism and its countercultural appeal. Certain elements in European chinoiserie already suggest an aestheticized valorization of the unrestrained licentiousness that Buddhism represented in Jesuit eyes. The subsequent literary reclamation of Buddhist thought following the oriental renaissance of the nineteenth century, evident in writers from Thoreau to Conrad and T. S. Eliot to Allen Ginsberg, suggests a continuity in its typically anti-establishment positioning within British and later American culture, a common thread of fascination linking the iconoclastic undercurrents of New England Transcendentalism and avant-garde poetics with the staid Catholicism of Matteo Ricci and his peers.[1]

The interpretive paradigm brought to bear on Chinese artistic influences in Britain likewise left a decisive mark on eighteenth-century culture. Quite apart from the naturalization of the chinoiserie style itself within contemporary stylistic idioms, the critical reaction to Chinese design as a form of aesthetic illegitimacy contributed to two complementary trends in the history of taste. On the one hand, the wild popularity of a markedly alien style in an age whose literary and artistic elites claimed for themselves the mantle of Augustan classicism provided the cultivated Man of Taste both with a safely identifiable nemesis and an added sense of urgency to the project of delineating a standard of beauty that would confirm his judgment and social status. On the other hand, just as modern attempts to censor films have inevitably augmented their box office success, the concerted critical effort to stamp out the chinoiserie craze no doubt enhanced its appeal for many a contrarian collector. In a similar vein, it may also have served to illuminate and even, perversely, to legitimate alternative modes of expression for a new generation of artists and writers who seized on the forbidden pleasures of its fantastic elements and unfettered exoticism as a source of inspiration. A survey of gothic fiction and romantic poetry fully attuned to the aesthetic dimensions of cross-cultural encounter would, I suspect, reveal unexpected traces of this inheritance.[2] The predominance of women novelists in the early history of the gothic may itself reflect the persistent coding of the aesthetic transgressiveness of chinoiserie as feminine and a corresponding identification on the part of aspiring women writers with gestures of literary defiance and experimentation. The classicist's reading of chinoiserie, in other words, may have inadvertently carved out a local space for a transformative and newly empowering creative vision in the same manner that the

Jesuit's reading of Chinese Buddhism established a new conceptual category pregnant with possibilities for the restless literary mind.

The political aftermath of the commercialist phase of the encounter explored in the final chapter is sufficiently well known to need little further elaboration. Both the Hegelian verdict on China's place outside the history of civilization and its seeming confirmation in the humiliations of the Treaty of Nanjing appear, in retrospect, as inevitable consequences of the discourse of stagnation, obstruction, and political illegitimacy that emerged in merchant and diplomatic renderings of Chinese culture and society over the course of the eighteenth century. It seems equally clear that the flowering of a complementary discourse of rights and political freedoms in the social movements and liberal political philosophy of the nineteenth century, with their rhetorical emphasis on progress, the free circulation of ideas, and the sovereignty of the individual, was to some degree preconditioned by the consolidation of a particular form of cultural self-consciousness through the commercialist engagement with China. If Matteo Ricci's reflections on China, in other words, provide an illuminating context for the epistemology of Descartes, surely those of Lord Macartney and John Barrow provide the same for the liberalism of John Stuart Mill.

What is perhaps less immediately apparent in considering the subsequent history of this encounter is the degree to which its underlying paradigms and habits of interpretation continue powerfully to determine Western responses to China even to the present day. The discussions on trade issues and human rights that have largely dominated these responses over the past decade have, from a historical perspective, an unmistakably familiar ring to them. Westerners tend to regard China's recent economic boom, for example, as predicated upon an increasingly "free circulation" of goods and capital entailed by the reversal of long-standing policies of "state interference" in the marketplace. The unremitting suppression of political dissent in the wake of the Tiananmen Square massacre, meanwhile, offends democratic sensibilities as a systematic obstruction of the free flow of ideas posited by the liberal ideal.[3] There are always echoes of missionary zeal in political efforts to "convert" other nations to the creed of Western-style free-market democracy. But the sense of uncanny repetition of historical patterns is heightened in this case on recognizing that the reform agendas being urged on China today are themselves the products of the eighteenth-century history of China's contact with the West. While it is perhaps naive to hope that the ideological lenses that mediate cross-cultural vision will ever become obsolete, to recognize their presence and grapple resolutely with their historical contingency would increasingly appear, as we enter the fifth century of this encounter, both an ethical imperative and a purely pragmatic precondition to more fully engaging with all that Chinese culture, among many others, has yet to teach us about ourselves.

Notes

INTRODUCTION

1. For current debates on the Marco Polo legend, see F. Wood, *Did Marco Polo Go to China?* John Lust identifies a small number of seventeenth-century books on China in which "an element of medieval storytelling" still persists, but he rightly argues that the appearance of credible, firsthand Jesuit accounts in this period was transformative (Lust, *Western Books,* vii). For an excellent treatment of medieval storytelling practices in the realm of the exotic, see Campbell, *Witness.*

2. On Western European conceptions of and responses to other cultures in the early modern period, see especially Marshall and Williams, *Great Map.* Other useful sources are Kiernan, *Lords of Humankind*; Daunton and Halpern, *Empire and Others*; Hulme, *Colonial Encounters*; and Hammond and Jablow, *The Africa that Never Was.*

3. Gibbon, *Memoirs*, 41, 143.

4. Ibid., 41–42.

5. Ibid., 42.

6. Ibid., 42–43.

7. Henri Cordier's monumental *Bibliotheca Sinica* lists nearly 1,500 Western books on China published between 1600 and 1799. John Lust has compiled a more accessible and recent bibliography of a sizeable subset of these sources, along with a helpful chart showing the breakdown of this output by country and century (Lust, *Western Books,* ix).

8. *The Decline and Fall* is itself peppered with allusions to Chinese history, one of which is prefaced by the unexpected claim that "the Chinese annals, as they have been interpreted by the learned industry of the present age, may be usefully applied to reveal the secret and remote causes of the fall of the Roman empire" (Gibbon, *Decline and Fall,* 3:261).

9. Gibbon, *Memoirs*, 169.

10. See Said, *Orientalism.* Two concise and instructive overviews of key developments and debates within postcolonial studies during the past twenty years are Gandhi, *Postcolonial Theory,* and Loomba, *Colonialism/Postcolonialism.*

CHAPTER I

1. Eco, *Perfect Language,* 18–19.

2. Ibid., 165, 215, 277. For an account of the tradition of venerating the representational clarity of mathematics that Leibniz draws on here, see Markley, *Fallen Languages,* 67.

3. Stillman, *New Philosophy,* 10.

4. Each of these claims is true to a certain extent, but they all require considerable qualification. For a detailed discussion of these issues, see DeFrancis, *Chinese Language.*

5. J. Cohen, "Universal Character," 239.

6. Mandeville, *Travels,* 143. The problem of the authorship of this immensely popular text has never been satisfactorily resolved, although it seems clear that it represents a compilation of other sources rather than an original or firsthand account. See, for example, Higgins, *Writing East*; and Seymour, *Sir John Mandeville.* The author(s) may have taken this particular image from the Book of Esther, and it is, in any case, a frequently recurring trope in oriental despot scenarios. Although writers of later periods typically do not succumb to this degree of geographic confusion, images of China often remain inflected to some degree by undifferentiated notions of "the East."

7. Mendoza, *History,* 1:53. Cf. Jer. 20.9 AV: "But his word was in mine heart as a burning fire shut up in my bones." Mendoza refers here to the legendary visit of St. Thomas the Apostle to China. The first documented Christian mission to China was that of the Nestorians in the seventh century. See Cary-Elwes, *China,* 9–37.

8. "Eloge de la Chine, comparée au reste de la terre, par un prétendu philosophe chinois, tiré de l'anglais," *Journal encyclopédique* 8 (Dec. 1, 1762): 123–29; quoted in Guy, *French Image,* 429–30. Translations of this and other passages from foreign language sources are my own unless otherwise noted.

9. On Max Weber's notion of charismatic leadership as a source of political legitimacy (exemplified for him, interestingly, by the historical role of the Chinese emperor), see Weber, *From Max Weber,* 245–52. Although there are certain affinities between my concept of legitimacy in representation and Weber's three-part typology of legitimate authority, I distinguish my usage of the term from the ideological readings offered by subsequent Marxian theorists. See, for example, Poulantzas, *Political Power,* 221–24.

10. The best-known contemporary theorist of this analogy is probably Sir Robert Filmer, who responded to mid-seventeenth-century controversies regarding the nature and origins of political authority with a passionate elaboration of the patriarchalist position that the authority of a king, far from being based on the consent of the governed, "is the only right and natural authority of a supreme father" (Filmer, *Patriarcha,* 11).

11. Snider, *Origin and Authority*, 3.

12. In addition to the books by Snider, Stillman, and Markley cited above, see Bono, *Word of God*; and Kroll, *Material World*.

13. See, for example, Stillman, *New Philosophy*; Markley, *Fallen Languages*, and *Two-Edg'd Weapons*, 30–55; and Vickers, "Restoration Prose Style," 3–76. For an account of Sprat's work as a defense of established interests, see P. B. Wood, "Methodology," 1–26.

14. Knowlson, *Universal Language*, 36; Bacon, *Works*, 4:54–55.

15. Bacon, *Works*, 4:61.

16. Ibid., 4:254–55.

17. Markley, *Fallen Languages*, 63; Snider, *Origin and Authority*, 73. Snider's book is an excellent source on the importance of myths of origin in establishing the legitimacy of the present both for Bacon and in seventeenth-century English culture more generally.

18. Bacon, *Works*, 3:396–97, 4:61. For original Latin, see Bacon, *Works* (London, 1826), 8:21.

19. Bacon, *Works*, 4:32; Farrington, "Temporis Parus Masculus," 201. All emphases in quotations are in the original unless otherwise noted. Keller offers a compelling reading of Bacon's matrimonial and sexual metaphors in *Reflections*, 33–42.

20. Sprat, *History*, 2, 61, 112–13. See Cope's introduction to this edition for useful historical background to Sprat's work.

21. Swift, *Gulliver's Travels*, 230.

22. See Keller, *Reflections*, 33–66; Bordo, *Flight to Objectivity*, 97–118; and Schiebinger, *The Mind Has No Sex*, 136–55.

23. Shakespeare, *The Tempest*, 1.2.56–57. I develop this idea of paternal anxiety and its narrative implications more fully in two articles: "His Master's Voice" and "Rhetorical Phallacies."

24. Keller sees in the matrimonial metaphors underlying Bacon's conception of this ideal a fantasy of securing scientific omnipotence through an oedipal "identification with the father which allows simultaneously for the appropriation and denial of the feminine" (Keller, *Reflections*, 41). For Snider, Bacon's recurrent figures of birth and generation provide the metaphorical foundation of his own canonization as the "father" of modern science (Snider, "Bacon, Legitimation," 119–38).

25. Cowley, "To the Royal Society," included in the prefatory matter to Sprat's *History*; and Sprat, *History*, 62, 111–12.

26. For a fascinating discussion of the broad-based fear of "female generativity" and the ascendancy of mechanistic reproductive theory in the seventeenth century, see Bordo, *Flight to Objectivity*, 108–12.

27. Locke, *Essay*, 508.

28. There has been considerable debate over the degree to which seventeenth-

century prose style was in fact influenced by the Royal Society and the rise of Baconian science. See, for example, Arakelian, "Myth," 227–45; Vickers, "Royal Society," and "English Prose Style," 1–76; and Markley, *Fallen Languages,* 1–8.

29. Wilkins, *Essay,* 1, 289, and Dedicatory Epistle 2. For a more detailed overview of the workings of Wilkins's system, see Emery, "John Wilkins' Universal Language," 174–85. For the historical background to the project, see Demott, "Sources," 168–81. The most thorough exploration of contemporary cultural contexts for the work is provided by Robert Stillman, who positions Wilkins in relation to Restoration discourses on economic theory and political legitimation (Stillman, *New Philosophy,* 179–262).

30. Wilkins, *Essay,* 17–18.

31. Wilkins, *Essay,* Dedicatory Epistle 5. Wilkins would seem indebted to Hobbes in the "Kingdome of Darknesse" chapters of the *Leviathan* for his view of the linguistic origins of religious error: cf. Hobbes, *Leviathan,* 424–25, 472–73.

32. Wilkins, *Essay,* 6–8, 19.

33. Ibid., 14–18.

34. Ibid., 1.

35. Slaughter, *Universal Languages,* 82, 186. Taxonomic systems of knowledge are central to Foucault's conception of the "Classical *episteme.*" See Foucault, *Order,* 71–77.

36. Markley, *Fallen Languages,* 81–82.

37. See Francus, *Converting Imagination,* 23, 28–30. For the relevant passages in Locke, see *Essay,* 395–96, 406–8, 490–508.

38. Swift, "A Proposal for Correcting, Improving, and Ascertaining the English Tongue," *Works,* 9:135.

39. Reddick, *Making of Johnson's Dictionary,* 14. On seventeenth- and early-eighteenth-century proposals for the formation of an English academy, see Landa, *John Oldmixon's Reflections,* Introduction, 1–2; and Wells, *Dictionaries,* 31–38.

40. Swift, "A Proposal," *Works,* 9:136–40.

41. Ibid., 140–43.

42. Ibid., 140–41, 147.

43. Quoted in Landa, *John Oldmixon's Reflections,* Introduction, 2; Johnson, "Preface to the English Dictionary," *Works,* 6:224, 246, 253.

44. Johnson, *The Plan of an English Dictionary, Works,* 6:206–7.

45. Johnson, "Preface," *Works,* 6:230.

46. Johnson, *Plan, Works,* 6:208.

47. See Demaria, "Theory," 167; and Wimsatt, *Philosophical Words,* 110.

48. Johnson, "Preface," *Works,* 6:225, 257.

49. Johnson, 6:231.

50. Johnson, *Plan, Works,* 6:213.

51. Johnson, "Preface," *Works,* 6:242, 251; Demaria, "Theory," 165. One need not look far to confirm the importance of genealogy as a source of legiti-

macy and authority in the broader cultural sphere. Johnson points to the parallel in this regard between the linguistic and political realms in the Preface: "Tongues, like governments, have a natural tendency to degeneration; we have long preserved our constitution, let us make some struggles for our language." Burke picks up the thread in his *Reflections on the Revolution in France* and weaves it into a mainstay of his argument. The Princess Sophia—or more precisely, her womb—was named "for a *stock* and root of *inheritance* to our kings" on the grounds of her descent from King James the first, and because "no experience has taught us, that in any other course or method than that of an *hereditary crown*, our liberties can be regularly perpetuated and preserved sacred as our *hereditary right* . . . the undisturbed succession of the crown [is] a pledge of the stability and perpetuity of all the other members of our constitution" (Burke, *Reflections*, 109–11 [emphasis added]).

52. Johnson's affinity for the methodological basis of Wilkins's taxonomy is suggested by a quotation from Hooker that he includes in the *Dictionary* under the definition of "distinction": "The mixture of those things by speech, which by nature are divided, is the mother of all error: to take away therefore that error, which confusion breedeth, *distinction* is requisite."

53. Cornelius, *Languages*, 2–3.

54. Ibid., 3. While Egyptian hieroglyphics attracted considerable attention in Europe during this period as well, their appeal stemmed largely from the typological mysteries they were thought to conceal, rather than the linguistic principles they embodied. Their usefulness was in any case limited by their indecipherability: although the German scholar Athanasius Kircher (1602–1680) made some progress toward correctly deciphering individual characters of the ancient Egyptian script, it was not until the 1820s that Jean-Françoise Champollion, using the recently discovered Rosetta Stone, made the breakthrough that enabled it to be read accurately for the first time. On the relation of hieroglyphics to the typological tradition, see Korshin, *Typologies*, 165–72. For a comprehensive history of the interpretation of hieroglyphics in this period, see David, *Le débat*.

55. Lach, *China*, 743.

56. Boxer, *South China*, xvii.

57. Mendoza, *History*, 1:121–22. I have modernized the spelling.

58. On the number of Chinese characters, see DeFrancis, *Chinese Language*, 84–92. For a discussion of the indispensability myth, see DeFrancis, *Chinese Language*, 177–88. For early testimony on the practice of palm writing, see Ricci, *Fonti Ricciane*, 1:37. The only English edition of Ricci's China journals, while a useful starting point, is based on an early Latin translation and adaptation of Ricci's Italian that at times deviates markedly from the original. I have therefore used my own translations in the quoted passages that follow. See Ricci, *China in the Sixteenth Century*.

59. Ricci, *Fonti Ricciane*, 1:36–37.

60. Cornelius, *Languages,* 28.

61. Ricci, *Fonti Ricciane,* 1:38.

62. Ibid.

63. Sprat, *History,* 113.

64. Ricci, *Fonti Ricciane,* 1:36, 44–45.

65. Mendoza, *History,* 1:109.

66. Bacon, *The Advancement of Learning, Works,* 3:399–400. Although hieroglyphs are sometimes used in the strictly pictorial manner that Bacon imagines, they are more commonly employed as phonetic representations. See note 54 above.

67. Bacon, *Novum organum, Works,* 4:32, 61, 254.

68. Bacon, *The Advancement of Learning, Works,* 3:400.

69. Wilkins, *Essay,* Dedicatory Epistle 2.

70. Wilkins, *Essay,* 13.

71. Ibid., 450–52.

72. Webb, *Historical Essay,* 29. Kircher, a notable exception, believed that Chinese characters derived from Egyptian hieroglyphics.

73. Ch'ên Shou-yi, "John Webb," 302; Webb, *Historical Essay,* Dedicatory Epistle 3.

74. The argument is summarized in the Dedicatory Epistle 3–4, and elaborated at length in the body of the essay. Webb's arguments concerning the origins and the special characteristics of Chinese seem to apply to both its spoken and written forms.

75. Ch'ên, "John Webb," 307, 314; Webb, *Historical Essay,* 26, 71, 116.

76. Webb, *Historical Essay,* 191.

77. Ibid., 146. On Bacon's skepticism regarding the recoverability of divine language and the "unbridgeable divide between the *verbum Dei* and the languages of man," see Bono, *Word of God,* 218–21.

78. Webb, *Historical Essay,* 167–68.

79. The isolationist reading of Chinese history has been largely discarded by modern scholars. See, for example, Gernet, *History*; Adshead, *China*; and M. H. Hunt, *Genesis,* 3–28.

80. Webb, *Historical Essay,* 142–43.

81. According to John Barrell, eighteenth-century English writers, in particular, regularly invoked the parallels between political and linguistic order, a rhetorical gesture that can be understood in the context of wider efforts to affirm and consolidate the unity of the nation (Barrell, *English Literature,* 110–75).

82. Mungello, *Leibniz and Confucianism,* 7. For a helpful overview of Leibniz's China studies and the sources available to him, see Lach, "Leibniz and China," 436–55; and Leibniz, *Writings on China,* 1–18. A bibliography of contemporary materials can be found in Lust, *Western Books.*

83. Leibniz to Antoine Verjus, Hannover, 2 December 1697, Widmaier,

Leibniz Korrespondiert, 55; Lach, *Preface to Leibniz' Novissima Sinica,* 75. For background on the Rites Controversy and Leibniz's reaction to it, see Mungello, *Leibniz and Confucianism,* 9–13. The controversy is also treated at some length in Chapter 2 of the present work.

84. See Roy, *Leibniz,* 123; and Lach, "Leibniz and China," 437. In his last published letter of this correspondence, Leibniz doggedly repeats a refrain that by this point has become a persistent theme when he writes, "I am curious to learn whether you have since made any progress in the decipherment of the Chinese characters. If not, there is no need to be discouraged: it will come with time" (Leibniz to Joachim Bouvet, Hannover, 13 December 1707, Widmaier, *Leibniz Korrespondiert,* 267).

85. Lach, "Andreas Müller," 565, 574. On the contemporary fascination with "keys" for deciphering religious and linguistic mysteries of all kinds, see Korshin, *Typologies,* 4–6, 89–92.

86. Lach, "Andreas Müller," 567–68 (his translation). Leibniz refers to Müller frequently in the Jesuit correspondence. See, for example, Leibniz to Bouvet, Hannover, 2 December 1697, Widmaier, *Leibniz Korrespondiert,* 60; Leibniz to Bouvet, Berlin, 18 May 1703, Widmaier, *Leibniz Korrespondiert,* 187; Leibniz to Bouvet, Hannover, 18 August 1705, Widmaier, *Leibniz Korrespondiert,* 218; Leibniz to Claude de Visdelou, Hannover, 20 August 1705, Widmaier, *Leibniz Korrespondiert,* 220.

87. Lach, "Leibniz and China," 437; Roy, *Leibniz,* 135. See also Leibniz to Bouvet, Braunschweig, 15 February 1701, Widmaier, *Leibniz Korrespondiert,* 141–42.

88. Leibniz to Bouvet, Braunschweig, 15 February 1701, Widmaier, *Leibniz Korrespondiert,* 143; Leibniz to Bouvet, Berlin, 18 May 1703, Widmaier, *Leibniz Korrespondiert,* 188. Bouvet apparently shared Kircher's view of the Egyptian origins of Chinese: see Bouvet to Leibniz, 28 February 1698, Widmaier, *Leibniz Korrespondiert,* 73.

89. Leibniz to Bouvet, Hannover, 2 December 1697, Widmaier, *Leibniz korrespondiert* 60; Leibniz to Bouvet, Hannover, 18 August 1705, Widmaier, *Leibniz Korrespondiert,* 218; Leibniz to Bouvet, Braunschweig, 15 February 1701, Widmaier, *Leibniz Korrespondiert,* 140. For further accounts of Leibniz's characteristic, see Cornelius, *Languages,* 98; Eco, *Perfect Language,* 269–84; and O'Briant, "Leibniz's Project," 182–91.

90. Lach, "Andreas Müller," 568 (his translation).

91. Mungello, *Leibniz and Confucianism,* 38.

92. Bouvet to Charles le Gobien for Leibniz, Peking, 8 November 1700, Widmaier, *Leibniz Korrespondiert,* 123. For an overview of late-Ming views on the *Yi Jing* that might have informed Bayer's speculations, see Goodman and Grafton, "Ricci," 123–40.

93. Needham, *Science,* 2:304, 315, 337.

94. Bouvet to Leibniz, La Rochelle, 28 February 1698, Widmaier, *Leibniz Korrespondiert*, 74. The impulse to recover the true, forgotten meaning of the hexagrams persists to the present day. A recent commentator promises "to restore the *I Ching* back to its legitimate form . . . and thus unlock the vital principles of the Yin and Yang dialectics" in order to "present an untarnished picture of the true heart of the *I Ching* while helping to right the wrongs that have persisted for so long a period of time" (Collins, *Fu Hsi*, viii–ix).

95. Leibniz to Bouvet, Braunschweig, 15 February 1701, Widmaier, *Leibniz Korrespondiert*, 135; Bouvet to Leibniz, Peking, 4 November 1701, Widmaier, *Leibniz Korrespondiert*, 149. For a more complete account of these two men's speculations on the relationship between binary arithmetic and the *Yi Jing*, see Mungello, *Curious Land*, 312–28. As far-fetched as the speculations of Leibniz and Bouvet may seem to readers today, they reflect an impulse that is still very much part of modern-day science. The eminent theoretical physicist Frank Wilczek claims that the structure of matter, including all of chemistry, the foundations of biology, and the structure of the universe, can be deduced by pure calculation given just six numbers (Wilczek, "Recipe").

96. Leibniz, *Writings on China*, 133–34.

97. See, for example, Leibniz to Bouvet, Braunschweig, 15 February 1701, Widmaier, *Leibniz Korrespondiert*, 135–36.

98. Leibniz to Bouvet, Berlin, 18 May 1703, Widmaier, *Leibniz Korrespondiert*, 185.

99. Mungello, *Curious Land*, 174, 201–2, 209.

100. Ibid., 209; Lundbaek, *Prémare*, 12.

101. Lundbaek, *Bayer*, 92. Translations of passages from Lundbaek's books are his own.

102. Ibid., 103, 105.

103. Ibid., 113–14.

104. Ibid., 115–18. Bayer's nine primary strokes are in fact variations on the simplest, one-stroke radicals as listed in modern Chinese dictionaries. They actually do have names and are understood as graphic building blocks of other characters, but they are not generally taken to have any meaning in themselves, and certainly no semantic value is preserved in their various recombinations.

105. Ibid., 194.

106. Ibid., 137.

107. Lundbaek, *Prémare*, 13. Subsequent page citations in the text refer to this work. For additional background on the figurist tradition, particularly among the Chinese Jesuits, see Rowbotham, "Jesuit Figurists," 471–85; von Collani, "Chinese Figurism," 12–23; and Lackner, "Jesuit Figurism," 129–49.

108. Lundbaek, *Prémare*, 42.

109. On the frequency and reliability of semantic and phonetic components in Chinese characters, see DeFrancis, *Chinese Language*, chaps. 6–7.

110. Lundbaek, *Prémare*, 155.
111. Ibid., 176–77. See also David, *Le Débat*.
112. Le Comte, *Un Jésuite à Pékin*, 232–33.
113. Du Halde, *Description géographique*, 269.
114. Ibid., 270.
115. Percy, *Miscellaneous Pieces*, 1:5–7, 10.
116. Ibid., 1:22–24.
117. Boswell, *Life of Johnson*, 3:339. On Johnson's views on China and things Chinese, see Fan Tsen-Chung, "Dr. Johnson," 18–19; and Porter, "Writing China," 98–101.
118. *Lettres édifiantes, 1702–1776*, 468–69.

CHAPTER 2

1. For a detailed treatment of some of the problems of translation faced by the early China Jesuits, see Dehergne, "Un Problème ardu," 13–44. L. Liu provides a theoretical account of issues of cross-cultural translation between East and West in *Translingual Practice*.
2. For a concise account of the transition during the Ming dynasty from an expansionist to a more defensive foreign policy, see Gernet, *History*, 398–422.
3. Ricci, *Opere Storiche*, 1:106, n. 5.
4. Dunne, *Generation*, 17–19.
5. Ricci, *Opere Storiche*, 2:420.
6. Ibid., 2:72.
7. Ricci, *Fonti Ricciane*, 1:337; Ricci, *Opere Storiche*, 2:104.
8. On the proliferation of schools of Buddhist thought in China dating from the Tang dynasty, see K. Ch'en, *Buddhism*, 297–364. On the "syncretic pragmatism" that characterizes Chinese folk religion, see Granet, *Religion*, 142–56. For a discussion of the role of illustrated pantheons of gods and spirits in Chinese popular religion, see Halén and Pedersen, *C. G. Mannerheim's Chinese Pantheon*, 12–22.
9. Gernet, *China*, 73–74. For a modern view of the comparative history of Buddhism and Christianity in China, see Küng and Ching, *Christianity*, 195–272.
10. On the traditional use of Buddhist temples as hostels and even havens for outlaws, see K. Ch'en, *Buddhism*, 263–64.
11. Granet, *Religion*, 143. For a brief overview of traditional Chinese folk religious beliefs and practices, see *The Cambridge Encyclopedia of China*, 294–96. Teiser offers a richly engaging anthropological reading of a widespread festival of renewal that captured many aspects of popular religious life that the early Jesuits would have observed (see Teiser, *Ghost Festival*).
12. Gernet, *China*, 73–76.
13. On the origins of the Latinized name "Confucius" and Western construc-

tions of the person and belief system associated with it, see Jensen, *Manufacturing Confucianism*, 1–134. Ricci claims to find the golden rule—"the second precept of charity"—in all of the classical texts of the literati, although in fact it is stated in a negative form in the writings of Confucius (see Ricci, *Fonti Ricciane*, 1:120, n. 4).

14. Ricci, *Fonti Ricciane*, 1:120. For a brief, useful overview of the Confucian belief system and of the problems involved in classifying it as either a philosophy or a religion, see Ching, *Chinese Religions*, 51–84.

15. On the congruence of Ricci's approach with the early patristic tradition set forth in Paul's sermon before the Athenians on their worship of "the unknown god" (Acts 17.15–33), see Jensen, *Manufacturing Confucianism*, 56.

16. Gernet, *China*, 29.

17. Standard sources on the history of the Jesuit mission to China are Dunne, *Generation*; Rowbotham, *Missionary and Mandarin*; Etiemble, *Les Jesuites en Chine*; Young, *Confucianism and Christianity*; and Mungello, *Curious Land*. There is a helpful biographical sketch of the founder of the mission in the *Dictionary of Ming Biography, 1368–1644*, s.v. "Ricci, Matteo." For a fascinating book-length biography that juxtaposes Ming China with Europe of the Counter Reformation, see Spence, *Memory Palace*.

18. On the pervasiveness of the Jesuit image of Confucius in eighteenth-century Europe, see Jensen, *Manufacturing Confucianism*, 7–11; and Appleton, *Cycle*, 37–52.

19. Gernet, *China*, 65.

20. For a brief treatment of neo-Confucian assimilation of Buddhist ideas and the *sanjiao* school, see Wright, *Buddhism*, 86–107; Fung, *Short History*, 266–80; and Ching, *Chinese Religions*, 156–62, 217. More detailed studies can be found in Yü, *Renewal*; and Berling, *Syncretic Religion*.

21. Ricci, *Fonti Ricciane*, 1:132.

22. Ricci, *True Meaning*, 401.

23. Ibid., 403.

24. Ricci, *Fonti Ricciane*, 1:108–9. Ricci's account of the "Lord of Heaven" refers to the imperial cult of heaven described in the *Book of Rites*: see Ching, *Chinese Religions*, 61–62. Ricci's attempts to establish the compatibility of Catholicism with a seemingly "alien" doctrine drew upon established precedents in Renaissance scholarship. See Goodman and Grafton, "Ricci," 95–148.

25. Ricci, *Fonti Ricciane*, 1:115. On the traditional role of the literati in China and the Chinese usage of the term, see Granet, *Religion*, 97–104.

26. Ricci, *Opere Storiche*, 2:207, 385.

27. Mungello, "Sinological Torque," 227. On the persistence of the interpretive desire to recover the "true meaning" of these texts among modern Western scholars, see Jensen, *Manufacturing Confucianism*, 14–19.

28. Ricci, *True Meaning*, 57.

29. Ibid., 63, 81–83.

30. See, for example, Faure, *Chan Insights*, 16.

31. On the history of Chinese critiques of Buddhism, see K. Ch'en, *Buddhism*, 213–96; Wright, *Buddhism*, 86–107; and Fung, *Short History*, 316–18. Scholars continue to disagree on the nature and degree of Chinese influences on Jesuit views of Buddhism: see Jensen, *Manufacturing Confucianism*, 51–52.

32. Ricci, *True Meaning*, 143, 241. On contemporary Catholic views of the evangelical methods of the "skilled quibblers and falsifiers of scripture" they saw in their Protestant brethren, see Sypher, "Image of Protestantism," 66.

33. Ricci, *Fonti Ricciane*, 1:122–23.

34. Ricci, *True Meaning*, 99, 103.

35. On the origins of the political structure of the Society of Jesus, see Letson and Higgins, *Jesuit Mystique*, 22–23.

36. Ricci, *Fonti Ricciane*, 1:108–9, 115.

37. Ibid., 1:120.

38. Ibid., 1:53, 117. On later Jesuit distortions of Ricci's views of the ancestral rites, see Jensen, *Manufacturing Confucianism*, 65–70.

39. Ricci, *Fonti Ricciane*, 1:124–25.

40. Ibid., 1:116; Ricci, *True Meaning*, 205. On the Hua-yen school of Buddhism with which such teachings are most closely associated, see K. Ch'en, *Buddhism*, 313–20.

41. See Ginzburg, *Cheese*, 4–21, 68.

42. Ricci, *Fonti Ricciane*, 1:126. On Catholic charges of Protestant sexual perversity and excess, see Sypher, "Image of Protestantism," 59–84.

43. Ricci, *Fonti Ricciane*, 2:30.

44. Ibid., 1:98, 124; Sypher, "Image of Protestantism," 71–72.

45. Spence, *Memory Palace*, 220.

46. Ibid., 244–45; Dunne, *Generation*, 163.

47. Ricci, *Fonti Ricciane*, 2:78–79. Charges that the arguments of religious opponents were little more than rhetorical games were not uncommon in Counter-Reformation Europe (see Martin, *Jesuit Mind*, 10).

48. Ricci, *Fonti Ricciane*, 1:125.

49. Ibid., 1:131.

50. Ibid., 1:131, 283–84.

51. Ricci, *True Meaning*, 137–39.

52. Dunne, Rowbotham, Mungello, and Etiemble are the best starting places for further reading on these debates; for a brief overview, see also the article "Chinese Rites Controversy" in *New Catholic Encyclopedia*.

53. Useful general histories of the Society of Jesus during this period include Bangert, *History*; Mitchell, *Jesuits*; and Martin, *Jesuit Mind*. In spite of the rivalries among missionary orders in China, there were notable instances of collabo-

ration, as, for example, between the Franciscan Antonio de Caballero and the Jesuit Jean Valat (see Mungello, "Sinological Torque," 219–22).

54. *Le Journal des Savans* 40 (Dec. 6, 1700): 474.

55. Ibid., 472–73.

56. Longobardi, *Traité*, 2:197. On Leibniz's reading of Longobardi, which was an important source for his "Letter on the Natural Theology of the Chinese," see Saussy, *Problem*, 37–46.

57. See Fung, *Short History*, 284–320.

58. Longobardi, *Traité*, 2:198–212.

59. Ibid., 2:206, 212, 216.

60. Ibid., 2:179–80.

61. Brisacier, *Lettre*, 42–43.

62. Fung, *Short History*, 146–49; Granet, *Religion*, 80–90.

63. Le Gobien, *Histoire*, 224–25.

64. Ibid., 225–27.

65. Sainte-Marie, *Traité*, 2:293, 387. Mungello provides a careful study of the author's life and work in "Sinological Torque," 217–26.

66. Sainte-Marie, *Traité*, 301–2.

67. Ibid., 299–301.

68. Brisacier, *Lettre*, 24.

69. Sainte-Marie, *Traité*, 411.

70. Brisacier, *Lettre*, 90–91.

71. *Le Journal des Savans* 40 (Dec. 6, 1700): 473–74.

72. François de Salignac de la Mothe Fénelon, letter to P. de la Chaise, Sept. 1702, in *Oeuvres de Fénelon*, 2:466–68.

73. Ibid., 2:468.

74. Le Comte, *Eclaircissement*, 14.

75. Luke 14.23 AV: "And the lord said unto the servant, Go out into the highways and hedges, and compel them to come in, that my house may be filled."

76. Bayle, *Oeuvres*, 2:377–78.

77. Ibid., 2:378–79.

78. The best general source on Voltaire's interest in China is Guy, *French Image*. For a detailed history of European translations of the Chinese orphan play, see Ch'ên Shou-yi, "The Chinese Orphan: A Yüan Play," 89–115. A modern English translation is available in J. Liu, *Six Yüan Plays*, 41–82.

79. Voltaire, "Relation du bannissement des jésuites de la Chine," *Dialogues*, 217–18.

CHAPTER 3

1. The best introductions to chinoiserie are Honour, *Chinoiserie*; and Jacobson, *Chinoiserie*. On the early history of porcelain in Europe, see Plumb,

"Royal Porcelain Craze," 57–69; and Gleeson, *Arcanum*. For a comprehensive overview of this period of British fascination with China, see Appleton, *Cycle*.

2. In this respect, chinoiserie resembles other important developments in eighteenth-century culture. The parallels and codevelopment with the rococo aesthetic have been thoroughly documented; see, for example, Jacobson, *Chinoiserie*, 59–88. It might also be read as an aesthetic counterpart to those culturally sanctioned fantasies of escape and transgression that enjoyed such prominence in the social life of eighteenth-century England (see Castle, *Masquerade*).

3. Impey, *Chinoiserie*, 11, 102–3.

4. Southey, *Letters*, 192; quoted in Davis, *Chinoiserie*, 20.

5. Booth, "'Self Portraiture,'" S96. For a brief but engaging general overview of Near and Far Eastern influences on eighteenth-century English arts and letters, see Humphreys, "Lords of Tartary," 19–31. Kowaleski-Wallace provides insightful close readings of less familiar china scenes in works by Anne Finch, Frances Burney, and Susan Ferrier, among others, in her book *Consuming Subjects*, 52–69.

6. See Knight, "Ironic Loneliness," 351; and Christopher Brooks, "Goldsmith's *Citizen*," 124–44.

7. Goldsmith, *Citizen of the World*, letter 33.

8. Ibid., letters 14, 33, 99. The genre of the oriental tale in England has received less attention than it perhaps deserves (see Conant, *Oriental Tale*; and Weitzman, "Oriental Tale," 1839–55).

9. For a discussion of Goldsmith's recombination of various conventional tropes of the foreign visitor and travel literature genres, see Booth, "'Self Portraiture,'" S92; and Deane, "Goldsmith's *Citizen*," 47–48.

10. Goldsmith, *Citizen*, letters 41, 45, 81. On the economic and cultural associations of silk in eighteenth-century English literature, see Landa, "Pope's Belinda," 215–35.

11. Goldsmith, *Citizen*, letter 14. On the history of collecting and the aesthetics of curiosity in eighteenth-century Britain, see Benedict, "Curious Attitude."

12. *Critical Review* 13 (1762): 397–400; quoted in Booth, "Goldsmith's *Citizen*," S85. The "character" Lien Chi is given in the opening "letter of introduction" serves as our guarantee of the credibility of all that follows. He repeatedly claims that the "unaffected" and "polite" resemble each other everywhere and clearly counts himself among their number (letters 33, 91). For a characteristic rhapsody on the glories of the Chinese nation, see letter 42: "When I compare the history of China with that of Europe, how do I exult in being a native of that kingdom which derives its original from the sun."

13. Goldsmith, *Citizen*, letters 45, 33. Christopher Brooks, "Goldsmith's *Citizen*," 127, 136.

14. On the relationship between eighteenth-century Gothic and chinoiserie styles, see Porter, "From Chinese to Goth," 46–58.

15. Nieuhof, *Embassy*, 149–50.

16. On the impact of these illustrations in the decorative arts, see Grigsby, "Johan Nieuhof's *Embassy*," 172–83.

17. For helpful discussions of the Beauvais tapestries, see Standen, "Story," 103–17; Jarry, *Chinoiserie*, 15–31; and Honour, *Chinoiserie*, 92–93. On the painters responsible for the original cartoons and a more detailed history of the tapestries' production, see Jarry, "La Vision de la Chine," 173–83.

18. The best introduction to Adam Schall's career in China is probably Spence, *To Change China*, 3–33. See also Jarry, "La Vision de la Chine," 176–77.

19. Jarry, *Chinoiserie*, 26–32. A set of these tapestries found its way as a gift to the Chinese emperor Qianlong, who was sufficiently pleased that he ordered the construction of a building to house them in his own miniature Versailles. See Bernard-Maitre, "Les Tapisseries," 9–10.

20. Chippendale's *The Gentleman and Cabinet-Maker's Director* was only the best known of these. See also, for example, Halfpenny, *Rural Architecture*; and Decker, *Chinese Architecture*.

21. Nieuhof, *Embassy*, 197; Halfpenny, *Rural Architecture*, notation to Plate 20.

22. Chambers, *Plans, Elevations, Sections*. A reproduction of Chambers's illustration of the House of Confucius appears in *The Gentleman's Magazine* of June 1773. There has been some debate over the identity of the architect: see Harris, *Sir William Chambers*, 33–34.

23. For background on Watteau's chinoiseries, see Jacobson, *Chinoiserie*, 62–68; Adhemar, *Watteau*, 94–98; and Michel, *Watteau*, 279–80.

24. Jacobson, *Chinoiserie*, 62–63; Honour, *Chinoiserie*, 88–90.

25. Halfpenny, *Rural Architecture*, Plates 9 and 17; annotation to Plate 17; Sayer, *Ladies Amusement*, 181; Chippendale, *Director*, annotations to Plates 26–28. For Humphreys's views of the Halfpenny's achievement, see "Lords of Tartary," 27.

26. Chambers, *Designs*, Preface.

27. Halfpenny, *Rural Architecture*, Plates 10 and 54.

28. Attiret, "Particular Account," 6; reprinted in Dodsley, *Fugitive*, 1:61–83.

29. Attiret, "Particular Account," 6, 38–39.

30. Chambers, *Designs*, 1–3.

31. Fénelon, "Socrate," *Dialogues*, 49.

32. Ibid., 47.

33. Ibid., 44–45.

34. On the prevalence of foreign fashions in eighteenth-century England and their social implications, see, for example, Brewer, *Pleasures*, 83–85; and Mackie, *Market*, 40–47.

35. Shaftesbury, "Advice to an Author," *Characteristics*, 1:217–18. On the ideological constructedness and class implications of Shaftesbury's seemingly ahistorical realms of truth and beauty, see Markley, "Style," 140–54.

36. Shaftesbury, "Advice to an Author," *Characteristics,* 1:219.

37. Burke, *Reflections,* 146. On the perceived relationship between luxury and civic virtue in eighteenth-century England, see Berry, *Idea of Luxury,* 126–76; and Brewer, *Pleasures,* 80–85. Sekora argues that luxury was the most significant social idea in eighteenth-century England (Sekora, *Luxury,* 9).

38. Goldsmith, "Orphan of China," 434. Murphy's script was based on Voltaire's adaptation of a Yüan dynasty music drama. See Ch'ên Shou-yi, "The Chinese Orphan: A Yüan Play," 89–115. A modern translation of the play is included in J. Liu, *Six Yüan Plays.*

39. *The Connoisseur* 73 (June 19, 1755); *The World* 205 (Dec. 2, 1756). For further discussion of the classicist backlash against the chinoiserie aesthetic in eighteenth-century periodical literature, see Honour, *Chinoiserie,* 125–32; Allen, *Tides,* 1:234–56; and Spector, *English Literary Periodicals,* 241–367.

40. *The World,* 117 (Mar. 27, 1755).

41. On the political dangers of aesthetic novelty, see Allen, *Tides,* 1:240; and also Tristram, "Sprawling Dragons," 8. On the class porousness of the chinoiserie style, see Christopher Brooks, "Goldsmith's *Citizen,*" 125–26. There is an ever-expanding bibliography on the social implications of the expanding role of fashion in the early modern marketplace. See, for example, Braudel, *Structures,* 311–33; McCracken, *Culture,* 31–43; and Mackie, *Market.*

42. Halfpenny, *Rural Architecture,* Preface; *The World* 117 (Mar. 27, 1755).

43. Sayer, *Ladies Amusement,* 4.

44. "Propriety," *The Compact Oxford English Dictionary.*

45. *The World* 117 (Mar. 27, 1755).

46. *The World* 26 (June 28, 1753).

47. Shebbeare, *Letters,* letter 56. On the traditional role of the imagination in the procreation of monsters, see Boucé, "Imagination," 86–100. The most famous case of a monstrous birth in eighteenth-century England is recounted in Todd, *Imagining Monsters.*

48. Lovejoy, "Chinese Origin," 101, 112.

49. Temple, *Works,* 3:229–30; reprinted in Hunt and Willis, *Genius,* 96–99. For the history of the English use of the term "sharawadgi," see Lovejoy, "Chinese Origin," 110–22. For an account of its possible Chinese etymology, see Chang, "A Note," 221–24.

50. Lovejoy, "Chinese Origin," 112–13. For a collection of key primary texts on eighteenth-century English gardening, see Hunt and Willis, *Genius.* For useful discussions of the English adaptation of the Chinese style in gardening, see Fan, "China's Garden," 21–34; Ge, "Eighteenth-Century English Misreading," 106–26; and Shou-yi Ch'ên, "Chinese Garden," 321–39.

51. Chambers, *Designs,* Preface and 14–19.

52. For an overview of Chambers's interest in gardening, see Bald, "Sir William Chambers," 142–75. For further background on the backlash against

Chambers and the role of Mason and Horace Walpole in the controversy over Chambers's presentation of Chinese gardening, see Chase, "William Mason," 526–27; and Porter, "From Chinese to Goth," 46–58. The significant political implications of eighteenth-century landscape gardening are laid out in Bending, "A Natural Revolution?"

53. Chambers, *Dissertation*, 12, 14, 19.

54. Chambers, *An Explanatory Discourse*, 145.

55. Chambers, *Designs*, 19; Chambers, *Dissertation*, 19.

56. Chambers, *Dissertation*, 11. Earlier exponents of some of Chambers's aesthetic ideas in the *Dissertation* include Addison, *Spectator* 412; Baillie, *Essay on the Sublime*; Hogarth, *Analysis of Beauty*; Burke, *Philosophical Enquiry*; and Whately, *Observations*.

57. Chambers, *Dissertation*, 38–39.

58. Ibid., 36, 44–46, 73.

59. Chambers, *Designs*, 18.

60. Chambers, *Dissertation*, 25–27, 40.

61. Shaftesbury, "Advice to an Author," *Characteristics*, 1:218–19. On the history and implications of disinterestedness as a component of the aesthetic attitude, see Bohls, "Disinterestedness."

62. Cawthorn, *Taste*.

63. Wycherley, *Country Wife*, 86.

64. D. Cohen, "Revenger's Comedy," 122–25.

65. See Cleanth Brooks, *Well Wrought Urn*, 94–95; Kowaleski-Wallace, *Consuming Subjects*, 52–53; Brown, *Ends of Empire*, 113, and *Alexander Pope*, 6–28. On the history of the trope of glass or china as an emblem of female sexuality, see A. Williams, " 'Fall' of China," 412–25.

66. Pope, *Rape of the Lock*, canto 3, ll.153–60, *Poetry and Prose*, 91–92.

67. On Pope's use of zeugma in trivializing the figure of Belinda and the commodity fetishism with which she is identified, see Brown, *Alexander Pope*, 18–19. The most thorough recent analysis of the sexual politics of Pope's poem and of the "subversively 'masculine' power" of Belinda's "ravishing" beauty is Pollak, *Poetics*, 77–107.

68. There are other instances of fashionable eighteenth-century commodities evoking a sense of female erotic power equally capable of provoking masculine anxiety: see Mackie, *Market*, 104–27. The analysis of this phenomenon in connection with chinoiserie might be elaborated further by a reading of a long pornographic poem published in 1740 under the title *A Chinese Tale*, ostensibly written by "a celebrated mandarine of letters" Sou ma Quang. The frontispiece depicts the Chinese maid of honor Chamyam masturbating before a mirror in a room cluttered with chinoiserie while her frustrated (male) lover looks on from his hiding place in a large china jar. The poem is a lavishly long-winded meditation on this scene.

69. *The World* 12 (Mar. 22, 1753).

70. On the emergence of the British taste for foreign foods and beverages and its implications for the global economy in the eighteenth century, see Walvin, *Fruits of Empire*. On the history and context of Hogarth's treatment of race, see Dabydeen, *Hogarth's Blacks*.

71. *The Connoisseur* 65 (Apr. 24, 1755). On the changing relationship between masculinity and fashion in the early eighteenth century, see Mackie, *Market*, 189–202.

72. Kowaleski-Wallace points out that the widespread assumption that women were the primary consumers of porcelain is unsupported by the historical record (Kowaleski-Wallace, *Consuming Subjects*, 57–58).

73. *The World* 38 (Sept. 20, 1753).

CHAPTER 4

1. Scott, *Tea Story*, 17.

2. Forrest, *Tea*, 27, 284. As tea was not cultivated commercially on a large scale in India until 1825, most of these imports came from China (Forrest, *Tea*, 105). For additional background on the development of the British taste for tea, see Walvin, *Fruits of Empire*, 9–31.

3. Kowaleski-Wallace, "Tea, Gender, and Domesticity," 140. For an expanded treatment of this topic, see the same author's *Consuming Subjects*, 19–36.

4. Hanway, *Essay*, 2:17, 35–36.

5. Ibid., 2:2, 39, 57, 154, 273.

6. Ibid., 2:257.

7. Ibid., 2:182. For an overview of the bullionist position and its relationship to mercantilism, see Screpanti and Zamagni, *Outline*, 23–27. For a more detailed historical analysis of the flow of bullion in the early modern world economy, see Wallerstein, *Modern World System II*, 105–12.

8. Hanway, *Essay*, 2:200–205, 276–77.

9. Earlier Dutch efforts at establishing a permanent trading presence in China had failed (see Wills, *Peppers, Guns and Parleys*). For a helpful overview of the history of trade between Europe and East Asia in the early modern period, see Impey, *Chinoiserie*, 29–50.

10. For a detailed treatment of the rise of protectionist sentiment in England, the place of the English East India Company in the controversies that it generated, and, more generally, the relationship between mercantilism and nationalism, see P. J. Thomas, *Mercantilism*, 1–16.

11. A good general source on the history of the English trade with China is Eames, *The English in China*. The essential primary documents on the conditions of trade at Canton are collected in Morse, *Chronicles*. On English apprehensions

regarding the continued viability of the China trade, see, for example, Morse, *Chronicles,* 5:93, 129.

12. I am thinking here in particular of Richard Hakluyt's accounts of English explorations, first published in 1589. In the dedicatory epistle, he writes: "He pointed with his wand to all the knowen Seas, Gulfs, Bayes, Straights, Capes, Riuers, Empires, Kingdomes, Dukedomes, and Territories of ech part, with declaration also of their speciall commodities, & particular wants, which by the benefit of traffike, & entercourse of merchants, are plentifully supplied" (Hakluyts, *Principal Navigations,* 1:4). A recently discovered addition to the corpus of early literary paeans to international trade as well as chinoiscric—is described in Knowles, "Cecil's Shopping Centre," 14–15.

13. The interpretation of early-eighteenth-century literature in its relation to contemporary economic theory and practice has itself been something of a growth industry in recent years. See, for example, Thompson, *Models*; Sherman, *Finance*; and Ingrassia, *Authorship.*

14. Defoe, *The Review,* 9.54 (Feb. 3, 1713); reprinted in Defoe, *Best of the Review,* 107.

15. Lillo, *London Merchant,* III.i.

16. Smith, *Wealth of Nations,* 83–87; see also Dickey's essay on "The Nature of Things" in the same volume, 220–25. On the seventeenth-century history of the idea of commerce as according with the natural order of things, see Appleby, *Economic Thought,* 242–79.

17. Lillo, *London Merchant,* III.i; see also Addison, *The Spectator* 69 (May 19, 1711).

18. Smith, *Wealth of Nations,* 136, 148. For Marx's views on China and the necessary role of European colonization in its modernization, see Marx, *Karl Marx on Colonialism.*

19. Defoe, *The Review,* 4.106 (Oct. 16, 1707), and 8.16 (May 1, 1711); reprinted in Defoe, *Best of the Review,* 133, 113. For a further elaboration of this theme, see also Defoe, *A Plan of the English Commerce,* 52

20. *Some Considerations,* 71–73.

21. Smith, *Wealth of Nations,* 165.

22. See Ames, "Lawyerus."

23. Defoe, *The Review,* 6.42 (July 9, 1709); reprinted in Defoe, *Best of the Review,* 142–44. For a detailed analysis of the context of Defoe's view, see Appleby, *Economic Thought,* 199–241.

24. *Some Considerations,* 73.

25. Great Britain, "Second Report," 91:53.

26. Macartney, *Embassy,* 213. For further background on the Macartney embassy, see Bickers, *Ritual*; the Chinese perspective on these events is presented in Hevia, *Cherishing Men.*

27. See, for example, Walter and Robins, *Voyage,* 320.

28. On the history of the seventeenth-century Dutch embassies to the Chinese court, see Wills, *Peppers, Guns and Parleys*. For an illuminating example of English insight into the need for cultural accommodation, see Staunton, *Historical Account*, 231–35.

29. Staunton, *Historical Account*, viii. Other editions published in the same year omit the explanation, while still others omit the frontispiece altogether.

30. Dundas, letter to Lord Macartney, Sept. 8, 1792; reprinted in Morse, *Chronicles*, 2:234, 237.

31. Dundas letter, Morse, *Chronicles*, 2:236.

32. Dundas letter, Morse, *Chronicles*, 2:240–41. A 1792 letter from King George "To the Supreme Emperor of China Kien-long worthy to live tens of thousands and tens of thousands thousand Years" repeats the themes of mutually beneficial circulation and exchange in the ambassador's instructions with scarcely any modification of context or language (see Morse, *Chronicles*, 2:244–47).

33. Hevia, *Cherishing Men*, 26–27, 201. On British reservations about military action, see, for example, the "Second Report," cited above.

34. Hevia provides an interpretive framework for the Macartney embassy based on the complementary discourses of the public sphere, notions of China and chinoiserie, and British self-identity (Hevia, *Cherishing Men*, 57–74). My own reading, by positing a more generalized interpretive apparatus, serves to position both the diplomatic phase of the encounter in relation to others that came before, and Hevia's three discourses in a different relationship to one another. Most notions of China in the period, I would argue, are themselves constituted through such interpretive apparatuses, which themselves have a constitutive role to play in the formation of European identities.

35. Dundas letter, Morse, *Chronicles*, 2:233. On Qing policies for receiving merchants and other emissaries from the "West Ocean kingdoms," as European countries were called, see Hevia, *Cherishing Men*, 52–55.

36. See Wills, *Peppers, Guns and Parleys* and *Embassies*. For a concise overview of early English attempts to trade with China, see Spate, *Monopolists*, 97–101.

37. Morse, *Chronicles*, 1:137–38.

38. Smith, *Wealth of Nations*, 159–60.

39. Staunton, *Historical Account*, 8–11.

40. Great Britain, "Second Report," 3–4.

41. Barrow, *Travels*, 2–4.

42. Ibid., 41, 59. Not surprisingly, Barrow's damning assessment of the state of Chinese maritime technology represents a reversal of the prevailing seventeenth-century view. The British diarist John Evelyn, writing before the ascendancy of the Royal Navy, described Chinese vessels as "jonks of such prodigious size, as seem like cities rather than ships" (Evelyn, *Miscellaneous Writings*, 654).

43. Macartney, *Embassy*, 81, 168, 266, 275.

44. Ellis, *Journal,* 198.
45. Ibid., 488–89.
46. Barrow, *Travels,* 4–5.
47. Ibid., 5–6, 100–101.
48. Ellis, *Journal,* 40–41, 440, 491.
49. Spacks, *Boredom,* 18–24.
50. Ellis, *Journal,* 40.
51. Macartney, *Embassy,* 191.
52. Eames, *English in China,* 82; Morse, *Chronicles,* 2:253.
53. Morse, *Chronicles,* 1:187, 5:83.
54. Ibid., 2:60.
55. Great Britain, "Second Report," 52–53. The Qing policies that led to these complaints were largely motivated by political fears of collusion between Chinese merchants and overseas powers (see, for example, Hevia, *Cherishing Men,* 49–50).
56. Staunton, *Historical Account,* 276–77.
57. Macartney, *Embassy,* 131–34. The ambassador refers twice to Chambers somewhat disparagingly, but seems clearly to have taken the architect as his model here.
58. Ellis, *Journal,* 133.
59. Walter and Robins, *Voyage,* 355–56.
60. Macartney, *Embassy,* 90. Writing fully two hundred years after Lord Macartney, Senator Paul Wellstone of Minnesota takes a remarkably similar view of the Chinese attitude toward this facet of the circulatory ideal: "A government that routinely violates its own laws to crack down on dissent is equally likely to cheat on market access agreements, fail to honor contracts or restrict the free flow of business information from abroad" ("Get Tough with China," A21).
61. Walter and Robins, *Voyage,* 368–69.
62. Barrow, *Travels,* 142.
63. Ibid., 152.
64. Morse, *Chronicles,* 2:245–47. The king's fraternal posturing is a useful reminder of the very real resemblances between Britain and China at the end of the eighteenth century: both were "expansive colonial empires" based on absolutist imperial discourses; nascent British pretensions notwithstanding, the Qing Empire, as Hevia points out, "was the largest, wealthiest, and most populous contiguous political entity anywhere in the world" (Hevia, *Cherishing Men,* 25–26, 31).
65. Morse, *Chronicles,* 2:236–37.
66. See Hevia, *Cherishing Men,* for an in-depth analysis of the conflicting interpretations of the Macartney embassy from the British and Chinese sides. Perhaps the best-known account of the tribute system itself is Fairbank, "Tributary," 129–49.
67. A good general account of both embassies can be found in Collis, *Great*

Within. In Staunton, *Historical Account,* see especially 304–37. In Ellis, *Journal,* see 50–51, 78, 92–171.

68. Staunton, *Historical Account,* 304–5.

69. Ibid., 307–8; Ellis, *Journal,* 119, 171. On the Dutch experience in China, see the two books by Wills cited above. Swift alludes to the Dutch reputation for mercenary accommodation of humiliating rituals when Gulliver, posing as a Dutch merchant, asks the Japanese emperor to be excused from his countrymen's usual practice of trampling on the crucifix (Swift, *Gulliver's Travels,* 261–62).

70. Staunton, *Historical Account,* 306–7, 337.

71. Ellis, *Journal,* 139–40.

72. Letter from Lord Macartney to the Chairman and Deputy Chairman of the Honorable East India Company, Dec. 23, 1793; reprinted in Pritchard, "Instructions," 387.

73. Barrow, *Travels,* 24.

74. Ibid., 116.

75. Ellis, *Journal,* 307, 122, 220. On this uprising and patterns of social unrest in early-nineteenth-century China, see Spence, *Search for Modern China,* 165–70.

76. Macartney, *Embassy,* 191.

77. Ibid.

78. Barrow, *Travels,* 3, 124, 355.

79. Macartney, *Embassy,* 227, 239.

80. Ellis, *Journal,* 198.

81. Walter and Robins, *Voyage,* 366.

82. *Farther Adventures* first appeared in 1719, several months after the original *Robinson Crusoe,* and twenty-nine years before the first edition of Walter and Robins's account of Anson's voyage. I will refer to the facsimile edition in three volumes published by William Clowes & Sons, London, 1974.

83. Defoe, *Farther Adventures,* 151–52.

84. Ibid., 156–57.

85. Ibid., 164–67. L. Liu offers a rewarding reading of the porcelain house scene as "a master allegory of eighteenth-century metaphysics" richly interwoven with the early modern history of porcelain in Europe (L. Liu, "Robinson Crusoe's Earthenware Pot," 752–54).

86. Hegel, *Philosophy of History,* 116.

EPILOGUE

1. On the oriental renaissance and the nineteenth-century engagement with Buddhism, see Batchelor, *Awakening*; and Schwab, *La Renaissance.*

2. I develop this argument at greater length in "From Chinese to Goth," 46–58.

3. *The Economist,* for example, attributes the economic boom in southern

China to Deng Xiaoping's open-door policy, which allowed "foreign goods [to] circulate freely" and "money, factories, managers and trade [to] flow through the channels opened by language and blood" ("South China Miracle," 19). At the same time, continuing conflicts over human rights are widely seen to arise from metaphorically complementary forms of obstruction in the political sphere: "Even as it opens up to market forces, China blocks the marketplace of ideas" (Platt, "Two Men's Paths," 6).

Bibliography

A Chinese Tale. London, 1740.

Adhemar, Hélène. *Watteau: Sa vie, son oeuvre*. Paris: P. Tisne, 1950.

Adshead, S. A. M. *China in World History*. New York: St. Martin's Press, 1988.

Aldridge, A. Owen. "The Perception of China in English Literature of the Enlightenment." *Asian Culture Quarterly* 14, no. 2 (1986): 1–26.

Allen, Beverly S. *Tides in English Taste: 1619–1800*. 2 vols. Cambridge, Mass.: Harvard University Press, 1937.

Ames, Richard. "Lawyerus Bootatus and Spurratus: Or, The Long Vacation." London, 1691.

Appleby, Joyce Oldham. *Economic Thought and Ideology in Seventeenth-Century England*. Princeton, N.J.: Princeton University Press, 1978.

Appleton, William W. *A Cycle of Cathay: The Chinese Vogue in England during the 17th and 18th Centuries*. New York: Columbia University Press, 1951.

Arakelian, Paul. "The Myth of a Restoration Style Shift." *The Eighteenth Century: Theory and Interpretation* 20 (1979): 227–45.

Attiret, Jean-Denis. "A Particular Account of the Emperor of China's Gardens near Pekin." Trans. Harry Beaumont. London, 1752.

Bacon, Francis. *The Works of Francis Bacon*. 14 vols. Ed. James Spedding et al. London, 1857–1874.

Baillie, John. *An Essay on the Sublime*. London, 1744.

Bald, R. C. "Sir William Chambers and the Chinese Garden." In *Discovering China: European Interpretations in the Enlightenment*, ed. Julia Ching and Willard G. Oxtoby. Rochester, N.Y.: University of Rochester Press, 1992.

Bangert, William. *A History of the Society of Jesus*. St. Louis, Mo.: The Institute of Jesuit Sources, 1972.

Barrell, John. *English Literature in History, 1730–80: An Equal, Wide Survey*. London: Hutchinson, 1983.

Barrow, John. *Travels in China*. London, 1804.

Batchelor, Stephen. *The Awakening of the West: The Encounter of Buddhism and Western Culture*. Berkeley, Calif.: Parallax Press, 1994.

Bayle, Pierre. *Oeuvres diverses*. 5 vols. Hildesheim: Georg Olms, 1964.

Bell, John. *A Journey from St. Petersburg to Pekin, 1719–22*. Ed. J. L. Stevenson. Edinburgh: Edinburgh University Press, 1966.

Bending, Stephen. "A Natural Revolution? Garden Politics in Eighteenth-Century England." In *Refiguring Revolutions: Aesthetics and Politics from the English Revolution to the Romantic Revolution*, ed. Kevin Sharpe and Steven N. Zwicker. Berkeley and Los Angeles: University of California Press, 1998.

Benedict, Barbara. "The 'Curious Attitude' in Eighteenth-Century Britain: Observing and Owning." *Eighteenth-Century Life* 14, no. 3 (1990): 59–90.

Berger, Willy Richard. *China-Bild und China-Mode im Europa der Aufklärung*. Cologne: Böhlau Verlag, 1990.

Berling, Judith. *The Syncretic Religion of Lin Chao-en*. New York: Columbia University Press, 1980.

Bernard-Maitre, P. Henri. "Les Tapisseries chinoises de François Boucher a Pékin." *Bulletin de la Societé de l'Histoire de l'Art français* (1951): 9–10.

Berry, Christopher J. *The Idea of Luxury: A Conceptual and Historical Investigation*. Cambridge: Cambridge University Press, 1994.

Bickers, Robert A., ed. *Ritual and Diplomacy: The Macartney Mission to China (1792–1794)*. London: Wellsweep Press, 1993.

Bodde, Kerk. *Chinese Thought, Society, and Science*. Honolulu: University of Hawaii Press, 1991.

Bohls, Elizabeth. "Disinterestedness and the Denial of the Particular: Locke, Smith, and the Subject of Aesthetics." In *Eighteenth-Century Aesthetics and the Reconstruction of Art*, ed. Paul Mattick. New York: Cambridge University Press, 1993.

Booth, Wayne C. "'The Self-Portraiture of Genius': *The Citizen of the World* and Critical Method." *Modern Philology* 73 (1976): S85–S96.

Bono, James. *The Word of God and the Languages of Man: Interpreting Nature in Early Modern Science and Medicine*. Madison: University of Wisconsin Press, 1995.

Bordo, Susan. *The Flight to Objectivity: Essays on Cartesianism and Culture*. Albany: SUNY Press, 1987.

Boswell, James. *Life of Johnson*. 6 vols. Ed. G. B. Hill and L. F. Powell. Oxford, 1934.

Boucé, Paul-Gabriel. "Imagination, Pregnant Women, and Monsters, in Eighteenth-Century England and France." In *Sexual Underworlds of the Enlightenment*, ed. G. S. Rousseau and Roy Porter, 86–100. Chapel Hill: University of North Carolina Press, 1988.

Boxer, C. R., ed. *South China in the Sixteenth Century: Being the Narratives of Galeote Pereira, Fr. Gaspar da Cruz, O.P., Fr. Martin de Rada, O.E.S.A. (1550–1575)*. London: Hakluyt Society, 1953.

Braudel, Fernand. *The Structures of Everyday Life: The Limits of the Possible*. Trans. Siân Reynolds. New York: Harper & Row, 1981.

Brewer, John. *The Pleasures of the Imagination: English Culture in the Eighteenth Century*. New York: Farrar Straus Giroux, 1997.

Brisacier, Jaques Charles de. *Lettre de Messieurs des Missions Etrangères au Pape, sur les idolatries et les superstitions chinoises*. Paris, 1700.

Brooks, Christopher. "Goldsmith's *Citizen of the World*: Knowledge and the Imposture of 'Orientalism.'" *Texas Studies in Literature and Language* 35 (1993): 124–44.

Brooks, Cleanth. *The Well Wrought Urn: Studies in the Structure of Poetry*. New York: Harcourt Brace Jovanovich, 1975.

Brown, Laura. *Alexander Pope*. New York: Basil Blackwell, 1985.

———. *Ends of Empire: Women and Ideology in Early Eighteenth-Century English Literature*. Ithaca, N.Y.: Cornell University Press, 1993.

Burke, Edmund. *A Philosophical Enquiry into the Origin of Our Ideas of the Sublime and Beautiful*. London, 1759.

———. *Reflections on the Revolution in France*. Ed. Conor Cruise O'Brien. London: Penguin, 1968.

Cambridge Encyclopedia of China. Cambridge: Cambridge University Press, 1991.

Campbell, Mary B. *The Witness and the Other World: Exotic European Travel Writing, 400–1600*. Ithaca, N.Y.: Cornell University Press, 1988.

Cary-Elwes, Columba. *China and the Cross: Studies in Missionary History*. London: Longmans, 1957.

Castle, Terry. *Masquerade and Civilization: The Carnivalesque in Eighteenth-Century English Culture and Fiction*. Stanford, Calif.: Stanford University Press, 1986.

Cathay Invoked. San Francisco: California Palace of the Legion of Honor, 1966.

Cawthorn, James. *Of Taste: An Essay*. London, 1771.

Chambers, William. *Designs of Chinese Buildings, Furniture, Dresses, Machines, and Utensils*. London, 1757.

———. *A Dissertation on Oriental Gardening*. London, 1772.

———. *An Explanatory Discourse*. London, 1773.

———. *Plans, Elevations, Sections, and Perspective Views of the Gardens and Buildings at Kew*. London, 1763.

Chang, Y. Z. "A Note on Sharawadgi." *Modern Language Notes* 45 (1930): 221–24.

Chase, Isabel. "William Mason and Sir William Chambers' *Dissertation on Oriental Gardening*." *Journal of English and Germanic Philology* 35 (1936): 517–29.

Ch'en, Kenneth. *Buddhism in China: A Historical Survey*. Princeton, N.J.: Princeton University Press, 1964.

Ch'ên, Shou-yi. "John Webb: A Forgotten Page in the Early History of Sinology in Europe." *Chinese Social and Political Science Review* 19 (1935–1936): 295–330.

———. "The Chinese Garden in Eighteenth-Century England." *T'ien Hsia Monthly* 2, no. 4 (1936): 321–39.

———. "The Chinese Orphan: A Yüan Play." *T'ien Hsia Monthly* 3, no. 2 (1936): 89–115.

Ch'ien, Chung-shu. "China in the English Literature of the Eighteenth Century." *Quarterly Bulletin of Chinese Bibliography* New Series 2 (1941): 7–48.

———. "China in the English Literature of the Seventeenth Century." *Quarterly Bulletin of Chinese Bibliography* New Series 1 (1940): 351–84.

Ching, Julia. *Chinese Religions*. Maryknoll, N.Y.: Orbis, 1983.

Ching, Julia, and Willard G. Oxtoby, eds. *Discovering China: European Interpretations in the Enlightenment*. Rochester, N.Y.: University of Rochester Press, 1992.

Chippendale, Thomas. *The Gentleman and Cabinet-Maker's Director*. London, 1754.

Cohen, Derek. "The Revenger's Comedy: Female Hegemony in *The Country Wife*." *Atlantis* 5 (1980): 120–30.

Cohen, Jonathan. "On the Project of a Universal Character." In *John Wilkins and 17th-Century British Linguistics*, ed. Joseph Subbiondo. Amsterdam: John Benjamins Publishing Co., 1992.

Collins, Roy. *The Fu Hsi Ching: The Early Heaven Sequence*. Lanham, Md.: University Press of America, 1993.

Collis, Maurice. *The Great Within*. London: Faber and Faber, 1941.

Colloque international de Sinologie (Chantilly 1974): La mission française de Péking aux XVIIe et XVIIIe siècles. Paris: Belles Lettres, 1976.

Colloque international de Sinologie (Chantilly 1977): Les rapports entre la Chine et l'Europe au temps des lumières. Paris: Belles Lettres, 1980.

Colloque international de Sinologie (Chantilly 1980): Appréciation par l'Europe de la tradition chinoise à partir du XVIIe siècle. Paris: Belles Lettres, 1983.

Conant, Martha Pike. *The Oriental Tale in England in the Eighteenth Century*. New York: Columbia University Press, 1908.

Conner, Patrick. *Oriental Architecture in the West*. London: Thames and Hudson, 1979.

Connoisseur. London, 1754–1756.

Cordier, Henri. *La Chine en France au XVIIIᵉ siècle*. Paris: H. Laurens, 1910.

Cornelius, Paul. *Languages in Seventeenth- and Early Eighteenth-Century Imaginary Voyages*. Geneva: Librairie Droz, 1965.

Cummins, J. S. *A Question of Rites: Friar Domingo Navarrete and the Jesuits in China*. Aldershot, England: Scolar Press, 1993.

Dabydeen, David. *Hogarth's Blacks: Images of Blacks in Eighteenth-Century English Art*. Athens: University of Georgia Press, 1987.

Daunton, Martin, and Rick Halpern, eds. *Empire and Others: British Encounters with Indigenous Peoples, 1600–1850*. London: UCL Press, 1999.

David, Madeleine V. *Le Débat sur les écritures et l'hiéroglyphe au XVIIe et XVIIIe siècles, et l'application de la notion de déchiffrement aux écritures mortes.* Paris: SEVPEN, 1965.

Davis, Howard. *Chinoiserie: Polychrome Decoration on Staffordshire Porcelain, 1790–1850.* London: Rubicon, 1991.

Dawson, Raymond Stanley. *The Chinese Chameleon: An Analysis of European Conceptions of Chinese Civilisation.* London: Oxford University Press, 1967.

———, ed. *The Legacy of China.* Oxford: Clarendon Press, 1964.

Deane, Seamus. "Goldsmith's *The Citizen of the World.*" In *The Art of Oliver Goldsmith*, ed. Andrew Swarbrick, 33–50. London: Vision Press, 1984.

Decker, Paul. *Chinese Architecture.* London, 1759.

Defoe, Daniel. *The Best of Defoe's Review.* Ed. William L. Payne. New York: Columbia University Press, 1951.

———. *The Farther Adventures of Robinson Crusoe.* London: William Clowes & Sons, 1974.

———. *A Plan of the English Commerce.* New York: Augustus Kelley, 1967.

DeFrancis, John. *The Chinese Language: Fact and Fantasy.* Honolulu: University of Hawaii Press, 1984.

Dehergne, J. "Un Problème ardu: Le nom de Dieu en Chinois." *Colloque international de Sinologie (Chantilly 1980): Appréciation par l'Europe de la tradition chinoise à partir du XVIIe siècle.* Paris: Belles Lettres, 1983.

Demaria, Robert. "The Theory of Language in Johnson's Dictionary." In *Johnson After Two Hundred Years*, ed. Paul Korshin, 159–74. Philadelphia: University of Pennsylvania Press, 1986.

Demott, Benjamin. "The Sources and Development of John Wilkins' Philosophical Language." In *John Wilkins and 17th-Century British Linguistics*, ed. Joseph Subbiondo, 168–81. Amsterdam: John Benjamins, 1992.

Dictionary of Ming Biography, 1368–1644. New York: Columbia University Press, 1976.

Dodsley, Robert, ed. *Fugitive Pieces on Various Subjects.* 2 vols. London, 1771.

Du Halde, Jean Baptiste. *Description géographique, historique, chronologique, politique, et physique de l'empire de la Chine et de la Tartarie Chinoise.* 4 vols. Paris, 1735.

Dunne, George H. *Generation of Giants: The Story of the Jesuits in China in the Last Decades of the Ming Dynasty.* Notre Dame: University of Notre Dame Press, 1962.

Eames, James Bromley. *The English in China.* London: Pitman and Sons, 1909.

Eco, Umberto. *The Search for the Perfect Language.* Trans. James Fentress. Oxford: Blackwell, 1995.

Ellis, Henry. *Journal of the Proceedings of the Late Embassy to China.* London, 1817.

Emery, Clark. "John Wilkins' Universal Language." *Isis* 38 (1947–1948): 174–85.

Etiemble, René. *L'Europe chinoise.* Paris: Gallimard, 1988.

———. *Les Jesuites en Chine: La querelle des rites (1552–1773).* Paris: Julliard, 1966.

Evelyn, John. *The Miscellaneous Writings.* Ed. William Upcott. London, 1825.

Fairbank, John K. "Tributary Trade and China's Relations with the West." *Far Eastern Quarterly* 1 (1942): 129–49.

Fan, Cunzhong. "China's Garden Architecture and the Tides of English Taste in the 18th Century." *Cowrie: A Chinese Journal of Comparative Literature* 1, no. 2 (1984): 21–34.

———. [Fan, Tsen-Chung]. "Dr. Johnson and Chinese Culture." *China Society Occasional Papers,* new ser. 6 (1945): 5–20.

Farrington, Benjamin. "Temporis Parus Masculus: An Untranslated Writing of Francis Bacon." *Centaurus* 1 (1951): 193–205.

Faure, Bernard. *Chan Insights and Oversights: An Epistemological Critique of the Chan Tradition.* Princeton, N.J.: Princeton University Press, 1993.

Fénelon, François de Salignac de la Mothe. *Dialogues des Morts.* Paris: Librairie Hachette, 1888.

———. *Oeuvres de Fénelon.* 33 vols. Ed. Augustin Caron and Jean Gosselin. Paris, 1827.

Filmer, Robert. *Patriarcha and Other Writings.* Ed. Johann P. Sommerville. Cambridge: Cambridge University Press, 1991.

Forrest, Denys. *Tea for the British: The Social and Economic History of a Famous Trade.* London: Chatto & Windus, 1973.

Foss, Theodore, and Donald Lach. "Images of Asia and Asians in European Fiction, 1500–1800." *China and Europe: Images and Influences in the Sixteenth to Eighteenth Centuries.* Ed. Thomas Lee. Hong Kong: Chinese University Press, 1991.

Foucault, Michel. *The Order of Things: An Archaeology of the Human Sciences.* New York: Vintage, 1973.

Francus, Marilyn. *The Converting Imagination: Linguistic Theory and Swift's Satiric Prose.* Carbondale: Southern Illinois University Press, 1994.

Fung, Yu-Lan. *A Short History of Chinese Philosophy.* Ed. Derk Bodde. New York: Free Press, 1948.

Gandhi, Leela. *Postcolonial Theory: A Critical Introduction.* New York: Columbia University Press, 1998.

Ge, Liangyan. "On the Eighteenth-Century English Misreading of the Chinese Garden." *Comparative Civilizations Review* 27 (1992): 106–26.

Gernet, Jacques. *China and the Christian Impact: A Conflict of Cultures.* Trans. Janet Lloyd. Cambridge: Cambridge University Press, 1985.

———. *A History of Chinese Civilization*. Cambridge: Cambridge University Press, 1996.

Gibbon, Edward. *The History of the Decline and Fall of the Roman Empire*. 7 vols. Ed. J. B. Bury. London, 1897.

———. *Memoirs of My Life*. New York: Penguin, 1984.

Ginzburg, Carlo. *The Cheese and the Worms: The Cosmos of a Sixteenth-Century Miller*. Trans. John and Anne Tedeschi. Baltimore, Md.: Johns Hopkins University Press, 1980.

Gleeson, Janet. *The Arcanum: The Extraordinary True Story of the Invention of European Porcelain*. London: Bantam, 1999.

Goldsmith, Oliver. *Citizen of the World*. London: J. M. Dent & Sons, 1934.

———. "The Orphan of China, a Tragedy, as it is performed at the Theatre-Royal in Drury-Lane." *Critical Review* (1759): 434.

Goodman, Howard, and Anthony Grafton. "Ricci, the Chinese, and the Toolkits of Textualists." *Asia Major*, 3d ser. 3 (1990): 95–148.

Granet, Marcel. *The Religion of the Chinese People*. Trans. Maurice Freedman. Oxford: Basil Blackwell, 1975.

Great Britain. "Second Report of the Select Committee, Appointed to Take into Consideration the Export Trade from Great Britain to the East Indies" [1791]. *House of Commons Sessional Papers of the Eighteenth Century*. 145 vols. Ed. Sheila Lambert. Wilmington, Del.: Scholarly Resources, Inc., 1975.

Grigsby, Leslie B. "Johan Nieuhoff's *Embassy*: An Inspiration for Relief Decoration on English Stoneware and Earthenware." *Antiques* (Jan. 1993): 172–83.

Guy, Basil. *The French Image of China Before and After Voltaire. Studies on Voltaire and the Eighteenth Century* 21 (1963): 1–468.

Hakluyt, Richard. *The Principal Navigations, Voyages, Traffiques, and Discoveries of the English Nation*. 16 vols. Edinburgh: E. & G. Goldsmid, 1885.

Halén, Harry, and Bent Lerbaek Pedersen. *C. G. Mannerheim's Chinese Pantheon: Materials for an Iconography of Chinese Folk Religion*. Helsinki: Finno-Ugrian Society, 1993.

Halfpenny, William, and John Halfpenny. *Rural Architecture in the Chinese Taste*. London, 1755.

Hammond, Dorothy, and Alta Jablow. *The Africa That Never Was: Four Centuries of British Writing About Africa*. New York: Twayne Publishers, 1970.

Hanway, Jonas. *An Essay on Tea. A Journal of Eight Days Journey*. 2 vols. London, 1757. Vol. 2.

Harris, John. *Sir William Chambers: Knight of the Polar Star*. London: A. Zwemmer, 1970.

Hegel, Georg W. F. *The Philosophy of History*. New York: Dover, 1956.

Hevia, James L. *Cherishing Men from Afar: Qing Guest Ritual and the Macartney Embassy of 1793*. Durham, N.C.: Duke University Press, 1995.

Hickey, William. *Memoirs*. Ed. Peter Quennell. London: Hutchinson, 1960.

Higgins, Iain. *Writing East: The "Travels" of Sir John Mandeville*. Philadelphia: University of Pennsylvania Press, 1997.

Hobbes, Thomas. *Leviathan*. Ed. Richard Tuck. Cambridge: Cambridge University Press, 1996.

Hogarth, William. *The Analysis of Beauty*. London, 1753

————. *Engravings*. Ed. Sean Shesgreen. New York: Dover, 1973.

Honour, Hugh. *Chinoiserie: The Vision of Cathay*. New York: Dutton, 1962.

Hook, Brian, ed. *The Cambridge Encyclopedia of China*. Cambridge: Cambridge University Press, 1991.

Hudson, G. F. *Europe and China: A Survey of Their Relations from the Earliest Times to 1800*. London: E. Arnold & Co., 1931.

Hulme, Peter. *Colonial Encounters: Europe and the Native Caribbean, 1492– 1797*. London: Methuen, 1986.

Humphreys, A. R. "Lords of Tartary." *The Cambridge Journal* 3 (1949): 19–31.

Hunt, John Dixon, and Peter Willis, eds. *The Genius of the Place: The English Landscape Garden, 1620–1820*. New York: Harper & Row, 1975.

Hunt, Michael H. *The Genesis of Chinese Communist Foreign Policy*. New York: Columbia University Press, 1996.

Impey, O. R. *Chinoiserie: The Impact of Oriental Styles on Western Art and Decoration*. London: Oxford University Press, 1977.

Ingrassia, Catherine. *Authorship, Commerce, and Gender in Early Eighteenth-Century England: A Culture of Paper Credit*. Cambridge: Cambridge University Press, 1998.

Isaacs, Harold. *Images of Asia: American Views of China and India*. New York: Capricorn Books, 1958.

Jacobson, Dawn. *Chinoiserie*. London: Phaidon Press, 1993.

Jarry, Madeleine. *Chinoiserie: Chinese Influence on European Decorative Art, 17th and 18th Centuries*. Trans. Gail Mangold-Vine. New York: Vendome Press, 1981.

————. "La Vision de la Chine dans les tapisseries de la manufacture royale de Beauvais: Les premières tentures chinoises." In *Actes du IIe Colloque International de Sinologie: Les Rapports entre la Chine et l'Europe au Temps des Lumières*, 173–83. Paris: Les Belles Lettres, 1980.

Jensen, Lionel M. *Manufacturing Confucianism: Chinese Traditions and Universal Civilization*. Durham, N.C.: Duke University Press, 1997.

Johnson, Samuel. *The Works of Samuel Johnson*. London, 1816.

Jones, Richard Foster. *The Seventeenth Century: Studies in the History of English Thought and Literature from Bacon to Pope*. Stanford, Calif.: Stanford University Press, 1965.

Jones, William. "Dissertation on the Chinese." In *Dissertations and Miscellaneous Pieces Relating to the History & Antiquities, the Arts, Sciences, and Literature, of Asia*, 2 vols, ed. William Jones, William Chambers et al., 1:209–34. London, 1792.

Journal des Savans. Paris, 1665–1949.

Keller, Evelyn Fox. *Reflections on Gender and Science*. New Haven, Conn.: Yale University Press, 1985.

Kiernan, V. G. *The Lords of Human Kind: Black Man, Yellow Man, and White Man in an Age of Empire*. Boston: Little, Brown and Co., 1969.

Kircher, Athanasius. *China Illustrata*. Trans. Charles D. van Tuyl. Muskogee, Okla.: Indiana University Press, 1987.

Knight, Charles A. "Ironic Loneliness: The Case of Goldsmith's Chinaman." *Journal of English and Germanic Philology* 82 (1983): 347–64.

Knowles, James. "Cecil's Shopping Centre: The Rediscovery of a Ben Jonson Masque in Praise of Trade." *TLS* (Feb. 7, 1997): 14–15.

Knowlson, James. *Universal Language Schemes in England and France, 1600–1800*. Toronto: University of Toronto Press, 1975.

Korshin, Paul J. *Typologies in England: 1650–1820*. Princeton, N.J.: Princeton University Press, 1982.

Kowaleski-Wallace, Elizabeth. *Consuming Subjects: Women, Shopping, and Business in the Eighteenth Century*. New York: Columbia University Press, 1997.

———. "Tea, Gender, and Domesticity in Eighteenth-Century England." *Studies in Eighteenth-Century Culture* 23 (1994): 131–45.

———. "Women, China, and Consumer Culture in Eighteenth-Century England." *Eighteenth-Century Studies* 29 (1995–1996): 153–67.

Kroll, Richard. *The Material Word: Literate Culture in the Restoration and Early Eighteenth Century*. Baltimore, Md.: Johns Hopkins University Press, 1991.

Küng, Hans, and Julia Ching. *Christianity and Chinese Religions*. New York: Doubleday, 1989.

Lach, Donald. *Asia in the Making of Europe*. 3 vols. Chicago: University of Chicago Press, 1965–1993.

———. "China and the Era of Enlightenment." *Journal of Modern History* 14 (1942): 209–23.

———. *China in the Eyes of Europe: The Sixteenth Century*. Chicago: University of Chicago Press, 1968.

———. "China in Western Thought and Culture." In *Dictionary of the History of Ideas*, 5 vols., ed. Philip P. Winter, 1:353–73. New York: Scribner, 1973.

———. "The Chinese Studies of Andreas Müller." *Journal of the American Oriental Society* 60 (1940): 564–75.

———. "Leibniz and China." *Journal of the History of Ideas* 6, no. 4 (1945): 436–55.

——, ed. and trans. *The Preface to Leibniz' Novissima Sinica.* Honolulu: University of Hawaii Press, 1957.

Lackner, Michael. "Jesuit Figurism." In *China and Europe: Images and Influences in the Sixteenth to Eighteenth Centuries,* ed. Thomas Lee, 129- 49. Hong Kong: Chinese University Press, 1991.

Landa, Louis, ed. *John Oldmixon's Reflections on Dr. Swift's Letter to Harley (1712) and Arthur Mainwaring's The British Academy (1712).* Augustan Reprint Society, ser. 6, no. 1. Ann Arbor, Mich., 1948.

——. "Of Silkworms and Farthingales and the Will of God." In *Studies in the Eighteenth Century,* 2 vols., ed. R. F. Brissenden, 2:259–77. Toronto: University of Toronto Press, 1973.

——. "Pope's Belinda, The General Emporie of the World, and the Wondrous Worm." *The South Atlantic Quarterly* 70 (1971): 215–35.

Le Comte, Louis. *Eclaircissement sur la dénonciation . . . des Mémoires de la Chine.* Paris, 1700.

——. *Nouveaux Mémoires sur l'état présent de la Chine.* Paris: 1696.

——. *Un Jésuite à Pékin: Nouveaux Mémoires sur l'état présent de la Chine, 1687–1692.* Ed. Frédérique Touboul-Bouyeure. Paris: Phébus, 1990.

Le Gobien, Charles. *Histoire de l'Edit de l'Empereur de la Chine.* Paris, 1698.

Leibniz, Gottfried. *Leibniz Korrespondiert mit China: Der Briefwechsel mit den Jesuitenmissionaren (1689–1714).* Ed. Rita Widmaier. Frankfurt am Main: Vittorio Klostermann, 1990.

——. *Viri illustris Leibnitii epistolae ad diversos.* 4 vols. 1734–1742.

——. *Writings on China.* Ed. and trans. Daniel Cook and Henry Rosemont, Jr. Chicago: Open Court, 1994.

Letson, Douglas, and Michael Higgins. *The Jesuit Mystique.* London: Harper-Collins, 1995.

Lettres édifiantes et curieuses de Chine par des Missionnaires Jésuites, 1702– 1776. Ed. Isabelle and Jean-Louis Vissière. Paris: Flammarion, 1979.

Lillo, George. *The London Merchant.* Lincoln: University of Nebraska Press, 1965.

Liu, Jung-en, trans. *Six Yüan Plays.* New York: Penguin, 1977.

Liu, Lydia. "Robinson Crusoe's Earthenware Pot." *Critical Inquiry* 25 (1999): 728–57.

——. *Translingual Practice: Literature, National Culture, and Translated Modernity—China, 1900–1937.* Stanford, Calif.: Stanford University Press, 1995.

Locke, John. *An Essay Concerning Human Understanding.* Ed. Peter H. Nidditch. Oxford: Clarendon Press, 1975.

Longobardi, Nicolas. *Traité sur quelques points de la religion des chinois.* Vol. 2, Paris, 1701. In *Viri illustris Leibnitii epistolae ad diversos,* 4 vols., ed. Kortholt. Leipzig: 1734–1742.

Loomba, Ania. *Colonialism/Postcolonialism.* London: Routledge, 1998.

Lovejoy, Arthur O. "The Chinese Origin of a Romanticism." *Essays in the History of Ideas*. New York: Putnam, 1960.

Lundbaek, Knud. *Joseph de Prémare (1666–1736), S.J.: Chinese Philology and Figurism*. Aarhus, Denmark: Aarhus University Press, 1991.

———. *T. S. Bayer (1694–1738): Pioneer Sinologist*. London: Curzon Press, 1986.

Lust, John. *Western Books on China Published up to 1850 in the Library of the School of Oriental and African Studies, University of London: A Descriptive Catalogue*. London: Bamboo Publishing Ltd., 1987.

Macartney, George. *An Embassy to China: Being the Journal Kept by Lord Macartney during his Embassy to the Emperor Ch'ien-lung, 1793–1794*. Ed. J. L. Cranmer-Byng. Hamden, Conn.: Archon Books, 1963.

Mackie, Erin. *Market à la Mode: Fashion, Commodity, and Gender in 'The Tatler' and 'The Spectator.'* Baltimore, Md.: Johns Hopkins University Press, 1997.

Mandeville, John. *The Travels of Sir John Mandeville*. Trans. C. W. R. D. Moseley. New York: Penguin, 1983.

Markley, Robert. *Fallen Languages: Crises of Representation in Newtonian England, 1660–1740*. Ithaca, N.Y.: Cornell University Press, 1993.

———. "Style as Philosophical Structure: The Contexts of Shaftesbury's *Characteristicks*." In *The Philosopher as Writer: The Eighteenth Century*, ed. Robert Ginsberg, 140–54. Selinsgrove, Pa.: Susquehanna University Press, 1987.

———. *Two-Edg'd Weapons: Style and Ideology in the Comedies of Etherege, Wycherlye, and Congreve*. Oxford: Clarendon Press, 1988.

Marshall, P. J., and Glyndwr Williams. *The Great Map of Mankind: Perceptions of New Worlds in the Age of Enlightenment*. Cambridge, Mass.: Harvard University Press, 1982.

Martin, A. Lynn. *The Jesuit Mind: The Mentality of an Elite in Early Modern France*. Ithaca, N.Y.: Cornell University Press, 1988.

Marx, Karl. *Karl Marx on Colonialism and Modernization: His Dispatches and Other Writings on China, India, Mexico, the Middle East and North Africa*. Ed. Shlomo Avineri. Garden City, N.Y.: Anchor Books, 1969.

McCracken, Grant. *Culture and Consumption: New Approaches to the Symbolic Character of Consumer Goods and Activities*. Bloomington: Indiana University Press, 1988.

Mendoza, Juan González de. *The History of the Great and Mighty Kingdom of China and the Situation Thereof*. 2 vols. Ed. Sir George T. Staunton. London: Hakluyt Society, 1853.

Michel, Marianne Roland. "Représentations de l'exotisme dans la peinture en France de la première moitié du XVIIIème siècle." *Studies on Voltaire and the Eighteenth Century* 154 (1976): 1437–57.

———. *Watteau: An Artist of the Eighteenth Century*. London: Trefoil Books, 1984.

Mitchell, David. *The Jesuits: A History*. London: Macdonald, 1980.

Morse, Hosea Ballou. *The Chronicles of the East India Company Trading to China, 1635–1834*. 5 vols. Taipei: Ch'eng-wen Publishing Company, 1975.

Mundy, Peter. *The Travels of Peter Mundy in Europe and Asia, 1608–1667*. 5 vols. Ed. Richard Carnac Temple. Cambridge: Hakluyt Society, 1907–1936.

Mungello, David. *Curious Land: Jesuit Accommodation and the Origins of Sinology*. Stuttgart: Franz Steiner Verlag, 1985.

———. *Leibniz and Confucianism: The Search for Accord*. Honolulu: University Press of Hawaii, 1977.

———. "Sinological Torque: The Influence of Cultural Preoccupations on Seventeenth-Century Missionary Interpretations of Confucianism." In *Christianity and Missions, 1450–1800*, ed. J. S. Cunnins. Aldershot, England: Ashgate, 1997.

Needham, Joseph. *Science and Civilisation in China*. 6 vols. Cambridge: Cambridge University Press, 1956.

New Catholic Encyclopedia. New York: McGraw Hill, 1967.

Nieuhof, Johan. *An Embassy from the East-India Company of the United Provinces, to the Grand Tartar Cham, Emperour of China*. London, 1669.

O'Briant, Walter H. "Leibniz's Project of a Universal Language." *Southern Humanities Review* 1 (1967): 182–91.

Percy, Thomas. *Miscellaneous Pieces Relating to the Chinese*. 2 vols. London, 1762.

Pillement, Jean. *L'Oeuvre de Jean Pillement (1727–1808)*. Paris: A. Guerinet, 1910.

Pinot, Virgile. *La Chine et la formation de l'esprit philosophique en France (1640–1740)*. Paris: P. Geuthner, 1932.

Platt, Kevin. "Two Men's Paths Toward Liberty in China." *The Christian Science Monitor*, Mar. 6, 1998, 6.

Plumb, J. H. *In the Light of History*. London: Allen Lane, 1972.

Pollak, Ellen. *The Poetics of Sexual Myth: Gender and Ideology in the Verse of Swift and Pope*. Chicago: University of Chicago Press, 1985.

Polo, Marco. *The Book of Ser Marco Polo*. Trans. and ed. Sir Henry Yule. London: J. Murray, 1921.

Pope, Alexander. *Poetry and Prose of Alexander Pope*. Ed. Aubrey Williams. Boston: Houghton Mifflin, 1969.

Porter, David. "From Chinese to Goth: Walpole and the Gothic Repudiation of Chinoiserie." *Eighteenth-Century Life* 23 (1999): 46–58.

———. "His Master's Voice: The Politics of Narragenitive Desire in *The Tempest*." *Comitatus* 24 (1993): 33–44.

———. "Rhetorical Phallacies: The Poetics of Misogyny in Jean de Meun's Discourse of Nature." *Mediaevalia* 22 (1998): 59–77.

———. "Writing China: Legitimacy and Representation, 1606–1773." *Comparative Literature Studies* 33 (1996): 98–101.

Poulantzas, Nicos. *Political Power and Social Classes.* Trans. Timothy O'Hagen. London: NLB, 1975.

Pritchard, Earl H. *Anglo-Chinese Relations During the Seventeenth and Eighteenth Centuries.* University of Illinois Studies in the Social Sciences 17 (1929): 1–244.

———. "The Instructions of the East India Company to Lord Macartney on His Embassy to China and His Reports to the Company, 1792–4." *Journal of the Royal Asiatic Society* (1938): 201–30, 375–96, 493–509.

Raven, James. *Judging New Wealth: Popular Publishing and Responses to Commerce in England, 1750–1800.* Oxford: Clarendon Press, 1992.

Reddick, Allen. *The Making of Johnson's Dictionary, 1746–1773.* Cambridge: Cambridge University Press, 1990.

Reichwein, Adolf. *China and Europe: Intellectual and Artistic Contacts in the Eighteenth Century.* Trans. J. C. Powell. London: K. Paul, Trench, Trubner & Co., 1925.

Review. London, 1704–13.

Ricci, Matteo. *China in the Sixteenth Century: The Journals of Matthew Ricci, 1583–1610.* Ed. Nicolas Trigault. Trans. Louis J. Gallagher, S.J. New York: Random House, 1953.

———. *Fonti ricciane: documenti originali concernenti Matteo Ricci e la storia delle prime relazioni tra l'Europa e la Cina.* 3 vols. Ed. Pasquale M. d'Elia. Rome: Libreria dello Stato, 1942–1949.

———. *Opere Storiche del P. Matteo Ricci, S.J.* 2 vols. Ed. P. Pietro Tacchi Venturi. Macerata: F. Giorgetti, 1911–1913.

———. *The True Meaning of the Lord of Heaven (T'ien-chu Shih-i).* Trans. Douglas Lancashire and Peter Hu Kuo-chen, S.J. St. Louis, Mo.: The Institute of Jesuit Sources, 1985.

Rouleau, F. A. "Chinese Rites Controversy." 18 vols. In *New Catholic Encyclopedia*, 3:611–17. New York: McGraw Hill, 1967–1988.

Rowbotham, Arnold H. "China and the Age of Enlightenment in Europe." *Chinese Social and Political Science Review* 19 (1935): 176–201.

———. "The Impact of Confucianism on European Thought of the Eighteenth Century." *Far Eastern Quarterly* 4 (1945): 224–42.

———. "Jesuit Figurists and Eighteenth-Century Religious Thought." *Journal of the History of Ideas* 17 (1956): 471–85.

———. *Missionary and Mandarin: The Jesuits at the Court of China.* Berkeley and Los Angeles: University of California Press, 1942.

———. "Voltaire, Sinophile." *PMLA* 47 (1932): 1050–65.

Roy, Olivier. *Leibniz et la Chine.* Paris: Librairie Philosophique J. Vrin, 1972.

Said, Edward W. *Orientalism.* New York: Vintage, 1979.

Sainte-Marie, Antoine de. *Traité sur quelques points importants de la mission de la Chine.* Vol. 2, Paris, 1701. In *Viri illustris Leibnitii epistolae ad diversos,* 4 vols., ed. Kortholt. Leipzig, 1734–1742.

Saussy, Haun. *The Problem of a Chinese Aesthetic.* Stanford, Calif.: Stanford University Press, 1993.

Sayer, Robert. *The Ladies Amusement; Or, the Whole Art of Japanning Made Easy.* London, 1762.

Schiebinger, Londa. *The Mind Has No Sex? Women in the Origins of Modern Science.* Cambridge, Mass.: Harvard University Press, 1989.

Schwab, Raymond. *La Renaissance Orientale.* Paris: Payot, 1950.

Scott, J. M. *The Tea Story.* London: Heinemann, 1964.

Screpanti, Ernesto, and Stefano Zamagni. *An Outline of the History of Economic Thought.* Trans. David Field. Oxford: Clarendon Press, 1993.

Sekora, John. *Luxury: The Concept in Western Thought, Eden to Smollett.* Baltimore, Md.: Johns Hopkins University Press, 1977.

Seymour, M. C. *Sir John Mandeville.* Aldershot, England: Variorum, 1993.

Shaftesbury, Anthony Ashley Cooper. *Characteristics of Men, Manners, Opinions, Times, etc.* 2 vols. Ed. John Robertson. London, 1900.

Shakespeare, William. *The Tempest.* Ed. Anne Barton. London: Penguin, 1968.

Shebbeare, John. *Letters on the English Nation.* London, 1755.

Sherman, Sandra. *Finance and Fictionality in the Early Eighteenth Century: Accounting for Defoe.* Cambridge: Cambridge University Press, 1996.

Sirén, Oswald. *China and Gardens of Europe of the Eighteenth Century.* New York: Ronald Press Co., 1950.

Slaughter, Mary M. *Universal Languages and Scientific Taxonomy in the Seventeenth Century.* Cambridge: Cambridge University Press, 1982.

Smith, Adam. *An Inquiry into the Nature and Causes of the Wealth of Nations.* Ed. Laurence Dickey. Indianapolis, Ind.: Hackett, 1993.

Snider, Alvin. "Bacon, Legitimation, and the 'Origin' of Restoration Science." *The Eighteenth Century* 32 (1991): 119–38.

———. *Origin and Authority in Seventeenth-Century England: Bacon, Milton, Butler.* Toronto: University of Toronto Press, 1994.

Some Considerations on the Nature and Importance of the East-India Trade. London, 1728.

"South China Miracle, The." *The Economist,* Oct. 5, 1991, 19.

Southey, Robert. *Letters from England.* Ed. Jack Simmons. London: Cresset Press, 1951.

Spacks, Patricia Meyer. *Boredom: The Literary History of a State of Mind.* Chicago: University of Chicago Press, 1995.

Spate, O. H. K. *Monopolists and Freebooters.* Canberra: Australian National University Press, 1983.

Spectator. London, 1710–1714.

Spector, Robert. *English Literary Periodicals and the Climate of Opinion During the Seven Years' War.* The Hague: Mouton & Co., 1996.

Spence, Jonathan. *The Memory Palace of Matteo Ricci.* New York: Penguin, 1985.

———. *The Search for Modern China.* New York: W. W. Norton, 1990.

———. *To Change China: Western Advisers in China, 1620–1960.* New York: Penguin, 1980.

Sprat, Thomas. *The History of the Royal Society of London.* London, 1667.

Standen, Edith A. "The Story of the Emperor of China: A Beauvais Tapestry Series." *Metropolitan Museum Journal* 11 (1976): 103–17.

Staunton, George. *An Historical Account of the Embassy to the Emperor of China.* London: John Stockdale, 1797.

Stillman, Robert E. *The New Philosophy and Universal Languages in Seventeenth-Century England: Bacon, Hobbes, and Wilkins.* Lewisburg, Pa.: Bucknell University Press, 1995.

Subbiondo, Joseph, ed. *John Wilkins and Seventeenth-Century British Linguistics.* Amsterdam: John Benjamins Publishing Co., 1992.

Swift, Jonathan. *Gulliver's Travels.* London: Penguin, 1985.

———. *Works of Jonathan Swift.* 19 vols. Boston, 1883.

Sypher, G. Wylie. "Faisant ce qu'il leur vient à plaisir": The Image of Protestantism in French Catholic Polemic on the Eve of the Religious Wars." *Sixteenth Century Journal* 11 (1980): 59–84.

Teiser, Stephen. *The Ghost Festival in Medieval China.* Princeton, N.J.: Princeton University Press, 1988.

Temple, William. *Works.* 4 vols. London, 1757.

Thomas, Gertrude. *Richer Than Spices.* New York: Alfred A. Knopf, 1965.

Thomas, P. J. *Mercantilism and the East India Trade.* London: Frank Cass & Co., 1963.

Thomas, Pascoe. *A Voyage to the South Seas.* London, 1745.

Thompson, James. *Models of Value: Eighteenth-Century Political Economy and the Novel.* Durham, N.C.: Duke University Press, 1996.

Todd, Dennis. *Imagining Monsters: Miscreations of the Self in Eighteenth-Century England.* Chicago: University of Chicago Press, 1995.

Tristram, Philippa. "Sprawling Dragons, Squatting Pagods, and Clumsy Mandarins." *The Georgian Group Journal* (1995): 1–8.

Vickers, Brian. *English Science, Bacon to Newton.* Cambridge: Cambridge University Press, 1987.

———. "Restoration Prose Style: A Reassessment." In *Rhetoric and the Pursuit of Truth: Language Change in the Seventeenth and Eighteenth Centuries,* ed. Nancy Struever and Brian Vickers. Los Angeles: Clark Library, 1985.

———. "The Royal Society and English Prose Style: A Reassessment." In *Rhetoric and the Pursuit of Truth: Language Change in the Seventeenth and Eighteenth*

Centuries, ed. Nancy Struever and Brian Vickers. Los Angeles: Clark Library, 1985.

Voltaire. *Dialogues et anecdotes philosophiques*. Ed. Raymond Naves. Paris: Editions Garnier Frères, 1955.

———. *Oeuvres complètes*. 66 vols. Paris, 1819–1823.

Von Collani, Claudia. "Chinese Figurism in the Eyes of European Contemporaries." *China Mission Studies (1550–1800) Bulletin* 4 (1982): 12–23.

Von Erdberg, Eleanor. *Chinese Influence on European Garden Structures*. Cambridge, Mass.: Harvard University Press, 1936.

Wallerstein, Immanuel. *The Modern World-System II: Mercantilism and the Consolidation of the European World-Economy, 1600–1750*. New York: Academic Press, 1980.

Walpole, Horace. "Mi Li: A Chinese Fairy Tale." In *The Castle of Otranto and Hieroglyphic Tales*, ed. Robert L. Mack. London: J. M. Dent & Sons, 1993.

Walter, Richard, and Benjamin Robins. *A Voyage Round the World by George Anson*. Ed. Glyndwr Williams. London: Oxford University Press, 1974.

Walvin, James. *Fruits of Empire: Exotic Produce and British Taste, 1660–1800*. Basingstoke, England: Macmillan, 1997.

Webb, John. *Historical Essay Endeavoring a Probability that the Language of the Empire of China is the Primitive Language*. London, 1669.

Weber, Max. *From Max Weber: Essays in Sociology*. Ed. and trans. H. H. Gerth and C. Wright Mills. New York: Oxford University Press, 1946.

Weitzman, Arthur. "The Oriental Tale in the Eighteenth Century: A Reconsideration." *Studies in Voltaire and the Eighteenth Century* (1967): 1839–1855.

Wells, Ronald A. *Dictionaries and the Authoritarian Tradition*. The Hague: Mouton & Co., 1973.

Wellstone, Paul. "Get Tough with China." *The New York Times* Apr. 5, 1999, A21.

Whately, Thomas. *Observations on Modern Gardening*. London, 1770.

Wilczek, Frank. "The World's Numerical Recipe." Lecture presented at the Institute for Advanced Study, Princeton, N.J., Jan. 2000.

Wilkins, John. *An Essay Towards a Real Character and a Philosophical Language*. London, 1668.

Williams, Aubrey. "The 'Fall' of China and *The Rape of the Lock*." *Philological Quarterly* 41 (1962): 412–25.

Williams, Glyndwr, ed. *Documents Relating to Anson's Voyage Round the World, 1740–1744*. London: Navy Records Society, 1967.

Wills, John E. *Embassies and Illusions: Dutch and Portuguese Envoys to Kiang-hsi, 1667–1687*. Cambridge, Mass.: Harvard Council on East Asian Studies, 1984.

———. *Peppers, Guns and Parleys: The Dutch East India Company and China, 1662–1681.* Cambridge, Mass.: Harvard University Press, 1974.

Wimsatt, W. K. *Philosophical Words.* New Haven, Conn.: Yale University Press, 1948.

Witek, John W. *Controversial Ideas in China and in Europe: A Biography of Jean-François Foucquet, S.J. (1665–1741).* Rome: Institutum Historicum S.I., 1982.

Wood, Frances. *Did Marco Polo Go to China?* London: Secker & Warburg, 1995.

Wood, P. B. "Methodology and Apologetics: Thomas Sprat's *History of the Royal Society.*" *British Journal for the History of Science* 13 (1980): 1–26.

World, The. London, 1753–1756.

Wright, Arthur F. *Buddhism in Chinese History.* Stanford, Calif.: Stanford University Press, 1959.

———. "The Chinese Language and Foreign Ideas." In *Studies in Chinese Thought,* ed. Arthur Wright, 286–303. Chicago: University of Chicago Press, 1953.

Wycherley, *The Country Wife.* In *Restoration Drama,* ed. Ronald Berman, 18–117. New York: Signet, 1980.

Young, John. *Confucianism and Christianity: The First Encounter.* Hong Kong: Hong Kong University Press, 1983.

Yü, Chün-fang. *The Renewal of Buddhism in China: Chu-hung and the Late Ming Synthesis.* New York: Columbia University Press, 1981.

Index